Seeing Hardy

Seeing Hardy

*Film and Television Adaptations
of the Fiction of Thomas Hardy*

by Paul J. Niemeyer

McFarland & Company, Inc., Publishers
Jefferson, North Carolina, and London

Frontispiece: Thomas Hardy, c. 1894.

Library of Congress Cataloguing-in-Publication Data

Niemeyer, Paul J., 1966–
    Seeing Hardy : film and television adaptations of the fiction of
Thomas Hardy / by Paul J. Niemeyer.
        p.   cm.
    Includes bibliographical references and index.

    ISBN-13: 978-0-7864-1429-1
    softcover : 50# alkaline paper ∞

    1. Hardy, Thomas, 1840–1928—Film and video adaptations.
2. Hardy, Thomas, 1840–1928—Fictional works.   3. Film
adaptations—History and criticism.   I. Title.
PR4757.F55 N54   2003
791.43'6—dc21   2002152177

British Library cataloguing data are available

Cover: Ray Stevenson as Clym and Catherine Zeta Jones as Eustacia in
Hallmark's television adaptation of *Return of the Native* (1994).

Manufactured in the United States of America

McFarland & Company, Inc., Publishers
  Box 611, Jefferson, North Carolina 28640
   www.mcfarlandpub.com

To my mother and father

Contents

Introduction:
Seeing Hardy, Knowing Hardy

Thomas Hardy was born shortly after the invention of photography; as a result, he is one of the first "great writers" for whose life we have a near complete photographic record. We first saw him in about 1856, when he would have been sixteen and perhaps beginning his apprenticeship with a Dorset architect, standing stiffly and holding his hat by his side, clearly trying to look as dignified and professional as any sixteen-year-old possibly can. Through seventy years of photographs we can watch him grow and mature: we can see the arrival of the full beard he wore at the height of Victorian fashion, accompanied by the gradual disappearance of the hair on his head; we see him as the respected writer at the peak of his career, bearded no longer but sporting a luxuriant mustache; and, finally, we see him as an old man, a stately grandfather figure whose deep wrinkles and sharp eyes bespeak years of experience and wisdom. The image of this latter Hardy is perhaps the one most people know best: photographs of Hardy as the "Grand Old Man" of English literature appear on or in modern-day copies of his books; and when his home town of Dorchester honored his memory with a public statue, it chose to depict him as a very old man, seated and staring down at the people who must, in return, look up at him. In all the years of making images of Hardy, one constant emerged: he always looked very, very serious.

Of course, this is the problem with just about every photograph made during the era of the plate process. The subject had to stay still as a wax-work for several minutes, often with his or her head held in place by a

1

Hardy in his eighties, "The Grand Old Man" of English literature.

harness that could have been put to use during the Inquisition. The ordeal was enough to make even the most good-humored individuals—Dickens, for instance, or Mark Twain—look as though they were about to have several teeth pulled. But even in the photographs of Hardy that were taken after plates were replaced by high-speed film and cumbersome cameras gave way to small Kodaks, he still looks serious, or dejected, or as if his mind is dwelling on thoughts that metaphorically take him outside the photographer's studio. Somehow, the pictures of Hardy seem to match the image of him that is generally thought to emerge from his novels, stories, and poems; his is a sober face, a sad face, the face of a tragedian. We know that the stiff and glum-looking Dickens we see in many photographs isn't the *real* Dickens—too many biographies and personal testimonies attest to his whimsical, mercurial, and fun-loving nature—but, for Hardy, those dour images just *fit*.

To avoid misleading anyone, I have to state up front that this study is not particularly concerned with the photographic images of Thomas Hardy the man; rather, its concern is with cultural and societal images of Hardy as a writer and of the kinds of novels he wrote. However, the photographs of Hardy and how we respond to them illustrate a notion that is at the heart of this study. Roland Barthes writes of a phenomenon he calls the "photographic paradox," which is that the photo *by itself* has no "code," no system of signifiers by which it can be understood as anything other than an "analogue of reality," but that the person or persons who perceive the photograph will "read" it according to a system of culturally generated and culturally understood signs.[1] Someone who does not know who Hardy was, has never heard his name, and has never read a word of his fiction or poetry, is likely to look at any of the photographs of Hardy and simply see a man who obviously lived a long time ago, and read his face as registering whatever he was feeling or thinking at that moment. However, for someone who knows Hardy's fiction or knows something about him personally, his photographs are likely to confirm or refute what that person already knows about him through biographies, critical studies, or through his actual works. If a person's culturally constructed image of Hardy is that of a sober Victorian gentleman who wrote tragic novels, then most of the photos of Hardy are likely to confirm that "reading" of his personality.

But where do culturally understood messages about authors come from in the first place? We can point to numerous sources: biographies, "required reading" in the classroom, academic criticism, societies to preserve the author's memory and to champion the reading of his or her books, conferences on the writer's works; the list goes on. However, the most pervasive, most easily understood, and most quickly absorbed means of disseminating cultural images of authors is through the film adaptations of their books. In the last century the cinema was the most popular and successful form of mass entertainment; and from its very inception film has been a medium that draws from all other media—especially from popular and "classic" novels. This fact has often had troubling implications for literary scholars, many of whom charge that film versions of novels automatically cheapen and distort the source material, misrepresent the author's goals, and essentially create false impressions of what the novel is about. Of great concern to some critics is what a film adaptation "does" to the image of the author. For instance, most adaptations of *Gulliver's Travels* tend to be made for children, and many critics have rightly argued that such approaches to this bitterly satirical novel give the false impression that Jonathan Swift was the eighteenth century's Lewis Carroll, an entertainer of boys and girls, who made up whimsical stories of tiny people and giants. However, when considering the "image" of an author that is presented by a film adaptation, a question that should quickly come to mind is this: does the film actually *create* this particular image, or did the filmmakers perhaps latch on to a *pre-existing* cultural image of the author and merely carry it into the film adaptation? Certainly, it is difficult to believe that film *alone* reconstituted *Gulliver's Travels* as a children's story; it is more than likely that early book versions of the story specifically adapted for young readers and play versions of *Gulliver* that were meant for children existed long before Swift's story made it to film.

With Thomas Hardy, the case can be made that his cultural image was certainly put into place long before he attracted the attention of filmmakers, and it can further be argued that films have had little impact in shaping how he has been perceived. In fact, it may seem strange to even embark on a study of film adaptations of Hardy's novels because, until the 1990s at least, they have been few and far between. As I explain in chapter one, several film versions of Hardy's novels were made during the silent era, but each one of those films is now lost or unobtainable and between 1929 and 1967 there were *no* film adaptations of Hardy's major works at all.[2] Several TV adaptations of Hardy's works were made in the 1970s, and at the end of that decade Roman Polanski's *Tess*—based on *Tess of the d'Urbervilles*—appeared; but then there was nothing more based on Hardy's novels until the mid–1990s. Unlike Dickens, Jane Austen, and the Brontës, Hardy has not been a particularly popular subject for filmmakers; so it could be said there aren't enough Hardy adaptations to merit a full-length study like this, and especially that the relative dearth of "Hardy films" means that they have had only a perfunctory impact on his cultural image. However, I believe that such suppositions would be false. This study takes into consideration six feature-length films and four television programs based on Hardy's novels, which is a good, substantial number of adaptations to consider—certainly there are more film versions of Hardy's novels in existence than there are adaptations of many other authors' works. Further, even though the number of adaptations from Hardy's works hasn't been as extensive as those from Dickens or Austen, the films are still numerous enough, and their viewership has been wide enough, to contribute to a cultural perception of Thomas Hardy and of what he wrote. As proof of this claim, I offer my own experience of gaining a cultural understanding of Hardy, which was largely dependent on my awareness of film.

In the late 1970s, when I was in junior high school, I encountered the name Thomas Hardy twice, as Lord Nelson's flag captain and as the author of a novel that inspired a *Masterpiece Theatre* serial my parents had watched, *The Mayor of Casterbridge*. Around 1980, Hardy's name began to appear in the news in connection with a new movie that was about to be released in America, *Tess*. I had little interest in seeing this film—I was in the first generation of American kids brought up by George Lucas and Steven Spielberg—but for whatever reason, *Tess*'s ad campaign made an impression on me. I vividly recall a commercial showing an image of Stonehenge looking more tumble-down than in the pictures I'd seen; and I remember Nastassia Kinski in Leigh Lawson's cart, protesting, "But I don't want to be kissed, sir!" Kinski's face was also hard to escape, as it stared out from posters, newspaper ads, and paperback books. I saw the film reviewed on Siskel and Ebert's old PBS program; heard other TV critics speculate about *Tess*'s chances at the Oscars and talk ominously about the fact that Roman Polanski couldn't return to the country; and I heard, or read, many film reviewers gloss the novel as Hardy's finest tragedy, even as his "masterpiece." In spite of all the hype and the praise, though, I still had no interest in seeing *Tess*. That desire essentially stayed in place until 1989, the year I finally read *Tess of the d'Urbervilles* and then experienced a patently stereotypical desire to "now see the movie."

What I saw amazed me. Polanski's film seemed to me to be remarkably faithful to the book—even though I couldn't overlook some key omissions—and it precisely embodied what I imagined the novel to "look" like. The actors were perfectly cast; the colors of the natural world—moving from muted to vibrant to dull gray—were in keeping with Hardy's depiction of nature; and the film's stately pace complemented the rhythm of the novel. For years, Polanski's *Tess* stayed in my mind as an ideal literary adaptation—and I still admire it both as an adaptation and as a film—but as I began to study Hardy's fiction in earnest, and as I began to realize that much of what I read *about* his fiction didn't always match what I *knew* about Hardy's fiction, I started to wonder if Polanski really *had* crafted a faithful version of Hardy's novel, or if I had actually read Polanski's film *back into* the novel. I may have read the book first, but I still knew the film from the clips and from the reviews; and the film was constantly on my mind *as* I read, for there on the cover of my used Signet edition of *Tess* was Nastassia Kinski. It is entirely possible that I accepted Polanski's film as faithful to the source because for ten years I'd been conditioned to accept it as faithful.

A major goal of this study, then, is to determine the degree to which cultural images of Thomas Hardy and his fiction have been created by film adaptations; or, what I believe is more precise, the degree to which the films capitalize on already-existing images of Hardy and disseminate them back into the culture at large. A central tenet I will be dealing with is that Hardy's novels are not driven by plot: rather, they are driven by the perspectives that are deployed by the characters and, sometimes, by the narrator; and this approach makes Hardy's novels multifaceted and generally unstable. Film, by contrast, is a relatively *stable* medium that depends on a more unified point of view than the ones that are deployed by Hardy; therefore, tension automatically exists between Hardy's novels and film form. I believe that Hardy's novels cannot be "faithfully" adapted to film because his technique of utilizing multiple perspectives and, as is often the case, multiple voices, does not readily lend itself to film. However, what *is* readily adaptable to film are the numerous "critical" versions of Hardy's works. Hardy's multifaceted approach has often baffled critics of his novels, and in an effort to make his works comprehendible, critics have often grafted particular readings on to specific works. Many of these critical readings have gained such popularity that they are accepted, often without question, not as *interpretations* of what Hardy wrote, but as the

work itself. This study will show that the filmmakers who have brought
Hardy's novels to the screen have often dramatized not Hardy's actual
novel, but the work as it has been apprehended through the lenses of the
critics; and it is largely in this sense that the films both embrace a cultural
understanding of Hardy and also return that reading to the culture from
which it sprang.

In making this argument, I am not necessarily breaking new ground.
This work was very much influenced by Peter Widdowson's *Hardy in History: A Study in Literary Sociology* (1989), which traces the construction
of Thomas Hardy's image by critics, by the schools, and by radio, television, and film. It was probably Widdowson's book more than any other
that convinced me there is much more to Hardy's fiction than pastorals,
tragedies, and meditations upon the workings of fate; it was probably his
book that convinced me to examine the role critics have played in shaping our perception on and understanding of both Hardy's fiction and
Hardy's own persona, as well as Hardy's own *personal* role in shaping these
images. While I was researching the earliest reviews of Hardy's novels, I
was surprised by how many of today's critical perspectives were actually
in place from the very beginning. Oftentimes, it seems that what we think
of as radical new approaches in the criticism of Hardy's fiction—such as
feminism and Marxism—are really just the latest offshoots of ways of reading those novels that began in the original reviews. Therefore, I found it
necessary to trace the critical history of each novel that I will examine in
this study and then consider the degree to which the novel supports or
rejects those critical readings. My approach differs from Widdowson's in
that he traces the critical history of Hardy's novels primarily to uncover
the critics' own attempts to apply humanistic, culturally "approved" values to the original novels. While Widdowson brilliantly demonstrates how
entrenched certain readings of Hardy's novels have become, he also seems
to fall into a trap he is presumably be trying to avoid—that of reading
Hardy *one* way. Widdowson's central argument is that the "true" Hardy,
the one who has been obscured by years of humanistic interpretations, is
essentially Marxist in his outlook; and it seems to me that a Marxist perspective is only one of many that Hardy typically deployed. To tie Hardy
down to creating only one "type" of fiction is not necessarily to misread
him, but to radically reduce him.

My own critical approach in this study derives from many disciplines.
Since I argue that Hardy's novels are multifaceted and that they are doing
many often contradictory things at the same time, I have relied on such
approaches as semiotics, deconstructionism, and reader response. My
approach to the films, however, is much more structuralist in nature; and

in discussing the films I specifically utilize a critical framework devised by Brian McFarlane, which he in turn adapted from the theories of Barthes. My approach creates something of a critical bricolage, but I believe that were I to utilize one critical apparatus in this study I would be forced to often warp and distort Hardy to fit my own interpretation. Furthermore, this study is a cultural critique that takes more than one medium into consideration; therefore I too need to utilize more than one critical framework in order to do justice to all media that are considered here.

I must also acknowledge that Hardy's use of multiple perspectives has been analyzed by many earlier critics. In fact, my central argument about the novels embraces some fairly common conventions, such as that Hardy often makes use of multiple figures who narrate large portions of the action, and that his novels are constructed in such a way that they often interrogate literary genres and even the language upon which they are built. I see this study as a complement to, if not an extension of, such works as J. Hillis Miller's indispensable *Thomas Hardy: Distance and Desire* (1970) and J. B. Bullen's *The Expressive Eye* (1986), which both examine the degree to which Hardy's novels are built upon the deployment of point of view. Numerous other studies have also dealt with the importance of visualization in Hardy's fiction, and these works are credited in the appropriate chapters.

Where I see this book as offering something truly new and unique is that this is the only full-length examination of not only Hardy's fiction, but how that fiction has been interpreted by critics and how both Hardy's actual novels and the critical and cultural interpretations of those novels are adapted into film form. To some degree, Widdowson also undertakes this project in *Hardy in History*, but he deals with film and television adaptations in only a portion of one chapter. A few essays have touched on how the film adaptations of Hardy's novels play upon cultural images of Hardy and his works—most notably, Roger Webster's "Reproducing Hardy: Familiar and Unfamiliar Versions of *Far from the Madding Crowd* and *Tess of the d'Urbervilles*" (1993)—but, for the most part, the essays that examine the film adaptations of Hardy are written by Hardy scholars who clearly disapprove of what the filmmakers have "done" to the author. There is a surprising number of harsh, dismissive, and often pedantic critiques that trot out all of the clichés that have long been used against film adaptations; and all too often admirers of Hardy tend to fault the filmmakers for not being true to the critic's own particular interpretation of the novel. One of the things I have sought to do in this study is to move away from the type of critique that bashes a filmmaker just for making a film that isn't "true" to every character, word, and semicolon in the novel; instead,

I have tried to examine those elements in the novels that *can* be adapted to film form, and I have attempted to bridge the gap between literary criticism and film criticism. Part of chapter two examines various theories on film adaptation and argues for a theory that does justice to both original novels and to the films that are based on them.

As I researched this project, one of the surprises was to discover how little has actually been published on the film and TV adaptations of Hardy's novels. There have been several articles written on Polanski's *Tess* (most of which are concerned more with Polanski himself), a handful of essays on John Schlesinger's *Far from the Madding Crowd,* but hardly anything on Michael Winterbottom's *Jude* and next to nothing on the TV movies and miniseries. The only book-length studies that consider the film adaptations of Hardy's novels are two unpublished dissertations, which I consulted before I began this project. The first, Shirley M. Haynie's "Resolving the Dilemma of Mixed Reviews: Faithful Film Adaptations of Thomas Hardy's *Far from the Madding Crowd* and *Tess of the d'Urbervilles*" (Southern Mississippi, 1990), is an interesting and valuable analysis of how film criticism as a discipline often seems to be ill-equipped to offer workable frameworks for testing the "fidelity" of literary adaptations; but the emphasis of Haynie's study is geared more toward film criticism in general and less specifically toward Hardy, so I was not able to make use of it here. The second dissertation, Christina Vick's "Cinematic Aspects and Film Adaptations of Selected Works of Thomas Hardy" (Texas A & M, 1990), argues that Hardy was influenced by the theater, and that the "theatrical" quality of his novels makes them highly adaptable to film form. While I found Vick's study to be interesting, Joan Grundy's *Hardy and the Sister Arts* (1979) is a much more extensive examination of the many visual arts from which Hardy borrowed.

The present study is a revision and rethinking of my original doctoral dissertation, which I defended at the University of Arizona in 2000. A great deal of credit for this book goes to the three members of my committee who helped bring the original project into being and who saw me through its initial stages: Professors Gerald Monsman, Suresh Raval, and Charles Scruggs. I owe Professor Monsman a special debt of gratitude for initially suggesting that I combine my interests in Hardy and film; and all three gentlemen are warmly thanked for remaining constant sources of advice and support. My friends Marty Kelley, Gail Shuck, James Champagne, Lisa-Anne Culp, Carol Nowotny-Young, Don McNutt, Yvonne Merrill, and Jill Weber helped make the arduous revising and rewriting process much easier. Leslie Dupont offered some good advice on the manuscript, and both Jim Champagne and my e-mail friend George Moss gave me some helpful suggestions about the title. Claire Brandt of Eddie Brandt's Saturday Matinee and the staffs at the British Film Institute and the Everett Collection in New York were of invaluable help in locating film stills. Finally, my mother and father, Joyce and Albert Niemeyer, remain my most trusted advisors, and I am in their debt for giving me the greatest gift I have ever received, a life-long love of the written word. This book is a product of that love.

What I hope the reader will come to recognize, as I myself came to see during the writing process, is that this book is not just concerned with how novels may be turned into films, but with how film has kept a particular writer alive and current. This book is as much a cultural history as it is a critical study: it takes into consideration how Hardy's novels were interpreted in his own time and how they have been kept relevant through generations of critical movements, and how various eras and different filmmakers have occasionally used Hardy to reflect upon their own times. Seeing Hardy oftentimes involves more than examining his works, his life, his thought, or even the films based on his novels: it involves seeing ourselves *in* Hardy, and ultimately knowing who we are as readers, as viewers of films, and as a culture.

Part One

Filming Hardy

1

"Strange Business":
Thomas Hardy, the Cinema,
and the Critics

In the summer of 1921, the Progress Film Company of Shoreham, Sussex, began shooting a motion picture version of Thomas Hardy's 1886 novel, *The Mayor of Casterbridge*. Much of the film was shot on location—or, to be precise, in those real places Hardy used as models for his fictional ones—and on July 2 the 81-year-old author witnessed the moviemakers at work.[1] Later, Hardy wrote to his friend Florence Henniker:

> This morning we have had an odd experience. The film-makers are here doing scenes for "The Mayor of C." & they asked us to come & see the process. The result is that I have been talking to The Mayor, Mrs. Henchard, Eliz[abeth] Jane, & the rest, in the flesh. ...It is a strange business to be engaged in.[2]

Also strange is that, at this time, Hardy would find the filmmaking process to *be* strange. By 1921, Hardy was not new to movies. He had first been contacted by a film company in 1911 about the rights to *Tess of the d'Urbervilles*[3]; and two years later the Famous Players Film Company of America would release a successful version of *Tess*, which Hardy privately viewed in his publisher's office. Two years later, Turner Films, Ltd., of Britain released a version of *Far from the Madding Crowd*; at its November premiere a souvenir booklet was provided for which Hardy wrote a summary of the novel.[4] As his letters show, Hardy was at least peripher-

13

Filming *The Mayor of Casterbridge* near Steyning, summer 1921. Hardy was present on the set when the production moved to Dorchester.

ally involved in negotiating the sales of the film rights to his novels, and he had for many years been adapting his own novels to the stage and had been dealing personally with actors, so it is surprising to learn of the wonder he felt at seeing one of his stories filmed. In his own mind, Hardy didn't merely chat with the actors—he spoke to his *characters*, real and "in the flesh."[5]

In many ways, Hardy's feelings about visiting the cast and crew on the set of *Mayor*—part wonderment, part dismissiveness toward a new medium he often found bewildering—are indicative of his attitude toward film as a whole. Essentially, Hardy understood that he had a personal stake in the movies that were based on his novels, if for no other reason than the success or failure of a given film would have an immediate impact on sales of the novel and more than likely influence how it was perceived by the general public. In 1911, after he was approached about filming *Tess*, Hardy wrote to his publisher, "I should imagine that an exhibition of successive scenes from *Tess* (which is, I suppose, what is meant) could do no harm to the book, & might possibly advertise it among a new class"[6]— which means that Hardy immediately understood the benefits of the book/movie tie-in. If the moviegoers who didn't usually read good literature (it's hard not to detect a tinge of snobbery in Hardy's comment) liked what they saw on the screen, they might seek out the source novel. Elsewhere, though, Hardy's enthusiasm for the potential of film to increase his book sales is tempered by the realization that a poor adaptation could damage both sales and the novel's reputation. After he signed the rights to *Tess* to Famous Players in 1913, Hardy suffered some remorse, wondering if he had inadvertently given the filmmakers the "power to tamper with the story to an extent, such as might injure its circulation[;] e. g. changing it from a tragedy to a story in which everything ends happily"; and he asked his publisher to add a clause to the contract stating that the filmmakers could omit individual *scenes*, but not take liberties with the actual *story*.[7] Likewise, when Hardy's publisher, Frederick Macmillan, was negotiating the sale of *Mayor* to Progress in 1921, Hardy suggested that, "in order to run no risk of injuring the sale of the book," the filmmakers should be contractually obligated to make "No alteration or adaptation ... such as to burlesque or otherwise misinterpret the general character of the novel."[8]

Ironically, despite his fretting over what filmmakers might do to his novels, Hardy's recorded comments on the films that were made reveal nothing short of indifference. He called the 1913 *Tess* a "scientific toy," and claimed that he could "say nothing to its relation to, or rendering of, the story."[9] It seems that, in the end, Hardy saw films only as a means of increasing his book sales; so why, then, did he become so swept up on the set of *The Mayor of Casterbridge* that he saw his characters seemingly come to life? So far as I know, no one has written on the effect of watching a film *being made*, but Christian Metz has contended that watching a finished film is like looking into a mirror in which the spectator sees everything reflected but the self—and this act of seeing in turn forces the subject to recognize himself or herself *as* a perceiving subject.[10] It is therefore possible that, on some level, Hardy realized the element really missing from the filmmaking process was, quite simply, *Hardy*. In his novels and in the plays he adapted from his own works, Hardy was palpably *there*; but when he watched a film based on one of his novels—or even when he viewed the filmmaking process—he found himself in the uncomfortable and paradoxical situation of not seeing *himself* in the film, but of observing his characters coming to life independent of him.[11] Perhaps this small phenomenon helps explain the ambivalence Hardy apparently felt toward the films based on his novels—and the ambivalence so many novelists have felt toward cinematic adaptations of their works.

Of course, whether or not Hardy was frustrated because he felt his own absence in these films is something that will never be known. If he did try to see himself in the adaptations it would only be appropriate, since spectators have long tried to see the original authors in films based on their works, and oftentimes they have even viewed film adaptations as a way of experiencing and understanding a writer—either as an artist or as a person, or both. Certainly, for years moviemakers have understood this desire, and they have often marketed literary adaptations by exploiting and building upon what is known not so much about the *novel*, but what is known about the *novelist*. For instance, Frank M. Laurence has argued that the popular image of Ernest Hemingway as a lover, adventurer, "tough guy," and, ultimately, writer, is largely the product of movie advertisements. Laurence claims that, by playing up the original novels' "autobiographical" elements and by promoting locations Hemingway wrote about, movie ads would tell the public "what [Hemingway's] writing was like. Movie publicity was a kind of vulgar literary criticism. Some of it was embarrassing, but it served to widen his name recognition within the public that might never have read a word he wrote."[12] This suggests that publicity can serve as a means for *conditioning*: the moviegoer enters the film expecting it to be a reflection of how the author wrote and lived. An obvious example of this kind of conditioning is in MGM's original theatrical trailer for *Doctor Zhivago* (David Lean, 1965), which begins with a lengthy biography of Boris Pasternak and moves into an exegesis of the suppression of the novel—and of Pasternak's artistic freedom—in the Soviet Union.[13] The filmgoer is thus invited to view *Doctor Zhivago* not just as a movie, but as a representation of what Pasternak lived through and as an indictment of a political system that suppressed his art. Similarly, publicists for films based on Hardy's novels have often tried to show that the film is faithful to some aspect of Hardy's life or experiences, usually by stressing that the movie is true to the locations and to the times in which Hardy lived. The trailer for *The Scarlet Tunic*,[14] based on Hardy's story "The Melancholy Hussar," proudly promotes that the film was shot in "*Hardy's Dorset*, where the story truly belongs."

As influential as movie ads may be in building an image of the original author, it is the films themselves that do the most to create these images. Frequently, the author becomes a character *in* the film, as is the case with Mary Shelley in James Whale's *Bride of Frankenstein* (1935). "Can you believe that bland and lovely brow conceived of Frankenstein?" Byron (Gavin Gordon) asks of the demure Mary (Elsa Lanchester)—a question that critics and readers have been asking for two hundred years. In the film, Mary is a portrait in duality, someone whose gentility masks an ability to create horror—a fact that is reinforced toward the end of the film, when the monstrous "Bride" is brought to life and she turns out to be played by none other than Elsa Lanchester. Interestingly, the "divided" author in the film is perhaps a reinforcement of the way Mary Shelley has long been viewed by critics and biographers. As Fred Botting explains, "as many identities are found for [Shelley] as there are splits identified in her mind. Polarised between precariously shifting and opposed limits that define her as a radical or a conservative, as artistically imaginative or passively fanciful, as a loving or hateful wife or daughter, the name 'Mary Shelley' engenders a multitude of different signifieds."[15] Apparently, no matter what the dividing lines are, Mary Shelley is popularly viewed as "split," and *Bride of Frankenstein* illustrates and perhaps codifies that division.[16]

Even when the author of the original novel is never mentioned or alluded to in a film adaptation, a director can still show that the film is *about* that author through such devices as casting and makeup. In the film of D. H. Lawrence's *Women in Love* (Ken Russell, 1969), Alan Bates is cast as Rupert Birkin; and though in the novel Lawrence gives only a sketchy physical description of this character, for the film Bates has been given a hairstyle and a full beard that make him look unmistakably like Lawrence himself. Since Birkin stands most firmly for connection between and among the sexes through either copulation or intense physical contact (as in the nude wrestling scene with Gerald Crich [Oliver Reed]), Bates/Birkin reinforces in the viewers' minds the popular image of Lawrence as the "priest of love," whose life and work was dedicated to promoting ardent sensuality.

Hardy, too, has been "portrayed" in two film adaptations of his novels—through "cameos" in John Schlesinger's *Far from the Madding Crowd* (1967) and in the Arts and Entertainment network's *Tess of the D'Urbervilles* (1998),[17] both of which will be discussed in the appropriate chapters—but, more than anything else, filmmakers have chosen to "portray" Hardy on screen by tapping into a certain cultural awareness of who Hardy was and of the "kind" of fiction that he wrote. As a canonized writer, Hardy has been absorbed into the general culture of Great Britain, and, to a lesser extent, into American culture: his poetry has been widely anthologized; his fiction is extensively taught in primary and secondary schools[18]; and his best-known novels exist in dozens of editions and are still widely read by the general public. Like all writers who maintain a certain currency or name value, Hardy has an identity both generated by what he wrote, and which exists independently from what he wrote. Someone who has never read a word of Hardy can still get an idea of who he was by hearing about him from those who have read his books, by encountering references to him in articles, or by reading about him in connection to writers Hardy has influenced. Today on the Internet, a person can find many websites devoted to Hardy—some of which host legitimate discussions of his life and work; many more of which offer photographic "tours" of the real Dorset locations that inspired his fiction. In short, popular conceptions of Hardy are "out there," familiar to many people; and the goal of this study is to determine how the film adaptations of Hardy's novels become means for experiencing Hardy's world, vision, and art—in essence, of *seeing* Hardy.

To understand how Hardy has been "seen" on film, it is worthwhile to examine how other popular or canonized authors have been made visible through cinematic adaptations. The most natural starting point is probably Charles Dickens—both because arguably more films have been made from his novels than from any other author's, and because at least as early as Eisenstein's famous essay, Dickens has been regarded as a novelist whose narrative techniques anticipate film form, an element that has in part made his novels adaptable to the cinema.[19] More importantly, as Mike Poole argues, "by a curious kind of slippage, Dickens has come to stand for the whole Victorian era in popular memory, and this means that adaptations of his work are often perceived as offering unmediated access to Britain's past."[20] True enough, but I would like to offer a qualification to Poole's statement: to most people, Dickens does not stand merely for the "Victorian era" in general, but for a specific *version* of the Victorian era—one filtered through the imaginative lenses of Dickens himself. We think of this particular version of Victoriana as "Dickensian," a term that comes readily encoded with a variety of images—orphans, beadles, Christmas celebrations, twisted and lawless London streets and alleyways, debtors' prisons, gaslight villains, good-hearted petits bourgeois, monolithic and heartless bureaucratic institutions, and so on. For readers, Dickensian qualities may also be further refined to include a complex plot that hinges on coincidence, disguised identities, and more than one *deus ex machina*; but even for those who have not read Dickens a sense of Dickensiana can be conveyed by the fact the illustrations from his novels are still widely produced—not just in editions of the novels themselves, but in history and reference books, on greeting cards, and so on—and these illustrations have done a great deal to solidify a general concept of what Dickens wrote.

The extent to which the illustrations have contributed to our understanding of Dickens can be seen by examining a pair of American film reviews that followed the release of David Lean's 1946 adaptation of *Great Expectations*. An anonymous reviewer in *Time* declares that "most Dickensians will love it. And countless people who can't take Dickens are likely to hurry back to that author with a new understanding."[21] In part, what makes this film so identifiably Dickensian for the reviewer is that, "In both casting and composition, there is a good deal of intelligent derivation from Dickens' inspired illustrators, Cruikshank and 'Phiz.'"[22] To this reviewer, Lean's *Great Expectations* becomes a way of experiencing and understanding Dickens in part because the film *looks* like what something by Dickens *should* look like. However, James Agee, writing in *Nation*, found the look of the film to be slightly untrue to the author of the novel:

> I ... wish that the Dickens illustrations had been studied still more faithfully and imaginatively—that the whole tone of the film had had a kind of India-ink darkness, psychologically as well as visually: for it seems to me they had hold of a story much more cruel and mysterious than the one that got told.[23]

Agee goes on to say that the film that would have emerged from such a study of the illustrations "would have been still more faithful to Dickens—or *my idea of him,* anyhow" (my emphasis).[24] Both reviewers' attention to the original illustrations is right on target, for Lean did, in fact, base the "look" of the film on the drawings that Hablôt K. Browne ("Phiz") made for Dickens's earlier works and, to a lesser extent, on Cruikshank's drawings for *Oliver Twist*[25]—a significant fact since *Great Expectations,* alone of the novels Charles Dickens wrote, is devoid of illustrations. Browne and Cruikshank have been so instrumental in putting into peoples' minds what a Dickens novel *is* that the director in all probability felt he had to be faithful to *their* versions of Dickens, and two critics evaluated Lean's film in this light. Agee even admits that the drawings have contributed to his notion of who Dickens himself was—a writer who delves into the dark and cruel aspects of the human psyche.

Lean's *Great Expectations* is a film that is generally considered to be faithful to its source novel in part because it capitalizes on familiar images and concepts associated with that author. However, if a filmmaker takes only the basic *idea* of the novel, or if only a few elements from the novel are filmed, a viewer may feel that he or she has been denied access to the original author and his book. Alfonso Cuarón's 1998 *Great Expectations,* for example, makes no attempts to seem authentically Dickensian: though it retains the story's original title and the bare outline of the plot, the movie is set in modern-day Florida and New York, thus necessitating a "look" far removed from Cruikshank and Browne; and Cuarón radically simplifies the story and changes the names of most of the characters. Not surprisingly, many critics complained that Dickens isn't "in" this film: for instance, *Variety*'s Todd McCarthy charges that "Dickens' story has been too pared down ... to the point where it comes close to seeming like just another success story with a few regrets piled up along the way."[26] However, critics who liked the film seemed to feel that the best—perhaps the *only*—way to enjoy this new *Great Expectations* was to exorcise the ghost of Charles Dickens. John Wraithall in *Sight and Sound,* for instance, says that the film's modernizing approach "might seem a perverse way to tackle Dickens, a writer whose vivid evocation of place and social milieu has generally lasted better than his coincidence-laden plots.... The result, if light on Dickens, is far more exciting than one can imagine a straight version being."[27] Generally speaking, because Lean chose to stay faithful to the Dickens we know from the illustrators, critics tend to perceive his *Great Expectations* as "authentic," something that supports what we *know* about Dickens; while the Cuarón film is generally held to be enjoyable only if Dickens is first taken out of the way.

In recent years, perhaps no films have done more to both play upon and to create an image of a particular author than have the adaptations of E. M. Forster's novels. In a short stretch of time (1984—1992), all but one of Forster's six novels were filmed, and three of those films were made by the team of producer Ismail Merchant and director James Ivory. This apparently sudden interest in Forster by both moviemakers and audiences resulted in a genuine phenomenon that brought Forster back into prominent view as a novelist. Many reviewers, in fact, seemed to approach the films as if they weren't so much *adaptations*, but as if they were Forster *himself*, revived from a cryogenic sleep and welcomed into a world that can now appreciate him. In 1992, David Ansen of *Newsweek* claimed that the films based on Forster's works show that he is an author for these "perplexed, inward-drawn times"[28]; while *Time*'s Richard Corliss, in his review of Ivory's *Howards End* (1992), practically calls Forster a prophet: "How modern, how very 1990s, the story of 1907 plays today. It is about real estate, and failing insurance companies, and the collision of feminism and domesticity, and the way the upper class misuses and misunderstands the masses."[29] Neither of these reviewers suggests the filmmakers might be tweaking Forster's novels and adapting them in such a way that they are *made* to shine a light on modern times, or that they themselves are reading the 1980s and 1990s *into* Forster's novels. In both reviews, the films are praised for "capturing" Forster and presenting him to modern audiences virtually unchanged. The common assumption is that the filmmakers have pulled off the task of not so much *adapting* Forster's novels, but *transferring* them to the screen, so that what is presented to the audience *is* the novel itself. It is telling that, in his review of Ivory's *Maurice* (1987), Ansen says the film fails to measure up to the same director's *A Room with a View*, not because of any problem with the script, acting, or direction, but because "the source isn't as good." The title of the review—"A Closet with a View: Forster's Secret Novel"—doesn't even convey that a *film* is under discussion.[30]

The matter of Forster's sexuality has also been incorporated into a few of the adaptations of his novels, and this too allows one to perceive the films as providing access to the original author. Though both Cairns Craig and Peter Hutchings have argued the adaptations of Forster have less to say about the Edwardian era than about our own desire to reflect

upon a supposedly simpler time,[31] Hutchings also—and perhaps unknow-
ingly—indicates that one of the films ultimately reproduces what most
people know best about Forster. One of Hutchings' most pointed criticisms
about *A Room with a View* is that,

> As the foppish Cecil Vyse, Daniel Day-Lewis is immediately identifiable
> as an 1890s-inspired version of his contemporary gay role in *My Beauti-
> ful Laundrette*, and the film plays upon an opposition between Cecil's
> effeminacy and George's more forthright, exuberantly physical hetero-
> sexuality. On this level, the film "outs" aspects of the novel, exposing
> homosexual undercurrents.[32]

Hutchings also brings up the casting of openly gay Simon Callow as
Rev. Beebe, claiming Callow's presence "obviously draws out the implicit
homoeroticism of the pond scene,"[33] in which Beebe and several young
men frolic naked. It could also be said that this bit of casting says a good
deal about Ivory's knowledge of what is going on under the surface of the
novel, since in Forster's manuscript versions of *Room*, Rev. Beebe is clearly
attracted to George.[34] The gay subtext of Ivory's *A Room with a View* is
perhaps a subtle, even nudging way of "outing" Forster himself.

An even more interesting example of "outing" the original author
occurs in Oliver Parker's 1999 adaptation of Oscar Wilde's 1895 play, *An
Ideal Husband*. Wilde himself had been the subject of Brian Gilbert's biopic
just the year before, so it could be that a newfound popular interest in the
playwright spurred this adaptation; but in Miramax's production notes
for the film, writer/director Parker states the decision to film the play was
made because of its "contemporary connections" to culture and politics.
Still, two of the stars, Rupert Everett, who plays Lord Goring, and Minnie
Driver, who plays Mabel Chiltern, both indicate that the film is a vehicle
for reflecting upon the persecution Wilde was forced to endure. Everett
calls Wilde "a very contemporary character," and says that "as we come of
[*sic*] the end of this millennium, a hundred years after he died, it's interesting to think of him and how much and how little things have changed."
Similarly, Driver says,

> At a time when you think someone would just be so angry at the way they
> were being treated, he comes out with this wonderful theme: we are none
> of us perfect. There is grace, beauty and love in imperfection. This is, I think,
> one of the gentlest and loveliest things Wilde could have said about the
> world. Especially at the time when he was being mercilessly persecuted.[35]

Neither star dares speak the name of the charge under which Wilde
was prosecuted; instead, both Everett and Driver—or the person who

edited and compiled their comments—suggest we read between the lines and reflect upon our own culture's treatment of gays and lesbians. Parker also hints at the presence of the gay playwright in some key ways: most obviously, Wilde is "outed" in a sequence where the Chilterns (Jeremy Northam and Cate Blanchett) attend a performance of *The Importance of Being Earnest,* and Wilde himself (Michael Culkin) appears at the curtain-call. During Wilde's famous address to the audience, the camera cuts between Wilde and the box in which Sir Robert and Lady Gertrude are seated. Gertrude asks her husband, "Is there in your life any secret honor or disgrace?" Sir Robert responds, "Gertrude, there is nothing in my past life that you might not know." Dramatically, of course, Lady Gertrude's question concerns the possibility that Sir Robert has sold government secrets; but their dialogue also points to the Wilde character on stage, and reminds us that Wilde's "secret life" would lead to his own disgrace (shortly after the premiere of *The Importance of Being Earnest,* as a matter of fact), and that this scandal is one of the things that keeps him of interest today.

For years, then, filmmakers have used various devices—authentic locations, images associated with authors, and common biographical knowledge—in order to make their films reflections on what we know about certain authors; and critics often affirm that knowledge in their reviews or construct their own alternative ways of viewing the author. Such efforts on the part of filmmakers and critics to make the author "visible" would seem to support Roland Barthes's contention that "the *explanation* of a work is always sought in the man or woman who produced it, as if it were always in the end, through the more or less transparent allegory of the fiction, the voice of a single person, the *author* 'confiding' in us."[36] By and large, in Western critical culture we do tend to conceive of a work of literature as the expression of a unique and individual mind, and as the property of the person who created it; and we seem to expect that the adapter of the novel to film will do something to acknowledge the presence—even the personality—of the individual who brought the original work into being.

This brings us back to Thomas Hardy and the issue of how the cinema has helped to construct an image of this author and his works. The task at hand is quite a bit different—perhaps easier—than it would be to study the ways an author like Dickens has been represented on the screen, since relatively few Hardy novels have been filmed. To make the task easier still, filmmakers have been interested only in a certain *kind* of Hardy novel—the kind that the author himself lumped into the category "Novels of Character and Environment" for the 1912 "Wessex Edition" of his works. The problem with analyzing the ways an author like Dickens has been represented is that there is simply too much to work with. It is safe to say that all of Dickens' novels—and many of his short stories—have been adapted to the screen, and some have been shot literally dozens of times. Through watching film versions of Dickens, a person can develop at least a passing—if, at times, uninformed—familiarity with the author and never have to read his actual books. Likewise, the seeming inevitability of a new film (or TV) version of *Jane Eyre, Wuthering Heights,* or *Pride and Prejudice* every few years says a great deal both about how familiar we are with these stories, and how much more we are willing to see in the books and in the people who wrote them. Hardy, however, has had only five novels filmed in the era of sound and color, and each was made only once (this does not, of course, include TV versions, which will be handled separately).[37] With so little of Hardy on the screen, his cinematic "image" is relatively confined.

It would be interesting to begin this discussion by focusing on the films Hardy himself saw or could have seen, and by considering the kind

Far from the Madding Crowd (1915), one of the lost silents based on Hardy's novels. *Left to right:* Farmer Boldwood (Malcolm Cherry) and Sergeant Troy (Campbell Gullan) fight as Bathsheba (Florence Turner) looks on.

of "Hardy" they created, but that task is now nearly impossible. The silent versions of Hardy's novels now exist only in fragments or have vanished altogether. Most disappointing, perhaps, is the loss of MGM's 1924 version of *Tess of the d'Urbervilles*, which was both updated to "modern" times and released with alternative endings—one tragic, the other happy (Hardy's opinion on this film, I believe, is unrecorded).[38] It is also interesting to speculate on the "could-have-beens," those Hardy films that never were. The Associated British Picture Corporation embarked on an adaptation of *The Mayor of Casterbridge* in 1949, but abandoned it as too expensive and as having no commercial potential in America[39]; and David O. Selznick tried for years to make his own *Tess*—conceiving it both as an epic on the lines of his own *Gone with the Wind* (1939) and as a vehicle for his wife Jennifer Jones—but he never got beyond a volume of production notes that his heirs later sold to Roman Polanski.[40] Since these aborted projects would have been made during the "golden ages" of both Hollywood and British film, it is fascinating to consider how Hardy would have been represented; but the critical response to the three major Hardy films that *were* made is sufficient to show how many movie reviewers conceive of Hardy and how they view the films as a means of understanding the author.

In examining a selection of contemporary reviews for *Far from the Madding Crowd* (John Schlesinger, 1967), *Tess* (Roman Polanski, 1979), and *Jude* (Michael Winterbottom, 1996) that were published in widely circulated newspapers and periodicals, it is amazing to note how many film reviewers become *de facto* Hardy critics. A good many reviewers seem to find it obligatory to comment on the source novels and occasionally to recite facts about Hardy's life, as if in so doing they are offering a standard of truth by which the films may be evaluated. At times, it even appears that some reviewers are less interested in evaluating the film than they are in pontificating on the quality of the source novel. A review of Schlesinger's *Far from the Madding Crowd* in *Saturday Review,* for instance, yields this backhanded compliment to Hardy: "Hardy's vision, while confined to the assumptions of his time, nevertheless has breadth and psychological acuteness; he was, at least, in the second rank of greatness."[41] The *Times* of London carps that "Hardy, obviously, is not the easiest novelist to adapt. His own dialogue, such as it is, is generally poor, and his construction rambling, with a heavy dependence on sheer coincidence to keep the story moving." In this reviewer's terms, Schlesinger's *Crowd* is disappointing because, "To film [Hardy], one must first dramatize him: seize the essential and re-create in film terms. The one thing one cannot do is what Frederic Raphael, the script writer here, does: passively drift along in his wake, presenting gems from Hardy transcripted with literal directness from the book."[42] Andrew Sarris, then a highly influential film critic for the *Village Voice*, found in the film an excuse to indict the long-dead novelist: "What does Thomas Hardy's 1874 novel tell us in 1967? That life is cruel and nature indifferent? That man's folly is fed by woman's capriciousness? Or is it merely the musty smell of Literature that motivated this super-production?" Sarris concludes, "We should forget Hardy as a screen subject as the French should forget Balzac."[43] Judging from these comments, one wouldn't think that a director, screenwriter, and cast are offering their own interpretations of Hardy, but that Hardy himself wrote the script and perhaps had a hand in the direction.

This tendency to critique the original novel through the film is visible again in the reviews of Polanski's *Tess*. Writing in *Cineaste*, Melanie Wallace claims "the complexities in Hardy, who was, above all, conscious of the classes and mores that ruled late Victorian England, become cumbersome in *Tess* [the movie], and what is lost, in the final analysis, is the pervasive sense of drudgery and poverty that the novel abounds with, as well as the realization that the tragedy of modern love is that it is unrequited."[44] Whether "drudgery and poverty" pervade the Talbothays Dairy sequences in Hardy's novel is debatable, as is the question of whether a character like Angel Clare is even capable or deserving of love—modern or otherwise; but Wallace is clearly disappointed that what she expects to see in the film isn't there. Another disappointed reviewer is Tom Milne, who finds *Tess* a *"reductio ad absurdum"* of Hardy, because Polanski doesn't understand that "Hardy constantly *implicates* Tess with the landscape, not least by his meticulous descriptions of the various long and painful journeys back and forth through Wessex on foot, which mirror her arduous path through life."[45]

More recently, Winterbottom's *Jude* initiated an entirely new round of reading the novel through the film, with many reviewers diligently reminding their readers that the original novel was a shocker that attacked the very society from which it sprang. Lawrence Van Gelder in the *New York Times* reports, "Hardy's 1895 work, with its portrayal of a society that crushed those who challenged its rules, drew so outraged a reaction from Victorian England that the author never again wrote a novel." The film *Jude* strikes Van Gelder as untrue to Hardy because "the role of society has been shrunk. From this imbalance emerges not a great tragedy but a tale of doomed romance."[46] Georgia Brown in the *Village Voice* says the novel "created a scandal for criticizing marriage. Hardy not only shows the bondage of sanctioned unions but then has Jude and Sue living together and having two children.... For this sin, they become the world's outcasts."[47] Brown's review chides Winterbottom for "lightening" the story, thereby robbing it of its impact.

These "pocket" critiques of the novels contained within the reviews do little more in themselves than show the reviewers' knowledge (accurate or not) of the source materials, and they usually provide yardsticks by which the reviewer measures the quality of the film. But the very presence of these critiques inside the reviews shows that many reviewers feel they must defer to the authority of the original novel when they are faced with a film adaptation. In many cases, it seems the film is not allowed to function on its own terms: it becomes, in fact, a representative of the novel itself. And, from time to time, the film becomes a surrogate even for the novelist. Just as a good deal of ersatz literary criticism makes its way into the reviews, so too does biography. *Time's* review of Schlesinger's *Far from the Madding Crowd*, for instance, begins by reminding us that,

> Before he became a novelist, Thomas Hardy was an architect. Though he seldom practiced his profession, he never quite abandoned its principles. Like Victorian buildings, his books were sturdily constructed, gloomy, and based on strong, pseudo-classic foundations—mostly imitation Greek tragedy. The film of *Far from the Madding Crowd* remains faithful to that arrangement—and therein lie its virtues and flaws.[48]

That Hardy was an architect is, of course, true; but why is this fact inserted into a film review? The reviewer's opinion aside, it is doubtful whether Hardy's first career influenced his writing beyond the creation of Christopher Julian, the architect-hero of *The Hand of Ethelberta* (1876); and certainly Henry James for one would quibble with the notion that Hardy's novels were built on sturdy foundations.[49] In fact, Hardy's episodic plots are reminders that he wrote while the serial and the triple-decker novel still flourished. What is ultimately off-putting about this review, though, is the contention that Hardy always wrote gloomy and tragic novels. This statement indicates the reviewer has read only the most famous of Hardy's works, but even then not all of them—and this certainly applies to *Madding Crowd*—are laden with doom. This biographical tidbit serves its purposes: to provide a starting point for a critique of Schlesinger's film, and to let the director off the hook. To this reviewer, the "flaw" in the novel is that Hardy's depiction of the countryside dwarfs his characters—and Schlesinger's film, in being faithful to Hardy, retains this fault.

Film critics were generally disinclined to read Polanski's *Tess* as a reflection of Hardy's actual life, but a few reviewers did see the novel as embodying something Hardy felt deeply—a sense of connection with and love for his native land—and at least two critics saw the film as trying to capture Hardy's own appreciation for nature. Robert Hatch, writing in *The Nation*, says Polanski "matches his pace to Hardy's progresses through the story, developing it, as it was written, in almost self-sufficient episodes, pausing for leisurely appreciation of the English countryside that the novelist so loved (the film was in fact shot in France)."[50] Stanley Kauffmann, however, found that the film's depiction of the countryside came up short compared to that of the "real" Wessex he himself experienced:

> Two summers ago I spent a few days in Dorset, which is most of Hardy's Wessex, three miles from Marnhull, which is Tess's Marlott; and, no doubt influenced by Hardy's vision, I saw that wonderful countryside as *living*— busy in its thriving and its cycles—rather than as a set of postcards. Polanski and his cinematographers show some rough farm work, but when they look at the countryside, it becomes picturesque, which is not how the characters often see it or what the tragedy needs.[51]

In both of these reviews, the reality Hardy *must* have experienced becomes for the writers a kind of reality they want to see reflected in Polanski's film. In this case, each reviewer seems to regard Polanski's *Tess* as a means to tap into Hardy's mind and feelings about nature, even though the landscapes Hardy wrote about have long since been altered by technological progress and were, in fact, being altered even as Hardy wrote about them, and even though *Tess* was shot across the Channel in France.

Lastly, though the reviewers of Michael Winterbottom's *Jude* tended to focus mainly on the outcry the original novel created, at least one reviewer saw the opportunity to recite some "relevant" biographical information that explains the creation of Hardy's novel and exposes its central themes:

> Hardy, who called "Jude the Obscure" a "tragedy of failed ambitions," started writing it right after the death of Tryphena Sparks, a cousin very like Sue Bridehead, with whom as a young man he had a tortured and unsatisfying affair. And, since the self-taught Hardy was, like Jude, an autodidact and ex-stonemason, the story is obviously a kind of mournful love poem, trembling with accusation and bitterness.[52]

Michael Millgate, in his 1982 biography of Hardy, disproves the popular notions that Sue Bridehead was based on Tryphena Sparks and that *Jude* became Hardy's meditation on their doomed love affair,[53] and the reviewer errs in saying that Hardy, son of a stonemason though he was, practiced the trade himself; but the use of these biographical legends says a great deal about this particular reviewer's approach to Winterbottom's film: he evaluates it as something that illuminates and perhaps provides access to the life of Thomas Hardy.

Once again, these reviews were all written around the time of the films' initial release dates, and all appeared in newspapers or periodicals that were widely distributed. The reviewers who in their columns explicated upon Hardy and his original novels, then, were in some respects presenting Hardy for the consumption of a large reading public. Just working from the reviews, some broad generalizations about Hardy the man and Hardy the writer can be drawn: he was a working-class figure from rural England, self-taught, unlucky in love but a lover of nature; and his cumbersome, often clumsy, frequently depressing, and always tragic novels still shocked his contemporaries with their sexual frankness, and today they remain of interest for Hardy's descriptive abilities, his evocation of nature, and for his concern for the poor and working classes. This, no doubt, fits the general picture of Hardy that many people who have read at least one of his novels already have: in fact, this description of Hardy isn't too far from the biographical blurbs that are printed at the front or back of just about every paperback edition of his novels.

At no point do I wish to suggest Hardy was someone entirely different from this quick biographical sketch. The data presented are essentially correct, if they are incomplete and radically simplified, but therein lies the rub: for the popular conception of Hardy is laden with commonplaces and stereotypes that are often never challenged and which are codified as authentic.[54] Peter Widdowson has created a thorough study of the ways Hardy has been reproduced in the popular imagination; and to Widdowson, the "positive commonplaces" about Hardy the writer may be broken down into

> his descriptions of "peasant life" and his "Shakespearian" rustic characters...; his creation of the myth of "Wessex"; his description and deployment of the natural environment; his nostalgia for a passing rural world; his poetic style; his "Greek" conception of tragedy, tragic characters, and Fate...; and the "universal" significance of his characters and settings.[55]

In the film reviews, we can see that many of the "Hardean" characteristics that Widdowson delineates—especially those about nature and tragedy—have either been identified by the reviewers as operating within the films, or the films have been criticized by the reviewers for not adequately embodying these Hardean qualities. Likewise, many of the film reviewers echoed some characteristic complaints about Hardy, which Widdowson also categorizes in his study. Accordingly, Hardy has long been faulted for

> violent sensationalism; artificiality of plot...; chance and coincidence;

"melodrama"...; "flat" and "unconvincing" characterization; awkward-
ness and pedantry of style...; "fashionable pessimism" or "gloom"; didacticism (or "ideas"); and Hardy's [failed] attempts to write about any society
other than rural "Wessex."[56]

As we have seen, many film reviewers also couldn't resist knocking
Hardy for crafting bad plots and for writing poor dialogue, for espousing
irrelevant—or just plain dated—ideology, and for simply being damned
depressing. These popular conceptions of Hardy—both positive and negative—are what many reviewers expected to, and sometimes *did*, see in the
films; and it is this Hardy they have recreated in their reviews. In some
respects, the film critics are contributing to a process of seeing Hardy that
began at least as early as 1912—and which had its beginnings with Thomas
Hardy himself.

To again follow Widdowson's argument, the basis of a good many
preconceptions about Hardy is the General Preface to the 1912 "Wessex"
edition of his novels and stories,[57] in which he explains how he created
Wessex and tells the reader what makes his fictional landscape significant:

> I considered that our magnificent heritage from the Greeks in dramatic
> literature found sufficient room for a large proportion of its action in an
> extent of their country not much larger than the half-dozen counties here
> reunited under the old name of Wessex, that the domestic emotions have
> throbbed in Wessex nooks with as much intensity as in the palaces of
> Europe, and that, anyhow, there was quite enough human nature in Wes-
> sex for one man's literary purpose [General Preface, p. 394].

Hardy goes on to say that his characters are "beings in whose hearts
and minds that which is apparently local should be really universal" (p.
394). There we have it, straight from the source: Wessex is a stage upon
which modern equivalents of Greek dramas (read: tragedies) are enacted
by rural characters who embody "universal" qualities. In two passages
Hardy makes a claim for himself as an author of pastoral tragedies; and
in the next paragraph he broadens his self-definition by declaring his novels have recorded "for [his] own satisfaction a fairly true record of a vanishing life" (p. 395). It would seem that this claim to realism would cancel
his claim to being a pastoral tragedian, but Hardy's self-characterizations
have rarely been questioned, and in fact some critics have suggested it is
Hardy's depiction of the passing rural world that *makes* his novels pastoral tragedies.

Hardy's image has been further codified through the General Preface by his categorizing his novels and story collections into three ranks:

the first being "Novels of Character and Environment," the second "Romances and Fantasies," and the last (I use the word deliberately)"Novels of Ingenuity." Hardy describes the first category as containing those books "which approach most nearly to uninfluenced works; also one or two which, whatever their quality in some few of their episodes, may claim a verisimilitude in general treatment and detail" (p. 393). What Hardy means by "uninfluenced works" is a mystery, since in the same preface he claims to be influenced by Greek drama; but his favoring of "verisimilitude" is striking, for the second and third categories of his fiction are so ranked because of their "not infrequent disregard of the probable" and the "artificiality of their fable" (p. 393). So Hardy is favoring realism, and it is this quality that has elevated seven of his novels to pride of place. Not surprisingly, the top category contains every novel generally considered to be, if not Hardy's best, then certainly his "best loved": *Tess of the d'Urbervilles, Far from the Madding Crowd, Jude the Obscure, The Return of the Native, The Mayor of Casterbridge, The Woodlanders,* and *Under the Greenwood Tree,* in this order; while the third category, "Novels of Ingenuity"—those Hardy says were "written for the nonce simply" (p. 393)—consist entirely of those novels that have at various times been dubbed Hardy's worst efforts in fiction: *Desperate Remedies, The Hand of Ethelberta,* and *A Laodecian.* Not surprisingly, the bulk of Hardy criticism has focused on the Novels of Character and Environment, and every film that was based on a Hardy novel came from the first category. Few authors have done more than Hardy to establish who they are, how they should be read, and what their "best" books are, so shouldn't Hardy be seen as the best authority here?

The answer is a qualified no. Hardy gives the impression in his General Preface that his novels are all part of an organic whole and that from the beginning he had a carefully planned scheme for Wessex in his head; however, many scholars have shown that Hardy subjected his novels to constant revision, changing place names, and adding or deleting information to make the locations in one novel conform to those in another.[58] Hardy's fiction of a uniform and coherent vision of Wessex in which all his dramas are played out is so seductive that his books that move the action away from Wessex—such as *The Hand of Ethelberta* (1876), with its many London sequences, and *A Laodecian* (1881), which trots all over Europe—seem atypical of Hardy, and are therefore easily marginalized in his canon. Also, by inviting his readers to see his novels as embodying themes from Greek tragedy, Hardy forces them to concentrate only on those books that do contain a general conception of tragedy—those that have been classified by the author as Novels of Character and Environment. As a result, such works as the farcical *The Trumpet-Major* (1880) and the broad comedy *Two on a Tower* (1882) must be perceived as lesser works, since they don't fit into the author's scheme of grand tragedy. But, again, this scheme is nothing more than an elaborate fiction: it is as if Hardy is disallowing himself to be read as anything other than a pastoral tragedian with an eye toward a vanishing way of life.

Why Hardy would go to such pains to create this image for himself is debatable; but a powerful explanation is offered by Widdowson, who believes that Hardy chose to privilege one "category" of novels and consign the rest to "lesser" status because those so-called minor novels are deeply concerned with matters of social class, and Hardy was desperate to conceal his own working class origins. Furthermore, the "minor" novels often deal with themes of art and artifice, themes that had by 1912 become reviled by Hardy's critics; and, finally, the minor novels contain a good deal of autobiography, and—again—Hardy wished to deflect attention from who he *was*.[59] To Widdowson, Hardy was deeply invested in obscuring his class roots and fitting into bourgeois British society; therefore, in the General Preface, he merely codified an image of himself that was already developing among the critical establishment, and he adopted a system of classifying his novels that some earlier critics had informally proposed.[60] Hardy, in Widdowson's reading, both accepts a way of being classified by society and allows society to reaffirm what it likes best about his fiction—its pastoral, tragic, and ultimately humanistic qualities.

Widdowson's explanation of how Hardy has been appropriated by popular culture is, I believe, entirely correct; but I am less convinced by his argument that Hardy's actions were mostly geared toward masking his class origins. Like George Wotton in *Thomas Hardy: Towards a Materialist Criticism* (Totowa, NJ: Barnes and Noble, 1985) and Joe Fisher in *The Hidden Hardy* (1992), Widdowson seeks to uncover a "truer" Hardy—the Hardy who has been concealed through years of being constructed along humanistic lines—and, essentially, to reclaim this Hardy for Marxist or materialist purposes. Certainly, all three of these studies are valuable and often brilliant, but I believe that, in their reliance upon one established critical framework, these critics fall into the same trap they try to discredit—that of reading Hardy *one* way. One of the tenets I hold in this study is that Hardy leaves himself open to being read numerous ways, for he is not so much engaged in concealment or subversion as he is in deliberate *contradiction*.[61] In December 1885, as he was working on *The Woodlanders*, Hardy made this notation:

> The Hypocrisy of things. Nature is an arch-dissembler. A child is deceived completely; the older members of society more or less according to their

penetration; though even they seldom get to realize that *nothing* is at it appears [F. E. Hardy, *Life,* p. 176].

This short passage, I believe, does more to explain Hardy's intentions as a writer and his actions as an artist than anything else he wrote. Hardy's novels are largely concerned with the issue of misapprehension: his characters are continually seeing signs and symbols and using their personal interpretations of these visual stimuli as a way of interpreting the world around them and making decisions about their lives and actions. Consider, for instance, the significance with which Jude invests Mr. Phillotson's departing words in the opening chapter of *Jude the Obscure* (1895). Phillotson's speech about the importance of a university education really applies only to himself, yet Jude perceives that the schoolmaster is talking to and about *him.* Jude's subsequent actions are directed by his mistaken assumption that a university degree will define his role in the world, and he reads each new "sign" along the way as confirming or rejecting his actions. However, Jude's perceptions do not mesh with the reality around him, and they also conflict with Sue's own perceptions, resulting in two people who blind themselves to other possible truths and realities. To some degree, the theme of misapprehension informs each of Hardy's novels, and at times (as will be shown in subsequent chapters) it seems Hardy deliberately wants his readers to misapprehend what he wrote.

Why Hardy would *want* readers to misapprehend his fiction is tied up in what seemed to be his conviction that a novel could be more than what its genre (or genres) dictated it be.[62] As readers and critics have long noted, at times it is difficult to say for certain what "kind" of fiction Hardy wrote because he would often set up a novel as one thing and abruptly reveal it to be something else. *Far from the Madding Crowd* (1874) seems to be a pastoral comedy that incorporates tragedy; while *The Woodlanders* (1887) puts the grim tragedy of Giles Winterborne in contrast with the near-sex farce of Fitzpiers and his three mistresses. One of Hardy's least-discussed fictional efforts, *The Trumpet-Major*, is—as its author liked to point out—a meticulously researched historical novel on the lines of Scott, but the plot seems to be borrowed from Restoration comedy. A more thorough explanation of how Hardy displaces genres will be offered in the next chapter; for now it will suffice to say that Hardy puts different genres in opposition in order to break down both those genres and how they have traditionally been interpreted. What he accomplishes is to question what genres and language mean, and how they are constructed. Hardy's General Preface also puts language in opposition, as here he calls his best works "uninfluenced" yet also influenced by the Greeks; and he declares that his

Wessex locations have all "been done from the real," even though "no detail is guaranteed" (p. 395). Hardy deconstructs his own preface and his own meaning, challenging the reader to question the language he or she uses to read meaning into the preface.

What I am working toward here is an interpretation of Hardy's novels along Bakhtinian lines: a typical Hardy novel, like *The* Novel of Bakhtin's description, "parodies other genres (precisely in their role as genres); it exposes the conventionality of their forms and their language; it squeezes out some genres and incorporates others into its own peculiar structure, re-formulating and re-accentuating them."[63] As such, a Hardy novel can generate numerous readings, none more or less "correct" than another[64]; yet a good deal of criticism has tried to rein in Hardy's novels and render them into coherent and unified texts. The problem is that criticism has largely tied Hardy down to doing just one or two things—creating pastoral tragedies, decrying the plight of the working class, subverting capitalism—when in fact his novels are usually doing several things at one time, simultaneously embracing and questioning all means of being read. If Hardy has an overall theme it is the fallacy of reading coherence into incoherent words, texts, and images, and the mistake of the individuals who guide their lives and actions according to these readings and misreadings.

If this interpretation of Hardy I am proposing is valid, a natural question arises: how can Hardy's novels possibly be filmed with any degree of accuracy or fidelity? As has been argued throughout this chapter, literary criticism has played a major role in constructing both an image of the author and of what that author wrote; and as we have seen in the reviews of three film adaptations of Hardy's novels, Hardy has a long-established image which filmmakers have largely adhered to—or perhaps, as some critics have charged, distorted. It is the contention of this study that Hardy's novels are extremely difficult to film *as written*; however, his stories may be filmed if they are first filtered through a given set of critical and cultural concepts *about* Hardy and his works. It is through seeing Hardy as he traditionally has been seen that a recognizable "Hardy" emerges through film, and that a "coherent" translation of his novels to film form can be made. Essentially, the goal of this study is to understand how Hardy has been seen through film (and, in chapter 7, how he has been seen through television), and how these ways of seeing Hardy make him comprehendible to culture at large. However, before any individual film or novel can be discussed, it is necessary to consider both what a film adaptation *is*, and *how* a filmmaker can go about adapting Hardy to film.

2

What You See Is More Than What You Get: The Problem of Adapting Hardy to Film

Thomas Hardy's reputation as a "cinematic" novelist is fairly well established, and it began in his own lifetime. In 1922, Joseph Warren Beach likened *The Mayor of Casterbridge* to a "movie" in its use of dramatic scenes that require only the barest exposition and dialogue.[1] Beach's argument was adapted with few changes by Lord David Cecil in the 1940s,[2] and Cecil is usually credited with being the first to identify Hardy's literary techniques with those of the cinema—though he is more properly the populizer of this approach. In the 1970s, Hillis Miller commented on Hardy's "cinematic" attention to detail[3]; but it was David Lodge in the middle of that decade who first specifically labeled Hardy a *cinematic* novelist, and who offered the best definition of the term—which is, I believe, of Lodge's own coinage. To Lodge, a cinematic novelist is one who "deliberately renounces some of the freedom of representation and report afforded by the verbal medium, who imagines and reports his materials in primarily visual terms, and whose visualisations correspond in some significant respect to the visual effects characteristic of film."[4] Lodge goes on to argue this definition applies to the fiction of Thomas Hardy because

> Hardy uses verbal description as a film director uses the lens of his cam-
> era—to select, highlight, distort and enhance, creating a visualised world

that is both recognisably "real" and yet more vivid, intense and dramatically charged than our ordinary perception of the real world. The methods he uses can be readily analysed in cinematic terms: long shot, close-up, wide-angle, telephoto, zoom, etc. Indeed, some of Hardy's most original visual effects have since become cinematic clichés.[5]

Lodge stresses that Hardy was not, of course, *influenced* by film (by coincidence, Hardy's last novel was published in 1895, the year usually given for the birth of the film industry), but that Hardy *anticipated* film form.[6] A similar claim was made by John Wain in his 1965 introduction to *The Dynasts*; and, in fact, Wain stops just short of crediting Hardy with *creating* the art of film. Wain argues that when Hardy set about to write about the Napoleonic Wars he could not find the proper existing vehicle— novel, epic poem, drama—to do justice to his vision, and as a result he was forced to create an entirely new means of expressing himself. In Wain's view, the resulting work is nothing less than a "shooting-script."[7] Like Lodge, Wain identifies several cinematic tricks in Hardy's writing—most notably the use of "panoramas" to describe the battles and "close-ups" in the dramatic sequences—and he even goes so far as to say that, "as in the cinema itself," the visual power of *The Dynasts* is so great "we care very little about the verbal quality of the script."[8] The most recent analysis of Hardy's proto-cinematic techniques was made in 1979 by Joan Grundy, who persuasively argues that Hardy was inspired by the same optical devices and amusements that also influenced many early filmmakers— panoramas, dioramas, magic-lantern shows—and that his deployment of these visual tricks in his writings not only anticipated film but provided him with a powerful metaphor he would employ in his novels and poetry: that life, like a magic-lantern show, is a series of shadows and illusions.[9]

The views of these critics all echo Sergei Eisenstein's famous theory that early filmmakers borrowed their visual and storytelling techniques from the great Victorian writers,[10] though Grundy is the only one to acknowledge Eisenstein in her argument. It would logically follow that, as Hardy's novels are widely seen to be cinematic, they would also be highly filmable; but, paradoxically, many critics feel that Hardy's cinematic qualities actually keep his novels from being the source of satisfying films. Lodge himself claims that "it is difficult for film adaptation to do justice to Hardy's novels precisely because effects that are unusual in written description are commonplace in film"[11]; and Neil Sinyard agrees, saying, "Hardy is so intimidatingly visual as to make the camera seem almost redundant: the director can only duplicate, not enhance."[12] Joy Gould Boyum believes that the problem with filming Hardy is simply that, once you get past his "much-vaunted pictorialism," you're left with melodrama, didacticism, artificial plots, and dated social themes—all things that are of little interest to modern audiences.[13]

What is interesting about all of the comments—excepting those of Boyum, who is a film theorist—is that, while they are very knowledgeable about Hardy, they seem limited in their understanding of film. Lodge and Sinyard flatly state that all a filmmaker can do is imitate Hardy's style, and they imply that imitation would, by its very nature, be static and boring. This is, of course, patently untrue. A good filmmaker can easily follow Hardy's written descriptions and create moments that make for good cinema and remain true to Hardy—as is evidenced by Roman Polanski's letter-perfect "strawberry" scene from *Tess*, which conveys both the interest of Hardy's narrator in Tess's mouth as well as the obvious sexual imagery of the fruit between her lips. Polanski here is clearly imitating Hardy, and the scene is anything but boring or static. Lodge also claims that Hardy's "cinematic" devices have since fallen into the realm of movie clichés, but this underestimates the film medium, for those devices—the long shot, the tracking shot, and so on—are part of the language of cinema. To suggest a film viewer would dismiss a good tracking shot as trite is like saying a novel reader would be bored by a descriptive paragraph simply because she's encountered descriptive paragraphs before. Again, it is the *quality* of what is filmed that is important; and all of the filmmakers who have

Tess (Nastassia Kinski) takes the strawberry from the hand of Alec (Leigh Lawson) in Roman Polanski's *Tess* (1979).

adapted Hardy have, to some degree or other, succeeded in capturing some of Hardy's visual power. In fact, the one constant among the three major films that will be analyzed in this study is that they have been praised for their camerawork and visual appeal. Lodge and Sinyard are, I believe, incorrect in their arguments that following Hardy's visual cues makes for a flat adaptation; however, it is clear that a filmmaker needs to do *more* than simply find visual equivalents to Hardy's written descriptions to create a good film. The question of *what* a filmmaker needs to do to successfully film a novel hits at the very heart of that disparate branch of film studies that can only loosely be labeled adaptation theory.

At this stage, I am putting Hardy somewhat into the background in order to discuss the mechanics of film adaptation. All too often, film versions of famous or classic novels become straw men for the critics: Joy Boyum rightly charges that literary scholars are apt to fault adaptations for being untrue to their source novels, and adherents to "pure film" theory are liable to dismiss adaptations for being unoriginal *as films*.[14] Essentially, I am approaching the Hardy adaptations from the standpoint of a "literary scholar," but I do not want to get involved in the tiresome exercise of comparing and contrasting the novels and films and carping because the filmmakers weren't faithful to every word of Hardy's prose. My interest is in determining how the films create cultural images of Hardy and of the kinds of fiction he wrote. To a good degree, I am operating under the assumption that a filmmaker *will* make changes — often major ones — to the source novels, both because changes are inevitable in the process of transferring a novel to film, and because such changes are often necessary in order to make "Hardy" more visible to the viewer. A further presupposition on my part is that the filmmakers are acting in good faith. As will be shown in the following three chapters, the filmmakers under discussion — John Schlesinger, Roman Polanski, and Michael Winterbottom — all felt they were being true to Hardy's "vision," and all sought to reproduce this vision faithfully, even if their films had to change Hardy's original story somewhat in the process. It is my intention to act in good faith as well: in this study, film will never be approached as a "lesser" art form than the novel; no film under discussion will be knocked for trivial deviations from Hardy; and major changes will be analyzed in light of *why* those changes were made and *what* they do in the film and to Hardy. Finally, the films will be analyzed not just in the light of Hardy's novels, but in light of the director's total output of films and in the context of the cultural and social movements in the cinema that helped shape the film itself. However, I recognize that it isn't enough to merely be respectful to the adaptation and to the adaptor. Definite terms for judging how a successful adaptation can be made must be established, and adaptation theory has struggled to find the right terms since its inception.[15]

The problem with adaptation theory, as I see it, is that it has labored since 1957 under the weight of the man who essentially founded adaptation studies, George Bluestone.[16] Bluestone's *Novels into Film* lays out several precepts about the differences between novels and films that affect adaptation, and these precepts have invariably been touched upon by every adaptation study to follow. Bluestone's basic tenets are that the novel is communicated through word-symbols and film is communicated through literal images, and these two basic forms are antithetical[17]; that film editing is equivalent to, but not the same thing as, the literary trope[18]; and—probably most famously—that "the novel has three tenses: the film has only one,"[19] meaning films always take place in the *present*, even if the action takes place in the past, while novels are always free to shift tenses.[20] In Bluestone's view, film originated as part hobby, part folk art: as early filmmakers began to experiment with the unique properties of the medium and to seek out their own subjects, they succeeded in creating film narrative, independent of the novel; while the novel itself is an assimilation of different kinds of *writing*. Bluestone argues that the novel takes in all written forms, and so it moved to an inevitable questioning of the words that make up its own being[21]—so that the fragmented modernist novel becomes the end product of *all* fiction writing. Bluestone's theory would therefore reject the Eisensteinian notion that film form early on borrowed its narrative techniques from the novel; and, in fact, Bluestone suggests the ties between novel form and film form based on certain similarities in their narrative structures are illusory. In the end, Bluestone flat-out rejects the idea that adaptation from novel to film is even possible: he argues that what the filmmaker "adapts is a kind of paraphrase of the novel—the novel viewed as raw material." He concludes that critics must recognize that the novel will inevitably be "destroyed" in the film version, but in this destruction "the filmist becomes not a translator for an established author, but a new author in his own right."[22]

This first major study on film adaptation, then, has as its central premise the notion that adaptation is fundamentally *impossible*; and Bluestone's arguments have had, for several years at least, some strong adherents.[23] One of the more thorough dismissals of the adaptability of novels to cinema was made by Jean Mitry in 1971. Like Bluestone, Mitry insists that the fundamental differences between novels and films are in time and tense; but, even more so than in Bluestone, Mitry's approach is firmly grounded in semiotics. "Time in the novel," he argues, "is constructed with words. In the cinema it is constructed with actions. The novel *creates* a

world while the cinema *puts us in the presence* of a world which it organizes according to a certain continuity. *The novel is a narrative which organizes itself in a world; the film, a world which organizes itself in a narrative.*[24]
Mitry, perhaps influenced by Barthes's theories on narrative, sees the characters, actions, and basic structure of any novel as springing from the
unique infrastructure of *the* novel form, and he argues that to remove any
of these elements from the novel and to then transfer them to film is to
rob those elements of their essential meaning.[25] Later, Edward Murray also
found novel form and film incompatible; but his view is that a novel's *style*
makes it inherently unadaptable. Murray asks, "How can a *literary style* be
communicated on the screen? Take away Henry James's seemingly endless fussy qualifications, or Conrad's almost too perfect English diction —
and what's left?"[26] Although his study does not use the term, it is essentially
semiotic in nature, for, like Mitry, Murray sees the novel's characters,
action, and psychology — all of which he lumps together into "style" — as
springing entirely from the way the author chooses and arranges words.
This all-important element of verbal style is, to Murray, a hindrance to
adaptation, since in a movie "'style' is almost ('almost' because dialogue
in a film is part of its style) wholly nonverbal."[27]

These assessments were all published as film studies was defining
itself, and before a few critics in the late 1970s and 1980s began to formulate
theories on the *mechanics* of adaptation as opposed to its *efficacy*; but the
prejudices and biases expressed by Bluestone and those who came after
are still current in many circles. A common view among many film theorists and critics in general is that film should be evaluated *as is,* and the
source novel should either be forgotten or merely viewed (in Bluestone's
phrase, which he borrowed from Balázs) as "raw material." This is perhaps
easy to do when the novel is little known; but when the film adaptation is
of a novel that has a good deal of name value on its own — a bestseller, a
cultural phenomenon, or especially a work of "classic" or "canonized" literature — it becomes far more problematic to disentangle the two media.

The biggest barrier to viewing "classic" film adaptations as separate
from their source novels is that all too often the adaptations insist on being
viewed *as* adaptations. In the previous chapter, I indicated the degree to
which movie advertisements have sold the films by trading on the novel's
or the author's reputation, and the attempts filmmakers have made to signal the author's "presence" in the film by imitating print images or by
evoking biographical data; and today, the most common way for an adaptation to defer to the source novel is to incorporate the author's name into
the film's title. *Emma* (Douglas McGrath, 1996) was widely advertised as
Jane Austen's Emma, though that is not the title that appears onscreen;

and during the making of Adrian Lyne's controversial new version of *Lolita*, the project was referred to as *Vladimir Nabokov's Lolita*, though when the film finally emerged in the United States in 1997, Nabokov's name did not appear as part of the title. However, both *Bram Stoker's Dracula* (Francis Ford Coppola, 1992) and *Mary Shelley's Frankenstein* (Kenneth Branagh, 1994) boldly display the author's names as part of their titles, both (presumably) as a way of differentiating themselves from earlier adaptations and establishing themselves as more "faithful" to the original novels than were previous films—even though each film takes major detours from its source. The Coppola film also became part of a now common tie-in venture that, to its small credit, at least exemplifies the free exchange between books and films: Signet Books issued both Bram Stoker's 1897 novel, *Dracula*, complete with the film's poster art and logo on its cover, as well as a novel entitled *Bram Stoker's Dracula*, written by Fred Saberhagen and James V. Hart, which was based on Hart's screenplay, which *itself* was based on the novel by Bram Stoker!

A further stumbling block to separating the film adaptation from its source is that, in recent years, it has been difficult for a film to appropriate a classic novel's title and make radical changes to the source without incurring the wrath of critics and audiences. Cuarón's modern-dress *Great Expectations* (see Chapter 1) was a modest critical success and a substantial box office hit, but it achieved its success without hiding its experimental agenda of seeing how Dickens's basic story would play itself out in a contemporary American setting. It made no pretensions to *being* Dickens's novel. In contrast, director Roland Joffé made the claim that his adaptation of *The Scarlet Letter* (1995) is both a reflection of Nathaniel Hawthorne's "divided mind" about sexual behaviors and is actually "the story that Hawthorne wished he could have told in 1850"[28]—meaning the film he created is truer to the novelist's intentions than even the original novel was. Joffé's film actually grafts 1990s attitudes and ideas on to both Hawthorne's novel and on to the colonial era in which it is set: the result is a good deal of screen time devoted to Hester and Dimmesdale exploring their sexual togetherness in scenes of passionate lovemaking and arty nudity, and the addition of several elements that are to be found nowhere in Hawthorne: a black slave for Hester, a heroic depiction of the Iroquois (both elements are designed, presumably, to comment on American racism), and a happy ending in which Hester, Dimmesdale, and Pearl escape from their narrow-minded Puritan community, signified by Hester's leaving the scarlet letter itself in the mud. The film was roundly ridiculed and the screenplay was dismissed as a politically correct assault on the novel, and audiences for their part stayed home. It is difficult to believe that Hawthorne's *Scarlet Letter*, which most Americans probably remember with some pain as required school reading, could generate such affection that people would want to defend it against the potential damage from a loose film adaptation; but the consensus seemed to be that most people *know* what *The Scarlet Letter* is *supposed* to be, and Joffé's film wasn't it.

It is also not too great of a stretch to say that, increasingly, the distinctions between novels and films are becoming so blurred that it is hard to say either medium can stand alone. As Hardy's own comment that a film version of *Tess* could encourage people to read the novel (see Chapter 1) shows, men and women have long come to works of literature by *first* experiencing them through film adaptations; and, in many cases, reading the book becomes a way of reliving the filmgoing experience. The explosion of interest in the works of E. M. Forster and Jane Austen in the 1980s and 1990s was sparked by the *initial* "rediscovery" of their novels by filmmakers. Today, bestsellers often make it to the screen within two or three years; and many contemporary authors have had their reputations "made" by having a hit film adapted from one of their books. With films and novels—and, occasionally and if they are alive, the original authors—so willing to work hand in hand with each other, and with audiences viewing films and novels as fairly interactive media, it has become very difficult to claim that a film version of a novel *must* be allowed to stand on its own.

It is perhaps with a recognition of the free flow between novels and films that Charles Eidsvik in 1975 called for a "politique des adaptations," a theory that explains how film adaptation mutually benefits literature *and* film. Eidsvik was perhaps one of the first critics to realize that novels and films operate in a dynamic that is both competitive and complementary: among his most interesting claims are that novel writers are apt to push themselves to be more experimental and daring in their works to keep their novels from easily being "co-opted" by a "kitschy" film adaptation; and that difficult and challenging novels force filmmakers to stretch the limits of film art and technology to create a movie that does justice to the novel.[29] In short, Eidsvik sees the adaptation as a *separate* art form that stimulates growth in the two media, and he demands the adaptation be taken more seriously for what it does. Whether because of Eidsvik or not, the most interesting theories on the mechanics of adaptation emerged in the fifteen years that followed his essay, and it is from these theories that my own approach to the film adaptations of Thomas Hardy will be drawn.

The Mechanics of Adaptation: Intertextuality

One of the most welcome additions to adaptation theory has been the intertextual approach, which has had the effect of reducing Bluestone's niggling complaint that novels and films are made up of entirely different sign systems that do not communicate with one another. Under the intertextual approach, novels and films—and other forms of art as well—are brought under the same umbrella: that of a text that is always *communicating*. Working largely from the semiotic theories of Metz,[30] Keith Cohen has sought to reduce the differences between the written word and the visual image by arguing that each are "signs aimed at communicating something. In this sense, word and image are each part of a larger system of signification—part of a *language*."[31] Cohen acknowledges that the word and the image are indeed different in that the word possesses a double articulation (it is both signifier and signified) while the image possesses a single articulation, so that "while the sign *table* elicits different mental images for different readers, the filmic image of a table results in the same mental image for every spectator"; but he argues there is a good deal of similarity between the written word and the film image because "in each case a mental image is created. Both novel and cinema *refer* to, or at least *evoke*, some global configuration that is summoned up by the receiver of their messages."[32]

By viewing novels and films not as conflicting forces but as agents within the same sign system, the adaptation can be seen not as something that leeches off the original novel, but as something that does much the same work as the original: simply put, both are communicating a message. In the particular study just quoted, Cohen is chiefly concerned with showing that "the same codes [in one form of media] may appear in more than one system,"[33] and he does not deal with adaptation *per se*[34]; but other critics have used intertextuality as the basis for practical theories on adaptation. For instance, Christopher Orr, largely working from Barthes's "The Death of the Author," suggests that the novel and its film adaptation *both* draw from the same "centers of culture." In Orr's terms, the literary source can be described as "one of a series of pre-texts which share some of the same narrative conventions as the film adaptation," so that "the art of adapting a text from another medium is, in effect, the privileging or underlining of certain quotations [Barthes's term for pre-existing narrative codes] within the film's intertextual space."[35] With this approach in mind, we could say that in his film of *Tess*, Polanski was not really *dramatizing* Hardy's critique of the way women were perceived in late Victorian England; rather, both Hardy and Polanski drew from the *same* cultural assumptions about women, resulting in a degree of correspondence between Tess in the novel and Tess in the film.

Given my argument that novels and films are becoming more fluid in their relations to each other—that each medium, in effect, is sharing more of its narrative space—it only makes sense that this study will, to a degree, be an intertextual one. However, intertextuality can be taken to a logical extreme that would render viewing adaptations *as* adaptations pointless. In Barthes's original system, from which Orr draws,

> a text is not a line of words releasing a single "theological" meaning (the "message" of the Author-God) but a multi-dimensional space in which a variety of writings, none of them original, blend and clash. The text is a tissue of quotations drawn from the innumerable centres of culture. ...[T]he writer can only imitate a gesture that is always anterior, never original. His only power is to mix writings, to counter the ones with the others, in such a way as never to rest on any one of them.[36]

It is with this system as a model that Barthes argues it is pointless for literary criticism to search for the imprint of the "author," for the author is merely a manipulator of signs, someone who delved into the realm of pre-existing codes and signifiers and arranged them into a pattern we call narrative. Look beyond the narrative and you'll find nothing more than the original signs and codes. And it is working from this system that Orr claims the film adaptor delves into the same realm of signifiers and comes out with a film that frequently makes gestures toward the original novel's signs and codes. From there, Orr says, it is up to the *viewer* to arrange the film's signs into something coherent and meaningful: "Every person in a given audience sees a different film. What makes one person's experience of the film richer or simply more interesting than another's are the cultural references at that person's disposal and the strategies he or she uses to organize those references."[37]

Granted, individuals see films differently, but it seems to me that Orr pretty much discounts the idea of culture being a *shared* experience. As I have been indicating throughout this study, culture *is* largely shared, and culture easily dictates a mass response. When Joffé's *Scarlet Letter* failed with both audiences and critics and was derided as a bastardization of Hawthorne, this was a *cultural* response—a sense shared by many people that the film was something false or *other* than what it was supposed to be. If it were the case that a novel and its film adaptation merely sprang from the same sign system and that all they share is a certain privileging of the same signs, such uniform reactions to film adaptations of classic novels would not exist: the movie could make whatever changes it wishes, and only the most pedantic among us would care. It seems to me that if Barthes is correct that the author is merely a manipulator of signs, that manipulation *itself* is done in a way that is still characteristic and recognizable of a particular writer, so that both the writer and what he or she writes becomes identifiable to—and absorbed by—the general culture.

Further, though I agree that both novels and films spring from the same "multi-dimensional" narrative space, it also seems that the signs and signifiers that comprise any given novel or film are always affected by history and by historical presuppositions about particular novels and about film in general. As Donald F. Larsson explains, any novel is part of the "historical matrix"—it is an element of a definite time, place, and culture—but the novel inevitably becomes distorted by subsequent readings and critical interpretations.[38] In other words, what had one meaning to the novel's original readers has another meaning for the next wave of readers, and then again for the next. More importantly (for this study, at least), Larsson argues that

> the degree of historical distortion in an adaptation is complicated further by the *cultural* history of the novel. Only rarely does a well-known work escape a popularization which incorporates the text as part of general mass culture with little or no regard for its actual content. In these cases, the text which is brought to the screen is less the novel itself than the novel as bowdlerized for public school texts, as fitted out for touring stage presentations, as enshrined in lovable characters (and even lovable authors) from the canons of Acceptable Literature.[39]

Larsson's sweeping statement that what is adapted is not the novel *as is* but a bowdlerization may seem to hark back to Bluestone's claim that the filmmaker really adapts a "paraphrase" of the novel, but there is a crucial difference: Bluestone sees film producers as cynically exploiting novels, merely digging out of them what can be quickly transformed into useable film material; Larsson argues it is culture at large that digs what it likes best out of novels and then codifies those elements: in effect, culture dictates how the novel is read, and film adaptations of that novel will more than likely be faithful to that cultural reading. A premise I am working with in this study is that both novels and films spring from the same sign system and that there is considerable interchange between signs, which makes adaptation highly possible; but the signs from each individual novel and film are codified by the forces of history and culture, so that the signs are invariably encrusted *with* history and culture.

To this point, I am still dealing with adaptation on a theoretical level: *what* is adapted may have been explained, but *how* adaptation takes place still needs to be discussed. The central issue here is how the signifiers from one form (the novel) may be transferred to another (the film) and what happens to those signifiers once they are transformed. Sadly, few adaptation theorists have tried to lay out a method for adaptation: as valuable as their arguments are, Cohen, Orr, and Larsson remain committed to explaining only a general theory of adaptation; and even Joy Boyum's lengthy and significant study doesn't really get down to the mechanics of adaptation. Only two studies, which appeared about a year apart, have really attempted to take a "systematic" approach to adaptations, and the results are radically different.

Griffith's Approach: Imitation

To take the most recent study first, James Griffith in 1997 sought to prove that there is little difference between the ways novels and films communicate; but where earlier critics had tried to find semiotic links between the two forms of communication, Griffith argues the word and the image are related in that they are both imitations of something *real*. Working from a quasi-Classical framework he dubs Neo-Aristotelianism, Griffith contends the novel is the end product of the author's *choices*: the novelist wishes to understand the "shaping cause" that calls the work into being, so the novelist uses all the tools of writing to help him or her realize that original cause. Further, the reader participates in the process of uncovery by using the "evidence" in the text to recreate the shaping cause.[40] To Griffith, the verbal and literary devices the author chooses to give shape to the novel are artificial representations of things that are real and concrete; and he feels this artistic mimesis is largely the same from one medium to another:

> [An] author has themes, moods, or effects to convey, for which he or she then invents an action to be portrayed with chosen techniques in words. The author makes choices more complex than finding a form adequate to the content. The material or medium does not signify much by comparison: the effects, actions, even some techniques may be communicated through the images and sounds of film, and communicated adequately to match the components of the novel.[41]

In Griffith's study, elements of novelistic "style" are stripped down and made subordinate to the novel's imitative *actions*, for "Stylistic touches have more or less importance to the effect of the whole novel, but the material cause never suffices alone for that effect."[42] The actions are important to Griffith both because they make up the structure of the novel, and because they are artificial and arbitrary—mere representations of a reality that is beyond the text. Griffith further argues that filmmakers create similar if not the same artificial actions to realize the shaping causes of their films; therefore, novels and films are doing largely the same work, and for a filmmaker to create an adaptation of a novel all he or she needs to do is imitate roughly the same choices that the original novelist made. The ideal film adaptation, in Griffith's terms, is "an adaptation of a good novel that faithfully imitates the aesthetic choices that make the novel a success, and thereby the film also." However, Griffith stresses that a good filmmaker should strive to imitate only those actions that create the overall *effect* of the novel; meaning the filmmaker should try to capture the novel's mood and tone, and not necessarily every detail from the novel. By imitating only the novel's *effect*, the filmmaker is free to make independent aesthetic choices that allow the film to work *as* a film.[43]

Frankly, it seems to me that Griffith doubles back on himself, arguing that filmmakers *can* imitate the same *actions*—which would, presumably, relate to plot, story, and certain narrative details—that the novelist made, but stressing that they *should* be faithful *only* to the "effect." This problem prevents me from fully endorsing Griffith's theory; but I recognize the value of considering "effect" in evaluating the relationship of the film adaptation to its source novel. The three filmmakers who will be most often discussed in this study have all tried to "imitate" Hardy's most significant effects, and have largely succeeded in conveying the mood or tone Hardy is usually said to have established in his original novels: John Schlesinger utilizes long, lingering takes of authentic Dorset countryside to convey the "pastoralism" of *Far from the Madding Crowd*; Polanski concentrates on faces to show the gradations of class and character in *Tess*; and Michael Winterbottom focuses on dull gray countryside and oppressive Gothic architecture to convey the somberness of *Jude*. I also find Griffith's scheme valuable because it supports a point I have been making. We can agree that any film version of a Hardy novel will not be authentic Hardy but rather *imitation* Hardy (or imitation Dickens or imitation Austen, whatever the case may be), but it still seems to me that what is imitated is Hardy's novel *as culturally apprehended*. In other words, if the general "effect" of *Jude the Obscure* is determined to be that of classical tragedy—and not that of, say, caustic satire (which is another possible reading of *Jude's* effect)—then the filmmaker is likely to imitate those actions in Hardy that most allow the novel to be read as a tragedy and ignore those that open the novel to being read as a satire. Winterbottom's *Jude*, then, would be an imitation not just of *Jude the Obscure*, but a codification of how the novel is popularly read.

McFarlane's Approach: A Barthean System

A much more practical approach to adaptation was proposed by Brian McFarlane in 1996. Like Orr before him, McFarlane takes his inspiration from Barthes, in this case, from Barthes's essay "Introduction to the Structural Analysis of Narratives." McFarlane embraces Barthes's theory that narratives are entirely made up of *functions* that fall into two groups: distributional and integrational.[44] As McFarlane describes it,

> To distributional functions, Barthes gives the name of *functions proper*; integrational functions he calls *indices*. The former refer to actions and events; they are "horizontal" in nature, and they are strung together linearly throughout the text; they have to do with "operations"; they refer to a functionality of *doing*. *Indices* denotes a "more or less diffuse concept which is nevertheless necessary to the meaning of the story." This concept embraces, for instance, psychological information relating to characters, data regarding their identity, notations of atmosphere and representations of place. Indices are "vertical" in nature, influencing our reading of narrative in a pervasive rather than a linear way; they do not refer to operations but to a functionality of *being*.[45]

The narrative functions are further broken down by Barthes into *cardinal plot functions* and *catalyzers*. In McFarlane's words,

> *Cardinal functions* are the "hinge-points" of narrative: that is, the actions they refer to open up alternatives of consequence to the development of the story: they create "risky" moments in the narrative and it is crucial to narrativity ... that the reader recognizes the possibility of such alternative consequences. The linking together of cardinal functions provides the irreducible bare bones of the narrative.[46]

The catalyzers

> work in ways which are complementary to and supportive of the cardinal functions. They denote small actions (e.g. the laying of the table for a meal which may in turn give rise to an action of cardinal importance to the story); their role is to root the cardinal functions in a particular kind of reality, to enrich the texture of those functions ... [they] "lay out areas of safety, rests, luxuries"; they account for the moment-to-moment minutiae of the narrative.[47]

By contrast, the indices do not involve physical actions. As McFarlane explains, Barthes subdivides this function into *indices proper* ("concepts such as character and atmosphere") and *informants* ("ready made" knowledge provided to the reader by the author, such as "the names, ages, and professions of characters, certain details of the physical setting," etc.).[48] The indices are crucial to the text in that they establish mood, tone, character, and the like; and they are important in that they indicate how the narrative should be *read*, but they do not in and of themselves move the narrative forward.

Barthes's system is remarkably simple and straightforward, and we can see how it works by looking at an important sequence from *Tess of the d'Urbervilles*. The death of Prince, the Durbeyfields' horse, in Chapter 4, is a cardinal plot function in that the narrative "hinges" on this event: the loss of income that will ensue from Prince's death forces Tess to go to the d'Urberville estate to look for financial help (which is itself merely a plot function). Once at The Slopes, she meets Alec, an action that qualifies as another *cardinal* plot function in that it leads directly to her being hired on to the property (and, of course, on meeting Tess, Alec is possessed with the desire to seduce her), and so on. The entire narrative of *Tess* consists of such "risky moments," and how Tess responds to them largely dictates the momentum of the plot. Such surrounding incidents as Tess's comment to her brother before the accident that they are living on a "blighted" star (p. 21), or even her nodding off on the cart qualify as catalyzers to the cardinal plot function of Prince's death, in that they "set the stage" for the action; while such elements as the blood that spurts from Prince's dying body, and the postman's scolding of Tess, are all *indices*—they add detail to the action and provide a way of reading what is going on.

McFarlane applies Barthes's system to film adaptation by arguing that the "functions proper" are entirely *transferable* to film—meaning they can be reproduced *in toto* in the film medium. McFarlane contends that a film adaptation may reproduce every single plot function from the novel, but "when a major cardinal function is deleted or altered in the film version of the novel (e.g. to provide a happy rather than a sombre ending), this is apt to occasion critical outrage and popular disaffection. The filmmaker bent on 'faithful' adaptation must, as a basis for such an enterprise, seek to preserve the major cardinal functions."[49] We can see the truth of this statement by considering the fact Polanski chose to omit the scene where Prince dies: in the film, Joan learns of Jack's "noble" ancestry and then promptly encourages Tess to present herself to the d'Urbervilles and "claim kin"; and then there is a cut to Tess in the coach en route to The Slopes. Hardy's basic plot function here is retained (in the end, it is primarily important that Tess get to the property and meet Alec); but by eliminating the *cardinal* plot function—the death of the horse—Polanski entirely changes Tess's *reason* for going to the d'Urbervilles. Furthermore, by eliminating this sequence Polanski creates more of an indictment of Joan

Durbeyfield's behavior toward her daughter than Hardy ever did. In this instance, Polanski's dropping of this cardinal function results in a lack of fidelity to Hardy because it significantly alters a portion of the story Hardy tells, although—as I explain in Chapter 4—Polanski's change to the story creates a complication that is in itself somewhat Hardean.

McFarlane goes on to argue that the catalyzers and some of the "indices proper" in the narrative are also transferable to film (for instance, when a director casts an actor who fits the description of the character as given by the author); but that indices by and large are *not* directly transferable to film, and it is only in this sense that adaptation—or, as McFarlane calls it, *adaptation proper*—begins. Like many film theorists before him, McFarlane argues that the novel "draws upon a wholly *verbal* sign system, the film variously, and sometimes simultaneously, on *visual, aural,* and *verbal* signifiers"; and that "the verbal sign, with its low iconicity and high symbolic function, works *conceptually,* whereas the cinematic sign, with its high iconicity and uncertain symbolic function, works directly, sensuously, *perceptually.*"[50] Where McFarlane differs from earlier film theorists is that he argues sign systems are only *parts* of novels and films, and do not constitute their sole identifying characteristics. McFarlane categorizes all verbal and visual/aural sign systems under the heading of narrative indices—they affect how the work is *perceived,* but they do not affect how the plot functions *act.* Since the novel's verbal indices do not readily meet the visual needs of film, the filmmaker must here *adapt* and find a way of communicating through film what has been communicated on paper. It is in the realm of "adaptation proper" that the filmmaker is freest to shape and mold the film into something personal—something that stands on its own as a film or as something that reflects upon the original novel.[51]

McFarlane's system for analyzing adaptations strikes me as the best of all approaches for several reasons. First, it is concrete and workable. It is a fairly easy matter to identify any novel's plot functions and to then determine if they have been retained in the film version. Second, McFarlane's approach acknowledges the shared narrative space of novels and films while allowing for the unique properties of both media. Third, McFarlane's system allows the film to be viewed both as an adaptation and as an original film: essentially, McFarlane shows that the filmmaker's freedom is in manipulating the novelist's plot functions and in finding cinematic indices to replace the novelistic ones. And it is at this point that I can bring this study firmly back to Hardy, for I believe that in Hardy's fiction, the *indices* are ultimately more important than the plot functions; and how the filmmakers choose to adapt the indices to film results inevitably in a cultural reading of Hardy.

Hardy's Plot Functions and Indices

In the first chapter I argued that the distinguishing feature of Hardy's fiction is his deployment of perspective. Broadly speaking, most significant actions (or cardinal plot functions) in his novels are seen through the eyes of a character or filtered through the perspective of a highly idiosyncratic omniscient narrator. A common feature in Hardy's fiction is that no two perspectives are entirely alike, so how the plot function is to be read is often thrown into doubt. Very often, more than one mode of reading will be put in conflict with another, so that it appears Hardy is breaking down the conventions of narratives and of language. What the "typical" Hardy novel *does* is raise questions: it questions language, it questions genres, it questions the ways people construct themselves, and it questions its own status *as* a novel. To illustrate how Hardy achieves this effect, I will analyze a key scene from a "representative" Hardy novel, *The Woodlanders*, and then isolate the problem that arises when one tries to adapt Hardy's indices to film.

Why use *The Woodlanders* to illustrate Hardy's narrative strategies? There are several reasons. First, it is a fairly unimpeachable source. *The Woodlanders* is usually acknowledged as one of Hardy's six "major" (or even "best") novels, so I am working with a well-known text that most readers would agree contains elements that are typically "Hardean." Second, despite its generally acknowledged "major" status, critics have long been unsure what to make of *The Woodlanders*: as Penny Boumelha observes, the novel "draws on genres so widely disparate as to be at times incompatible."[52] Critics have tried to peg *The Woodlanders* as a pastoral, a melodrama, a farce, a protest against divorce laws, or as a mixture of any of the above[53]; yet for years the novel has resisted most attempts at classification. Perhaps because it is so difficult to determine just *what The Woodlanders is*, a good many critics have left it alone: of all Hardy's "major" works, it has perhaps received the least attention. It is precisely *The Woodlanders*'s capacity to open itself to many readings yet resist them all that convinces me this novel is perhaps the best illustration of Hardy's narrative approach. Finally—and most importantly—*The Woodlanders* clearly illustrates how important in Hardy's fiction the act of *seeing* is to catalyzing—and even generating—plot functions.

Significantly, what is arguably the first—and certainly not less than the second—cardinal plot function in *The Woodlanders*[54] is made clear to the reader through the devices of dialogue, seeing, and eavesdropping. In Chapter 3, as Marty South is delivering the gad-spars to the timber merchant George Melbury, she finds herself inadvertently listening to

Melbury's late-night conversation with his wife, where he recounts his old "wrong" against Giles Winterborne's father and his decision to make amends "by letting his daughter marry the lad; not only that but [Melbury had given] her the best education he could afford, so as to make the gift as valuable a one as it lay in his power to bestow" (p. 49). One of the most striking qualities of this scene is its artificiality: it resembles a theater piece in which two characters stand upstage and dispense vital plot information while a third character lurks backstage, listening in; but, as has been commented on by numerous critics, this mode of overhearing is one of the most common features in Hardy's fiction.[55] More importantly, what the characters *perceive* during the process of overhearing more often than not affects what they do. In the case of the scene from *The Woodlanders*, the plot is affected in two ways: first, both the reader and Marty are given a glimpse into Melbury's own process of perceiving—which leads, in turn, to his actions. The old timber merchant fears that in trying to make Grace "good enough" for Giles he has actually made her *too* good for him. From this point his actions will largely be directed toward finding a way to keep Giles from marrying Grace—even though a formal courtship has never been arranged, and the subject has never even been formally broached with Giles (there is a rather general understanding between the two men). Melbury's acts are directed by his *perceptions* of who Giles is and who Grace must turn out to be.

Second, after overhearing Melbury's conversation, Marty chooses to live a life of renunciation. She gives up all hope that Giles will marry her, and she decides to cut off her hair and sell it. The hair is intended to make a wig for Felice Charmond, and it will play a vital role in Felice's later "exposure"; and Marty will further affect the plot in that she tries to—and eventually will—convince Giles to join her in embracing a tragic view of the world. One moment of overhearing, then, puts into motion the events that immediately touch upon the lives of six major characters—Giles, Grace, Melbury, Marty, Felice, and, later, through Grace and Felice, Fitzpiers. The cardinality of this plot function should be clear; but, as was established earlier, plot functions are always surrounded by catalyzers and indices—devices outside the plot that indicate how the functions should be read. In the case of the sequence from *The Woodlanders*, Hardy deploys a device of multiple perspectives that throw the meaning of this plot function into doubt. After Melbury announces that he will send for Grace, the narrator comments,

> Melbury perhaps was an unlucky man in having the sentiment which could make him wander out in the night to regard the imprint of a daughter's

footstep. Nature does not carry on her government with a view to such feelings; and when advancing years render the opened hearts of those who possess them less dextrous than formerly in shutting against the blast, they must inevitably, like little celandines, suffer "buffeting at will by rain and storm."

But her own existence, and not Mr. Melbury's, was the centre of Marty's consciousness, and it was in relation to this that the matter struck her as she slowly withdrew.

"That, then, is the secret of it all," she said. "I had half thought so. And Giles Winterborne is not for me!" [p. 50].

Hardy provides two narrative indices here that ostensibly seem to harmonize with each other and open the incident to being read as a tragedy. Marty's perspective is plain enough: she views the information she has just received as a personal disaster, a sign to renounce her hopes. The narrator would also seem to be encouraging the reader to interpret what has happened tragically, for he compares Melbury to the flower in Wordsworth's "The Small Celandine"—a plant that, when young, folds up in the cold and rain; but when it is old, exposes itself to those very same destructive natural forces. Going by Wordsworth, then, Melbury can be read as having entered the stage in his life when he has to give himself up to the decaying powers of Nature, to tragically resigning himself to losing those faculties he took for granted in his youth. This is certainly a strange reading in light of the melodramatic and artificial circumstances in which the passage appears, and especially in light of the fact that Melbury emerges in the novel as something of a traditional comic figure: the stuffy father who wishes to prevent his daughter from marrying beneath her station.

In just one passage, then, it can be seen that a cardinal plot function is largely brought into being by *perspective*. The perspectives multiply (from Marty to Melbury to Hardy's narrator to Wordsworth), interact with each other, and perhaps cancel each other out. What *happens* in the story is obvious, but through the device of multiple perspectives, Hardy seems to question *why* it happens: Melbury acts in accordance with his own suppositions about a situation, Marty acts according to the words she hears, and the narrator alludes to a nature poem to modify the action for the reader. The authority behind this plot function is never one thing or another—it is made up of several things, all ultimately the products of *words*: either spoken (Melbury's) or written (Wordsworth's). Yet the word is hardly a reliable basis for taking an action, as is made manifest in the novel after Giles loses the life-hold on his house and finds the taunting doggerel Marty has scribbled on his wall: "O Giles, you've lost your dwelling-place, / And therefore, Giles, you'll lose your Grace." Reading these words fills Giles with "a terrible belief that they were turning out to be true, try to regain Grace as he might" (p. 139). Giles, therefore, writes to Melbury renouncing any claim to Grace's hand; and even after Grace secretly alters the word "lose" to "keep" on the graffito, Giles chooses to believe Marty's explanation that "some idle boy altered it" (pp. 140–1). From this point on, Giles leads his own life of tragic renunciation, moving to a hut in the forest and becoming an outsider to Little Hintock society. He has been given two texts—Marty's standard one and Grace's revised version—and he chooses to live by Marty's defeatist version as opposed to Grace's hopeful one.

Again, *The Woodlanders* has largely frustrated the attempts of critics to classify it. The reason, I believe, is because Hardy so thoroughly deploys multiple perspectives that the novel can accommodate multiple interpretations. The book can be read as a tragedy, since the perspectives of Giles, Marty, and—to a degree—the narrator are indeed tragic; and since the life of renunciation Giles chooses leads to his death. The novel is also open to being read as a pastoral,[56] or even as a celebration of pagan fertility rites, since it contains such pastoral descriptions as this one of Giles:

> He looked and smelt like Autumn's very brother, his face being sunburnt to wheat-colour, his eyes blue as corn-flowers, his sleeves and leggings dyed with fruit-stains, his hands clammy with the sweet juice of apples, his hat sprinkled with pips, and everywhere about him the atmosphere of cider which at its first return each season has such an indescribable fascination for those who have been born and bred among the orchards [p. 235].

However, what is frequently not commented upon is that this perspective on Giles is largely Grace's: At this stage she is experiencing her first doubts about her marriage to Fitzpiers, and the sight of Giles at work on the apple-press awakens in her a desire to escape, to again become the "crude country girl of her latent early instincts" (p. 236). In fact, Grace's view of Giles as "Autumn's very brother" stands in complete contrast with the narrator's descriptions of Nature, such as this famous passage from Chapter 7:

> They went noiselessly over mats of starry moss, rustled through interspersed tracts of leaves, skirted trunks with spreading roots whose mossed rinds made them like hands wearing green gloves; elbowed old elms and ashes with great forks, in which stood pools of water that overflowed on rainy days and ran down their stems in green cascades. On older trees still than these huge lobes of fungi grew like lungs. Here, as everywhere, the Unfulfilled Intention, which makes life what it is, was as obvious as it could be among the depraved crowds of a city slum. The leaf was deformed, the curve was crippled, the taper was interrupted; the lichen ate the vigour of the stalk, and the ivy slowly strangled to death the promising sapling [p. 83].

This is a powerful passage, yet its sentiments—that an "Unfulfilled Intention" is *blindly* shaping the events in the country and the city—are entirely opposed to those Hardy earlier expressed in another famous passage, where he seems to express belief in a *seeing* and *Fulfilled* Intention: "And yet their lonely courses formed no detached design at all, but were part of the pattern in the great web of human doings then weaving in both hemispheres from the White Sea to Cape Horn" (p. 52). This narrative ambiguity calls into question whether or not the characters' lots are assigned to "Fate"; yet Hardy's invocation of that troublesome "Unfulfilled Intention," as well as other passages—such as "the finger of fate touched [Grace] and turned her to a wife" (p. 204)—gives rise to the novel being read as a dissection of the working of fate; and *The Woodlanders* has frequently been considered the novel in which Hardy first conceived of the Imminent Will, which he would later develop more fully in *The Dynasts*.[57] Further, Grace's failure to obtain a divorce from the philandering Fitzpiers despite a new and more liberal law has led some to conclude Hardy was commenting on the need to reform divorce laws—or that he was simply attacking the societal institution of marriage.[58] Lastly, such elements as Grace learning of Fitzpiers's infidelity from Felice while the two of them are lost in the woods and the incident of three women rushing into Fitzpiers's bed chamber when they think he is on his deathbed have led many to conclude the novel is a melodrama or a farce.[59] I believe the reason none of these interpretations of the novel have stuck or been accepted as codifying is because they are all, to some degree, *correct*: just as Hardy uses perception to generate and create actions, he also uses it to construct genres. To read the Giles/Marty plot is to read a pastoral tragedy; to read the Grace/Giles/Fitzpiers/Felice story is to read a romantic melodrama, and so on. The genres in *The Woodlanders* constantly abut against each other, yet none becomes dominant; as a result, one cannot say to *which* genre the novel belongs. In the end, *The Woodlanders* questions the powers of language and perception to create a reality for the characters; and it questions the ability of language to construct a form that can really define or contain the novel.

If it were the case that this use of multiple perspectives was restricted to *The Woodlanders*, this study could go no further. It is my contention that Hardy's deployment of multi-voicedness is his dominant mode of expression: the actions of his characters—and, hence, the plots that are constructed through those actions—are largely dictated by what they *see*, *read*, and *interpret*; yet perspective in Hardy is hardly ever reliable: Hardy's use of multiple perspectives allows his novels to be read in numerous ways, so that they cannot be reined in by one dominant mode of reading. *The*

Woodlanders is the only one of Hardy's major novels to defy classification; but, as the next three chapters will argue, Hardy's other fictional works—specifically, *Far from the Madding Crowd, Tess of the d'Urbervilles,* and *Jude the Obscure*—should also be thought of as novels that cannot really be classified. However, each one of these books has to some degree been absorbed by the general culture; and it is the case that one or two of the genres the novels employ are usually accepted by critics and readers as the "true" and/or "only" voices of these novels, while the other modes of viewing that are generated and deployed in the novels have been silenced or pushed into the margins.

How, then, will the material that has just been laid out be applied to a discussion of the film versions of Hardy's novels? Once again, this will largely be a matter of considering how a given novel's plot functions have been *transferred* to film and how its indices and/or catalyzers have been *adapted.* However, as has been established in this chapter, Hardy's indices are largely made up of multiple perspectives, so the novels generate numerous simultaneous readings and interpretations. Although it is possible for a film to present multiple perspectives—Kurosawa's *Rashomon* (1950) is probably the most famous example—it is a much harder task for film to replicate *simultaneous* perspectives such as those that are deployed throughout *The Woodlanders* and in Hardy's other fictional works. It is my contention that, when faced with Hardy's multiplicity of perspectives, the filmmakers largely (and perhaps wisely) chose to adapt only a few narrative perspectives; and these have invariably been those modes of viewing that have given rise to the most popular and familiar interpretations of the novels—and of Hardy himself. To put it simply: rather than trying to adapt a Hardy novel *in toto*—which would probably be impossible and would more than likely result in an unsatisfying film—the filmmakers have sought to adapt the version of the novel (and the version of *Hardy*) we know and are familiar with. Their reasons for doing so are numerous, not the least of which—as the widespread public and critical rejection of Joffé's *The Scarlet Letter* shows—is that culture at large probably *expects* a familiar Hardy. What inevitably results is a film that is faithful not so much to Thomas Hardy, but to our cultural perceptions of who he was and what he wrote.

Two questions remain: First, is it the case that a "familiar" film version of a novel and of the novelist is necessarily bad or reductive? No: all of the films I am considering have a great deal of merit, and Polanski's *Tess* actually succeeds in creating a good deal of convergence with Hardy's novel. The second question, though, is simply this: *So what?* Why does it matter if films create a comfortable and familiar version of Hardy and his fiction? The answer is that, in the end, such films perhaps say more about *us* than they do about Hardy: they tell us about our capacity for reading, understanding, and interpreting. By giving us the Hardy we know or at least expect, the films ratify our tastes and desires; they validate our critical interpretations; they codify our cultural assumptions. The drawback is that a familiar Hardy is also a safe Hardy: when the full scope of his vision is hemmed in, Hardy offers little that challenges or questions our dominant ways of thinking; and a writer who says only what we want to hear becomes little more than a masseuse, soothing our pains but offering no cures.

Part Two

Filmed Hardy

3

Far from the Madding Crowd:
How Schlesinger Contained
the Uncontainable

I

Far from the Madding Crowd (1874) is the seminal novel in Thomas Hardy's career and in the creation of his popular and cultural image. It was his first big success, his first major achievement as a writer, and it was the novel his Victorian readers hoped he would write again and again[1]—a desire that nettled Hardy because, he later wrote in his *Life,* he "had not the slightest intention of writing for ever about sheepfarming, as the reading public was apparently expecting him to do, and as, in fact, they presently resented his not doing."[2] *Far from the Madding Crowd* is also central to Hardy's reputation for no other reason than it is the first true "Wessex" novel. Something in this locale struck a chord with his readers—as it continues to do today— so much so that Michael Millgate reports that as early as 1877, "Hardy's imaginative world had already impressed itself on his contemporaries."[3]

The grip of that imaginative world has not been loosened. *Far from the Madding Crowd* has never been out of print, and it remains one of Hardy's most widely published and popularly read novels. This popularity, of course, has long made *Crowd* attractive to dramatists and filmmakers. In 1886 the book became the first of Hardy's novels to be adapted for the stage[4]; in 1915 it became the second of Hardy's novels to go before the motion picture camera[5]; and in 1967 it became the first of Hardy's novels to be filmed in the era of sound, color, and wide-screen technology.

What keeps this novel alive, and why has it proved such a popular source for playwrights and moviemakers? The answer, I believe, is that what made the book such a hit in 1874—the very thing Hardy complained of—is what keeps it fascinating to readers today: its pastoralism and sense of rustic charm. Carl J. Weber, in his introduction to the 1937 Oxford edition of *Crowd*, perhaps speaks for all the millions who have enjoyed the novel:

> (T)here can be no doubt that one reason why this novel attracted so much attention in 1874 was the authoritative way in which the author spoke of nature. He *knew*; and in nature-study his novels provide a liberal education. So many English novelists had been exclusively concerned with the city, or the city's point of view, that to turn to Thomas Hardy was to receive a ticket for a welcome vacation in the country. Few first-class novelists had ventured to take the feet of their readers far from city streets; Hardy invited his audience to wander along country lanes and by-paths, and there he brought out the beauty and significance of sky and storm, of bird and tree.[6]

Easy as it is to snicker at Weber's comparison of reading *Crowd* to taking a touristy vacation, on a fundamental level he is absolutely correct. Since 1874, *Far from the Madding Crowd* has been known as a novel that celebrates "Nature," and one of the most durable readings of the novel is as a variant on the "classic" pastoral or Arcadian romance.[7] This way of reading *Crowd* largely stayed in place until the 1970s, when many critics tried not so much to divorce the novel from the pastoral tradition but to show that Hardy *reinvented* the pastoral in his novel—in effect, arguing that *Crowd* is still a nature novel, but a different *kind* of nature novel. Michael Squires, for instance, argued that Hardy "modified" the pastoral by infusing its traditional mythos with realism (loosely defined as relating to misfortunes and death) in order to *enhance* the traditional pastoral values that are in the novel[8]; while John Alcorn read the novel as celebrating humanity's role as part of the biological process, an interpretation that actually harks back to Arcadia, since, Alcorn argues, "In Hardy, man's unconscious life is anchored immediately and constantly in physical nature—not only in man's own animality, but in the whole external world of organic life."[9] Even Merryn Williams, in her materialist/Marxist critique of the novel, still evokes a sense of pastoralism where she writes that *Crowd*'s characters "are subordinated to the novel's central preoccupation—*the care of the land and flocks*, and the maintenance of the community in a condition of health" (emphasis mine).[10] Williams' view was somewhat amplified in 1988 by John Goode, who welcomes reading a certain "pastoral potential" in *Crowd*, for "one way of reading the novel, given this original [pastoral] image, is to see it as a fable of the recuperation of the organic moment by the survival of the values of work and love through the self-destructive modes of capitalist farming and romantic love."[11] In short, Hardy's "new" kind of pastoral—as identified in all of these readings—still has at its heart the concerns of the classic pastoral.

With perhaps the notable exception of Robert Langbaum in *Thomas Hardy in Our Time* (1995), few critics today analyze *Far from the Madding Crowd* strictly as a nature novel. Recent scholarship has tended to focus on the construction of gender roles, the deployment of the masculine gaze, and the novel's uses of language.[12] Still, in many contemporary studies on the novel, a tenacious pastoral strain can still be detected. Susan Beegel, for instance, focuses on male sexuality rather than Nature, yet her analysis of Gabriel Oak practically crowns him the pastoral king. Beegel shows that Gabriel is equipped with "phallic" instruments—"the sheep shears, trochar, marking iron, ricking rod, and flute"—which are, in fact, "instruments of salvation, objects which change death into life," for Gabriel uses his tools to cleanse the sheep of their wool and to save them when they are bloated. Furthermore, "The farmer's work in this novel is a procreative process—he or she joins with others to cause the flocks to multiply and the earth to bear fruit."[13] However, the most pastoral of all recent readings is in Shirley Stave's *The Decline of the Goddess*, a feminist study that does in fact declare that Gabriel is a nature god and that Bathsheba is a pastoral queen, whose very body is a metaphor of the natural world: "Within her life (Bathsheba) enacts the rhythms of the natural year, becoming the visible embodiment of nature."[14] The survival of the pastoralist strain in the criticism perhaps shouldn't be a surprise, since, when Hardy proposed the novel to Leslie Stephen, he clearly described it as a "pastoral tale." Readers who liked—and who still like—the novel for its depiction of Nature are in all possibility responding to what Hardy most wanted them to. His later tart comment in the *Life* about the demands of the "reading public" is tinged with Frankensteinian regret.

Beyond Nature, there is another key element to *Crowd*'s continued appeal, something that is as true today as when Weber wrote about it in 1937:

> *Far from the Madding Crowd* is a good novel with which to begin the study of Thomas Hardy. Not only was it his first real success, but it is wholly free from the results of the social reformer's zeal which came to mar somewhat the artistry of Hardy's last two novels, and it is equally free from the depressing and cheerless atmosphere which some readers find in the tragedies written after this novel. ... The student who begins with *Far from the Madding Crowd* need *not* feel sure the end will be tragic; and whatever

may be true of later and more somber titles, here he will find no philosophical or religious load of scepticism to carry. Here Hardy wrote for pure delight.[15]

It's debatable how much "pure delight" Hardy took in writing after four failed attempts to establish himself; however, Weber captures the ambivalence that many readers felt and continue to feel about Hardy's novels. The most common complaint about Hardy is that he is depressing, and *Far from the Madding Crowd* is certainly less so. As Elizabeth Drew wryly observes, "For Hardy, a story with only three deaths in it, one life sentence and a final marriage between the two chief characters can almost claim to be a comedy."[16] Comedy it isn't, but many readers do say they enjoy this book more than Hardy's "darker" novels; often readers who don't like Hardy as a rule like *Far from the Madding Crowd*; and people who read *Crowd* first among Hardy novels occasionally feel disappointed by the books that follow. In some respects, it is a novel that not only invites readers to find a haven from the city, but to find a haven from the rest of Hardy's fiction.

To put it bluntly, then, what *Far from the Madding Crowd* does is make its readers feel *good*, both in terms of what it presents and how it is set apart from Hardy's other novels. A reader is led to feel that in reading about Weatherbury and the surrounding Wessex countryside, a kind of "inner" Arcadia can be reached; and in Hardy himself one can find the supreme English pastoralist he is often called. Small wonder, then, that dramatists and filmmakers have turned so often to this friendliest and most appealing of Hardy's novels, or that they have tried hardest to reproduce its most salient feature—its evocation of Nature. It was precisely this desire to "escape" dramatizing the problems and pressures of the modern world that sparked director John Schlesinger's desire to put the novel into cinematic form. Schlesinger's first two films, *A Kind of Loving* (1962) and *Billy Liar* (1963), were both gritty, black-and-white graduates from the school of social realism (the "kitchen-sink" dramas) that had revolutionized British filmmaking. In 1965, he was completing his third film, the social satire *Darling*, when,

> After being confronted day after day, reel after reel with the questionable lives of the jet setters in *Darling*, ... Schlesinger suddenly blurted out one day in the dubbing theater that it was time they went back to "something more romantic about another age" for their next project. He continued by saying that it would be refreshing to make a film set in the rural England of the previous century about people who enjoyed simple pleasures like sitting around singing songs at a harvest supper and in general were able to cope with whatever life meted out to them.[17]

A willful passionate girl and...
the three men who want her!

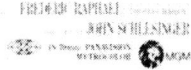

METRO
GOLDWYN
MAYER
A JOSEPH
JANNI
PRODUCTION

JULIE CHRISTIE   **TERENCE STAMP**
                                      PETER FINCH
                                      ALAN BATES

"FAR FROM THE MADDING CROWD"

Original theatrical poster for *Far from the Madding Crowd* (1967).

Shot in color and released in 1967, Schlesinger's *Far from the Madding Crowd* showcases a love of "rural England" in just about every scene. The film's depiction of Nature also became one of its main selling points: the American theatrical trailer opens with Julie Christie frolicking through a vast field of wildflowers on a bright summer day, while a narrator intones, "In this place of calm and beauty, of deep and primitive emotions, the woman Bathsheba Everdene lived. And here she gave herself to three men."[18] In the connections between the place, the "deep and primitive emotions," and Bathsheba's "giving" of herself, it is clear that—in the minds of the MGM publicity department, at least—Nature, emotion, and characters are all bound inextricably together. In these few seconds of trailer, an entire tradition of reading *Far from the Madding Crowd* has been concisely and neatly captured.

Of course, it would be foolish to suggest that critics have been wrong to focus on the importance of Nature in *Crowd*, or that the filmmakers were misguided in trying to be faithful to the feature people most commonly associate with the novel. However, there is the "Nature" that Hardy wrote about, and there is "Hardy's Nature," which is largely the creation of critics and which has become a part of the cultural history of the novel. What is frequently missed by casual readers and critics alike is that Nature in Hardy's *Crowd* is important mainly in that the characters' responses to it catalyze many of the novel's plot functions. In several crucial instances, a character will attempt to contain Nature by seeing it as something human—a reflection of that person's own wants and desires—and then act according to what that person perceives to be *in* Nature. However, Nature always proves itself to operate in a realm of its own, outside of human concerns; and when the characters come to realize this, they push their actions into other directions. This presentation of Nature can also evoke a mimetic response in the *reader*: Nature in this book is so seductive that it is easy to read the novel *as* a simple pastoral; but, by looking beneath the surface appeal, one can see that Hardy's depiction of Nature resists easy literary classifications. Ultimately, the only way to "contain" Hardy's Nature is for critics to alter it and to transform it into a different kind of Nature—a kind readily understood in cinematic terms.[19]

II

Far from the Madding Crowd's ability to seduce a reader with lovely pictures of rural life can perhaps best be found in one of its most famous passages, from Chapter 22: "The Great Barn and the Sheep-Shearers." Here Hardy transforms the ancient barn into a kind of living monument to functionality that, in opposition to church or castle, is unchangeable; for, "unlike and superior to either of those two typical remnants of mediæ-valism, the old barn embodied practices which had suffered no mutilation at the hands of time" (p. 195). While the workers shear the sheep inside the barn, tradition takes on the air of timelessness:

> This picture of to-day in its frame of four hundred years ago did not produce that marked contrast between ancient and modern which is implied by the contrast of date. In comparison with cities, Weatherbury was immutable. The citizen's *Then* is the rustic's *Now*. In London, twenty or thirty years ago are old times; in Paris ten years, or five; in Weatherbury three or four score years were included in the mere present, and nothing less than a century set its mark on its face or tone. Five decades hardly modified the cut of a gaiter, the embroidery of a smock-frock, by the breadth of a hair. Ten generations failed to alter the turn of a single phrase. In these Wessex nooks the busy outsider's ancient times are only old; his old times are still new; his present is futurity.
>
> So the barn was natural to the shearers, and the shearers were in harmony with the barn [p. 196].

The allure of this passage is in its vision of not only timelessness, but stability: sheep-shearing remains unaffected by outside forces or techno-logical changes, so it survives intact from generation to generation, its value as *labor* subsumed by its role as tradition and devotion. Shearing is made further appealing by the fact it is distinctly *of* the country; there-fore, the passage hints that in the immutable countryside, a sense of permanence and stability can be attained. This passage has often been read as a metaphor for the novel itself, with Gabriel Oak as the embodiment of the permanence of Weatherbury, and Sergeant Troy representing the "busy outsider" whose town ways and attitudes threaten to disrupt the peace and calm of the area.[20] Yet, as inviting as the sheep-shearing pas-sage is, it occurs in a context that suggests that neither the barn nor Weath-erbury nor Oak himself represents a means of escape from the "city" and all it stands for. As the passage in the barn continues, country values are shown to be entirely dependent upon the city:

> Cainy now runs forward with the tar-pot. 'B. E.' is newly stamped upon the shorn skin, and away the simple dam leaps, panting, over the board into the shirtless flock outside. Then up comes Maryann; throws the loose locks into the middle of the fleece, rolls it up, and carries it into the back-ground as three-and-a-half pounds of unadulterated warmth for the win-ter enjoyment of persons unknown and far away, who will, however, never experience the superlative comfort derivable from the wool as it here exists, new and pure—before the unctuousness of its nature whilst in a

living state has dried, stiffened, and been washed out—rendering it just now as superior to anything *woollen* as cream is superior to milk-and-water [p. 198].

The labor of the sheep-shearer may be ancient, but it does not exist in a vacuum: the sheep are merchandise, stamped as the property of Bathsheba Everdene, and the duty of the shearers is to put the wool into the service of commerce. Though Hardy's narrator clucks his tongue over the eventual alteration and transformation of the fleece into a product that can be used by "persons unknown and far away," he does not rob the new material of value, for what is new and pure cannot stay that way forever: the wool is of superlative comfort only *here*, at this moment; and it is superior to woollen only *just now*. Weatherbury may seem to be frozen in time, free from the pollution of the outside, but its commercial products cannot exist in a timeless state—they must be altered and made serviceable to outside consumers in order for the work that is done in Weatherbury to survive. The lure to the country that Hardy creates may be key to the novel's appeal, but it is ultimately a trap: whenever a character appears to be in ideal communion with the land—or whenever Hardy's narrator suggests that such communion is possible—Hardy immediately brings the character or the reader back down to the realm of the mundane or the ordinary; in short, to the realm of the *human*, which the novel argues is where peoples' attention and focus should always be. Nature, when it is invoked, is inevitably revealed as something more—and, at times, less—than it appears.

What Hardy creates in his Nature is a pattern of "deception" that reverberates throughout *Far from the Madding Crowd*; and this pattern is in fact at the very heart of the novel. Throughout the story, characters like Gabriel and Bathsheba look into Nature and form an impression of it based on what they perceive to be in it; and at some stage each person tries to organize his or her life according to what Nature apparently dictates. This is a project that is automatically destined to fail, for Hardy constantly deconstructs the notion of a coherent and readable Nature by showing that the only "messages" it offers—if messages they indeed are—are contradictory or ambiguous. This is evidenced as early as Chapter 2, in the first full description of a natural setting:

> Norcombe Hill—not far from lonely Toller-Down—was one of the spots which *suggest* to a passer-by that he is in the presence of a shape *approaching* the indestructible as nearly as any to be found on earth. It was a featureless convexity of chalk and soil—an ordinary specimen of those smoothly-outlined protuberances of the globe which may remain undisturbed on some great day of confusion, when far grander heights and dizzy granite precipices topple down [p. 57; my emphases].

This is an early example of Hardy's characteristic deference to the perspective of an anonymous third-person viewer. Norcombe Hill becomes indestructible and capable of withstanding the Apocalypse *only* if an individual is capable of seeing it in those terms. However, as the highlighted words show, individual perspective is largely a matter of what Hardy would later call "seemings, or personal impressions" (*Jude* p. 39)—there is no guarantee that the individual viewpoint is correct or even valid: the only certainty that Hardy presents is that the hill is "featureless," a blank; and it is within that very blankness that one may read Norcombe Hill as a symbol of endurance and eternity.[21] Hardy's deference here to the third-person figure is the first instance in the novel of someone trying to shape Nature and make it comprehensible to the human mind, to impose order upon the natural world. This desire to "order" all surroundings is, in effect, the desire of all people, as Hardy states shortly afterward:

> The instinctive act of humankind was to stand and listen, and learn how the trees on the right and the trees on the left wailed or chaunted to each other in the regular antiphonies of a cathedral choir; how hedges and other shapes to leeward then caught the note, lowering it to the tenderest sob; and how the hurrying gust then plunged into the south, to be heard no more [p. 58].

Again, the emphasis here is upon the individual spectator—embodied in the entire species—who tries to impose order on the "differing" powers and natures of the surrounding world. What is most evident is the *dis*cord of Nature—contradictory impulses that are both harsh and gentle, and which simultaneously seek to create sound and to crush it out of existence—which itself clashes with mankind's need to put Nature into *ac*cord. In effect, trying to read the dissonant sounds of Nature as an organized choir is to render the natural world itself *human*, recognizable to human minds and in sympathy with the human condition. But this is an entirely faulty reading of the world, as Hardy demonstrates when he puts his anonymous viewer on a hilltop to observe the motion of the stars:

> The poetry of motion is a phrase much in use, and to enjoy the epic form of that gratification it is necessary to stand on a hill at a small hour of the night, and, having first expanded with a sense of difference from the mass of civilized mankind, who are dreamwrapt and disregardful of all such proceedings at this time, long and quietly watch your stately progress through the stars. After such a nocturnal reconnoitre it is hard to get back to earth, and to believe that the consciousness of such majestic speeding is derived from a tiny human frame [p. 58].

Transcendence, in Hardean terms, is bifurcated: while it is possible to become one with natural phenomena, this harmony is attainable only if a person *first* renders the experience in abstract terms by seeing Nature as poetry. By themselves, the stars do nothing; but when they are transformed into something manageable and identifiable to the mind, they can become a vehicle for transcendence. But even here, Hardy invests his pattern with a great deal of irony, for to become one with natural phenomena is to risk losing oneself, to find oneself stranded beyond the bounds of the physical earth and disconnected from the human realm. It is this sense of irony, and, in fact, a general sense of distrust toward Nature that is *Far from the Madding Crowd*'s most prominent catalyzer—Nature must always be read with an eye toward its variety of meanings, and with the knowledge that what Nature communicates refers only to itself: people cannot look to it as a guide to their own lives and doings. In effect, Hardy's Nature is like the moor at the time of the coming of winter—"its irregularities were forms without features; suggestive of anything, proclaiming nothing, and without more character than that of being the limit of something else—the lowest layer of a firmament of snow" (pp. 134–5).

That the characters are determined to bend and mold Nature to fit their own perceptions is most evident where they attempt to interact with Nature and where they inevitably see something of themselves reflected in its workings. Ironically, the first person to attempt to reign in Nature and make it a reflection of his own wants and desires is Gabriel, the one character most usually assumed to be in tune with Nature. Gabriel will eventually become the character who is *most* capable of understanding the world around him; but in the early chapters of the novel, he easily falls into the trap of humanizing Nature and becoming lost within his own fancies. With his mind filled with images of the recently spotted Bathsheba, Gabriel, like the anonymous figure on the hillside, allows himself to overdetermine the significance of the sky, and this makes him the target of Hardy's light mockery:

> Being a man not without a frequent consciousness that there was some charm in this life he led, he stood still after looking at the sky as a useful instrument, and regarded it in an appreciative spirit, as a work of art superlatively beautiful. For a moment he seemed impressed with the speaking loneliness of the scene, or rather with the complete abstraction from its compass of the sights and sounds of man. Human shapes, interferences, troubles, and joys were all as if they were not, and there seemed to be on the shaded hemisphere of the globe no sentient being save himself; he could fancy them all gone round to the sunny side.
>
> Occupied thus, with eyes stretched afar, Oak gradually perceived that what he had previously taken to be a star low down behind the outskirts

of the plantation was in reality no such thing. It was an artificial light, almost close at hand.

To find themselves utterly alone at night where company is desirable and expected makes some people fearful; but a case more trying by far to the nerves is to discover some mysterious companionship when intuition, sensation, memory, analogy, testimony, probability, induction—every kind of evidence in the logician's list—have united to persuade consciousness that it is quite in isolation [p. 62].

At the start of this passage, Gabriel is like a tiny figure in the corner of a landscape painting, who is, paradoxically, also the observer of that same painting. He is acutely aware that his life as a farmer and shepherd is—in the eyes of Hardy's readers, at least—one that is filled with "charm"; therefore, he appears obligated to lose himself in the role of quaint observer of natural phenomena. But his awareness of the stars hinges upon his seeing them only as if they are in a painting; as a result, they become an extension of the human, and he becomes lost in egocentrism. Gabriel's reverie drives him away from the concerns of the world around him, and also drives him further within himself, to see himself as the world's only "sentient being," and to foolishly confuse the light of a simple lamp with the light of a star. Gabriel adds to the problem by reading the light as a talisman for his own need to find companionship. He follows the light to a shed on the neighboring plantation, where, in spying upon the occupants, he again sees Bathsheba and determines that she will fulfill the egocentric desires that were revealed while he was lost in contemplating the sky (pp. 62–3). What Gabriel fails to recognize—and which his later failure to win Bathsheba's hand will teach him—is that Nature reveals nothing about human relationships; it lies outside the realm of human understanding. Gabriel's failure to recognize this fact is mirrored in the actions of the calf in Mrs. Hurst's shed, who looks "idiotically at the two women, which showed that it had not long been accustomed to the phenomenon of eyesight, and often turn(ed) to the lantern, which it apparently mistook for the moon, inherited instinct having as yet little time for correction by experience" (p. 63). Gabriel's mistake is one of youth, and as the novel progresses, he will grow away from viewing Nature as the mirror of the human condition and will instead see that it signifies only itself. However, in the workings of Nature Gabriel will eventually come to recognize humankind's need for *irony*.[22]

In *Far from the Madding Crowd*, the only way that Nature impacts human experience (beyond, of course, creating phenomena like the storm that destroys Boldwood's crops) is by serving as a vehicle through which people may recognize the inherent irony of the human condition. Essentially, when characters acknowledge that Nature is multifaceted, constantly work-ing against itself and signifying only itself, they return to the realm of the human, where they may come to see the artificial yet highly effective way in which human society acts. When Gabriel convinces himself that a "star" has brought him to Bathsheba, Hardy creates an ironic situation which is appar-ent to the reader, and which *should* be evident to Gabriel. He sees the truth only when he presses his marriage proposal, at which time Bathsheba awak-ens him to the truth of their social differences:

> "Mr. Oak," she said, with luminous distinctness and common sense, "you are better off than I. I have hardly a penny in the world—I am staying with my aunt for my bare sustenance. I am better educated than you—and I don't love you a bit: that's my side of the case. Now yours: you are a farmer just beginning, and you ought in common prudence, if you marry at all (which you should certainly not think of doing at present), to marry a woman with money, who would stock a larger farm for you than you have now" [p. 81].

Gabriel is rejected not for who he *is*—at this stage, a promising and prosperous farmer—but for who he *is not*: an educated man possessed of indefinable qualities that Bathsheba can love. The *substance* of Gabriel—his clearly definable properties—hold little allure for Bathsheba; and Gabriel will come to recognize that in the social sphere, artificiality—rep-resented by the societal roles he will play—becomes the most important trait.[23] By mastering his societal roles, Gabriel is capable of bringing soci-ety under his control: by the end of the novel, he is wealthy, has command of two farms, and is married to Bathsheba. Gabriel gives up trying to con-tain Nature by making it more human; instead, he recognizes Nature for what it is: dissonant, chaotic, at odds with itself, and reflective only of itself—and succeeds in containing the human element by recognizing its inherent irony.[24]

The importance of the ironic perspective can be seen in Gabriel's early "mixed" feelings for Bathsheba. Though Gabriel sees in her the form that will fill the void within himself, he also recognizes her basic artificial-ity, and his attitude toward her in this sense opens him up to a new way of "viewing." Bathsheba is first seen looking into a mirror and practicing her smile, which Hardy calls "a performance in the sight of sparrows, blackbirds, and unperceived farmer who were alone its spectators" (p. 54). Why she is performing is not explained, but through the "cynical infer-ence" of Gabriel Oak, a correct and accurate portrait of Bathsheba emerges:

> She simply observed herself as a fair product of Nature in the feminine kind, her thoughts seeming to glide into far-off though likely dramas in

which men would play a part—vistas of probable triumphs—the smiles being of a phase suggesting that hearts were imagined as lost and won. Still, this was but conjecture, and the whole series of actions was so idly put forth as to make it rash to assert that intention had any part in them at all [p. 55].

Though Gabriel's viewpoint is "idle conjecture," it will eventually be proven correct: Bathsheba *will* order her life as a "drama" in which men will play a very great part; she does play at winning and losing the hearts of others; and she does indeed see herself as a child of Nature, whose very thoughts and actions are reflected in and by the topography around her.

The second time Gabriel sees Bathsheba she is again performing before Nature: "[A]s if to assure herself that all humanity was out of view, [she] dexterously dropped backwards flat upon the pony's back, her head over its tail, her feet against its shoulders, and her eyes to the sky. The rapidity of her glide into this position was that of a kingfisher—its noise-lessness that of a hawk" (p. 65). The use of animal imagery and Hardy's assurance that the "performer seemed quite at home anywhere between a horse's head and its tail" (p. 66) serve to enforce in the eyes of Gabriel and the reader that Bathsheba *is* one with Nature; it is in this sense that Shirley Stave can argue that Bathsheba is outside of human society and inside a mythic realm, where she becomes an "agricultural goddess."[25] This "nature child" version of Bathsheba is a popular figure, and, not surprisingly, she appears in Schlesinger's film. But reading the actions of the character as "natural" are troublesome, for if Bathsheba's behavior is part of Nature, why does Hardy stress that she is involved in an extremely artificial activity—the performance? And why does Bathsheba perform without a human audience? The answer is perhaps revealed when Gabriel informs Bathsheba that he has seen her display on the horse, and we are told that his "want of tact had deeply offended her—not by seeing what he could not help, but by letting her know that he had seen it. For, as without law there is no sin, without eyes there is no indecorum; and she appeared to feel that Gabriel's espial had made her an indecorous woman without her own connivance" (p. 69). Contrary to Stave's interpretation, Bathsheba *is* aware of socialization, represented here by Gabriel; and that, by performing in and to Nature, she feels she can escape society. Nature to Bathsheba is a realm where she will not be judged or held accountable for her actions.

Throughout the novel, Bathsheba is determined to follow her own course in life—a characteristic that has won for Hardy both admiration for his feminist sympathies, and criticism for his inability to allow Bathsheba to truly become independent.[26] However, it is not so much that Hardy is trying to present Bathsheba as emancipated, but that she is a woman who believes she is acting according to the dictates of a "higher" order, one that can be located in the mysteriousness of Nature. For instance, when she realizes that Boldwood has fallen in love with her because of the Valentine she sent him as a joke, Bathsheba feels that her action has violated a natural order of which she is part: that Boldwood is in love with her is "a triumph; and had it come naturally, such a triumph would have been the sweeter to her for this piquing delay. But it had been brought about by misdirected ingenuity, and she valued it only as she valued an artificial flower or a wax fruit" (p. 169). Because she has pretended at love, the emotion she elicits from Boldwood has no natural value to her. However, when she discovers she is in love with Troy, she believes that her impulses spring from a natural order that invests her feelings with value, a notion that Hardy all but destroys:

> Though in one sense a woman of the world, it was, after all, that world of daylight coteries and green carpets wherein cattle form the passing crowd and winds the busy hum; where a quiet family of rabbits or hares live on the other side of your party-wall, where your neighbour is everybody in the tything, and where calculation is confined to market-days. Of the fabricated tastes of good fashionable society she knew but little, and of the formulated self-indulgence of bad, nothing at all.... Her love was entire as a child's, and though warm as summer it was fresh as spring. Her culpability lay in her making no attempt to control feeling by subtle and careful inquiry into consequences. She could show others the steep and thorny way, but "reck'd not her own rede" [pp. 243–44].

All Bathsheba knows is impulse, and this has been learned from observing Nature, a fact that reduces her to a child-like condition. Though Hardy cynically alludes to the "fabricated tastes of good fashionable society," they are exactly what Bathsheba needs to defend herself against men like Troy. By relying upon Nature/impulse to guide her actions with Troy, Bathsheba winds up deceiving herself: she forces herself to believe that Troy "*cannot* be bad" (p. 253) in spite of the evidence she sees; and even at the worst of times in their marriage—the revelation of Troy's gambling debts, the confrontation over Fanny's body—Bathsheba reveals a reluctance to trust anything other than her most hopeful impressions.

Bathsheba often attempts to find validation for her actions or feelings in Nature itself, but there she is inevitably met with indifference and confusion. After Bathsheba flees from Troy, she awakens in what at first appears to be an Arcadian setting that could be an anodyne to the turmoil she's escaped:

> There was an opening towards the east, and the glow from the as yet unrisen sun attracted her eyes thither. From her feet, and between the

beautiful yellowing ferns with their feathery arms, the ground sloped downwards to a hollow, in which was a species of swamp, dotted with fungi. A morning mist hung over it now—a fulsome yet magnificent silvery veil, full of light from the sun, yet semi-opaque—the hedge behind it being in some measure hidden by its hazy luminousness [p. 363].

But no sooner does Hardy suggest that in this place of beauty and enchantment Bathsheba can find the balm to ease her mind, than he invokes Nature's contradictions, which horrifies Bathsheba and brings her back to the realm of human concerns:

But the general aspect of the swamp was malignant. From its moist and poisonous coat seemed to be exhaled the essences of evil things in the earth, and in the waters under the earth. The fungi grew in all manner of positions from rotting leaves and tree stumps, some exhibiting to her listless gaze their clammy tops, others their oozing gills. Some were marked with great splotches, red as arterial blood, others were saffron yellow, and others tall and attenuated, with stems like macaroni. Some were leathery and of richest browns. The hollow seemed a nursery of pestilences small and great, in the immediate neighbourhood of comfort and health, and Bathsheba arose with a tremor at the thought of having passed the night on the brink of so dismal a place [pp. 363–4].

This instance, when the natural world turns from one of red and yellow leaves and a pleasant haze into a swamp overgrown with repulsive fungi, stands as Bathsheba's moment of growth. For the first time, she truly recognizes the duality of Nature, and she especially sees that it does not address her own needs. In a minor but related incident, Bathsheba expects the approaching Liddy to be swallowed by the swamp, but Liddy easily crosses it (p. 365). This simple action becomes significant to Bathsheba because by it she recognizes the *surface* of the thing is illusory: what appeared unstable and dangerous is, in fact, an adequate means of support. This is a moment that snaps Bathsheba into recognizing the irony of her own situation as well as the irony behind all human institutions. Where she once found surety in her marriage to Troy, she now recognizes it as an artificial social rite, one which Troy previously dismissed to her by saying, "A ceremony before a priest doesn't make a marriage" (p. 361). Bathsheba physically demonstrates her awareness of her ironic state— wife/not wife, widow/not widow—by faithfully maintaining the grave of Troy's "true" wife, Fanny (Bathsheba "wiped the mud spots from the tomb as if she rather liked its words than otherwise" [p. 381]) and by accepting that, in spite of all seeming evidence of his death at sea, Troy will eventually return to make her live out the farce of her marriage. Bathsheba, in effect, ratifies the artificiality of society by exploiting its artificiality: by maintaining Fanny's grave, she calls into question the definition of a wife, and by refusing to play the role of widow—even so much as setting a proper time for mourning—she holds the institution up to ridicule.

Finally, although Bathsheba has relied upon language and words as tools and weapons—she talks herself into and out of situations—she comes to recognize her own ironic status as *woman* when she tells Boldwood, "It is difficult for a woman to define her feelings in language which is chiefly made by men to express theirs" (p. 412). Language and social structures are artificial things that impose meaning and order on the human realm.[27] Nature cannot respond to verbal ordering, but human beings can and do. Bathsheba, through deploying irony, has come to recognize her status as a woman and as a person. By the end of the novel, Bathsheba—like Gabriel—has grown: she no longer confuses the *image* of the thing for what it *is*; and it is precisely her capacity to grow and develop as a human being that eventually leads to her marriage with Gabriel:

> Theirs was that substantial affection which arises (if any arises at all) when the two who are thrown together begin first by knowing the rougher sides of each other's character, and not the best till further on, the romance growing up in the interstices of a mass of hard prosaic reality. This good-fellowship—*camaraderie*—usually occurring through similarity of pursuits, is unfortunately seldom superadded to love between the sexes, because men and women associate, not in their labours, but in their pleasures merely [p. 458].

It is *experience*, then—growing and developing an understanding of reality—that allows people to connect. To see this, people have to put aside the illusions of both Nature and society and look into themselves.

So, then, is Nature in *Far from the Madding Crowd* just a cipher, a thing people must turn away from? Does Nature communicate anything at all? Clearly, Hardy *does* show that Nature is a communicator, but what it communicates pertains primarily to itself. In the novel's most widely praised chapters, which feature the coming of the storm and the storm itself, Gabriel clearly listens to, observes, reads, and interprets what Nature has to say. A migrating toad is a "direct message from the Great Mother" (p. 300), the slug that has retreated indoors is "Nature's second way of hinting to him that he was to prepare for foul weather" (p. 300), and the behavior of the sheep is enough to convince him that the storm is on its way. Gabriel is capable of using this information to save Bathsheba's ricks, but how does this ability to read Nature help him to read the human condition? It doesn't. Gabriel understands that the messages that Nature is sending pertain to itself: he is capable of utilizing the information to prevent

damage to a profitable crop, but he does not see the storm as communicating anything about the people around him and the situations they are
in. In fact, the only person to see the storm as a kind of judgment is Boldwood, whose evocation of the story of Jonah and the gourd (p. 316) is
clearly meant to parallel the devastation he has faced at the hand of blind
chance. It is Gabriel's ability to keep the realms of Nature and the human
separate—to read them for what they have to say about themselves, in and
of themselves—that makes him the novel's source of authority.

Far from the Madding Crowd ultimately rejects the concept of pastoralism as it is conventionally understood: Nature is outside human com-
prehension and no aid to those who aspire to a better place or who wish
to find a realm of higher understanding. When the characters seek to tame
Nature or to make it "more like themselves," they wind up lost in self-
delusion. It is only when a person is capable of separating Nature and the
human, reading each for what it is and understanding how each operates,
that a person becomes truly cognizant of the condition of mankind. Yet
the novel's cultural identity as a simple pastoral—or just as escapist lit—
remains largely intact; and this identity was not challenged by John
Schlesinger's 1967 film; in fact, it was codified.

III

The cinematic *Far from the Madding Crowd* has long been regarded
as an ugly step-child, whether it is analyzed as an adaptation of the Hardy
novel or considered as a representative film of John Schlesinger's vast body
of work. The movie's reputation stems in no small part from its original
reception. When it premiered in England in October 1967, it was met with
mixed reviews and respectable box-office returns; but its performance in
the all-important American market was disastrous: reviews were bad (opening notices were "crucifying," in Schlesinger's words[28]), attendance was even
worse, and MGM, in an effort to salvage the film, would make extensive
cuts in its original 169-minute running time. Within a few years, Schlesinger
was distancing himself from *Crowd*, calling it the "least personal" of all his
films.[29] In the time since its premiere, criticism of the *Far from the Madding
Crowd* film has yielded several commonplaces: it is too long, too slow, too
glossy, and too enamored with cinematic tricks (such as the use of slow-
motion to convey Boldwood's first infatuated sight of Bathsheba at the
cornmarket, and the distorted lens to represent the drunken Joseph Poorgrass's "multiplying eye"). Most critics tend to applaud Peter Finch's Boldwood, to carp that Alan Bates's Gabriel is ineffective (he is "a rather wooden
piece of background furniture," according to James Welsh[30]), and to

criticize Terence Stamp's Troy and especially Julie Christie's Bathsheba as being too "mod" and "1960s" to be credible figures from the mid-Victorian era. However, critical opinion is mixed as to whether or not the film succeeds at adequately reproducing Hardy. Rita Costabile, in taking the film and its director to task, declares that "Schlesinger's difficulties derive directly from his failure to grasp the complex relationship between men and nature that is the principal theme of the novel"; and that, by "shooting for color and composition rather than vitality, Schlesinger overidealizes and sentimentalizes nature, misunderstanding its subtle, and sometimes destructive, encounters with man."[31] On the opposite end of the scale, Gene D. Phillips complains that the film's faults lie in the director's *too faithful* adaptation of an already flawed novel:

> Like Hardy's other novels, *Far from the Madding Crowd* is basically a gaslight melodrama, in which Hardy often does not provide clear-cut motivations for his characters' actions. We are drawn to probe beneath the surface of the characters for the motives that lurk behind their actions. But Hardy gives us little help, and the film, in being faithful to the novel, follows his lead.[32]

Only Fran E. Chalfont argues that the movie actually *complements* the Hardy novel and *deepens* it by visualizing such details as the chain of events that keep Fanny Robin from appearing at her own wedding.[33] In some respects, these three critical views represent the inherent problems faced by anyone who tries to analyze a film adaptation of a work of literature: it is tempting to damn the director for either not "understanding" the novelist's intentions, or for being too slavish in adapting the novel; and it is difficult to see the liberties a director may take as enhancing the original text. I believe that Schlesinger did, in fact, have an affinity with Hardy that he brought to his version of *Far from the Madding Crowd*; however, it is in his very desire to *be* faithful to Hardy (or at least Hardy as he is generally perceived) as well as to the Victorian era, and in his effort to find *realistic* film images to visualize Hardy's metaphoric treatment of Nature, that Schlesinger winds up creating both a safe, contained version of Hardy as pastoralist, and a familiar picture of Hardy's world as a place where Nature blesses those who live according to its dictates.

That Schlesinger should favor a realist approach is only appropriate, since he is largely a product of the social realist movement in British cinema; and in 1967, he was still very much under its sway. Social realism, of course, gave us the "Angry Young Man" whom the Welfare state had educated out of the working class, but who had not succeeded in breaking down the class and economic barriers to greater prosperity. Such films as

Room at the Top (Jack Clayton, 1958), *Look Back in Anger* (Tony Richardson, 1959), and *Saturday Night and Sunday Morning* (Karel Reisz, 1960) were marked by familiar elements like a working-class antihero who usually expressed his disaffection through sneering wit, aggressive sexuality, and chauvinism often bordering on misogyny; harsh, unsentimental depictions of bleak northern cities and landscapes, usually with a focus on the effects of industrialism on the land; and—most importantly—authentic regional dialects. Initially exciting and invigorating, this style of filmmaking had run its course within three or four years, and Angry Young Men and kitchen sinks became cliché; but the new trend toward realism allowed British cinema to open up in terms of its depiction of sex and class relationships, and in its willingness to tackle difficult subject matter like political corruption, abortion, and homosexuality.[34] For all its influence, though, social realism didn't come to Britain without ancestors: take away the Angry Young Man's venom and misogyny and replace his desire to make money with a more spiritual calling, then the person who emerges is a similarly disaffected young man who had appeared in the 1890s: Jude Fawley.

John Schlesinger's first feature film, *A Kind of Loving* (1962), fits neatly into the "kitchen sink" cycle; and, in Robert Murphy's terms, it is "the most realistic, least melodramatic" of the genre—in no small part because the hero and heroine of the film "are almost painfully ordinary."[35] Schlesinger was in many respects the perfect man to come into the realist genre, as he had previously worked as a documentary film maker, first on British television and then in the cinema. To his early features, Schlesinger brought a sense of documentary realism, often utilizing handheld cameras to "spy" on the action of his principals, filming on location and in real buildings as opposed to sets, and in hiring local people to serve as extras and to play small roles. What Schlesinger often captures is a sense of the mundane and ordinary, but his focus on ordinariness makes his protagonists that much more human. In *A Kind of Loving*, Schlesinger is clearly interested in the *work* his characters do; therefore, a good many scenes show Vic (Alan Bates) at his drafting table, and Ingrid (June Ritchie) clattering away with her fellow secretaries in the typing pool. In a much later film, *Sunday, Bloody Sunday* (1971), Schlesinger uses documentary-like techniques to show Dr. Daniel Hirsh (Peter Finch) dispensing medical advice to patients—no patients actually figure in the story—and to later capture a bar-mitzvah ceremony that ultimately serves to remind Daniel that he has largely lost his connection to his Jewish roots. Schlesinger's realist/documentary techniques establish a sense of connection between characters and their environment, and between the audience and the characters.

Also, out of all the British directors to emerge from the social realist movement of the 1950s and 1960s, Schlesinger was perhaps the ideal person to handle an adaptation of Hardy, as the three films he made before *Crowd* and the two he made after it—films that I label "early" and which I feel represent Schlesinger at his best and most consistent[36]—all show a thematic affinity with Hardy. In a 1971 interview, Schlesinger sounded a definite Hardean note in his statement, "I am especially interested in the problems that people have in finding security and happiness in life, and the need for accepting second best when that is all they can hope for"; and he explained his attraction to *Far from the Madding Crowd* was owing to the fact that "Hardy observed human relationships very truly. He saw life as an endurance contest and felt that when fate or providence—call it what you will—strikes you down, you must pick up the pieces and force yourself to go on. Here is a real affirmation of existence."[37] This is an extremely sensitive take on Hardy, an author who is too easily pegged as a doom-laden pessimist; and it would seem that Schlesinger was at least passingly familiar with Hardy's statement that "the universe is an imperfect machine, and ... to do good with an ill-working instrument requires endless adjustments and compromise."[38] We can see this theme of "make what you can with what the world gives you" played out in Schlesinger's early films. *A Kind of Loving* is, in many respects, a more upbeat and certainly less satirical version of the Jude-Arabella relationship. Like Jude, Vic is a well-educated man from the lower class; unlike Jude, he has worked his way into a white collar job as a draftsman, but he is still stifled by a desire to reach higher goals—represented by his dreams of going to Paris and by his constantly flipping through a book of snapshots of idealized naked women. Also like Jude, his sexual urges tie him to a life he hates: his first sexual encounter with Ingrid leaves her pregnant, and even though Vic realizes they are not a well-matched pair, he decides to do the honorable thing and marry her. Only the story's "happy" ending—with Vic and Ingrid resolving to muddle through in hopes a "kind of loving" will emerge—keeps the film from being a modern *Jude*.

A Kind of Loving was released as the kitchen sink cycle was growing stale, and as the directors who had made the seminal films in the genre began to experiment with other forms: in 1963, Tony Richardson branched out to the broad farce of *Tom Jones*, and Lindsay Anderson augmented social realism with a heavy dose of psychological realism in *This Sporting Life*. Similarly, Schlesinger's 1963 film, *Billy Liar*, juxtaposes social realism—represented by the humdrum life of Billy (Tom Courtenay)—with an examination of the character's "inner" state of being, which manifests itself in wild, escapist fantasies. Once again, this is a *Jude*-like story of the need for escape, albeit in a comic and fantastic manner; however, Billy, like Vic, is tied down to one place by his class and his own personal weaknesses. Schlesinger's next film, *Darling* (1965), a satirical story of a jet-setting young woman (Julie Christie) who seeks to bury the "boredom" she feels for life under a series of lovers and the hedonistic pleasures offered by the "swinging London" of the 1960s, would seem to be the antithesis of Hardy, but it nevertheless inspired Alexander Walker's observation that Schlesinger's subsequent adaptation of *Far from the Madding Crowd* was pointless, since the director had effectively already filmed the same story:

> Hardy's 'Darling,' one Bathsheba Everdene, reproduces the same feminine dissatisfactions as she seeks fulfilment with three men: Alan Bates, as her devoted herdsman nursing his love with dumb-ox loyalty, is the Dirk Bogarde character (a reporter and aspiring novelist) of the other film; Terence Stamp, as truculent Sergeant Troy, is strikingly like the sexual swaggerer played by Laurence Harvey in *Darling*; Peter Finch, the bachelor landowner who is said to lack 'passionate parts,' duplicates the impotent Italian prince whom 'Darling' married. Once Julie Christie had been cast, the dice was [*sic*], too: try as the film-makers might, it was impossible to keep the one film from recalling the other—to [*Crowd*'s] detriment.[39]

Though *Darling* does contain a rather "Hardean" love triangle, the model for this film would seem to be not so much *Far from the Madding Crowd* as *The Return of the Native*: for Julie Christie's Diana Scott, like Eustacia Vye of the novel, turns to the various men in her life in hopes they will deliver her from a life of boredom into one of romance and adventure. Just as Eustacia's refusal to compromise on a life with Clym leads to her attempted escape and subsequent drowning, so too does "Darling's" inability to settle lead to a symbolic death—in the form of her marriage to an Italian nobleman who showers her with material comforts, but starves her of affection.

Schlesinger's final two films from his early period are also his best meditations on Hardean themes. *Midnight Cowboy* (1969) returns to a *Jude*-like storyline, as Joe Buck (Jon Voight) wanders from Texas to New York to Florida trying to live out his naïve dream of becoming a successful hustler, only to find that his innate humanity makes *him* the victim in a cold and cynical world, and also that his cowboy persona, built on his faulty impression of what will "sell" with women, is, in fact, an out-dated joke. Just as Jude and Sue are figuratively chased through Upper Wessex by the representatives of conformity and religious hypocrisy, Joe and Ratso Rizzo (Dustin Hoffman) continually move from flea-bag hotels to a squatters' hovel to homelessness, avoiding religious fanatics and sharper hustlers on the way. Even the slow physical decline of Ratso and his death on the bus just as it nears Miami, where he believes his health will be restored, recalls Jude's death at Christminster—at the center of the place where he thought his dreams would come true, yet far removed from the fulfillment of those dreams.

Finally, *Sunday, Bloody Sunday* (1971) showcases another Hardean love triangle, with the bisexual Bob (Murray Head) flitting between the gay Daniel and divorced career woman Alex (Glenda Jackson), each of whom jealously guards Bob's attention. The film has often been criticized—even by Schlesinger himself—for Bob's seeming emptiness, but it is precisely this quality that makes him a Hardean character: Daniel and Alex pour their hopes *into* Bob, believing him to be the source of their own happiness. Bob is like Hardy's "Well-Beloved," an elusive figure that manifests itself to Pierston in the form of three generations of women: so long as Pierston clings to the illusion *in* the woman, he appears—if only to himself—to remain young and vital. Bob's departure for America at the end of the film leaves Alex and Daniel—again like Pierston when he realizes he has passed over many viable opportunities for happiness during his pursuit of an unobtainable ideal—facing their own loneliness and dealing with their decision to cling to an illusion rather than attempting to connect with a substantial and caring human being.

Temperamentally and thematically, then, John Schlesinger was well-suited to bring a Hardy novel to the screen. However, just as there is a tension between Schlesinger's original plan to create a small-scale, intimate film of *Crowd* and MGM's dictate that it be a splashy epic on the lines of David Lean's *Lawrence of Arabia* (1962) and *Doctor Zhivago* (1965),[40] so too is there a tension between Schlesinger's stated desire to make a film that faithfully conveys Hardy's vision, and his own impulses as a realist director. During filming, Schlesinger confessed, "Perhaps I failed to get the cosmos [i.e., Hardy's conception of man's place in the universe] into the picture, but I have tried to convey the feeling of time and place and show how ordinary men and women lived in a farming community a hundred years or so ago."[41] This desire to faithfully recreate the age is visible in a good deal of period detail and in the abundance of Victorian cultural information, technology, and bric-a-brac. There are authentic English folk songs and bawdy military ballads; a beach scene with bathing machines and period entertainment in the form of public story telling; lingering shots of a horse-drawn combine and a steam-powered wheat thresher; and a scene at the Greenhill sheep fair, where in a public booth Cainy Ball (Freddie Jones) has a tooth pulled. Such details fulfill Schlesinger's goal of being faithful to the period, but they also recall Brian McFarlane's view that a cinematic recreation of a long-dead novelist's contemporary environment far too often "produce[s] a distracting quaintness. What was a contemporary work for the author, who could take a good deal relating to time and place for granted, as requiring little or no scene-setting for his readers, has become a period piece for the film-maker."[42] This is indeed true of Schlesinger's *Far from the Madding Crowd*, for the very Victorianness of the picture tends to shift the viewer's focus from what is happening on screen. For instance, the scene in which Bathsheba and her maids sift through old Farmer Everdene's cluttered den opens on a close-up of a large, greasy stain high up on the back of a chair. To a good many viewers, this is probably just a spot of dirt, and many must wonder why it is the central image of the scene. To someone with a working knowledge of Georgian and early Victorian fashion and furniture, however, the spot is immediately recognizable as a stain from the greasy hair pomade that was popular during the first decades of the nineteenth century. The den, we can assume, has been a masculine domain for decades—but how many viewers have this information at hand? Also, many critics have noted that it is difficult to pin down exactly *when* Hardy's novel is supposed to take place, but no such problem is in the film: the date of death on Fanny's tombstone is October 9, 1866. Ultimately, its very historical accuracy lends to *Far from the Madding Crowd* a museum-like quality: its milieu is firmly entrenched in a specific time, losing all immediacy.

Just as Schlesinger sought to make his film authentically Victorian, so too does he strive to make the film authentically *Hardy*. The film was shot in "Hardy country," in Dorset and Wiltshire; and, in keeping with Schlesinger's tradition of recruiting local people to appear in his films, regionals were hired as extras, and actors from nearby repertory companies were given small roles. The locals were also pressed into double-duty by helping the lead actors learn the Dorset dialect—though the effect is less than satisfying. Frederic Raphael's screenplay is generally faithful to the novel, retaining a good number of the cardinal plot functions and generous passages of dialogue, and including sequences that wouldn't seem to make for good cinema, such as the shearing supper. But the film also contains images and sequences apparently inspired by other Hardy novels, perhaps in an effort to appeal to the serious Hardy scholars and fans, who are, after all, the only people who would understand the references. The film begins with a long pan that starts at the seaside and slowly moves over the rolling hills of a heath, until the camera spots a tiny Gabriel with his sheep and dogs, a gesture that recalls the famous opening chapter of *Return of the Native*, with its "cinematic" pan over Egdon Heath that terminates upon the discovery of a solitary wanderer. Troy at one point is

Julie Christie as Bathsheba, surrounded by authentic Hardy countryside.

seen leaving Weatherbury in a reddleman's wagon, another nod to *Native*. When Fanny goes to the wrong church on her wedding day, she finds a military band at practice; the musicians here, as well as the ones that later appear at Bathsheba and Gabriel's wedding, recall the Mellstock Quire from *Under the Greenwood Tree*. Boldwood's threshing machine and a scene of farm workers lazing in the sun bring to mind similar scenes from *Tess*. In the novel, Bathsheba marries Troy in Bath; but in the film, this very real location is replaced by the fictional Budmouth, which figures in a number of Hardy's novels. Schlesinger even plays up to Hardy's well-known fascination with the presence of history in the land by situating the sword display sequence in the earthen ramparts of Maiden Castle, an Iron Age hill fort, and by placing the cockfighting scene at Horton Tower, a ruin in southeast Dorset.[43] Schlesinger even out-Hardys Hardy in Grand Guignol: in the novel, Bathsheba's opening of Fanny's coffin is a nearly subdued affair, with her merely unscrewing the lid and beholding the dead girl and her child; but, in the film, Schlesinger heightens the melodrama by illuminating the room only with Bathsheba's single candle, and by showing Bathsheba slowly prying the lid open with a crowbar. The shot of the bloodless Fanny, with a shriveled blue baby under her chin, delivers a jolt on the lines of Jude's discovery of his hanged children. Finally, the film makes its ultimate gesture at being authentic Hardy at the Christmas party, where Boldwood is seen addressing an elderly servant named Gunney—who is revealed to be a near-double of the octogenarian Thomas Hardy.

Interestingly, most of these "Hardean" additions—the new locations, the characters who work the earth—relate to the film's depiction of Nature, and this is no accident, for Schlesinger's *Far from the Madding Crowd* also seeks to faithfully capture Hardy's view of the role of Nature in human affairs. But therein lies the rub, for in Hardy's novel, Nature rarely affects the operation of the novel's cardinal plot functions—characters look *into* Nature, and then act according to what they believe are Nature's dictates. Hardy's Nature really only catalyzes the plot functions. Once again, catalyzers do not easily lend themselves to direct transference from novel to film, and this is especially true of Hardy's treatment of Nature in *Far from the Madding Crowd*. How does a director film someone looking into Nature, seeing something of herself reflected in its operations, and then acting *according* to that perception? It is extremely difficult: just depicting someone looking *at* Nature tends to merely state the obvious. For instance, in the novel, Gabriel must interpret a number of signals—clouds, thunder, migrating toads, sheltering slugs, huddled sheep—before he can convince himself that a storm is coming, and that it will be devastating. By the time he comes to this conclusion, the men he must warn are already drunk and passed out. In the film, however, Gabriel is seen merely looking *at* ominous storm clouds and being buffeted by the wind, and then he goes into the barn to warn the revelers that a storm is coming. The clouds are so dark and the wind is so fierce that Gabriel's warning seems superfluous: one can only wonder why neither Troy nor anyone else can recognize the oncoming storm. Schlesinger is neither untrue to the text nor does he distort it—in fact, the material leading up to the storm and the actions Gabriel and Bathsheba take to save the ricks come straight from the novel and are beautifully realized on film (though it's hard not to feel cheated because Schlesinger does not show the storm hitting in all its cinematic fury)—but the fact of the matter is that Schlesinger here is content to let the camera record only what is put in front of it. The storm clouds convey mainly that it will rain, and this is plain for everyone to see. This is an inherent problem when it comes to photographing Nature: the image, absent of human occupation, is often static. How, then, can a camera capture mankind's attempts to make an ambiguous Nature a reflection of human wants and aspirations?

Schlesinger solves this problem by making it a non-issue. The film essentially begins at chapter 4, with Bathsheba's rejection of Gabriel's marriage proposal (their friendship is in place by the time the action starts). The major plot function has been faithfully retained, but without the information contained in chapters 1 through 3, its meaning is entirely different. What has been lost is Gabriel's confusion of the lamplight with a star that leads him to his love and Bathsheba's various performances in front of Nature: the characters are not victims of their own self-deceptions. Also, by eliminating the sequence in which Bathsheba saves the sleeping Gabriel from suffocation, the film omits the crucial element of camaraderie that will, in the end, help bring the couple together.[44] However, Schlesinger does try to show the characters' connection to Nature in terms of his use of light and darkness. When Gabriel sees Bathsheba on horseback, it is bright daylight and the green heath and the presence of the sheep create a springtime feel; however, when Bathsheba rejects Gabriel's marriage offer, the scene is again outdoors, but it is now dusk and the characters are bathed in gray. Gabriel's hopes are expressed through sunshine and images of spring, while the dashing of those hopes is conveyed through the coming of night. In this sense, Nature seems to mirror the pain that Gabriel is feeling. The association of Nature with Gabriel's isolation continues in subsequent scenes. Immediately after Gabriel walks away from Bathsheba, resolving to never ask for her hand again, there is a cut to an overhead shot of Gabriel's dogs herding his sheep into a circle. As the camera moves slowly up into space, and as the dogs and sheep continue to swirl into a wriggling mass, the animals begin to resemble microbes, signifying perhaps the pettiness of human ambitions. Shortly thereafter, Gabriel is seen watching Bathsheba leave for Weatherbury on a gray, rain-slicked road. Water imagery is significant in this film: Bathsheba's departure through water seems to punctuate Gabriel's "soaked" ambitions; and this association of water with drowned hopes is emphasized soon afterward by the sight of the waves washing over the broken bodies of the sheep Gabriel's dog has run over the cliff.

The action in the first reel embodies how Nature is presented in the film. Since Hardy's ambiguous Nature does not lend itself well to cinematic effects, Schlesinger apparently chose to compensate by using the interplay of light and darkness and the occasional use of water imagery to convey Nature's role in human affairs. In the film, light becomes associated with springtime, regeneration, and sexuality; while darkness is usually invoked whenever sexuality is reined in by the threat of marriage. In the opening sequences, Gabriel's infatuation with Bathsheba is conveyed both by the wistful look on his face, and by the fact his infatuation is complemented by the spring-like setting; however, when he tries to socialize his "natural" sexual desire by channeling it into a marriage proposal,

Nature signals its disapproval by turning dark and ominous. Bathsheba's departure for Weatherbury on a gray, cloudy day, and the water washing over the dead sheep tend to reinforce the death of Gabriel's dream. This depiction of Nature fits neatly into a familiar pastoral pattern, with Nature approving of unfettered sexuality and disapproving the encroachment of civilization and socializing customs; and this theme will be replayed throughout the film in the images Schlesinger chooses.

Patterns of light and darkness are used not only to signify Nature's "feelings" about particular scenes, but as a means of characterization. For instance, light is predominantly associated with Julie Christie's Bathsheba. Before she marries Troy, Bathsheba usually wears white and yellow (which makes her assumption of black crepe after Troy's supposed "death" at sea genuinely startling), and the fact that Christie is blonde—Bathsheba in the novel has dark hair, something she feels is a negative contrast to the blonde Fanny Robin—tends to tie her in with images of sunshine and golden wheat. Her "springtime" qualities are also illustrated through some subtle but meaningful changes that Raphael makes in his script: during the shearing supper sequence, Bathsheba's song is changed from "A Winning Tongue Had He," which anticipates the arrival of the soldier Troy, to "Bushes and Briars," a traditional pastoral in which the subject of the song waits "for the coming of (her) dear" amidst singing birds and skipping sheep. The way the sequence is handled—with Bathsheba at the head of a fully-laden table, Gabriel accompanying Bathsheba's song on his flute, and numerous intercuts of children playing in the grass—tends to emphasize that Bathsheba is the presiding figure—perhaps even the deity—in a springtime cult. These associations of Bathsheba with springtime and frolic no doubt inspired Alexander Walker's pithy comment that, as Bathsheba, Christie "sang radiantly, paid her workers radiantly, even milked the cows radiantly."[45] In fact, Bathsheba literally *is* radiant during the sheep-washing sequence. While Bathsheba, on horseback, supervises the labor of Gabriel and other shepherds, Boldwood rides up to her, and through his perspective, we see Bathsheba's face with the sun behind her wide straw hat, disseminating the light and bathing her features in a blinding glow. Significantly, this stands as a moment where Nature seems to be approving of Boldwood's love for Bathsheba; however, when he asks to speak with her, the two ride off into a nearby forest. When the couple is completely blanketed under the shade of the trees, Boldwood makes his proposal, and he is rejected. Bathsheba then walks out of the forest and into the light, while Boldwood, his face grim, stays in the darkness, suggesting Nature's continued disapproval of his attempt to socialize unfettered love. The action and dialogue contained in the scene are entirely

Fanny (**Prunella Ransome,** *right*) presses Troy (Terence Stamp, *on horseback*) for a wedding date.

faithful to Hardy; the one difference is that Bathsheba's rejection of Bold-wood in the novel takes place in the open, by the riverside, and Nature provides no commentary on what has transpired.

Similarly, Schlesinger associates Troy with images of light and spring-time. Troy is first seen on horseback, splendidly bedecked in full-dress uniform (including a plumed silver helmet), and leading his troops down a country lane. He is called away from his men by Fanny Robin (Prunella Ransome), who asks him when he'll marry her. This scene is roughly anal-ogous to chapter 11 in the novel, but it is played and photographed entirely differently. In the novel, Fanny calls to Troy from outside his barracks win-dow; when he answers, she cannot see him, and he is in fact confused as to her identity, at first demanding, "What girl are you?" (p. 137). The hid-den Troy—who no doubt is with another woman—evades Fanny's attempts to force him to name a wedding day. By contrast, in the film, Troy is outdoors and in the open. Though Schlesinger apparently tries to convey some of Troy's deceitfulness by shooting the scene on a gray day, this attempt is undermined by the colorful soldiers, the tender background music, by Troy and Fanny standing face-to-face, and by some very playful dialogue. Troy is treated as something of a rogue, but by introducing him on a country lane, in a scene that is often gentle and touching, he becomes a less deceitful, more romantic figure. The viewer is even allowed to sympathize with Troy during the scenes where he waits for Fanny at the church. As Troy nervously paces, a pair of elderly women in the pews begin loudly whispering that he has been jilted; and we feel his sense of humiliation grow. Troy's subsequent rejection of Fanny seems less harsh than it otherwise might.

However, it isn't until he is paired with Bathsheba that Troy likewise becomes a springlike figure. Though their first meeting is as described in the novel—in the darkness, when Troy's spur becomes tangled in her nightgown—his first appearance to Bathsheba in the light of day is in her garden, where she is hiving bees. Unlike in the novel, where Troy puts on Bathsheba's bee-keeping outfit in order to win her confidence,[46] Troy stands behind a showy display of bright flowers, where he seduces Bathsheba with a loving oration on her beauty. The buzzing bees, the flowers in bloom, the brightness of Troy's red uniform jacket, the lush background music, and the perpetually glowing Bathsheba all collaborate to create an image of springtime and procreation. This image is reinforced in the sword-exercise scene at Maiden Castle, where the massive ramparts dip into a series of suggestive clefts. The display is considerably expanded from its literary counterpart, with Troy running up and down the slopes and waving and thrusting his sword with a look of ecstatic fury on his face. At one point, Bathsheba's point of view is represented, and Troy is transported to the head of a charging cavalry, his sword pointed straight ahead. The sequence climaxes with Troy thrusting his sword into the ground, a gesture that speaks for itself. At this point, it must be noted that Terence Stamp and Julie Christie are ideally cast if only for their physical beauty: Stamp, with his cold blue eyes and roguish grin, becomes the epitome of manliness and sexual virility; whereas Alan Bates as Gabriel is saddled with a chinstrap beard that makes him look like a stern Mennonite, and Peter Finch—50 at the time and not the 41 that Hardy's Boldwood is said to be—looks far too old and staid to be any kind of a sexual threat to Bathsheba. The physical appeal of these actors and characters tends to feed the film's romantic feel, and, according to Roger Webster, fits into a dialectic that is purely 1960s pastoral. Webster claims that "Terence Stamp's Zapata moustache and Julie Christie's hairstyle are very much 1960s icons, and could easily belong on pop album sleeves from the period"—an observation that is significant

because "there is an underlying theme in much of the (1960s) popular culture of back to nature which constitutes a form of pastoralism: the songs
and album covers of groups such as 'The Incredible String Band' or the
Woodstock pop concert tradition can be seen as 'alternative' versions of pastoral without stretching the term unduly."[47] Whether Troy and Bathsheba
are meant to be symbols of 1960s-style pastoralism or not, it is nevertheless clear that in their youth, beauty, and exuberance, they are to be seen
as figures of springtime and regeneration.

Just as Schlesinger uses light to characterize Nature's approval of
unfettered sexual togetherness, so too does he use darkness and images of
water to indicate Nature's disapproval of attempts to rein in sexuality
through socialization. In each of the scenes where Boldwood proposes to
Bathsheba, he is somehow disconnected from pure, natural light: his first
proposal is made in the shade of the forest; his second is made indoors.
As in the novel, Boldwood confronts Troy at night and learns of
Bathsheba's elopement; and as in the novel, he walks away from the scene
and into "the hills and downs of Weatherbury like an unhappy Shade in
the Mournful Fields by Acheron" (p. 292), but Schlesinger adds the
significant detail of storm clouds lowering over Boldwood's head. It is also
worthwhile to note that, just as Bathsheba has been associated with springtime and Troy with spring and summer, Peter Finch's Boldwood is clearly
associated with autumn: not simply in terms of his age, but in that he is
dressed throughout the film in grays and blacks. The film also makes a clear
connection between Boldwood and industrialism: even though at one
point he is seen sowing seeds with his workers, he also introduces the
thresher to his farm. While his men eye the machine like an interloper,
Boldwood hops on top of it and declares, "Come on! It won't hurt you!"
Boldwood's house is also more of an imposing manor than a rich farm
house, with a lavish front gate, rich decor, and an army of servants. Boldwood is a threat both to the pastoral union of Bathsheba and Troy and to
the simple farming methods employed by Gabriel and the Weatherbury
peasants.

Significantly, the darkness that is employed to represent Nature's disapproval of socializing institutions comes to dominate the film once Troy
and Bathsheba marry; and Schlesinger further signals Nature's disapproval
through the evocation of water images. The end of the romantic hopes of
both Gabriel and Boldwood is punctuated by Bathsheba driving away
from them in her cart and splashing through puddles of water. When
Bathsheba meets Troy on the beach at Budmouth, their words are drowned
out under the sounds of crashing waves. It is as if the waves are trying
to silence an act—Troy's social union with Bathsheba—that should be

literally unspeakable. However, there is a hint that Bathsheba is making a sacrifice of herself: the only voice heard in the scene is that of the beachside barker, who thrills the crowd with a tale of Captain Cook's witnessing a human sacrifice; and the deadening power of society is demonstrated by the relegation of Troy and Bathsheba to the background as a group of black-clad elders walk into the foreground. These solemn, Grundyite figures obscure Troy and Bathsheba as surely as the city encroaches upon the pristine countryside.

After his marriage becomes public, Troy sheds his bright uniform and dresses entirely in gray. From this point on, Troy is almost always photographed at night, in the shadows, under a gloomy sky (as when he walks away from the castle after losing at cockfighting), indoors, or—in the cartoonish Dick Turpin sequence—in disguise. Once Troy has been socialized, he literally becomes a shadowy figure, losing the light he had when he was associated with Fanny and the unwed Bathsheba. In keeping with the imagery of the movie, he also becomes a character associated with water. The storm scene can be viewed as Nature's direct condemnation of the marriage, as it hits only when the now civilized Troy begins to pass around the liquor, his "wedding present" to the men. Nature's disapproval of human authority is witnessed in an amusing moment when a banner reading "OUR VICAR" blows into the mud, followed by a quick cut to the vicar himself, lying drunk and passed out on the barn floor. More seriously, water is later shown to be a sign of Nature's disapproval of Troy's abandonment of Fanny: the camera focuses on a leaf dripping water onto Fanny's coffin, something Costabile dismisses as "a trite metaphor (of) a crying leaf."[48] However, it is not so much that Nature *weeps* for Fanny as that it *disapproves* of Troy. This point is made even clearer when a torrent of water from the "gurgoyle's" spout washes away Troy's elaborate garden atop Fanny's grave. In the novel, Troy interprets the washed-out grave as a kind of judgment: "The sight, coming as it did, superimposed upon the other dark scenery of the previous days, formed a sort of climax to the whole panorama, and it was more than he could endure" (p. 377); however, this is merely his *impression*, his reading Nature as responding to his own guilt and self-loathing. Hardy shows this to be a faulty impression when Bathsheba re-plants the flowers on the grave and orders Gabriel to have the gurgoyle's spout turned in another direction. By leaving out this information, the film implies that Nature does indeed disapprove of Troy's actions: he has violated "natural" law both by marrying and by failing to take care of Fanny. When Troy apparently drowns himself (the film does not show Troy being picked up by a passing ship), it appears that Nature is covering him under its own obscuring waves.

Troy (Terence Stamp) and Bathsheba (Julie Christie) contemplate the loss of their premarital happiness.

Just as darkness seems to envelop Troy after the wedding, so too does it envelop Bathsheba, but there is the promise that her "spring-like" qualities give her the ability to regenerate. Although she, too, is primarily dressed in dark colors and photographed inside for much of the rest of the film, Schlesinger does give Bathsheba a moment of release that signifies she will be able to come back to life after the autumn and winter of Troy.

After she confronts Troy over Fanny's body, Bathsheba runs from the house, and, as in Chapter 44 of the novel, she awakens in the forest to the sound of a young boy practicing his psalter. However, the crucial detail that Bathsheba wakes up on the edge of a swamp—the area that allows her to realize how faulty her way of seeing the world is—has been altered: she wakes up on the edge of a lush green glen. Bathsheba is photographed in the dark foreground, under the shade of the trees, but in the background is a blue sky, a rich green carpet of grass, a horse happily rolling on its back, and the cherub-like child rehearsing a prayer. The meaning is clear: while Bathsheba may now be stuck in darkness, it is an easy thing for her to move into the regenerative light.

Finally, Schlesinger adds a detail to his imagery that further enhances his pastoral theme: that of time, symbolized in the film by the overabundance of clocks and the sounds of ticking. Clocks come to represent marriage, as they are only utilized in the scenes where marriage is an issue. The first time the ticking of clocks comes into play is where Boldwood sits at his table, solemnly eating dinner and contemplating the Valentine on his mantlepiece. As Schlesinger intercuts shots of the dining Boldwood, his well-disciplined dogs, and the Valentine, the ticking becomes almost nerve-wracking. The sound apparently even gets to Boldwood, who strides from his seat, grabs the Valentine, and throws it into the fireplace. The camera lingers on the burning words "MARRY ME" and the scene—and the sound of the clock—fades out. On the morning after their wedding, Troy presents Bathsheba with a beautiful clock/music box topped by a spinning soldier, and this gesture would seem to characterize their love; however, the sounds of the clock become mocking later in the film when Bathsheba confronts Troy over his gambling debts, and then confesses that their marriage was a mistake. The ticking of clocks is also heard over the scene when, after Troy's disappearance, Boldwood presses Bathsheba to marry him and receives her promise that she will give her answer at Christmas, and, again, at the Christmas party, when Bathsheba finally promises to marry Boldwood after six years. The significance of the sounds of the clocks only becomes apparent when they are heard again after Boldwood shoots Troy dead: then, as the camera moves in on Boldwood's agonized face, the ticking of the clocks gives way to sound of hammering—and Schlesinger cuts to the interior of a prison, where Boldwood's coffin is being nailed together.[49] Marriages, then, are limiting: once sexuality has been socialized into the marriage union, the youthfulness associated with sexuality begins to decay, terminating in death.

Schlesinger manages to bind all of his film images together in a melancholy coda that was apparently deleted from American prints of the film for years.[50] After the wedding of Gabriel and Bathsheba, the couple are seen together inside Bathsheba's study. Gabriel stands by the window, looking out onto a rainy night. He and Bathsheba regard each other and smile; then Bathsheba turns to her newspaper and the sound a clock chiming can be heard. Gabriel checks his watch (a sign, I believe, of Gabriel's being socialized or domesticated—Bates's Gabriel has never used a watch to this point; and, in the first chapter of the novel, Gabriel tries to make sense of his notoriously unreliable watch, and then never uses it again), and the camera pans to the corner of the room, where Troy's music box/clock is on display. The camera slowly zooms in on the small soldier figure, spinning on top of a castle parapet, and then freezes. The impression the viewer is left with is that, in spite of the gaiety that was seen at Bathsheba and Gabriel's wedding, the forces of Nature—darkness, rain, the rapid ticking away of time—will serve to quash the couple's happiness, and a new springtime—perhaps a new lover—will emerge to take its place.

In the final analysis, Schlesinger's *Far from the Madding Crowd* is a film that succeeds in transferring Hardy's *word* to the screen; but in terms of reproducing Hardy's *intent*, his way of seeing the world, it is something altogether different. In his very gestures to make the film authentic—authentically Victorian and authentically Hardy—Schlesinger takes away the immediacy of the story and turns it into something quaint. Moreover, by replacing Hardy's difficult-to-film literary treatment of Nature with a cinematic treatment of light and darkness, and through an emphasis on images associated with water and time, Schlesinger creates a film that is more in keeping with a traditional pastoral than what Hardy created. This is not to argue that the film is bad because of it—Julie Christie's eager-beaver Bathsheba aside, Schlesinger's *Crowd* offers uniformly excellent performances, and it is admirable for no other reason than its wish to *be* faithful to Hardy. Moreover, the film is indeed visually beautiful, but again its visual strengths tend to reinforce the standard image of Hardy as pastoralist. It is, then, not surprising that many contemporary critics claimed that the most authentically Hardean thing about the film was not its story or its period detail, but in the way Schlesinger and cinematographer Nicolas Roeg captured Nature. A review in *Sight and Sound*, for example, embodies a fairly common view that to be faithful to Hardy is to be faithful to his sense of place:

> Just as the desert was the real subject of the first part of *Lawrence of Arabia*, so the Hardy country is the real subject here. ... [The film's painterly] allusions, together with the images of sowing, sheep-dipping and harvesting, emphasising as they do the Arcadian character of the story, create both feelings of timelessness and of a time from which an urban

audience is totally cut off. It is here, it seems to me, that the specific appeal of the film lies. The actors may not all be convincing in their parts and the story may be pretty thin, but pastoral myth for the smokebound consumer is as potent as it was in the time of Beaumont and Fletcher.[51]

Schlesinger's *Crowd* does deserve to be praised for its pastoral qualities because it is, indeed, a pastoral—a film that privileges unfettered love and sexuality in an Arcadian setting while it warns against encroaching socialization and industrialism. The mistake that some critics have made, however, is in assuming that these qualities derive originally from Hardy. Hardy's novel is only a pastoral on the surface: it appears to advocate the joys of communion with Nature, but in the end it shows that people must look within to find the strength they need. In creating a film that makes gestures toward being authentically Hardean yet endorses common cultural ways of reading Hardy, John Schlesinger renders the author safe, familiar, and comfortably contained.

4

Tess by Hardy, *Tess* by Polanski: Convergence and Fulfillment

I

> In any attempt to define or to collect "the essential Hardy," [*Tess of the d'Urbervilles*] would inevitably be one of the principal sources. So that when one speaks of *Tess*, one speaks to a striking degree of Hardy, and one can scarcely speak of Hardy without speaking of *Tess*.[1]

So writes Arnold Kettle in a 1966 introduction to *Tess of the d'Urbervilles* (1891), and few probably would quibble with this statement. If one novel is immediately identified with Thomas Hardy—and if the name of Hardy immediately recalls the title of one particular work of fiction—that novel is more than likely *Tess*. To Kettle, the qualities that make the book "essential" to Hardy's reputation and achievement as a writer are its fame and popularity; the familiarity of the person on the street with its plot and themes; Tess's cultural status as a "mythological" character; and—most importantly—the fact *Tess* conveys Hardy's "deepest sensibility and ultimate commitment, the view of life that his art in its total historical, and therefore human, context expresses."[2] It can perhaps be argued that Kettle's criteria here are essentially New Critical (though his most famous study of *Tess* is one of the first substantial Marxist analyses of the novel[3]), and therefore passé in these post-structuralist times, when texts are rarely to be categorized on lists of artistic achievements; but it is hard to deny that Kettle got it right. The novel's fame and popularity are undeniable; its plot is indeed well known; and Tess Durbeyfield herself is famous enough that a typical crossword puzzle clue is "Hardy

94

heroine, four letters." Kettle's belief that *Tess* contains Hardy's most complete artistic statement on life, however, would likely be shot down by the modern critic—both for the apparent assumption that artistic achievement *can* be measured, and especially because the issue of *what* Hardy was trying to "say" in *Tess* (if he was trying to say anything at all) is one of the most contentious areas in all Hardy scholarship. *Tess* has probably been subject to more critical scrutiny and dissection than any of Hardy's novels, in order to uncover just what the author was getting at; and the character and mind of Thomas Hardy himself have similarly been subject to the critical scalpel so as to determine why he wrote what he wrote. Why *Tess* and Hardy should be so scrutinized is easy to explain: Hardy's narrator appears to be offering an intimate, personal, and even loving depiction of Tess herself, while he also seems to be actively pushing the reader away from not only Tess but from a coherent understanding of the narrative. Hardy at times gives the impression that he has locked Tess away in some private recess—suggested strongly by the epigraph from *Two Gentlemen of Verona*: "Poor wounded name! My bosom, as a bed, / Shall lodge thee"—and issued a challenge to reader and critic alike: to find and understand Tess is to find and understand Hardy, and vice versa.

Through more than one century of trying to uncover the author of *Tess* in *Tess*, a complicated image of Hardy has emerged: we see the

The publicity shot used in the advertising of *Tess*. The image of a woman at a window (*here*, Nastassia Kinski) is characteristic of Polanski.

pastoralist, pessimist, tragedian and supreme artist he is frequently called; but the Hardy of *Tess* has also been labeled a Darwinist, a Zolaist, a naturalist, a modernist, a socialist, a conservative, a satirist, a lover of women, a hater of women, a neo-pagan, an anti-religionist, a sadist, a pervert, and a writer who didn't know how to control his own materials. No one consistent "Hardy" emerges from the critical heritage of *Tess*—unlike the fairly codified "Hardy" that is produced by the critical history of *Far from the Madding Crowd*—but, strangely enough, this same discordant history of interpreting Hardy within *Tess* has, in and of itself, created a stable image of Hardy as *subject* for critical discourse. The simple fact that critics have for decades tried to uncover traces of Hardy's innermost self within *Tess* creates an image of Hardy as the artist who cannot be divorced from his work and is to be located within every word on its pages; and *Tess* itself becomes a kind of philosopher's stone that, if correctly interpreted, reveals the truths inside the person of Thomas Hardy. It is indeed difficult to separate Hardy from *Tess*—in the popular imagination, they are one and the same.

It is because *Tess of the d'Urbervilles* is so commonly seen as the conduit to Hardy's most personal self that makes Roman Polanski's 1979 film, simply titled *Tess*, such a fascinating adaptation; for Polanski's *Tess*—like so many of that director's films—made Polanski himself the subject of critical scrutiny and discussion (in no small part because this was his first film after he fled America on charges of statutory rape), so that this *Tess*, too, is widely seen as a text that opens itself up to being read as offering insight into the mind of its creator. This convergence of thought in the critical histories of Hardy's *Tess* and Polanski's creates a degree of confluence between the two works; but Polanski's adaptation of the novel still seeks to preserve some of the traditional ways of seeing Hardy, and these interpretations are, of course, important to the critical history of *Tess of the d'Urbervilles*.

One phenomenon in the "critography" of *Tess* the novel is that Hardy is often made into a straw man that readers and critics can use to support their own particular readings. Historically, those who are favorably disposed toward the novel often manufacture a Hardy they can defend from criticism—the "good little Thomas Hardy," to use Henry James's term,[4] who created a work of beauty in spite of some serious flaws in craftsmanship; while those who dislike the novel, or find it impossible to overlook its flaws, tend to point to certain distasteful elements in "Hardy's" thinking or personality that explain what is wrong with the book—thus giving us the "decadent" Hardy of the 1890s, and the rather lurid scoptophiliac who has emerged in much recent criticism of the novel. At times, reading the critical history of *Tess* is like reading the transcripts of a court trial, with Hardy as defendant and *Tess of the d'Urbervilles* as the evidence that will be used to acquit or condemn him.

The process of trying Hardy through *Tess* first began when Hardy was forced to severely alter or altogether omit from the manuscript a few passages relating to religion and sex in order to serialize it in a popular "family" magazine. Hardy's difficulty in finding a publisher for the unexpurgated text and his subsequent bowdlerization of *Tess* have long been cited as evidence of the narrow-minded, puritanical attitudes that dominated Victorian publishing houses, and of the fear in which writers and publishers held the critics and reading public[5]; and Hardy's particular troubles have been seen as proof that he was a literary rebel who enjoyed shocking the status quo. John Goode even suggests that Hardy may have "sent the novel to publishers certain to refuse it in order to generate an atmosphere of controversy before its publication."[6] *Tess* certainly did create controversy, and a few of its first critics leveled their strongest charges against the perceived immorality of the author. The anonymous critic in *Saturday Review* for January 16, 1892, practically accused Hardy of being a pornographer, saying the novelist's warning in his preface about the restored "adult" chapters "reminds us of those artists who have exhibitions of pictures open to the public, but who hang over an inner sanctum containing their choicest works a placard marked 'For gentlemen only.'"[7] There is a persistent myth that such moralistic charges were the norm in early criticism of *Tess;* and again we can see that Hardy was largely its progenitor. After Mowbray Morris savaged *Tess* in print, Hardy wrote in his diary, "Well, if this sort of thing continues no more novel-writing for me. A man must be a fool to deliberately stand up to be shot at."[8] He later included this response in his *Life,* which has had the effect of suggesting Morris's review was typical, and of foreshadowing an important event in Hardy's career. After all, Hardy *would* later abandon novel-writing, and the popularly received reason would be his inability to stomach bad reviews.[9] In fact, reviews that attacked *Tess* on moral grounds were a minority. Most contemporary critics treated the book seriously and showed great deference to Hardy's skills as a writer; and a few reviews were even laudatory.[10] Even Mrs. Oliphant, despite reservations about *Tess*'s "naughty chapters," afforded the novel grudging respect. However, one common complaint tends to surface in the early reviews, and it concerns Hardy's use of language. It is this aspect of *Tess*—more than its treatment of sex or religion—that has made it controversial, and which has been the focus of numerous claims for, and charges against, Hardy as a thinker and as a human being.

The first critics of *Tess* were probably most offended by the subtitle, *A Pure Woman, Faithfully Presented*; and the common complaint is that Hardy used the words "pure" and "purity" without understanding either their intrinsic meanings, or how those words may in any way be applied to Tess Durbeyfield. Moreover, to some critics, the subtitle was a thrown gauntlet, Hardy's declaration of war against respectable readers. The reviewer in the *Independent* of February 25, 1892, bluntly states, "Tess was not a pure woman. Pure women do not, save in novels, drop into the arms of men that they do not love." The reviewer goes on to indict the mind of the novelist himself, writing,

> In Mr. Hardy's belief we have arrived at a point in civilization where it is not necessary for a girl to lose purity before she becomes the mistress of a man she does not love and does not intend to marry. Even after she has married the man she loves, she may return to the arms of her seducer and still be pure![11]

Many critics who were not offended by the morality of the novel also took issue with Hardy's notion of purity, but the common charge among them was that Hardy simply failed in his attempt to redefine the term, or that by insisting his heroine was "pure" he created an inconsistent character. R. H. Hutton in the *Spectator* of January 23, 1892, makes the not unreasonable point that Hardy's redefinition of purity is nothing radical—in fact, it is downright conventional:

> …Mr. Hardy, instead of illustrating his conviction that there is no Power who guides and guards those who are faithful to their best lights, has only illustrated what every Christian would admit, that if fine natures will not faithfully adhere to such genuine instincts as they have, they may deteriorate, and will deteriorate, in consequence of that faithfulness.[12]

So, to the *Independent*, Hardy's moral failings make him a poor artist, while to Hutton, Hardy's artistic failings make him a poor moralist; but these two opinions ably illustrate how loaded are the terms "pure" and "purity" in *Tess*, and a good deal of criticism has been directed toward deciphering Hardy's precise meaning and intent in using these words. D. H. Lawrence, in a typically colorful reading, suggests Tess's purity is connected to her aristocratic blood; that she is "herself always."[13] While Lawrence's interpretation of Tess's aristocratic purity has not been particularly popular, some critics have followed in his wake by arguing that Tess is fundamentally true to something in herself, or to herself *as woman*. Simon Gatrell argues that Tess may be classified as "essential woman, wholly woman, as pure woman"[14]; but both Kathleen Blake and Rosemarie

Morgan suggest that, in using the term "pure woman," Hardy was establishing in the readers' minds a generic, literary archetype, which he then proceeds to dismantle—with greater or lesser degrees of success.[15] Since the publication of J. T. Laird's *The Shaping of Tess of the D'Urbervilles* in 1975, many critics have focused both on the fact that the novel's subtitle was an eleventh-hour addition, and that Hardy's numerous revisions to the novel had the effect of diminishing Tess's sexual nature and the blame she shares in her own fall, to suggest that Hardy was, in fact, only interested in placating the tastes of his publishers and readers. Both Mary Jacobus and Penny Boumelha have argued that, in his efforts to make Tess more "conventionally" pure, Hardy largely defeated his own purpose. To Jacobus, Hardy's program was to turn Tess into a blameless victim; therefore, he strips her not only of an active role in her own tragedy, but robs her of "sexual autonomy and the capacity for independent being and doing."[16] Alternatively, Boumelha notes that, as "Tess is purified, so there is also a far-reaching and wholesale blackening of Alec and Angel that transforms them unequivocally into rake and hypocrite."[17] Both suggest that Hardy's insistence on Tess's purity guided him toward endorsing a conventional interpretation of purity, thus making himself a servant to Victorian cultural ideology.

By far, the most popular way critics have found for defining Tess's purity is by showing that it is intimately associated with Nature and the natural world.[18] This association stems, perhaps, from Hardy's own "Preface to the Fifth and Later Editions," where he tries to defuse the criticisms against his "sub-title adjective" by arguing that those who are offended by it are guilty of ignoring "the meaning of the word in Nature, together with all aesthetic claims upon it, not to mention the spiritual interpretation afforded by the finest side of their own Christianity" (*Tess*, p. x). Unfortunately, Hardy's defense is far from clear; and it raises an entirely new complication in trying to understand *Tess*, as Bernard J. Paris notes:

> Using nature as a norm, we see that Tess's sexual relation with Alec is good (in any event, not reprehensible) and that the convention which condemns Tess's act has no validity. Copulation is the law of life; the birds and rabbits that Tess regards as innocent behave as she did.
> The argument for Tess's purity from the goodness of her intentions implies that her sexual relations with Alec were bad; the argument for Tess's purity from nature as moral norm regards her relations with Alec as innocent. Indeed, calling Tess's experience a liberal education makes it sound rather attractive—or, at least, valuable.[19]

Paris charges that Hardy's defense of Tess's purity creates "a confusion of many standards"[20]; and while I prefer not to use the word *confusion* in relation to Hardy's own thinking, it is true that, in *Tess*—more than in the earlier *Far from the Madding Crowd*—Nature is multifaceted and even deceptive, and if Hardy is offering it as a standard by which Tess is to be judged, confusion is likely to result in the mind of the reader. Where he first invokes Nature as a power or entity, Hardy offers a direct critique of Wordsworth's conception of Nature as beneficent and good by juxtaposing it with the poverty of the Durbeyfield children: "Some people would like to know whence the poet whose philosophy is in these days deemed as profound and trustworthy as his song is breezy and pure, gets his authority for speaking of 'Nature's holy plan'" (p. 4). In the anti-pastoralism—or at least anti-Romanticism[21]—of this passage, Nature is characterized as not only harsh and brutal, but is essentially defined by a kind of blind sexual determinism that results in "six helpless creatures, who had never been asked if they wished for life on any terms" (p. 4). This sexual determinism surfaces frequently in the novel: when Hardy's narrator asks why Tess "was doomed to be seen and coveted that day by the wrong man, and not by some other man, the right and desired one in all respects" (pp. 30–1), he quickly answers his own question: "Nature does not often say 'See!' to her poor creature at a time when seeing can lead to happy doing; or reply 'Here' to a body's cry of 'Where?' till the hide-and-seek has become an irksome, outworn game" (p. 31). The narrator is nowhere more explicit in associating Nature with a blind sexual urge than where he eulogizes Tess's baby as "Sorrow the Undesired—that intrusive creature, that bastard gift of shameless Nature who respects not the social law" (p. 75). Certainly, if Nature is the standard by which Tess should be judged, she is pure indeed: in her sexual relationship with Alec (however it is defined), her overwhelming attraction to Angel, and in her subsequent return to—and murder of—Alec, she is operating according to the dictates of Nature's drive to find the right mate.

Many critics have fastened on to this depiction of a highly sexed Nature and have persuasively argued that Hardy's intention was largely to dramatize a "Darwinian" view of the natural world. Laird demonstrates that Hardy didn't bring the Darwinian theme to the surface of the text until he made some key "insertions" for later editions of 1892 and 1895[22]; but at least one critic of the first edition—the anonymous reviewer in the *Athenaeum* of January 9, 1892[23]—identified the ideology of Huxley as operating within the novel, and for years thereafter critics have been interpreting *Tess of the d'Urbervilles* along Darwinian lines. The number of *Tess* studies that focus on heredity, survival of the fittest, evolution, and devolution is astonishing, as are the numbers of ways these topics have been read into Hardy's "world view." Consider, for instance, the "debate" that took place in two issues of the *Southern Review* in the mid–1970s, when two different critics applied "Darwinism" to *Tess*. First, Peter Morton argued that Hardy supplemented his reading of Darwin with Weismann, so that "Hardy's use of Weismann's belief that the germ-plasm, the material principle of heredity, is the sole biological reality, leads him to impose on the reader the temporal insignificance of the individual carrier of it." The d'Urbervilles/Durbeyfields, Morton argues, are in the process of de-evolving owing to a failure to adapt to new surroundings and new situations, and Tess merely carries on this process: the novel, then, is marked by its "rigid determinism, its total pessimism and its fidelity to one coherent scientific vision of the world."[24] Writing in direct response to Morton, J. R. Ebbatson contends Hardy's Darwinism was actually flavored more with Huxley than with Weismann, so that Hardy saw potential in evolution, not barefaced determinism: Tess is a character aligned with "Nature" who experiences the potentialities of growth and evolution through the organic process, but she is eventually done in by a counter-force, that of the "claustrophobic, life-denying moral law of human society."[25] As these examples indicate, applying Darwinian and post-Darwinian thought to Hardy's *Tess* is no easy matter. Several questions arise: Are evolution and natural selection in themselves deterministic and tragic, or does Tess's tragedy lie in her being prevented from experiencing the benefits of evolution? Is Tess the last in a line of a degenerate race, or the potential starting point for a new kind of life? It is also evident that, although these critics make a strong case for Hardy-as-Darwinist, they also strengthen two popularly held views of Hardy. In the reading of Morton, Hardy uses Darwin to bolster his tragic, pessimistic, and deterministic world view; while Ebbatson suggests that, in order to further his attack on society, Hardy dramatizes society's inability to appreciate and understand Tess as a new kind of organism.

If critics have been puzzled for years over what Hardy meant by "purity" and "nature," they have similarly been perplexed by what he was trying to say about women; and to this day *Tess of the d'Urbervilles* raises controversies over what it (allegedly) reveals about Hardy's attitudes toward them. To many of the first reviewers, there was no doubt that Hardy's sympathies were entirely on the side of women who had been wronged by a hypocritical, masculinist society,[26] and that he identified with women on a deep, personal level. Joseph Warren Beach in the 1920s went so far as to say that Hardy was so involved with Tess because he must have been "drawing from the life."[27] More recent critics, such as Margaret Higonnet and Marjorie Garson, have argued Hardy's "feminist" sympathies sprang less from a personal identification with women, than from a true ideological desire to render a woman's experience as accurately as a man could, and, paradoxically, to expose the dangers of men trying to read and interpret women's experiences.[28] Rosemarie Morgan makes one of the most persuasive cases for Hardy's feminist sympathies, saying Hardy has armed Tess not with dialogue, which is associated with masculinist discourse, but with *actions*—and through her actions she takes control of her own fate and parodies man's interpretations and expectations of her.[29]

To Marxist critics, Hardy's depiction of women is of particular interest, since these critics have located in Tess's plight a reflection of the situation of the working class in a capitalist economy.[30] Terry Eagleton, for instance, writes that "Tess's society has little use for her personality: it takes her body for sexual or economic profit, so that her consciousness is forced either to detach itself dreamily from material circumstance, or shrink itself within the harsh limits of mindlessly mechanical activity." In Eagleton's reading, Tess reduces herself to "impassive objectivity," negating her own being before society destroys it altogether.[31] This concern with Tess's body as material object is also the subject of John Goode's study, which considers Tess's "impure" status crucial to the interests of the hierarchical power structure, for "Monogamy, as Engels argued, is only necessary for woman since there is no other way of ensuring that her progeny have a single father and hence no other way of preserving the values of property."[32] Similarly, in a recent essay, Jennifer Wicke argues that *Tess* is in many respects "a story of going to market": not only is Tess herself valued as a marketable sexual commodity, subject in turn to the sexual "standards" dictated by the marketplace, but so too is Hardy's novel a commodity, its form and content dictated by the demands of consumer culture.[33]

For the most part, Marxist analyses of *Tess* tend to fit into a long-established tradition of seeing Hardy: again, the author is said to be chronicling the decline of a world that was somehow better than the world at hand, or condemning the effects of mechanized society on the individual. However, the critics who are interested in how Tess's body becomes a commodity have, I believe, struck upon something truly original, and together with many feminist critics they have made a persuasive case that Hardy uses the female body as a kind of "text" that culture, men, or even Hardy himself can inscribe with meaning and/or use as a kind of trade good.[34] Unfortunately, several other critics—often in the names of feminism, Marxism, or cultural/materialist criticism—have focused on Hardy's apparent "interest" in Tess's body and have leveled charges against him that are every bit as pernicious as those that were made against him in the 1890s, and this has led to what I believe is a damaging if not absolutely harmful way of seeing Hardy. Hardy has long been open to charges that he was "in love" with Tess, or that Tess became for him the fulfillment of his feminine "ideal." Biographers have forwarded the candidacy of any of a number of women with whom Hardy was infatuated as the original model for Tess; and in the late 1970s John Bayley became one of the first modern critics to suggest Hardy's supposed infatuation with Tess actually becomes part of the mechanics of the novel.[35] Views of Hardy as a romantic dreamer who tries to create in Tess his "ideal" woman or recreate a lost love are fairly benign, but there is a growing trend in some criticism to cast aspersions upon Hardy's "interest" in Tess, if not to openly accuse the author of perversion. Janet Freeman, for instance, draws no distinction between Hardy the writer and his narrator, and she contends that his ability to see Tess correctly is crucial to Hardy's own identity:

> Hardy's own eye remains trained on "beautiful Tess," following her history with singleminded concentration. This occupation is at once his discipline and his virtue—the form his existence takes inside the novel. As it is Tess's destiny to be seen, so it is Hardy's destiny to see: he does so unwaveringly, better than anyone else, his presence as observer continually felt.[36]

In Freeman's reading, Hardy's personal role in the novel is to protect Tess from being perceived incorrectly by either the characters or the readers; and once she dies, Hardy's own dependence upon her—and what I can only label as his scoptophiliac nature—is made apparent:

> For without Tess to look at, Hardy's one skill [of seeing] is useless. All his purity and privilege evaporate. His presence in the novel, after all, his identity as the only perfectly attentive eye, depends on having Tess to observe: she is the instrument that calculates for him his own peculiar value. And to what greater, more significant, use could anyone be put? Losing Tess brings Hardy's need for her out in the open and makes plain the fact that his own way of looking—for all its close attention—is yet another form of possession.[37]

Judith Mitchell characterizes *Tess* as a novel in which "we are privileged to participate directly in the emotions and fantasy life of the doting, gloating narrator as he scrutinizes his nearly perfect heroine."[38] Part of Hardy's "fantasy life," presumably, is his interest in "cruelty and suffering of a particularly detailed kind,"[39] as Tess is put through all forms of hell and attains no sense of "self-knowledge." *Tess*, in Mitchell's opinion, "shares to an uncomfortable degree the pathological appeal of much male pornography."[40] One of the strongest charges against Hardy is made by James Kincaid, who says that Hardy, like his characters and like his readers—both

Victorian and modern—
takes erotic pleasure in the
spectacle of the manipulation, torture, and death of
Tess[41]; and that the novel is,
in fact, "a titillating snuff
movie we run in our own
minds. The novel offers us
the terrifying suggestion
and demonstration that our
own lives are nothing more
than this criminal movie in
the head, made over in the
flesh."[42]

Scoptophiliac—porno-
grapher—snuff movie director? If Hardy was really so
demoralized by the charges
made against him by the
early reviewers of *Tess* and
Jude that he gave up novel
writing, what would *these*
charges have done to him?
Criticisms such as these not
only do little to enhance our

Thomas Hardy: the controversial novelist in
1891.

understanding of *Tess* as a novel, they needlessly assassinate Hardy's character. It is hard to finish these assessments and not emerge with a picture
in mind of Hardy as a dirty old man lurking around school yards or duck-
ing into peep shows. Furthermore, charges against Hardy as either a
pornographer or a pervert sound suspiciously close to similar charges made
by reviewers in the 1890s who accused Hardy of corrupting the minds and
morals of polite society. So Hardy remains in the popular conscience a
social rebel and outcast; but these modern critics suggest society was perhaps right in condemning him.

Needless to say, I have offered only a small and select sampling of the
ways *Tess* and, by extension, Hardy have been interpreted; and there are
more examples I could cite, but that would belabor the point. The reviews
and analyses provided here should be enough to establish that *Tess* as a
novel generates numerous readings, but it seems the text almost stub-
bornly refuses to confirm any one particular way of reading. Both Morton and Ebbatson make sound cases for Hardy's affinities with Darwin,

but neither can agree on what *kind* of Darwinian statement Hardy was trying to make; therefore, they supplement the novel by looking *outside* the
text to what Hardy presumably read, and Hardy's background reading
becomes a kind of authority for interpreting *Tess.* Similarly, the novel's
alternately adoring and abusive depiction of Tess has had the result that,
in the early part of the twentieth century, critics focused on Hardy's "positive" feelings toward women and argued he was mourning the abuse good
women all too often suffer, while critics toward the end of the century
have dredged up "unsavory" aspects of Hardy's personality to suggest the
author abused his creation *because* he loved her. It could be said that these
differing interpretations are simply the result of changes in critical thought
and of diverse schools of theory, but *Tess* has always been a special case.
This novel is extremely hard to pin down, and it is hard to make most of
its concepts adhere to any particular critical philosophy. Hardy's language
in *Tess* is extremely multifaceted and ambiguous, and he deploys it in such
ways that the novel opens up numerous "blank spaces" where the reader
is lured into constructing the plot along certain generic lines, only to have
the plot all but disintegrate. Oddly, critics have never been blind to just
how problematic the language of *Tess* is. In the first book-length study of
Hardy's novels, Lionel Johnson demanded of *Tess,* "I want definitions of
nature, law, society, and *justice*: the want is coarse, doubtless, and unimag-
inative; but I cannot suppress it."[43] Since Johnson's time, many critics have
tried to precisely define Hardy's slippery terms, but more often than not,
what they have created in their definitions is a new "version" of the novel
that essentially ignores Hardy's ambiguities and counter-readings.

Interestingly, many mid-twentieth century critics who recognized
Tess's ambiguities sought to smooth over them by suggesting they are the
result of flaws in Hardy's own thinking or in his approach to art. Such critics have argued that the only way to get a coherent reading out of *Tess* is
to ignore the novel's "blemishes" and focus on its "true" strain of discourse. Dorothy Van Ghent advised readers to ignore Hardy's "philosophy" and focus on his imagery in order to discern a story of individual
consciousness pitted against cosmic indifference,[44] while Kettle suggests
ignoring the same things so that the reader can create a coherent story
about the destruction of the English peasantry.[45] The result of both views
is that "good little Thomas Hardy"—the talented but undisciplined artist—
is recreated: Hardy could create good art, Van Ghent and Kettle argue, but
his damned silly habit of injecting personal philosophy into the novel
spoils the show. Post-structuralist critics, however, have been more inclined
to look at *Tess* in its totality—"flaws and all"—and argue that Hardy knew
precisely what he was doing in creating such a problematic book. Both Ian

Gregor and Peter Casagrande have found a kind of unity in *Tess*'s many contrasts: in Gregor's terms, they present a kind of flux and reflux that is part of natural life, and thus confirms his view that Hardy's works constitute a "great web" of interconnected activity; Casagrande contends Hardy's entire aesthetic in *Tess* is one in which beauty may be found in ugliness, suffering, death, and incoherence—if only readers will open their minds to it.[46] In recent years, some critics have suggested that the meaning of the novel, or just of Tess herself, is "overdetermined" by Hardy; that the author has presented multiple causes for Tess's fate or multiple ways of reading her character in part to expose the inadequacy of the novel form as a device for containing or conveying human experience.[47] My own view, again, is that Hardy deployed multiple perspectives in the novel to create a multifaceted structure; but for now I need to return to my initial concerns of what kind of Hardy is created through the critical history of *Tess*, and what the implications of this history are to Polanski's film.

Two things should be evident from the criticism of the novel: first, very traditional, even stereotypical, images of Hardy are confirmed by many reviewers and critics. Second, there is a lack of agreement among the critics as to what "kind" of novel *Tess* is, but they do tend to agree that as a work it is important, powerful, flawed, often hard to grasp—and, above all, that it is a text to be argued over. It is in the very fact that *Tess* generates so much discussion and dissent, that almost every sentence and paragraph in the book has been analyzed and fought over, that a dominant image of Hardy has emerged: that of the artist as *provocateur*, the creator whose work is intended to shock, disturb, and create controversy, but which also leads to an understanding of his innermost self. Both the popularity of, and the critical response to, *Tess* have bestowed upon Hardy the image of a literary celebrity whose novel is as much about himself as it is about a fictional Wessex peasant girl.

Since *Tess* is so closely connected in the popular and critical imaginations with Hardy himself, it might seem that a film version of the novel would be impossible: how does one film *Tess* without "Hardy" being so intimately a part of it? To some extent, the 1979 motion picture of *Tess* solves this problem in the same way John Schlesinger solved it in *Far from the Madding Crowd*—by evoking familiar images and motifs associated with Hardy; but, in a strange way, the film succeeds best at evoking Hardy not by deliberately bringing him into the film, but by a kind of accidental consonance through the persona of the director, Roman Polanski, and through his deployment of themes that are common to his own works. Polanski is routinely labeled an *auteur,* a director whose personality is stamped on every aspect of the film; and the label is easy to apply, since on almost every one of Polanski's films he shares in the producing and screenwriting duties, and on occasion even acts. Moreover, Polanski is a true celebrity, and his films have regularly been analyzed in terms of what they have to say about his life. This is certainly true of Polanski's *Tess*—which is, after all, the story of a teenage girl who is either raped or seduced by a worldly man, directed and co-written by a worldly man who claims to have seduced a teenage girl but was charged with raping her.

Polanski's film puts several of the novel's cardinal plot functions and catalyzers into the background or even eliminates some, and in this respect cannot be considered entirely faithful to its source; but the fact Polanski's *Tess* is so commonly viewed as a conduit to the artist behind it generates a certain degree of confluence with Hardy's novel. But this is perhaps a surface phenomenon. It is in how Polanski adapts those same plot functions and catalyzers—which both provide the basic structure of the novel and create ambiguous or even blank spaces where the reader can both participate in the narrative and seemingly uncover the "true" Hardy—that actual convergence between the novel and the film takes place. The plot of Hardy's *Tess* is largely generated by the ways in which Tess and Hardy's own readers perceive the truth behind language—the same language Hardy's critics have found so problematic; while Polanski operates along similar lines as Hardy, only calling into question the truth behind the visual images that are used to structure the film. That Polanski could bring *Tess* to the screen and still convey some sense of the novel Hardy wrote is remarkable, for *Tess of the d'Urbervilles* constantly collapses on itself as Hardy questions both the authority of the words that his characters use to construct Tess, and which he and his readers use to construct the novel. In many respects, Hardy's *Tess* is a self-reflexive work in that it is most strongly concerned with the act by which the novel is always defined—reading; and it is with an act of reading that I will begin this discussion.

II

It is often argued that the person of Tess is largely constructed by how she is read and perceived by others, and that Tess's "fight" in the novel is partly against such constructions of herself. However, I am not sure that adequate attention has been given to how thoroughly and aggressively Hardy interrogates the *authority* that lies behind the words and the perceptions that are used to construct Tess; or to the issue of how Hardy uses questionable—if not corrupted—forms of official discourse to both generate the novel's plot and to establish false patterns of reading. *Tess of the d'Urbervilles* operates on two levels: it is, on the narrative level, an examination of the power of corrupted discourse to shape the lives of individuals; and it is, on the textual level, an exercise in its own power to *generate* discourse, which is always in danger of being corrupted by the reader. It is in this latter respect that *Tess* produces multiple interpretations, inspires critical debate about Hardy's "meaning" in the novel, and leads readers to construct their own "versions" of *Tess* and of Hardy himself.

One of the best instances of how the act of reading both generates plot functions and creates "risky" areas of interpretation occurs in the "sign painter" sequence from Chapter 12,[48] where an artisan asks Tess to stand by as he performs a task:

> He set down her basket and the tin pot, and, stirring the paint with the brush that was in it, began painting large square letters on the middle board of the three composing the stile; placing a comma after each word, as if to give pause while that word was driven well home to the reader's heart,

THY, DAMNATION, SLUMBERETH, NOT.
2 PET. ii. 3.

> Against the peaceful landscape, the pale decaying tints of the copses, the blue air of the horizon, and the lichened stile-boards, these staring vermillion words shone forth. They seemed to shout themselves out, and make the atmosphere ring. Some people might have cried "Alas, poor Theology!" at the hideous defacement—the last grotesque phase of a creed which had served mankind well in its time. But the words entered Tess with accusatory horror: it was as if this man had known her recent history; yet he was a total stranger [p. 62].

To Tess, the words seem to expose her relations with Alec to public view, and they cause her to question her own perceptions of God's law. She says of the words, "I think they are horrible! ... Crushing! Killing!" (p. 62); and after she leaves the sign painter she says to herself, "Pooh—I don't believe God said such things!" (p. 63). Tess rightly realizes it is only the *words* of the sign painter that condemn her, and that they are substituted for God's authority. However, even though God may be absent, the authority of those same words on Tess remains in effect. She later becomes aware of the glances and whispers of her fellow parishioners, and she reads into their looks and words a condemnation of herself: "She knew what their whispers were about, grew sick at heart, and felt that she could come to church no more" (p. 66). It is as if the "accusatory horror" of the painter's words have been made real. Tess tries to substitute for church a kind of communion with Nature; but by this time the authoritative words of others have so saturated her thinking that she uses them to define the way God-in-Nature judges her: "A wet day was the expression of irreme-diable grief at her weakness in the mind of some vague ethical being whom she could not class definitely as the God of her childhood, *and could not comprehend as any other*" (p. 67; my emphases). Hardy's narrator imme-diately assures the reader that Tess's impressions here are "based on shreds of convention, peopled by phantoms and voices antipathetic to her," and that these images form "a cloud of moral hobgoblins by which she was terrified without reason. It was they that were out of harmony with the actual world, not she" (p. 67); but Tess, of course, is incapable of hearing the narrator's words: she continues to perceive herself as "a figure of Guilt intruding into the haunts of Innocence" (p. 67). The twin powers of authoritative words from the Bible and the gazes of others in the church affect Tess's perceptions of herself and of the world around her, and put her on a course of action where she tries to escape both the words and glances of others.

Not only is the sign painter sequence important in that it demon-strates the power of authoritative words, it opens up a space for the reader to inject a crucial, and previously non-existent, element into the novel. The sign painter scene marks the first appearance in the novel of Christ-ian dogma as a genuine force. In the entire first phase of *Tess,* scarcely one word is uttered by either a character or by Hardy's narrator about God, the church, theology, moral behavior, or any of the Christian virtues. The first page of the novel, of course, introduces Parson Tringham; but he is seen only as antiquarian and amateur genealogist: the only hint of Tring-ham's spiritual office is his advice to Jack to "chasten yourself with the thought of 'how are the mighty fallen'" (p. 3). The Clare brothers are intro-duced as students of religion, but Hardy treats their beliefs only lightly. Between the passage with the Clares and the appearance of the sign painter, the only references to religious matters are Abraham's innocent questions as to whether God lives on the other side of the stars, and if the dead horse Prince has gone to heaven (pp. 21, 24); and—most famously—in the nar-rator's rhetorical stance in The Chase: "where was Tess's guardian angel? where was the Providence of her simple faith? Perhaps, like that other god of whom the ironical Tishbite spoke, he was talking, or he was pursuing, or he was in a journey, or he was sleeping and not to be awaked" (p. 57). It is only at the start of Phase the Second—when the sign painter inscribes his vermillion words on the stile—that Tess begins to perceive the stain of sin on her behavior, and the power of organized religion becomes an issue in the book and to Tess. The appearance of the sign painter and his words at this stage have the effect of making Tess read his accusatory words *back* into her own history; likewise, it is easy for the reader to assume that the painter represents society's accusatory voice and eyes, which *must* have been with Tess from the start of the novel—when in fact they had never been seen before.

If the painter sequence summons Christian dogma into *being* in the novel, it also serves to question both the source and the authority of that dogma. Hardy's cry of "Alas, poor Theology!" is perhaps meant to be taken both as a lamentation against what the painter does to theology, and as an indictment of this man's thinking: he is guilty of espousing literally *poor* theology, for what he inscribes on the stile is actually a misquotation from 2 Peter.[49] This fact—and the painter's divorcing the passage from its original context—render the words grotesque. 2 Peter is basically a defense of Pauline Christianity against the claims of rival Gnostic sects (giving weight, perhaps, to Hardy's charge that the passage represents "a creed which had served mankind well *in its time*"); and contained within the text is a warning to the faithful against heeding the words of these false prophets: "And through covetousness shall they with feigned words make merchandise of you: whose judgment now of a long time lingereth not, and *their damnation slumbereth not*" (2 Pet. 2:3; my emphases). Perhaps the painter—or Hardy himself—merely changed the pronoun from third-person plural to second-person singular (and accusatory) in order to present a sufficiently blood-curdling passage; but why misrepresent this *particular* passage, and why draw from a text like 2 Peter in the first place? Perhaps Hardy means for the biblical passage to be read as a metaphor for Tess's personal story: Alec does in fact make "merchandise" of Tess, and he will later appear in the novel as a preacher—in effect, as a false prophet who steers Tess from one course in life to another course that leads to her execution. Or perhaps Tess is meant to be a sort of "Gnostic"—which would fit the views of those who see her as an "ideal pagan" or as a priestess of Nature—but that raises the question of whom, exactly, Tess steers from orthodoxy; and if her damnation indeed "slumbereth not," what are we to make of Hardy's contentions that she is a "pure woman" and that at the end of the novel she reaches "fulfillment"? Despite the power of the words from 2 Peter to terrify Tess, in no sense do they apply to her or to her situation.[50] It is only in their status as official discourse—as words from the Bible—that they gain authority over her.

That the painter should utilize a passage from 2 Peter in the first place is also significant, for Hardy was far too astute a biblical scholar to be blind to the knowledge that this particular epistle has, from the early Christian era, frequently been viewed with suspicion or even outright skepticism;

and it has often been grouped in the New Testament Apocrypha.[51] However, John Calvin in the sixteenth century and Robert Jamieson in Hardy's own lifetime argued the text is genuine simply because it was included in the New Testament; in their reasoning, the compilers of the Testament would not have practiced fraud, and that they *must* have possessed some (now lost) knowledge of 2 Peter's authenticity.[52] In effect, during the historical process, the ultimate authority behind 2 Peter has been displaced: the canonicity of the text has become its true authority, while the truth behind the words is lost. Tess, then, receives a twice-corrupted message: its original source is questionable and its meaning is further garbled by the painter; yet this message has been imbued with Biblical and cultural authority, and therefore the message is capable of shaping Tess's self-perception.[53]

Finally, this sequence is important in that it suggests to the reader that there is an underlying structure that apparently neatly ties together the actions of some characters. The painter tells Tess that—although he is no longer of his "persuasion"—he was converted by Mr. Clare (p. 63). Later it will be revealed that Mr. Clare also inspired the religious work in Alec d'Urberville (pp. 241–2), and his creed will be identified as the force against which Angel tries to construct his own life and actions. Since Mr. Clare is so instrumental in "activating" these characters who all will harm Tess in some way, it is easy to assume Hardy means for him to stand for ineffective and even dangerous religious authority[54]—a view that simplifies both Mr. Clare and his role in the novel. Admittedly, Hardy's characterization of the parson is not free from satire; but the narrator also admits, "One thing [Mr. Clare] certainly was; sincere" (p. 124). It is this quality of sincerity that makes Mr. Clare admirable in Angel's eyes, and in the narrator's. Just as there is in Hardy's narration a strain of discourse that allows the reader to construct Mr. Clare in a mocking, satirical way, there is a counter strain that reveals the parson as admirable for his willingness to absorb pain for the sake of others. Mr. Clare tells Angel that he has at times been attacked by drunken men he had tried to convert, and he believes that, by being beaten, "I have saved them the guilt of murdering their own flesh and blood thereby. And they have lived to thank me, and praise God" (p. 131). There is neither satire nor scorn here: in fact, in his willingness to suffer for others, Angel's father is obliquely allied with Christ—and, to some extent, with Tess. That the sign painter and Alec become poor apostles for this ersatz Christ is not Mr. Clare's fault: by his own admission, the painter has moved away from Mr. Clare's "persuasion," and Alec's conversion comes fully two or three years after he hears Mr. Clare preach—without the parson taking an active part in the conversion process. Furthermore, it has often been argued that when Angel rejects Tess, he demonstrates that all along he has been in line with his father's narrow and dogmatic thinking. However, Hardy shows that Mr. Clare is narrow-minded in his blind love for the *word*, but in his *deeds* he is a figure that can be regarded as "heroic." When Angel rejects Tess, it is because he refuses to suffer a single blow to his pride; and so he causes Tess to suffer. Angel does not apply his father's rigid dogmatism to Tess: Angel *misreads* the magnanimous portion of his father's creed and uses that misreading to bring pain. It is in rebelling against the self-sacrificing deed that Angel shows himself to be an ally of the crushing, killing word.

What ties the actions of characters like Alec, Angel, and the painter together is their rejection of deeds and their acceptance of the authority that has been built up around words. Such dogmatism is exemplified by the Marlott vicar, who can admire Tess's self-administered baptism of the dying Sorrow, but who refuses the baby a Christian burial out of wounded personal pride and for fear of allowing anyone else to know he has approved of a non-clerical baptism (p. 76). To the vicar, the deed must give way to custom, technicality, and dogma, all of which are part and parcel of *received* Christianity, the authority of which lies in the Word. In her own analysis of the force of language in *Tess*, Charlotte Thompson locates the cultural authority for the Bible's words in the margin glosses, "so that to lose the margins is to be left with only the letter and not the spirit of the text"[55]; but to Hardy the page headings probably would be far more important than the glosses, for it is in the headings that translators and scholars imposed a particularly Christian meaning upon the original texts. It is only in the chapter headings that the Old Testament books of Isaiah, Ezekiel, and Zechariah predict the Kingdom of Christ; and only in the headings that the Song of Solomon ceases to be about physical love and becomes an analogy for Christ's love of the Church—a reading that Hardy will later have Sue Bridehead ridicule in *Jude the Obscure* (*Jude*, p. 206). Likewise, *Tess* deals with the issue of original words that have degraded in value and meaning, yet are held up as authoritative by the culture at large—even if that culture has to graft new meanings upon old words to prop up the authority. In the case of Mr. Clare's words, we can see that between the transmission of his messages, their reception by Alec, Angel, and the sign painter, and the way these characters apply those messages to Tess, a good deal of degradation and slippage has occurred. The words received by Tess are garbled and their sources of origin are out of her reach, but because the messages are delivered to her by authority figures, they hold enormous sway over her.

Appropriately, the first action of the novel is largely brought into being by the process of a message being transmitted, degraded, and then

acted upon. Tringham's history of the d'Urbervilles is rich with information about Sir Pagan d'Urberville, the Knights Hospitallers, Oliver
Cromwell, and Charles II (pp. 1–2). However, by the time Tess learns of
her genealogy, the information has been filtered through two intermedi-
ary sources—first through Jack, who is at least tipsy when he hears it, and
then through Joan—and Joan's version is certainly different from Tringham's:

> "...We've been found to be the greatest gentlefolk in the whole county—
> reaching all back long before Oliver Grumble's time—to the days of the
> Pagan Turks—with monuments and vaults and crests and 'scutcheons,
> and the Lord knows what-all. In Saint Charles's days we was made Knights
> o' the Royal Oak, our real name being d'Urberville" [p. 13].

Joan's words have the effect of parodying Tringham's, rendering his
elevated discourse into gobbledegook, and they also highlight the foolishness of Joan's scheme to send Tess to Trantridge to "claim kin" with the
rich d'Urbervilles; but more than being a parody, these words are corrupted discourse. The sequence of events that move the message from
Tringham's lips to Tess's ears resembles the old party game of "Pass It On":
the first person whispers a message to the second person, who then tries
to repeat that same exact message to a third, and so on, the fun of the game
being to see how radically the message has changed by the time the last
person receives it. Tess actually treats Joan's information as if it were part
of a game, a fact she signals by her terse question, "Will [the knowledge]
do us any good, mother?" (p. 13). However, what befalls Tess is far from a
game. The causes that bring her to Trantridge—and to the attention of
Alec d'Urberville—can be characterized as misunderstood genealogical
information mixed with Joan's half-understood mystical/mythical lore
from *The Compleat Fortune-Teller*, all given authority by Tess's sense of
responsibility for getting the horse killed. It is perhaps incorrect to say that
Tringham's revelation of the family's history puts Tess on the course she
will follow: by the time Tess acts, Tringham's message has been degraded
almost beyond recognition. Tess is acting on an authority she neither
knows nor understands.

Between the two cardinal plot functions of Tess's meeting Alec and
her seduction or rape by him in The Chase, the novel can be seen as undermining the authority of the Word. Tess learns to distrust what has been
told to her or what she has read, while, simultaneously and paradoxically,
Hardy exposes the reader's need to trust in the authority of the narrator's
words. Essentially, Tess learns by experience to be a skeptical reader, which
will inform much of her behavior starting in Phase Two; however, Hardy

shows that, in a teleological sense, the word can never be completely undermined, for readers must continually invest the word *with* authority. This
is Tess's essential dilemma: try as she might to avoid being read, seen, and
interpreted by others, she always will be—even if it is only by the reader
of Hardy's novel.

Upon Tess's arrival in Trantridge, Hardy allows both Tess and the
reader to immediately understand the falsity of the words upon which
Tess's mission has been built. Based on what she has heard of the
d'Urbervilles, Tess expects to find an old family living in an ancient house;
but her first sight of The Slopes and the surrounding property is one in
which everything "looked like money—like the last coin issued from the
Mint" (p. 27). The newness of everything fills Tess with doubt as to the
legitimacy of her kin; and Hardy's narrator confirms her suspicions to the
reader by informing us that Alec's father, after "[c]onning for an hour in
the British Museum the pages of works devoted to extinct, half-extinct,
obscured, and ruined families appertaining to the quarter of England in
which he proposed to settle," purchased the old name and added it to his
own (p. 27). The original referents of the title—the true d'Urbervilles—
have become obscured; in effect, they have degraded in value, but the title
itself retains its original power and prestige. In this way, Hardy shows that
names, like words, can retain their surface power even after their original
referents have become displaced. Tess initially ascribed to the name
d'Urberville one set of meanings, but upon meeting Alec she realizes her
previous methods of reading and apprehending the name are false, and
she must negotiate new ways of perceiving both the name and, eventually, her role as Tess *of* the d'Urbervilles.

After allowing this degree of convergence between Tess's perspective
and the reader's, Hardy then challenges the reader to construct the plot
along lines that are predetermined not so much by Hardy, but by the
reader's own expectations for how this novel *should* develop. The character of Alec seems to be designed to spark a specific reaction that will largely
shape how his role is to be perceived. The most common complaint about
Alec is that he is a figure straight out of Victorian melodrama. His curl-
ing black mustache and his "Well, my beauty" dialogue are typically cited
as evidence of Alec's stage origins; and his visible attempts at seducing Tess
have all the earmarks of the stock cad: snatching kisses, voicing empty
flattery, and snooping at her from behind the drapes. His behavior is so
blatant and obvious, and Tess's reactions to it are so unyieldingly negative, that one can easily conclude that the only way this broadly drawn
bounder could have Tess *is* by raping her; yet there seems to be a possible
counter-reading of his behavior that Hardy relegates to the margins of the

text. After we have witnessed the most theatrical of Alec's antics, the narrator informs us that

> A familiarity with Alec d'Urberville's presence—which that young man carefully cultivated in her by playful dialogue, and by jestingly calling her his cousin when they were alone—removed much of her original shyness of him, without, however, implanting any feeling which could engender shyness of a new and tenderer kind [p. 46].

What this "playful dialogue" is we never learn, but certainly it is persuasive enough that Tess ceases to view Alec with disgust, even if she does not entirely warm to him. Hardy allows for the possibility that there is a human and appealing Alec lurking beneath the Lothario figure, but his humanity has been so marginalized in the text that a reader has little choice but to construct Alec according to the stronger narrative clues Hardy has provided—those that cast him as a stereotypical seducer. Basically, Hardy is trading upon the readers' familiarity with the figure of the stock cad; however, he refuses to confirm that this particular reading of Alec is correct, and it is largely because of this that the character—and Hardy's motives behind his creation—have become controversial. Rather than state point-blank what happens to Tess in The Chase, Hardy displaces the incident in favor of a series of apostrophes that throw the entire incident into doubt. After questioning the whereabouts of Tess's "guardian angel" and of "Providence," the narrator mourns:

> Why it was that upon this beautiful feminine tissue, sensitive as gossamer, and practically blank as snow as yet, there should have been traced such a coarse pattern as it was doomed to receive; why so often the coarse appropriates the finer thus, the wrong man the woman, the wrong woman the man, many thousand years of analytical philosophy have failed to explain to our sense of order. One may, indeed, admit the possibility of a retribution lurking in the present catastrophe. Doubtless some of Tess d'Urberville's mailed ancestors rollicking home from a fray had dealt the same measure even more ruthlessly towards peasant girls of their time. But though to visit the sins of the fathers upon the children may be a morality good enough for divinities, it is scorned by average human nature; and it therefore does not mend the matter.
>
> As Tess's own people down in those retreats are never tired of saying among each other in their fatalistic way: "It was to be." There lay the pity of it. An immeasurable social chasm was to divide our heroine's personality thereafter from that previous self of hers who stepped from her mother's door to try her fortune at Trantridge poultry-farm [pp. 57–8].

Wading through Hardy's explanations for what happens to Tess is like asking who killed Cock Robin. God is to blame. Or fate. Or heredity.

Or a tragic mindset. Or Tess's culture. If truth be told, the incident "was to be" for no other reason than in a story of a pure young girl who meets a young rake, the result will be either the violation of the woman or the preservation of her purity—and this particular story concerns violation. The reader has been invited to see the interaction between Alec and Tess in strictly conventional terms, but in throwing the nature of the violation into doubt and assigning its cause to several potential forces, Hardy undermines our own stereotypes of both his characters *and* of this type of novel.[56] Critics and readers to this day are troubled by the implications of Alec's character and of what happens in The Chase, precisely because Hardy tears us away from secure zones of interpretation, a fact Hardy exposes when Tess demands of Joan, "Why didn't you tell me there was danger in men-folk? Why didn't you warn me? Ladies know what to fend hands against, *because they read novels that tell them of these tricks;* but I never had the chance o' learning in that way, and you did not help me" (p. 64; my emphases). Honestly, Tess doesn't need to have read a novel to know to wipe off Alec's kiss or to jump out of his rig—but the novel-reading public *does* know of the dangers in such men-folk as Alec, and they have known of those dangers since Richardson published *Clarissa* in 1748.[57] That Hardy establishes Alec as the heir to Lovelace and then dismantles this comfortable way of reading him has the effect of undermining the authority of an established novelistic convention. We see the familiar figure, but his understood meaning has been displaced.[58] After the incident in The Chase, Tess learns to question received information; the reader, however, will still be called upon to trust Hardy's words.

Phases Three and Four—the Talbothays Dairy sequences—are reckoned by most readers to be their favorite portions of the novel, and this is, I believe, because Hardy creates a sense that these sequences *belong* to the reader. The narrator is not as intrusive in these phases as he was in the first two, and much of Hardy's writing is given over to passages of lyrical beauty and exacting if not romanticized details of life on a dairy farm. Moreover, the plot functions are relatively few (in a nutshell, they are Tess's arrival at the dairy; Angel's first notice of her; Angel's offers of marriage; Tess's inadvertently slipping her confession letter under Angel's rug; and Tess's wedding night confession); so there is little sense of the story being artificially manipulated by Hardy. In these phases, the narrative informants are usually more important than the mechanics of the plot, but these informants are also highly instrumental in allowing the reader to construct a kind of false—or merely personal—narrative for the novel. If one were to forget Tess's past with Alec and focus only on the plot functions I outlined above, *Tess* would appear to be built on the lines of a standard romantic comedy, with lovers being brought together, separated by an obstacle (in this case, a secret), and then marrying. Moreover, Angel and Tess are constantly implicated with the setting, so that their developing love appears to be pastoral in nature.[59] Such moments demand that the story of Angel and Tess be read as the stuff of pastoral romance, and as 110 years' worth of criticism attests, many readers have done just that. However, in constructing this portion of the novel as a pastoral, the reader inadvertently falls into the same trap as does Angel Clare—that of relying on the authority of the *Word* to bring coherence to what really cannot be defined.

When Angel first notices Tess, he himself defines her in pastoral terms, as "a fresh and virginal daughter of Nature" (p. 95), and he later thinks of her as a being from "unconstrained Nature, and not from the abodes of Art" (p. 136). However, Angel's conception of Nature *is* an entirely artistic and literary one.[60] When Angel calls Tess a Rachel in comparison to the other dairymaids' Leahs (p. 113), he assigns her a pastoral role straight out of Bible literature—as the shepherd-girl from Genesis. In a particularly famous passage, Angel transforms Tess into a variety of characters out of pastoral myth:

> She was no longer the milkmaid, but a visionary essence of woman—a whole sex condensed into one typical form. He called her Artemis, Demeter, and other fanciful names, half-teasingly—which she did not like because she did not understand them.
> "Call me Tess," she would say askance; and he did [p. 103].

Angel's reading of Tess as if she were a character out of an old tale leads him to believe he knows and understands her as a generic "type."[61] Though he specifically alludes to Greek goddesses, it is plain that Angel really sees Tess as a kind of Miranda or Perdita, a noblewoman cast into the wild who needs a man to educate her and reawaken her dormant nobility. Moreover, Angel's belief that he already knows Tess's story turns him both deaf and blind to the actual story she tries to narrate. Tess is anxious to tell Angel her "history," but he responds to her as if she is about to recap the plot of a novel: "Tell it if you wish to, dearest. This precious history then. Yes: I was born at so and so, Anno Domini—" (p. 147). Tess gets no farther than relating her father's idleness and drunkenness before Angel grows dismissive: "Yes—yes. Poor child! Nothing new" (p. 147). Small wonder Tess doesn't get much further in telling him of her past: since Angel sees her as a generic type whose story reveals "nothing new," there is little sense in going on with it.

The most interesting thing about Angel's desire to read Tess's life as a well-known story is how closely it parallels the desire that is likely to be evoked in the reader. Just as Angel constructs Tess's life as a pastoral romance, so too do the handful of plot functions and rich narrative informants create the illusion that Phases Three and Four make up the pastoral romance of *Tess*. Hardy even creates the illusion that the landscape is transformed by Tess's presence, as when she first enters the Valley of Great Dairies: "Her hopes mingled with the sunshine in an ideal photosphere which surrounded her as she bounded along against the soft south wind. She heard a pleasant voice in every breeze, and in every bird's note seemed to lurk a joy" (p. 81). All the expected fictional devices of a pastoral romance are in place, and this raises a question: why are Angel's attempts to impose a literary reading of Nature onto Tess wrong, while the narrator's attempts to connect her to Nature are somehow right? Earlier I considered just how problematic is the concept of "Nature" in this novel, and how critics have tried to grapple with Hardy's meaning. A simple way of eliding this problem is to admit that the only thing Hardy's Nature truly *is* is an elaborate series of tropes. We never see Nature as it is, but as Hardy *designates* it to be at any given point in the novel. That Hardy constantly changes the meaning of Nature should serve to emphasize that Nature in this novel is *always* a fictional construct; as such, the words used to build it simply stand in place of reality, and risk being misconstrued *as* reality. Angel's use of classical allusions have the effect of displacing the reality of both the natural world and of Tess; likewise, when a reader imposes a pastoral or even Darwinian interpretation on the whole of Hardy's "Nature" and on to Tess's role in the natural order of things, the complicated and multifaceted story Hardy is presenting becomes displaced and a new, readily understood story grows up in its stead. In this respect, every reader is a potential Angel, acting upon the narrative clues Hardy provides and then drawing upon a storehouse of knowledge to make Tess—and *Tess*—coherent.[62]

The extent to which Hardy plays upon the reader's desire to create a pastoral love story can be demonstrated by the simple fact that so many people find it easy to ignore that the love story is undercut even before it is allowed to develop. Hardy never shields the reader from the fact Angel has feet of clay: he is characterized by "something nebulous, preoccupied, vague, in his bearing and regard" (p. 89); and both his desire to take up farming because it will leave him at "intellectual liberty" (p. 92) and his plan to educate Tess to become a suitable wife mark Angel as a dilettante. What is remarkable is that despite these warning signs, readers are still often shocked and disappointed when Angel rejects Tess. The reason the reader is lured into thinking Angel is the perfect match for Tess is both because a pastoral romance demands a pastoral hero, and Angel is as close as this novel gets to one, and because Hardy so clearly builds Angel to stand in opposition to Alec. Alec's seductive *actions* are made plain on paper and his most seductive *words* are hidden away, while Angel's "seduction" of Tess is conveyed almost entirely through his words, and his actions toward Tess are relatively sedate. What is more, if Alec's designations of Tess as a "crumby" cottage girl (pp. 31, 41) and as an "artful hussy" (p. 41), as well as his mocking use of "cousin" when he addresses her, are meant to turn the reader's sympathies away from Alec, Angel's more poetic designations for Tess tend to win the reader to Angel's side. We *want* Tess to be Artemis and Demeter, just as we want her past to melt away and for her romance with Angel to develop. That Hardy seems to pull the rug out from under Tess's feet is one of the factors that has left him open to charges of cruelty; but, frankly, Hardy does more to dash the *reader*'s hopes for how the story will turn out: Tess herself has always been searching for an alternative reading to the situation she's in.

As is evidenced by Tess's silencing of Angel's allusions to her with the simple "Call me Tess," she is constantly resisting Angel's attempts to turn her into a story—both because she recognizes that her actual story does not fit his conception, and because she knows stories are often the end result of corrupted discourse. Dairyman Crick's tale about Jack Dollop— the country rake who becomes trapped in a churn by the mother of a girl he's seduced—is funny to everyone who hears it (or who reads the incident in Hardy's novel), but Tess recognizes that an important element of the story—the seduced girl—has been displaced: "She was wretched—O so wretched—at the perception that to her companions the dairyman's story had been rather a humorous narration than otherwise; none of them but herself seemed to see the sorrow of it; to a certainty, not one knew how cruelly it touched the tender place in her experience" (p. 106). Of course, Tess reads a great deal of personal significance into this story; but that "tender place in her experience" allows her to understand that the true subject of the story is the seduced woman, and that this figure has been worn away, leaving only the farce of Dollop in the churn. Likewise, Tess's attempts to retain her essential "self" in the face of Angel's desire to "read" her shows her own fear of being displaced or revalued, and of a new story growing up in her place. Tess's alertness here to ever-devolving language is something to which Hardy's own readers should be alert: for just as it is easy for Crick's listeners to forget that the comedy of Jack Dollop has displaced the tragedy of the girl, it is easy for Hardy's readers to displace Tess's actual history with the pastoral romance that is suggested in the Talbothays section. To read *Tess* is to be aware that words can always transform and degrade, that every text can displace a previous text; and to use words to create a sense of reality is to risk misreading and even destroying that reality. These are facts Tess learns in the final phases of the novel, when she herself moves from reader to writer, and finds herself grappling with the authority of words.

Just as the plot of *Tess of the d'Urbervilles* is set in motion by Tess's reception of corrupted words, the novel is hurtled to its conclusion by the absolute *failure* of words. *Tess* turns on two related events: Tess's misplacing the confession letter, and her maintaining silence after she discovers the mistake. As H. M. Daleski observes, it is Tess's silence alone that really affects the story—for it is her keeping quiet that causes Angel to feel she has deceived him, and which results in his leaving and in everything else that follows.[63] So a question is automatically raised: why even include the incident of the misplaced letter at all? Tess could have simply maintained her silence without ever trying to write and still made her wedding night confession, and the story wouldn't be changed at all. It is also strange that Tess, who has been presented primarily as a reader, should shift gears and become a *writer*—for as a writer she is put in a position to wield the same words she does not entirely trust. It seems that Hardy has tried to put some of the narrative burden on to Tess's shoulders: in places she attempts to narrate her own story, and, as a result, she is in a complex position of knowing the story she tries to tell could be misread, and of trying to circumvent those possible misreadings.

Tess's ability to effectively narrate is hampered by her realization that any attempt by a woman to narrate is liable to be corrupted by the (usually male) receiver: "This question of a woman telling her story—the heaviest of crosses to herself—seemed but amusement to others. It was as if people should laugh at martyrdom" (p. 141). The degree to which she can narrate her own story is further complicated by the fact it isn't clear if Tess can ever narrate *as herself*. Despite her open resistance to Angel's attempts to educate her, Tess's "natural quickness, and her admiration for [Angel] ... led her to pick up his vocabulary, his accent, and fragments of his knowledge, to a surprising extent" (pp. 137–8). Angel's success at transforming Tess—even if that transformation is mostly in terms of her language and surface behaviors—is confirmed later, when Alec asks Tess, "How is it that you speak so fluently now; who has taught you such good English?" (p. 244). What Tess has most picked up from Angel is his language and a good deal of his perspectives, which is appropriate since, as we have already seen, Angel is a character who is strongly tied to language and literary constructs. It is natural to assume that as Tess adopts Angel's perspectives and behaviors, she will also pick up his habit of deferring experience to the Word: it is as if Tess determines the only way she can get

Angel's attention is by giving him what he's always wanted—a literal *story* about herself.[64] That Tess's efforts end up under the rug literalizes the theme that when words are placed on top of experience, the word can hide or displace what has happened.

That Tess keeps her silence after her attempt to communicate through the word has failed is indicative of her problematic status in relation to words. Tess attempts to write to Angel after she learns that he asked Izz to accompany him to Brazil; but she cannot finish the letter, reasoning to herself that since Angel had offered to share his life with another woman "so soon after he had left her ... how could she write entreaties to him, or show that she cared for him any more?" (p. 231). Later, Tess thinks of writing to Angel's parents for help; but "that sense of her having morally no claim upon him had always led Tess to suspend her impulse to send these notes" (p. 231). What prevents Tess from writing in both cases is her feeling that she lacks authority: Angel has not only rejected Tess, he nearly put another woman in her place; therefore, Tess believes she has no claim either upon Angel or on his family, and no right to articulate her grievances or appeal to their good will. Any words Tess would attempt to utilize to narrate her story would be unauthoritative: first, because hers is a woman's story; and, second, because she has lost whatever authority Angel gave her.

At the start of this chapter I stated that Hardy gives the impression he has locked Tess away in a private recess, which might lead a reader to conclude there is an essential "Tess" to be found by searching for her in either the text or in Hardy's biography. Certainly, Hardy seems most invested in hiding Tess away during The Chase sequence, and in that we never get to read Tess's confession letter or hear her verbal confession to Angel. Hardy has been severely criticized for these narrative ellipses, but they are in keeping with his seeming desire to preserve Tess's essentiality. To put what has happened to her into words would be to risk exposing the truth to degradation, misreading, or misapprehension. The only thing we know for certain about Tess's experience is that it results in her pregnancy; otherwise, Hardy seems to want to *negate* our expectations of Tess's experience. Likewise, most of Tess's personal actions following The Chase sequence are directed toward negating others' readings of her; so the result of these twin negations is that Tess is transformed into a narrative blank space. Peter Widdowson charges with a great deal of justification that "Tess *has no character at all*: she is only what others (most especially the author) construct her as; and so she is herself merely a 'series of seemings' or 'impressions.'"[65] This is perhaps an extreme position, considering Tess if anything *is* characterized by her reactions to people and to events, and even her desire to not be read gives her some character; but Widdowson's interpretation shows just how thoroughly Tess becomes displaced in her own novel. It is possible that, in preserving Tess's essentiality, Hardy has his cake and chokes in trying to eat it; for while Tess's hidden self may keep others from correctly reading her, it is so completely hidden that apparently even Tess cannot locate it.

Tess's attempt to locate her own authority is complicated even more by the fact that, as the novel moves from the fifth to the final phase, the narrator becomes determined to plot Tess's story on a downward trajectory. The narrator all but absented himself from the previous two phases, giving the reader the illusion of contributing to the narrative process; but in Phase the Fifth the narrator returns in full force, shaping the plot along mechanistic and deterministic lines. Flintcomb-Ash becomes the site where the novel comes full circle: familiar faces reappear, and events are replayed in a sinister fashion, creating a Sophoclean sense that the past is rising up against Tess. However, even though Hardy deliberately turns the tables on Tess, she is for the first time shown to be consciously in control of creating and deploying her own image—of writing her own text. To ensure against "aggressive admiration" she makes herself dowdy (p. 219); she dresses herself "very charmingly as a simple country girl with no pretension to recent fashion" before her attempted visit to Angel's parents (p. 232); and, most importantly, she writes letters to Angel—and for the first time, *we* are allowed to read what she writes. Tess emerges a full—or, at least more full—character in these sequences ... but to what end? When Marian sees Tess's altered face she assumes that Angel has been beating her (p. 221); and the authority Tess takes upon herself by dressing in a way that will appeal to the Clares evaporates once she overhears Mercy Chant and Angel's brothers discussing his "ill-conceived" marriage (pp. 235–6). And Tess's letters, until the very last one, are filled with self-recriminations and go unanswered by Angel. There is a sense of pointlessness to Tess's attempts to gain authority over her own story and image: it is as if, in spite of how she presents herself, she is destined to be read as a victim (by Marian), as a simple peasant (by the Clare brothers), and as a fallen woman—a view reinforced by Angel's silence. Finally, despite the changes that have presumably taken place over the years since Alec last saw her, he still interprets her as a seductive—and highly seducible—woman. It is as if, by the final phase of the novel, all the ways of reading Tess—including the narrator's—come together and effectively squash Tess's own attempts to narrate herself. When Angel finds Tess in Sandbourne, he realizes that "his original Tess had spiritually ceased to recognize the body before him as hers—allowing it to drift, like a corpse upon the current, in a direction dissociated from its living will" (p. 299). Tess has become the blank space she has effectively been throughout the novel—an empty vessel that is open to being read and interpreted. And, ultimately, the reading of herself that Tess ratifies is the one that the reader is likely to have imposed on her from the end of the first Phase—that of the wronged woman who is now entitled to take her revenge.

Tess of the d'Urbervilles—in my interpretation, at least—has been such a difficult book to categorize precisely because it simultaneously embraces and rejects means of *being* categorized. *Tess* constantly implicates the authority of words in generating classifications, genres, interpretations, belief systems, and ways of apprehending who people—or perhaps just fictional characters—are. However, Hardy does not argue with the power of words to create a sense of reality. In fact, critics have long used their own words to create a text of *Tess* that is every bit as real as the text Hardy created: the various Darwinist *Tesses*, feminist *Tesses*, and Marxist *Tesses* are perhaps just "coherent" versions of *Tess* that displace the original. Likewise, the "Hardy" who has emerged through the criticism of *Tess*—the elusive public artist who reveals everything and nothing about himself through his great work, and who challenges all who come to the work to find him lurking within—has a fixed place in the public consciousness. Of course, this public artist is not who Hardy actually was. In 1979 another public artist made a film of *Tess*, and critics have often combed through this film in an effort to find traces of the man who made *it*. Since both Hardy's *Tess of the d'Urbervilles* and Roman Polanski's *Tess* have this "accidental" consonance, this phenomenon demands immediate treatment in the next section. Otherwise, Polanski's adaptation of *Tess* manages to converge with Hardy's novel in more complex and interesting ways; and what emerges is perhaps not so much a means of seeing Hardy *himself*, but of seeing the ideological goals of the novel accurately presented, and perhaps even fulfilled.

III

Just as the critical readings and interpretations of *Tess of the d'Urbervilles* have created images of Thomas Hardy that are read back into the novel, so too have the early films of Roman Polanski—as well as his scandalous and even tragic private life—solidified an image of this filmmaker that many critics have seen present in his own version of *Tess* (1979).[66] Polanski's *Tess* has been analyzed as a film that deploys themes and motifs that are familiar throughout his work, and, more often than not, as a commentary on the charge of statutory rape that led to his flight from America. The fact Polanski was sexually involved with Nastassia

Kinski—herself a minor at the time of their relationship—before he cast her as Tess has also worked its way into some commentaries on the film. Certainly, it is nearly impossible to divorce Polanski's personal circumstances from *Tess* because they directly affected its look: *Tess* had to be shot in Normandy instead of in England, from which Polanski could have been extradited; and Polanski himself pushes a personal identification with the material by beginning with the on-screen dedication, "To Sharon." This is, of course, Polanski's wife, Sharon Tate, who apparently brought Hardy's novel to his attention, and who was murdered along with her unborn baby and several friends on the order of Charles Manson in 1969. This crime continues to titillate and to generate interest, and Polanski's name continues to be associated with it. The film of *Tess* openly invites itself to be read in three ways: as an apology (in both senses of the word) for Polanski's life and previous films, as a valediction for Sharon Tate, and as a reminder that Polanski himself is a victim both of the Manson family and of the fallout from his sexual behavior. These personal identifications are so strong that it is fairly easy to take Hardy altogether out of the picture (so to speak) and consider the film entirely to be "Polanski's *Tess*."

Even so, few critics have been able to analyze *Tess* without considering how much it owes to Hardy. Prior to the film's release, many critics were convinced that he was simply not the right person to adapt a Hardy novel, or that Polanski would dwell on the literary *Tess*'s blood and violence to such an extent that the film would be less a literary adaptation than a horror movie.[67] David Ansen was one of the few critics who went into *Tess* convinced of a certain "affinity" between Hardy's *Tess* and the kinds of films Polanski makes; and he emerged convinced not only that *Tess* affirms the director's connection to Hardean themes, but that a new dimension in Polanski's filmmaking had been brought out by Hardy:

> It's not surprising that Roman Polanski should be drawn to the dark, raging injustices of Thomas Hardy's *Tess of the d'Urbervilles*. Exiles and outcasts have been central to Polanski's films, and Hardy's tragic Victorian heroine is no exception: victimized by men, shunned by the church, used by her impoverished family to cash in on their claims to aristocracy, caught in the jarring dislocations of the Industrial Revolution, this beautiful, innately noble farm girl is eventually driven to murder. One could imagine Polanski, the savage absurdist, spinning Hardy's tale into a black existential void. But *Tess* turns out to be a new departure from him. Stately, solemnly beautiful, it is a rigorously classical film—faithful to the novel's reticence, outrage and deep compassion. Indeed, in its grave lyricism and impeccable craftsmanship, *Tess* may put the viewer more in mind of David Lean ... than the man who made *Repulsion* and *Chinatown*.[68]

Ansen's review supports Polanski's own assertion that he chose *Tess* as a film subject in order to break away from the kinds of films he had previously made. "When I made my first films I had the tremendous desire of imposing myself," Polanski said in 1980. "I don't need that anymore. I don't need to prove myself. ...A decade ago, I was promoting realism. I did scenes of violence and sex because the general hypocrisy didn't allow that. Now violence has been exploited to such an extent that I am tired of it and nostalgic for romance."[69] Despite Polanski's stated attempt to not "impose" himself in *Tess*, many reviewers felt the presence of Polanski— both as maker of scandalous films and as subject for scandalous headlines—was all too visible in his adaptation of Hardy, and a good deal of personal repugnance toward Polanski appears in their reviews. Perhaps the strongest example of this type of reaction is in Jane Marcus's tellingly named "A Tess for Child Molestors," which constantly links Polanski with the "villain" of Hardy's novel. Marcus charges in her opening paragraph that the director "takes liberties with Hardy's book the way Alec d'Urberville takes liberties with Tess," and then goes on to make her comparison even more explicit:

> Polanski's film is a long, slow rape by the scriptwriter [*sic*] of Thomas Hardy's text, a long, slow rape by the camera of Nastassia Kinski's lovely face, and a long, slow rationalisation by the rapist imagination that that's how it is with helpless, hopeless victims. They never fight back.

In Marcus's assessment, Hardy's Tess is a strong figure who, by killing Alec, "revenges all the women wronged by men," while Polanski's Tess is weak and passive, a "cherubic eleven-year-old stilted figure" whose "pretty mouth" inspires the director's many "obscene" close-ups. Moreover, Marcus charges that Polanski entirely disempowers Tess by not showing the scenes where she assumes "male" authority by baptising her baby, and especially where she "justifiably" kills Alec. Marcus's condemnation of Polanski is made complete by associating him not just with Alec, but with those powers of "Fate" that Marcus believes Hardy most hated:

> [Hardy] subtitles his novel "A Pure Woman," taking the part of a male sympathiser of heroic womanhood. Polanski is a voyeur of victimisation who infantilises our Tess. Hardy makes it clear that the 'President of the Immortals' who has his sport with Tess is the author's enemy. Polanski is angling for a seat as Vice-President of the Immortals. His demand for sympathy for the victimised Tess turns tragedy into melodrama for voyeurs.[70]

Marcus, of course, was responding to the most recent and most notorious event in Polanski's life; but from almost the very beginning of his career critics have sought to read Polanski's biography into his films. Why they should do so is easy to understand: Polanski's life has generally been exciting and interesting, and, at least until he fled the United States, much of it was lived in a highly public fashion. A Jew raised in Poland in the 1930s, Polanski survived both the Holocaust (though his mother did not) and Soviet-style Communism; came first to Europe and then to America to make highly acclaimed and profitable films; dated beautiful women; and lived a life of freewheeling excess.[71] Polanski's life has the rags-to-riches quality of a Horatio Alger story; and his well-known distaste for Communism and his embrace of Western culture—including its decadent side—tap into Americans' deep-seated sense of political and social superiority, as well as our fascination with—and repugnance for—hedonism. Beyond this, though, is the fact that Polanski occasionally does invite the viewer to see a particular image of himself in his films. Probably the first of Polanski's pictures to be seen as offering access into his own life was *The Fearless Vampire Killers* (1967),[72] a horror spoof in which Polanski himself appears in the role of the vampire killer's assistant. Oddly, Polanski's character, Alfred, is essentially the romantic lead; but he is made into the target of an outrageously homosexual vampire and is also a Peeping Tom who frequently spies on the heroine (Sharon Tate). It has not been lost on critics that Alfred is basically Polanski's version of himself as director and celebrity. He is coveted by fans, critics, and admirers and made vulnerable to their gazes and desires, while as a director he captures intimate images of people, much as do Peeping Toms. The fact Polanski himself photographed Tate in the nude for *Playboy* to promote *Vampire Killers* has furthered the image of Polanski as a man who uses the power of the intrusive camera both to express his own interest in voyeurism and to explore—if not exploit—our own.

After the Manson killings, many news commentators suggested that they were either the result of the fast company Tate and Polanski kept, or the actions of a person who'd been inspired by the gore and violence that had supposedly been a part of Polanski's films—especially *Vampire Killers* and *Rosemary's Baby* (1968). Of course, Polanski had nothing to do with the killings—the victims were selected almost at random—but they have given rise to one of the most persistent assumptions about the content of his films. It was not uncommon in 1969 for the crime scene to be described as resembling "something out of a Polanski movie," and such simple-minded assessments have had the long-term effect of tainting Polanski's films as bloody, violent, and cruel—when in fact his use of violence is fairly restrained (especially by the standards of today), and his horror films usually emphasize tension over mayhem. Polanski's 1971 film of *Macbeth*—

the first picture he made after the Manson killings—was widely criticized for its violence, and the violence in turn was often interpreted as Polanski's response to the killing of his wife. What's more, the fact that the film was produced by Hugh Hefner's Playboy Enterprises and that Lady Macbeth performs her sleepwalking scene in the nude were seen by some as evidence that Polanski the hedonist and voyeur was still at work. Polanski's personal life had become such an issue that *Macbeth* itself seemed to be of secondary interest. By the time *Tess* appeared, critics were well accustomed to viewing Polanski's films as devices that put the life of the director on display.

But what *is* a "typical" Polanski film, once the persona of the director is taken out of the equation? This is a question that Polanski himself refuses to answer; and he has even dismissed the notion that he consciously dramatizes unified themes and ideas.[73] This is a common position taken by many artists—even Hardy frequently said that he was trying to create "impressions" of things in general, and that he wasn't trying to create unified themes—but Polanski perhaps has a point. In his body of work, Polanski deals with a variety of interests and works within several film genres; enough so that, when his films are watched in chronological order it often seems that they were directed by different people. Part of this effect springs from the fact that Polanski has always been an international director, working in the U. K., the U. S., Italy, France, and Tunisia, with casts and crews changing from country to country. Polanski's internationalism makes it difficult to connect his work to any particular national or cultural movements in filmmaking. Even his early Polish films don't seem to fit into a recognizable national framework. During the time Polanski made his student films and *Knife in the Water (Noz W Wodzie,* 1962), his first feature, Polish films were expected to reflect the principles of Soviet realism, and Polanski's interests in depicting violence and in avoiding "positive" proletarian values brought him condemnation from Eastern Bloc critics. His "British" films—*Repulsion* (1965), *Cul-de-Sac* (1966), and *Vampire Killers*—are unlike most films that came out of the U. K. during that period, avoiding kitchen sink melodrama, Hammer-like monstrosities, "Carry On" spoofery, or James Bond-style action. Even Polanski's first "American" film, *Rosemary's Baby,* did not fit into any of the Hollywood trends of the late 1960s: in fact, it inspired an entirely new sub-genre, that of the "demonic possession" or "devil child" movie. Polanski has always made the kinds of movies he's wanted to, and the country in which he makes his films doesn't necessarily matter—so long as the country is willing to fund the project.

Still, as stylistically and thematically diverse as Polanski's films are, they are unified by characteristic concerns and interests, and by the very fact that the films *are* so diverse. On first glance, a Polanski film may be very easy to define—as horror film or as thriller—but it is usually the case that Polanski utilizes the trappings of a particular genre only explode those very same trappings and generic classifications. *Chinatown* (1974), for instance, is popularly thought of as an "old fashioned" private eye movie that harks back to such film noir classics as *The Maltese Falcon* and *Murder, My Sweet*. The photography, the period detail, and the music all evoke this particular genre, as do the scenes of private eye Jake Gittes (Jack Nicholson) tailing suspects and spying on houses. What ultimately destroys *Chinatown's* generic affiliations, though, are its pessimism—the heroine dies and the villain not only lives but becomes even richer and more successful—which stands in contrast to the usual private eye film's detached cynicism, and the physical frailty of its hero. Gittes is constantly beaten and tortured; he is nearly drowned in a public cistern; and—in perhaps the film's most famous scene—his nostril is split by a thug (played by Polanski), and he goes through half the film with a ridiculous bandage on his nose. Most B-movie private eyes endure their share of torture, too, but they usually emerge victorious: Gittes's tortures become a kind of degradation that emphasizes the hopelessness of his position within the film.

If Polanski directs antithrillers as opposed to straight thrillers, then his horror movies can perhaps be regarded as antihorrors. Beyond parodying horror conventions, as he does in *Vampire Killers*, and, perhaps, in the often inexplicable *The Ninth Gate* (2000), where Polanski best manages to subvert the genre is by using point of view camerawork to suggest that terror is not imposed on the individual by outside forces—either human or supernatural—but that it is a force imposed from within by the individual's psychological neuroses. *Repulsion* takes place largely inside the mind of a placid, shy, quiet woman named Carol (Catherine Deneuve) who, left alone in her apartment for the weekend, is besieged by a variety of terrors: mysterious phone calls, walls that yield to the touch and split open, men who try to—and even succeed in—raping her, hands that emerge from the walls and caress her. The film is a disorienting experience for the viewer, because for long stretches of time Polanski does not make it clear what is real and what Carol imagines. Later in the film, Polanski tears the viewer out of Carol's mind and puts him or her into the mind of Carol's first victim. When Carol beats her suitor to death with a heavy candlestick, she swings it directly at the camera (Barbara Leaming reports that Deneuve was in reality swinging at Polanski, who'd bullied her until she was in a state of rage[74]), replicating not only the victim's point of view, but, in Virginia Wright Wexman's words, creating "the cinematic equivalent of Grotowski's stage devices, which insist that the audience participate in the performance."[75] By using the camera to duplicate what either the eye or the mind sees, Polanski both distorts reality and shows that actual violence can be the end product of imagined horrors.

Rosemary's Baby is an even more interesting exercise in using the camera to convey a possibly disturbed mental state. Polanski has professed that he considers the concept of "Satan as evil incarnate" as contrary to rationalism, and that he tried in the film to suggest "the possibility that Rosemary's supernatural experiences were figments of her imagination. The entire story, as seen through her eyes, could have been a chain of only superficially sinister coincidences, a product of her feverish fancies."[76] *Rosemary's Baby* is actually a deeply ambiguous film, leaving open the possibility that every person around Rosemary (Mia Farrow)—including her husband, neighbors, and doctor—is a member of a coven who've arranged for Satan to impregnate her; or that Rosemary's pregnancy results in a psychosis that causes her to mutilate her own body and has led her to believe that the people around her are plotting against her and her unborn baby.[77] (The final scene, with the coven gathered around a black-draped cradle, as well as Rosemary's horrified reaction to her own child, pretty much destroys this carefully constructed ambiguity.)

In his autobiography, Polanski mentions that at the time he made *Rosemary*, he was influenced by R. L. Gregory's book *Eye and Brain: The Psychology of Seeing*, which, in Polanski's words, has as one of its theories that we "see far less than we think we see because of past impressions already stored in our minds." Polanski cites as proof of Gregory's theory that many viewers have been convinced that they actually *saw* Rosemary's baby at the end of the film—when in fact the only hint of a palpable demonic presence in the whole picture is a pair of cat-like eyes that figure in Rosemary's "nightmare" of being raped by the devil.[78] Polanski's technique of allowing viewers to draw their own conclusions by throwing into question what it is they are looking at would be used to some extent in *Tess*; and it is one of those elements that strikes me as somewhat Hardean. Just as Hardy in *Tess of the d'Urbervilles* questions the authority of the words that are used to construct the plot, Polanski frequently undercuts the reality of what his camera records by showing that the image may convey something other than what the viewer at first believed. What makes a "typical" Polanski film typical, then, is that it is largely concerned with redefining and even subverting genres, and with questioning points of view. His characters are frequently rendered helpless by the events that unfold around them, and the viewer is made to feel a similar kind of helplessness in having the familiar props of the genre taken away.

Two more things need to be taken into consideration about Polanski's films: voyeurism and his depiction of women. Barbara Leaming's critical biography of Polanski—tellingly subtitled *The Filmmaker as Voyeur*—identifies the desire to look at what is forbidden as not only the director's major theme, but as a desire on the part of the spectator that Polanski exploits in order to make his own persona visible in his films.[79] Leaming identifies several instances in Polanski's films where characters observe moments of violence, criminal behavior, and erotic acts: to her, these are all incidents that have parallels in Polanski's life, and, by filming such moments, he not only creates an image of himself but exposes our own desire to take pleasure in what we see. Leaming's study illustrates the phenomenon of critics *wanting* to read Polanski's life into his films, but she is actually on safe ground where she writes of Polanski capturing our own desires to see what is forbidden. Film, of course, has always played on our feeling that we are overhearing and spying upon something that is "real," and many studies have been written on the voyeuristic properties of the medium. To most critics, the moments in Polanski's films where characters are looking out of windows, looking through keyholes, glancing through cracks in walls, and so on, are scenes in which characters become like cameras—they capture private moments. Polanski perhaps best captures the theme of voyeurism in *Bitter Moon* (1992), where Nigel (Hugh Grant) finds himself compelled to listen as the invalid Oscar (Peter Coyote) narrates his tales of sexual adventure; and as Oscar speaks, his stories are visually related to the viewer in flashbacks. Nigel is alternately disgusted and titillated by Oscar's frank tales of sexual excess, while the flashbacks depict sex scenes that border on soft-core porn. Polanski seems to be testing the viewers' limits, much as Oscar is testing Nigel's.

That *Bitter Moon* should be concerned with spying on sex acts is appropriate, for in Polanski's films it is not so much violence but sex and the female form that are most often spied upon—although violence frequently does accompany the sex. For instance, in *Vampire Killers*, Alfred peeps at Sarah while she is bathing, and he next spies on her being spanked as a punishment for bathing *too much*; and in *Rosemary's Baby*, the soft-focus sex scene that keeps Rosemary and Guy (John Cassavetes) in discreet silhouette is later parodied by the much more graphic scene of her "dream rape," in which Rosemary's naked body is displayed before the equally naked coven members—who are, perhaps, the doubles of the people in the audience. There can be no doubt that Polanski's invitations to the viewer to spy on women and on sex acts can be disturbing: after all, we are usually asked to partake in pleasure and pain. To some critics, though, Polanski's "voyeuristic" tendencies are not just disturbing—they are sexist and perverted. Molly Haskell, for instance, charges that Polanski is only interested in having his viewers see a certain "type" of woman—"the anesthetized woman, the beautiful, inarticulate, and possibly even murderous somnambule." In Haskell's reading, Polanski is invested in capturing the images of women only to expose the "threat" that they represent:

> In Polanski's tortured, paranoid universe, the woman, simply by being susceptible of "impregnation" by something outside her, is a potential carrier of evil. His blonde heroines all become instruments of the devil and fulfill his fears of evil, just as the lobotomized actresses he chooses to play them fulfill his ideas of women. Polanski is a perfect example of the artist whose vision of women is not formed according to what he sees, but conversely, whose women are chosen as they conform to his preconceptions.[80]

It is hard to deny that Polanski *does* often depict women as either placid or homicidal (some would say his Tess is both), and that he has a definite female "ideal" he continually puts on the screen. Most of Polanski's lead female performers are blonde, and they usually have wide, childlike eyes, full lips, and often girlish physiques. Catherine Denueve, Sharon Tate, Mia Farrow, Francesca Annis (Lady Macbeth), and Nastassia Kinski all seem to be cut from the same cloth—and all at one time or other in their films must either be subjected to a form of sexual degradation or be made to go through scenes in a trance-like state. Interestingly, Emmanuelle Seigner, who starred in *Frantic, Bitter Moon,* and *The Ninth Gate,* is a near-double for Kinski; and though the characters she plays are never placid, she has performed in the most explicit sex scenes Polanski has ever filmed. She also became Polanski's third wife. Whether Polanski is bedeviled by adolescent, pornographic, and hate-filled fantasies about women is not for me to say; but his almost monolithic depiction of women has helped construct part of Polanski's image, and, as we've seen, that image is hard to divorce from his films.

When examining how critics have constructed their own versions of Polanski, it is hard not to be struck by how familiar it all sounds. Just as Polanski uses the film medium to deflate generic boundaries and to question points of view, so too did Hardy use words to much the same effect. Just as Polanski has been accused of an unhealthy interest in female bodies and of being a scoptophiliac, so too has Hardy. And just as Polanski's films have been seen as offering access to his life, so too have Hardy's novels—especially *Tess*—been read as veiled autobiography. There is, then, a certain consonance between the novels of Thomas Hardy and the films of Roman Polanski that exists on the level of *reception.* Effectively, this is a kind of "false" consonance, but it nevertheless establishes that Polanski's vision as a filmmaker is perhaps ideally suited to Hardy's vision as a novelist. In fact, as David Ansen's review of *Tess* suggests, Polanski's vision is perhaps a darker and more absurdist offshoot of Hardy's own. However, when Polanski adapted the novel he often ignored fidelity and left many of Hardy's narrative functions out—an approach that, ironically, does more justice to Hardy's novel than would a more "faithful" approach.

Most studies that examine Polanski's *Tess* in relation to its source novel zero in on the fact that some of the novel's most memorable sequences are not in the film—and the opinion of a good many is that the film suffers for these losses. The most obvious omissions are the scene where Prince the horse is killed; the sign painter sequence; Sorrow's baptism; Angel's somnambulistic "burial" of Tess; Alec's conversion to Methodism and his subsequent de-conversion; and the tableau at the end where Angel and Liza-Lu watch the execution of Tess, and then walk off hand in hand.[81] All of these moments from the novel have frequently been labeled as melodramatic, sensationalistic, or as heavy-handed contrivances; and most critics of the film have tended to agree with Nell Kozak Waldman that Polanski must have dropped them because "no modern director would risk such a perilous strain on his audience's suspension of disbelief."[82] The common thought is that in bringing *Tess* to the screen, Polanski did away with Hardy's more fantastic elements to make the story more "real," and to some Hardy scholars, this "realism" causes grave offense. Gladys Veidemanis, for instance, faults *Tess* because it "leaves out all the superstition, coincidences, and allusiveness of the novel and, hence, fails to convey its legendary and mythic dimensions. The film is strictly realistic. All the improbabilities have been removed, including the concatenation of accident and chance by which Hardy's plot unfolds."[83] Other critics have charged that, by making *Tess* a "realistic" film, Polanski simplified Hardy's story, or that he dumbed it down, or robbed it of its essentiality—charges some would also make against Polanski's treatment of Tess herself.

Knowing the novel as well as I do, I have to admit that every time I watch the film I am jarred because the scene of Prince's death isn't there, and because Alec returns as himself and not as an evangelist. But does the loss of such material mean that the film is actually diminished, or that by the elimination of these elements the film has automatically been made into a "realist" text? No doubt Polanski did eliminate some sequences because they might play as ridiculous on film, but it seems to me that most of the moments from the novel that were eliminated are those that, if filmed, would likely impose a strict reading on the film that Polanski perhaps wished to avoid. It is entirely possible that Polanski wanted to throw much of what is being seen into doubt—to force the viewer to question what is being depicted onscreen—and, while this gesture is characteristically Polanskian, it is also in keeping with Hardy's effect of having the reader question much of what he or she is reading.

The most significant omission, in my view, is that of Tess's encounter with the sign painter. No doubt this sequence could have been used in the film, and it could have been shot more or less as Hardy wrote it. However, the scene with the painter would likely carry an entirely different ideological weight on film than it does in the book. Tess's encounter with the sign painter largely serves the purpose of establishing patterns of reading: she eventually identifies the painter's words with God, church, and society, and she tries to construct herself against such words, while for the reader, the sequence marks the moment when he or she is challenged to negotiate the authority of words in the novel *itself.* Had the sequence been filmed, Polanski could easily have shown Tess's disgust at the words the man paints, and the director no doubt could have tied those words in with such figures of religiosity as the Vicar of Marlott and Mercy Chant; but how would a *viewer* be given the sense that the painter's words are degraded, and that they fit into an overall pattern of degraded discourses and texts?

In contrast, the other significant omission—the death of Prince—has the effect of complicating the way the film should be viewed, rather than simplifying it. It is clear from the start of the film, when Jack encounters Parson Tringham, that the horse is already dead and that the family is suffering because of it. By reversing the incidents of the novel—making the death of the horse come *before* the Durbeyfields learn of their ancestry—Polanski does two things. First, he takes away the sense that "Fate" and heredity are primarily responsible for what happens to Tess. In Hardy's novel, the positioning of Tringham's information *first* in the story does create a sense of fate at work, for everything that follows largely springs from what Tringham says: the news causes Jack to get drunk, which keeps him from driving the cart, which forces Tess to drive it, which gets the horse killed, which sends Tess to the d'Urbervilles to act on Tringham's information. The film, however, turns Tringham's information into a possible solution to an existing financial crisis: Joan (Rosemary Martin) immediately realizes—without the aid of *The Compleat Fortune-Teller*—the potential value of the news. Tess goes to the d'Urbervilles not because either fate or some cause born of heredity forces her to, but because of monetary need.

The second thing Polanski does in eliminating the scene of the horse's death is that he takes a portion of the narrative away from the viewer.

Prince's death is significant to everything that happens in the first two or three reels, but the incident is literally *not* in the picture. The "true" beginning of the film actually occurred *before* Polanski's camera started rolling: the encounter between Jack and Tringham is a "false start," and its positioning at the beginning of the film proper causes the viewer to run the risk of inflating the significance of Tringham's information, making it the *primary* cause of what follows, rather than an auxiliary event. Jack's receipt of the news does indeed start the film, yet this moment isn't the true start of the action; and though the scene emphasizes the heredity of the Durbeyfields as an important concept ("I'm Sir John d'Urberville, that's who I am," Jack [John Collin] intones as the parson rides off), this concept is quickly deflated by the suggestion that—in Joan's hands—heredity is nothing more than another commodity. Polanski defers and undercuts the sources of Tess's tragedy: he causes the viewer to question the importance not just of what Tringham says, but of heredity *itself* and the role it plays in what happens to Tess.

The drawback to Polanski's elimination of the scene where Prince dies is that Tess is denied a personal role in what happens to the family and to herself. What makes the death of Prince cardinal to the novel's plot is that it instills in Tess a sense of responsibility: it is her own feelings of guilt that make Tess reluctantly agree to follow her mother's suggestion and go to the d'Urbervilles. With this sense of personal responsibility gone from the film, Tess does seem to be a mere victim: she is put into a position where she will be "coveted by the wrong man" by circumstances that are entirely outside of her control. In this respect, those who claim Kinski's Tess is entirely passive and meekly accepting of what happens to her are correct.

The sign painter sequence and the scene of the horse's death are—to my mind, at least—the only two *cardinal* plot functions that have been eliminated; otherwise, most of the omitted sequences are really just catalyzers or informants. Angel's sleepwalking scene may be fascinating, but it doesn't really advance the plot; and Polanski perhaps provides an acceptable substitute for the sequence in the scene where Angel (Peter Firth) walks away from the house after Tess has confessed her past to him. Firth's movements create the sense of sleepwalking, and his monotone delivery furthers the illusion that he is in a trance—or that he's convinced himself his wife is dead. Likewise, it is mainly important to the plot of Hardy's novel that Alec reappear at Flintcomb-Ash: that he shows up as an evangelist and then reverts to form is perhaps an over-visualization of the fact Alec presents himself as a changed man—maybe he even believes in his heart that he has changed—but he soon shows himself to be the man he always has been. Polanski actually complicates Hardy's depiction of Alec (Leigh Lawson) by having him reappear in pretty much the same clothes he wears as when Tess left him, and as the action unfolds, suggesting that Alec reverts to his *true* social status. In his final scenes in the Sandbourne hotel, Alec comes across less like the charming seducer he was earlier, and more like a fussy upper-middle-class husband from a play by Noël Coward. It seems that Alec, in settling down into this version of domesticity, has reverted to the dull, bourgeois snobbery that perhaps was the defining trait of his mercantile ancestors.

Another major complaint about Polanski's omissions is that by not showing the scene where Tess baptizes her baby (unnamed in the film), he denies the viewer the chance to see Tess take control of a situation for herself, and even—as Marcus argues—to usurp masculine authority. Perhaps this is so, but in not filming the baptism Polanski creates an ellipsis in the film that is actually quite Hardean. After we see Tess kneeling before the Bible and praying that God "spare" her child, there is a cut to the vicarage, where Tess arrives to relate the details of the baby's baptism and death. One of Hardy's most common narrative devices is to *not* show a significant action; instead, he has a character *narrate* the event to a listener. By eliminating the baptism, Polanski takes away the *visual* significance of the act: the viewer—like the vicar—must respond only to Tess and to the words she uses.

The omission of some of Hardy's scenes, then, are certainly not arbitrary, and they don't necessarily make *Tess* into a realistic film. No doubt *Tess* is less concerned with its own artificiality than is *Tess of the d'Urbervilles*; but Polanski fashions his own kind of anti-realism that is perhaps more appropriate to film form than is Hardy's anti-realism, but which also creates a kind of convergence with the novel. By putting significant events out of view, Polanski forces the audience to contend with a character's dialogue or with the image that is on the screen. Very often, the viewer is removed from stable ground and made to question the veracity of what Polanski has filmed. Furthermore, the film is filled with ellipses—there are broad leaps in time and quick shifts in scene, as when Tess leaves Alec on the road, and then there is a jump of at least nine months, when Tess has a baby—so that, like the novel, the film appears to be filled with "blank spaces" where the viewer is invited to "fill in" the story. Dianne Fallon Sadoff has said that such gaps are really for the benefit of those who've read the novel: they will know what *should* fill in the gaps, and this allows viewers to both participate in the narrative process of the film, and reminds them that "Polanski himself read *Tess* and knew it nearly by heart."[84] This is an interesting argument, but if it is taken to its logical conclusion, it means that Polanski's *Tess* is unintelligible to anyone who *hasn't* read the novel. In fact, the "blank spaces" in *Tess* tend to open the film up to interpretation from *anyone*. Perhaps someone who knows the novel *will* conclude, for instance, that Tess has to go to Flintcomb-Ash because her family has spent the money Angel gave her (plot details that are absent from the film); but a viewer who is unfamiliar with the novel is likely to draw different conclusions—that Angel left Tess desolate, or that Tess retreats into this dreary landscape as a form of self-punishment. Whether the viewer knows the novel or not, indeterminate moments like these do allow the viewer to participate in the narrative of the film. However, Polanski will eventually assert his control over the narrative, forcing the viewer to contend with the power of film form to create a sense of reality.

Even though Polanski does omit a good deal of Hardy material, the screenplay—written by Polanski himself, in collaboration with Gérard Brach and John Brownjohn[85]—is mostly faithful to the novel in that it preserves the majority of Hardy's plot functions. Furthermore, Polanski, like John Schlesinger, *does* at times try to make the film "Hardean" by consciously evoking the "Hardy" we all know—or at least think we know. Though he could not film in authentic "Hardy country," Polanski still tries to be faithful to Hardy's "period" and to the world that Hardy might have known. The film is firmly set in the 1880s (the year of death on Jack Durbeyfield's tombstone is 1888), and Polanski takes a great deal of pride in pointing out in his autobiography that all of the "nineteenth-century farm machinery, early railroad cars, and other rare old props" are authentic.[86] Co-producer Timothy Burrill reports that the location work in France actually enhanced *Tess*'s historical accuracy, since the kind of small-field farming depicted in the film is no longer practiced in England.[87]

There are also a few moments in the film that point directly to the presence of Hardy and to the unique fictional world he created. The four-man band that leads the May Day dancers at the start of the film seems inspired by the Mellstock Quire of *Under the Greenwood Tree*; and references to such Wessex locations as Casterbridge and Weatherbury abound—though the front gate of the mansion that Angel and Tess break into while they're on the lam has on it a "To Let" sign that puts the realtor's office in the very real location of Dorset. Probably the strangest reference to Hardy in the film comes in the form of what I take is a bizarre inside joke: one of the hens that Tess cares for is named Phena, and Phena, of course, was the pet name of Hardy's old love Tryphena Sparks. However, where *Tess* is most self-consciously "Hardean" is in its focus on human faces. Early on, Parson Tringham (the appropriately named Tony Church) asks to examine the face of Jack; and as the camera holds on Jack's face, allowing us to see his missing teeth and grizzled, haggard features, Tringham says, "Yes, that's the d'Urberville nose and chin—a little debased." This scene is the first of many that make "debased" physiognomies central to the shot: at Rolliver's, Polanski scans the grotesque faces of the drinkers, and later we see that Mrs. D'Urberville's blind eyes are set at odd, disconcerting angles. The old woman who waits on Tess and Angel at the Wellbridge house continually displays her wide, toothless grin; and in one scene she is accompanied by her staring, open-mouthed son. Even the woman who discovers the fugitives Angel and Tess in bed toward the end of the film has a turned-up nose that gives her a porcine look. These figures, who— with the exception of the caretaker's son—are old and ugly, are perhaps meant to stand in contrast to the young and attractive actors who play Tess, Alec, and Angel, to remind us that what is young and beautiful must eventually age and degrade. In a larger sense, though, Parson Tringham's opening comment that Jack's features are degraded remnants of an

The wedding of Angel and Tess (Peter Firth, Nastassia Kinski).

earlier, more noble "type" points to the issue of biological descent, and invites us to contemplate the film's grotesques as the products of *devolu-tion*. Since *Tess of the d'Urbervilles* has popularly been read as a medita-tion on Darwinian themes, the "devolved" grotesques in Polanski's *Tess* seem to fit in with this kind of reading.

A common assumption about *Tess* is that the film's specific subjects for criticism are entirely derived from Hardy's novel—and many critics have made this case—but, upon close examination, the film's attacks are actually more Polanskian than they are Hardean. One of the most popu-lar assumptions about Hardy's *Tess* is that it is a salvo against the institu-tion of religion; but, as we have seen, Hardy is more concerned with the authority of the *words* that are wielded by the church, and not so much with the power of the church itself. In fact, Hardy shows through the char-acter of Reverend Clare that religion can actually be a positive force. Many critics feel that Polanski's film replicates Hardy's negative depiction of reli-gion, but his attack is actually far more general and sweeping than is Hardy's. The role of Mr. Clare (David Markham) is very limited here: all we really learn of him is that he disapproves of Angel's chosen work, and that he believes his son should marry the "truly Christian" Mercy Chant (Arielle Dombasle). Rev. Clare's willingness to put his faith on the line and to risk his own skin to save someone else's are gone: he is merely a stiff representative of religious authority. Likewise, the Vicar of Marlott is lit-tle more than a caricature: when Tess comes to him to tell about the bap-tism, he is dressed in a beekeeper's outfit, which, with its wispy black veil and broad-brimmed hat, seems to be a feminized parody of a cleric's vest-ments; and Richard Pearson as the vicar affects a prissy manner that stops just short of camp. During the scene of Angel and Tess's wedding cere-mony, the camera focuses on the Bible in the priest's palsied hands, sug-gesting that it is not the *word* that is unstable; rather, the fault is with the authority that props the word up. Finally, Polanski's critique of religion seems to affect his presentation of Tess herself. Perhaps in an attempt to illustrate the "simple faith" that Hardy only alludes to in The Chase scene, Polanski frequently shows Tess in the act of prayer, and she invokes the name of God quite a bit. In The Chase, Tess knocks Alec down, and when she sees that she has wounded him, she sinks to her knees, clasps her hands, and begs for forgiveness—either from God or from Alec. When Tess writes her confession letter to Angel, we hear her say in voice-over, "I must be guilty because the Lord saw fit to take my child." This bit of narration, of course, is not in the novel; nor is the sequence where Tess, en route to her aborted trip to see Angel's parents, kneels before the Cross-in-Hand mon-ument and prays, only to have a bandy-legged old peddler tell her that there's a curse on the place and that praying there will bring her bad luck. All of these scenes may, on the surface, seem to replicate a "Hardean" critique of the church and of religiosity in general, but in fact these moments all fit into Polanski's tendency—best illustrated in *Rosemary* and in *Pirates* (1986)—to ridicule organized religion as a sham, and to show its most devoted adherents as having faith in a dangerous lie.

Likewise, Polanski seems to replicate a popular cultural view of Hardy's novel as a protest against the conditions of the working class, but Polanski actually creates a dialectic that suggests that *all* of the classes are equally responsible for what happens to Tess. By keeping Alec an "aristocrat" from beginning to end and by downplaying the way the Stokes made their fortune, Polanski indeed invites us to read Alec's relations with Tess in a somewhat Marxist fashion: Alec is the aristocracy, which exploits the proletariat Tess for financial and sexual gratification. However, Polanski exposes Alec as being distinctly bourgeois at the core; thus he implicates middle-class values in Tess's tragedy. Furthermore, Polanski undercuts Marxist readings of his film by implicating Marxist beliefs in Angel's rejection of Tess. In a sequence that has brought complaints for its lack of historicity, Polanski focuses on a copy of Marx's *Capital and Capitalist Production* at Angel's bedside.[88] Angel's desire to turn himself into a farmer, then, is born not so much from his illusions and from his desire to construct himself against his father's religion, but from a definable political ideology. Though Wexman argues that when Angel rejects Tess he is returning "in part to the repressive religious morality he has learned from his straightlaced country-parson family,"[89] Polanski actually shows that Angel retreats into his own *personal* politics. In fact, the words Angel uses to rebuke Tess and her entire pedigree sound like those of a stereotypical Soviet official from a Cold War satire: "I cannot help associating your lack of firmness with the decline of your family. Decrepit families imply deficient willpower and decadent conduct. I thought you were a child of nature, but you were the last in a line of decadent aristocrats." In using such doctrinaire terms to reject Tess, Angel expresses not so much his belief that Tess has destroyed his romantic illusions about women, but that she has smashed his *political* ideal of doing away with a society that has been divided along class—and, perhaps, gender—lines. By allying Alec with both the middle class and with the aristocracy, and by associating Angel with emergent socialism, Polanski creates an interesting critique of the political and economic forces that contend over Tess: the capitalist/industrialist upper class indeed exploits and rapes her because she is poor and a woman, but the forces of social revolution that should save her actually reject her because she isn't enough of a proletarian for their tastes.

Polanski even suggests that the poorest and most exploited classes have a hand in what happens to Tess. Despite his claims of "slavin' away" and of working "like a beast in the field," Jack Durbeyfield is clearly little more than a lazy reprobate. Interestingly, when Tess tries to tell Angel of her past, she does not focus on Jack's drunkenness, as she does in the book, but on his *idleness*. The film even takes away whatever sympathy a viewer might feel for Jack based on his poverty by hinting that, in addition to spending whatever money he has on drink, he is also abusive. At Rolliver's, where Jack is showing off the d'Urberville crest on his old spoon, he leans toward Joan and growls, "You'd better find that damned [family] seal, or I'll do ye a mischief!"[90] Given Jack's laziness, drunkenness, and potential violence, as well as Joan's almost comic scheming, it cannot be said that Polanski's treatment of Tess's family and of their social situation is an entirely sympathetic one. In fact, the Durbeyfield parents are clearly given a share of the blame in what happens to Tess—as are Alec, Angel, their respective classes and ideologies, and their religions and politics. Polanski overdetermines Tess's fate, much as Hardy does. The difference, however, is that Polanski points to entirely *human* causes for what happens to Tess: there is no sense that what happens to her "was to be," or that the creator of the film text artificially brings her fate into being simply because we expect it.

Polanski's attempts to *deliberately* invoke an image of Hardy, then, is pretty much a hit-or-miss affair, and the thematic "affinities" that many critics have identified as existing between the novel and the film are usually more Polanskian than they are Hardean. How, then, does Polanski create a true sense of consonance with Hardy's novel? This is achieved, I believe, through his deployment of visual images. *Tess* is most often praised for its visual beauty; but many critics have complained that the film's look is actually more important than anything that happens on screen, and that *Tess* as a result is dull and emotionless—"a series of leisurely Barbizon School landscapes," as Pauline Kael quipped.[91] Others have charged that Polanski has done little more than create a pastoral romance à la Schlesinger, and a few particularly literal-minded critics have fussed that the look of the film, pretty though it may be, is still far more French than English.[92] The film is indeed attractive, but Polanski rarely captures a beautiful image simply *because* it is beautiful. More often than not, the images Polanski records stay in the mind because he captures a haunting and overwhelming sense of *absence*.

Polanski seems to have adopted the technique Terrence Malick used in *Days of Heaven* (1978) of emphasizing elliptical narrative, privileging images of nature over the advancement of the plot, and utilizing a rich soundtrack to advertise his own control over the motion picture.[93] The viewer's attention is constantly being manipulated so that he or she must consider what is *not* there on the screen. Although *Tess* has its moments of spring-like activity (such as in Alec's garden at The Slopes, and even in the threshing scene where Liza-Lu appears holding Tess's baby) and of wintery gloominess (represented most strongly by the image of Tess and Marian [Carolyn Pickles] digging for turnips through the ice and mud), the overall treatment of Nature in the film is muted and even somber. In most of the outdoor scenes, the sky is an empty white, and the camera frequently captures flat, limitless landscapes on which few trees and houses—and usually no people—appear. The most prevalent image in the film is that of the road; and Polanski invariably photographs roads so that they disappear into the horizon, giving the sense that they lead nowhere. There are also, remarkably, few scenes of town life in the film. Marlott is seen only in the distance, in the scene where Tess tells Alec that she was born "just over there"; otherwise, we see the town only in bits and pieces—the outside of the Durbeyfield house, the outside of the vicarage, the fairgrounds. There is no feeling that Marlott has a "heart," or any place for the people to gather. The Slopes and Talbothays Dairy all seem to be literally in the middle of nowhere. Even Angel's hometown of Emminster always appears to be deserted: when Angel rides into town to visit his parents, the only people on the street are Mercy Chant and her students. Later, when Tess comes into town, no one at all is on the streets, and the wind is heard ominously whistling around cracks and corners. The silence is broken by the church bell, and the townspeople exit the church as a group, their voices a low babble. In this scene, Polanski seems to first be playing off a cliché of the western, where the hero comes into town, only to find it empty because the townsfolk are afraid to show themselves; and then the sudden procession of solemn people from the church—who promptly disappear into places unseen by the camera, again leaving Tess alone—owes something to science fiction or horror. The people who emerge from the church could very well be zombies. The scene of Tess's entrance into Emminster is one of the eeriest moments in the film, and it achieves its effect by emphasizing the absence of human habitation and by dulling the sounds of voices on the soundtrack.

Though the visual style of the film emphasizes absence, its soundtrack is alive with *presence*. It is rich, full, and even distracting. During most of the outdoor scenes in the first half of the film, the sounds of animals are important: at The Slopes, the cries of peacocks and other birds are so loud that in at least one scene Tess's explanation to Alec of why she has come is partially muffled, while during the Talbothays sequences, Tess and

Alec actually say very little to each other, but such sounds as lowing cattle and crowing roosters punctuate their scenes together. Polanski's use of these noises at times gives the film a sense of verisimilitude—as in real life, incidental sounds *do* drown out what we say—but it cannot be denied that the soundtrack frequently calls attention to itself. In the garden scene, it sounds as if the microphones have been placed in a nearby meadow, too far away to catch the dialogue between Tess and Alec but close enough that a cow is heard loud and clear. Moments like this emphasize the fact that what we are seeing is *not* real, that there is a human hand turning the volume knobs up and down and making us hear what Polanski selects. What Tess and Alec say to each other in the garden *should* be of most importance to the story; that it can scarcely be heard is disorienting, and it calls into question the importance of what has been photographed.

As the film progresses, the sounds of animals on the soundtrack begin to disappear, and at times the soundtrack becomes nearly silent. What helps make the scene of Tess's visit to Emminster so ominous is that we hear nothing more than the wind, which is temporarily broken by the tolling of the bell. Even after people appear, their words are no more than a dull hum: it is impossible to understand even what Mercy is saying to Angel's brothers when she finds Tess's boots. When Tess is propositioned on the road by Farmer Groby, his dialogue is very clear ("You weren't too proud to cock a leg for [Alec]," he says); otherwise, the only sound we hear is the clop of his horse's hooves on the road. Moments like this— where human voices are often indistinct, and where an almost unnatural quiet seems to dominate—emphasize Tess's isolation. If the film's earlier use of rich, vibrant sounds places Tess in a vital and active world, its later emphasis on silence serves to divorce her from that world.

In the final third of the film, the most prominent sounds come from machines: the clock that loudly ticks throughout the scenes of Angel and Tess's disastrous honeymoon; the roaring threshing machine at Flintcomb-Ash; the snapping hedge clippers that are heard at the Sandbourne hotel, while Tess is presumably upstairs killing Alec; the squeal of the train whistle that cuts short the scream of the landlady when she discovers Alec's blood seeping through the ceiling. In some ways, the soundtrack *itself* begins in a pastoral mode, rich in the noises of "Nature," and then it gradually gives way to the sounds of machines and of advancing industrialization. The only *visual* hint of mass industrialization in the film is the threshing machine at Flintcomb-Ash, but the soundtrack alone opens up the possibility that nature is gradually being contained and even devoured by the power of machines.

What Polanski achieves through his deployment of images that create a sense of absence and in his use of the soundtrack is, instead of a film that is as "strictly realistic" as Gladys Veidemanis and others charge, one that has a heightened sense of artificiality. Polanski is constantly drawing the viewer's attention away from the mechanics of the plot by focusing on a lonely or even ambiguous image, or on discordant noises on the soundtrack. Combined with the fact that a few significant events occur literally offscreen, Polanski creates the effect that much of the story takes place outside the limits of the camera and at such a distance from the viewer that he or she becomes less an eyewitness than an intruder who might be able to overhear just enough to understand what is being said. In such moments as in the garden scene, where it is difficult to understand what is being said, or in the sequence where the viewer is denied the opportunity to see Tess baptize her own baby, the viewer is actually pushed away from the story. Again, the spectator supplies what Polanski does not make readily visible onscreen. Still, it is not just in the "blank spaces" of the narrative alone that the viewer is invited to participate in the creative process; Polanski very much uses the character of Tess as a blank space, and the fact that Nastassia Kinski as Tess has been interpreted as anything from a figure of sexual independence[94] to a fantasy figure for child molesters attests to how thoroughly Polanski allows the viewer to construct his or her own version of Tess.

There can be little doubt that, true to Jane Marcus's charge, Polanski does fetishize portions of Tess's/Kinski's anatomy: he holds the camera on Tess's lips as she takes Alec's strawberry in, and in the scene where Tess bares her breast to suckle her baby, it is hard not to feel that there isn't a certain seductiveness in the slow, deliberate way with which she unbuttons her blouse. It is also occasionally difficult to take Kinski's performance seriously: she speaks so softly that at times she sounds like a little girl, and at times her German accent clashes with her affected Dorset dialect. Her response to the vicar when he tells her he can't bury the child— "Then I don't like you, and I won't come to your church any more!"—is delivered in a high squeak that makes the moment unintentionally funny. Sequences such as these give weight to the critical charges that Kinski was cast only for her looks; but if one looks beyond the flaws in Kinski's performance and beyond Polanski's adoration of her face (which, as many critics have pointed out, isn't entirely unlike Hardy's own obsession with Tess's looks), it is possible to see that Tess is positioned not as a dumb object to be ogled and admired, but as an enigma that the viewer must contemplate and attempt to understand. Tess registers few emotional reactions and reveals very little of her own character, so that Polanski actually makes Tess herself a nullity and a point of contention: he calls upon the viewer to construct his or her own version of Tess, and how that person responds to her largely dictates how that viewer will perceive the film.

Peter Widdowson charges that, by "freeing Tess from her historical determinants and by locating her in the film principally in her own emotional space, Polanski reproduces her as the existential heroine of his own time and tragic vision, as someone trying to live an authentic life in an inauthentic society"[95]—and that this "existential" viewpoint reproduces an entirely modern reading of the novel. However, it seems to me that Polanski's Tess largely *has no* identity, because what Polanski is concerned with is the way human and artificial means of perception ultimately rob the individual of identity. As in the novel, Tess is constantly being perceived by those around her: Alec and Angel continually stare at her, taking her in with their eyes; Farmer Groby casts leering sidelong glances at her; and the camera idealizes her. But Tess in the film very seldom *responds* to the looks she receives. Hardy's Tess often fights back against Alec, and while she is en route to Flintcomb-Ash she becomes so tired of the glances of men and of their comments about her looks that she cuts off her eyebrows and wraps a scarf around her face to make herself ugly. In the film, though, when men stare at Tess or compliment her, she usually looks down, or—in the case of Groby's crude come-on—she simply walks away. It is difficult to tell just from Kinski's performance *how* Tess feels about this kind of treatment: her face usually registers no emotion, and she says very little about how she feels beyond expressing a vague wish to die.

Interestingly, Polanski manages to make The Chase scene ambiguous, not so much because he conceals what happens to Tess, but because he makes her own reaction to it entirely unknowable. The scene is draped in artificiality: though it takes place at night, Polanski uses a day-for-night filter that turns the scene an unnatural blue. When Alec kisses Tess, she pushes him off the horse, and he ends up cutting his head open on a tree stump. This is the first direct depiction of violence in the film, and, ironically, the blood that is spilled is not Tess's but Alec's. It is actually possible that this moment foreshadows Alec's own death (he will die as a consequence of what he is about to do to Tess), just as his carving into a rare roast during the scene of his first meeting with Tess presages his murder; but the moment *could* be read as something that justifies his violation of Tess: she has drawn first blood, and now he is entitled to win something back. However, it is difficult to tell if this is what Polanski means, for what happens next is completely obscure. While Alec tries to comfort Tess, she either falls into a stereotypical swoon or simply falls asleep. Alec gently lays her on her back and begins kissing and stroking her. Tess's eyes are closed the whole time, and she appears to be kissing him back unconsciously, as if she is in a dream. As Alec grows more forceful, Tess seems to struggle, but it is impossible to tell if she's fighting or enjoying what is happening. Finally, fog rolls in and covers the pair—an obvious but reasonably effective device. What, then, does The Chase scene mean in this film? As is the case with the novel, we cannot say for certain if Tess is raped or seduced, and our lack of certainty is because Tess's personal response is so muted that we cannot tell what, exactly, is happening to her.

Likewise, the nature of Tess's relationship with Alec over the next few weeks is thrown into doubt by Tess's failure to register emotion. After The Chase scene, there is a montage of Alec's and Tess's life together: Alec presents Tess with a beautiful new hat, which she looks at with an expression that could be gratitude or bewilderment; Alec takes Tess out rowing on a river, and she looks at him from under her new hat, her expression suggesting either contempt or fear—or both; and we see Tess in her garret, trying to drown out Alec's knocking on the door and begging her to let him in. The first two scenes in the montage could easily have come from a romance—the image of two lovers in a boat is a time-honored cliché— but Tess's enigmatic expressions and their occurrence after what may very well be a rape scene, tend to make these moments bizarre and even phony; and Tess's desire to shut Alec out is also shrouded in ambiguity: does she lock him out because she feels guilty, or because she can no longer stand letting her violator continue to violate her? What happens to Tess may at first glance seem to be crystal clear, but Tess's lack of definable response throws everything into doubt. We don't understand what happens in The Chase because we don't understand *her.*

Surprisingly, Tess's own *words* in the film would seem to make her complicit in what Alec has done to her. In the letter Tess writes to Angel, she says in voice-over that her "guilt" is proved by the fact God took her baby. The film also has Tess *narrate* her affair with Alec to Angel, something the book elides entirely. While Angel listens, Tess stares into the fire and tells her husband that "It was fate that drove me to work for false relations ... I became his mistress in his bed, without love." Polanski's decision to have Tess *tell* what happened to her has been severely criticized; but when it comes right down to it, what does Tess's "confession" really say? She blames "fate" for what happened to her, while Polanski clearly shows that she was motivated by economic need, and she calls herself Alec's mistress when the evidence of Tess's own behavior does not back this up. What is really important here is the effect that her words have on *Angel,* and it is evident they have destroyed his own perceptions. Polanski is actually far harder on Angel than is Hardy: when Angel sends Tess to her family, there is no indication that he has left her with money, and in the scene his attitude remains cold. Tess's departure from Angel is played in front of a fence on which someone—perhaps a passing evangelist—has painted in red letters, "BLESSED ARE THE MERCIFUL." Angel's behavior is cruel and arbitrary, but once again, Tess's reactions to his treatment are difficult to gauge. It is not entirely clear if we should join Polanski in despising Angel for his treatment of Tess, or join with Tess in believing that her suffering is justified.

Finally, Tess is so subdued in the scenes between her telling Angel that she has killed Alec and her capture at Stonehenge that it is not clear if she has indeed lost her mind, or if she simply feels no guilt over a very justifiable act. All of the emotion in these scenes is given to Angel. Later, in the scene where Angel and Tess finally consummate their love in the house they've broken into, Angel even takes on the role of the woman: he buries his head in Tess's lap in a gesture of submission, and, as Wexman points out, Tess "takes the initiative by raising Angel's head," thereby initiating their lovemaking.[96] Wexman argues that Tess in this scene reaches erotic fulfillment—an acceptance of her own need for physical love; but, frankly, it is Angel who is fulfilled here, for Tess's gesture of loving him allows him to expiate the guilt he feels over having left her. And it is the fact that Angel's erotic fulfillment is important that we can understand what Polanski has been doing all along: making Tess the vessel for fulfillment of desire. Polanski implicates the viewer in wanting to see Tess undressed; and it is that desire—on the part of Alec, Angel, Farmer Groby, and the rest—that has led Tess to the gallows. Polanski makes his film an indictment of the very desire to see, and he perhaps punishes the viewer by denying that "last glimpse" of Tess. She walks away from the camera, while a closing scroll reads, "Tess of the d'Urbervilles was hanged in Wintoncester, aforetime capital of Wessex."

Tess is not, it must be said, a perfect film: the dubbing of the French actors is awful, and its leisurely pace does grow ponderous at times. But it is a film that does considerable justice to Hardy—not because it perfectly replicates the "period" of the novel or because it succeeds in evoking a number of characteristically "Hardean" moments, but because it is concerned with the power of artificial means of production to create reality and to shape peoples' lives. Ultimately, Polanski indicts the power of the film image to create and destroy the individual, as much as Hardy condemns the power of his own words to do the same thing. It is in Polanski's deployment of the visual image that he manages to create not only a degree of convergence with Hardy's novel, but to fulfill Hardy's purpose.

5

Hardy's *Jude the Obscure* and Winterbottom's *Jude*: Coherence and Codification

I

Perhaps no novel has done more to create a cultural image of Thomas Hardy than *Jude the Obscure* (1895). It has entered popular culture as Hardy's "most depressing" work; a salvo against the hypocrisy of Victorian socio-sexual mores, the book that was so harshly reviewed the author gave up fiction-writing forever. More than any other Hardy novel it has a story completely independent of the one contained in its pages: the pillorying of "Hardy the Degenerate"; the parodying of the novel as *Jude the Obscene*; the bishop who threw the book on the fire (Hardy's response to this act—"probably in his despair at not being able to burn me" [*Jude*, p. 40]—has become something of a punchline); Hardy's realization that he had taken the novel form as far as he could. Just the title *Jude the Obscure* conjures in many minds the image of a deeply pessimistic author whose dark, despairing, and highly sexualized view of the human condition was roundly rejected by conservative, strait-laced Victorian society.

Of course, this image of Hardy did not spring up by itself. Hardy's 1912 "Postscript" to *Jude* is a defense against critics he says have ignored the book's "real" story of "shattered illusions" and instead focused on the "twenty or thirty pages of sorry detail deemed necessary to complete the narrative, and show the antitheses in Jude's life" (p. 40). He also presents *Jude* as a moral and sensible work, and does admit that the whole unpleasant business completely cured him of "further interest in novel-writing" (p. 41). Hardy makes himself into Jeremiah, or perhaps Cassandra, railing against a society that misreads and ignores what he has to say, and it is this Hardy who is kept alive by several major currents that run through the criticism of *Jude the Obscure*. Hardy the Prophet is popularly held to be making in *Jude* his most comprehensive fictional statement that humankind is forever buffeted by the twin forces of society and fate—neither of which will allow Jude and Sue to live the kind of unconventional life they want—and that these forces lead people invariably toward a tragic end. Critics who have read and continue to read *Jude* as an indictment of society or a treatise on fate continue the process of creating a stolid image of Hardy as the eternal pessimist, the grim tragedian ever shaking his fist against a "Crass Casualty" that forever obstructs the sun and the rain. *Jude* can and does accommodate such readings, but too often these interpretations deflect attention from the ultimate business of this novel—that is, *being* a novel.

Jude the Obscure is unique among Hardy's fiction because, as many have pointed out, it is his most richly allusive work[1]; as such, I feel, it is his most self-consciously dialogistic. Hardy employs varying styles, viewpoints, themes, allusions, and ideas; and ultimately this slumgullion stew of language breaks down the authority of the artistic and literary modes of expression in which characters like Jude and Sue have wrapped themselves, and even breaks down the novel form that Hardy employs. The almost symbiotic connection between *Jude the Obscure* and the written word poses serious problems in terms of creating a film adaptation, which will be shown; but it has also proved a challenge to some critics of the novel, who, when faced with the multiplicity of *Jude*'s viewpoints, have concentrated on the most obvious ones: those that critique society and apparently assign mankind's troubles to fate.

Why have the critics chosen to focus on these aspects of the novel? One explanation is put forth by Joe Fisher, who believes that Hardy's novels are built on two layers. On the "surface" is a text designed to appeal to the publishers and to the reading public, while below that is a "hidden" text that is radically subversive of the consumer culture in which the novel was produced.[2] Accordingly, critics have either responded to the immediately visible text, or reacted to what they detect moving underneath its surface. This argument is appealing, but I feel it doesn't quite apply to *Jude*.[3] If anything, the novel has been considered subversive since day one: just about every analysis of *Jude* identifies some form of "attack" on one social system or another. I am also not entirely convinced that the novel is "layered"; rather, it seems to be made up of *strands*—some interweaving and crisscrossing, some running side by side, and some undoubtedly loud and colorful in comparison to the quieter and more subdued. No doubt the loudest strands are those dealing with marriage and sex: Arabella is drawn so broadly, Jude's sexual frustrations are made so acute, and Sue's apparent frigidity is so baffling, that these issues demand immediate attention. *Jude's* earliest critics were most drawn to its matrimonial and sexual elements, and the debates they had in 1895 and 1896 have become part of the novel's cultural history. In fact, many of today's critics are still reacting to *Jude's* original reviewers or working within critical frameworks that those reviewers helped establish.

The natural starting point for any discussion of the critical response to the treatment of sex in *Jude* is Margaret Oliphant's review in *Blackwood's* (January 1896), which is most famous for branding the novel "an assault on the stronghold of marriage."[4] Oliphant is usually thought of as one of *Jude's* most Grundyistic critics, but she is actually deeply concerned with what she believes is Hardy's stereotyping and manipulating of female characters to create an attack on matrimony. She charges that Hardy, like other writers of the time, depicts women only as "temptresses" and shows that "it is now the woman who seduces—it is no longer the man."[5] Oliphant's interest in how the novel depicts women and how women affect men in the social sphere makes her sound far more modern than other critics of the 1890s, and she seems downright enlightened compared to the critics who followed. In 1912, Lascelles Abercrombie argued that "any kind of woman would be the ruin of Jude," as all women hold him back from realizing both himself and the ability to reach his goals.[6] Later, D. H. Lawrence in his *Study of Thomas Hardy* (1936)—which is both praised and damned by current feminist critics[7]—allows Hardy's women something no other critic had: a sexual identity of their own; but in the end he still sees women mainly in terms of Jude's story. To Lawrence, Arabella is possessed of healthy female sexuality, which she uses to make a "man" out of Jude; but Sue is a woman who "was born with the vital female atrophied in her: she was almost a male."[8] While Jude's "balance" of masculine and feminine attributes gives him a sense of "wholeness," Sue's "over-balance" of male attributes symbolically robs her of a body; and Jude's fault is that he fails to appreciate Sue as a unique being. In short, Abercrombie and Lawrence argue that one of *Jude's* strongest themes is that Jude needs to connect to something within *himself*; and that women serve either as the barrier or as the key to self-discovery.[9] This view has not entirely been abandoned: in his 1961 "Afterword" to the Signet *Jude the Obscure*, which is still in print, A. Alvarez called Sue and Arabella the platonic "white and black horses" that draw the chariot of Jude's soul.[10]

More recent feminist criticism has largely rescued Sue—and, occasionally, Arabella—from being seen primarily in relation to Jude's story; and it has also revealed that Hardy uses Sue in part to critique the roles that late Victorian culture forced women to play. In Mary Jacobus's ground-breaking 1975 reading, Sue's story is seen as one of revolt—both against conventional society and for "the right to give or withhold herself as she chooses."[11] In 1978, Kathleen Blake convincingly argued that Sue's seemingly schizophrenic behavior is actually an accurate depiction of the mindset of many feminists of the 1890s: she represses her sexuality in order to escape being seen simply as a sexual object.[12] In the past few years, feminist criticism of the novel has addressed not only the roles women play in society and in relation to men, but how society forces men to behave in regard to women and toward themselves. Elizabeth Langland, for instance, claims that Jude succumbs to masculine discourses of scholarship, chivalry, and manliness; and, in trying to live by these codes, he is first trapped into marriage by Arabella's false claim of pregnancy, and then he casts himself in the societal role of seducer after Sue's collapse toward the end of the novel.[13] Similarly, James M. Harding's Freudian treatment of the novel has Jude misreading female sexuality as a kind of "castrated" masculinity, and this fear of the feminine causes him to transfer his desires to Christminster as a means of escaping that threat.[14]

Just as in the early reviews of *Jude the Obscure* we can see the first examples of feminist criticism of the novel, so too can we find the beginning of a tradition that sees *Jude* solely as an attack on societal institutions. An anonymous critic in *Saturday Review* (February 8, 1896) calls the novel a "tremendous indictment of the system which closes our three English teaching universities to what is, and what has always been, the noblest material in the intellectual life of this country—the untaught"[15]; and many subsequent critics have viewed *Jude* as a "problem" novel that exposes the harsh and arbitrary machinations of social systems. The novel thus becomes an angry exposé that is less concerned with reform than with condemnation. This traditional way of reading *Jude* continues today in much Marxist criticism. For instance, Terry Eagleton argues that "Jude's labour-power is exploited literally to prop up the structures which exclude him. His work is restorative of the old world rather than productive of the new, devalued to 'copying, patching and imitating.'" This "old world" ideology is so pervasive that it needn't actively crush those caught in its workings—the self (Jude) ultimately acts as "its own censor, anxiously desiring its own extinction."[16]

Finally, *Jude* has long been seen as Hardy's last attempt in fiction to work out a cohesive theme about the helplessness of mankind in the

"Jude at the Crossroads." An illustration by William Hatherall for the novel's 1895 run in *Harper's.* This image captures the bleakness that many people feel is at the heart of *Jude the Obscure.*

clutches of blind, unfeeling fate. An anonymous reviewer in *Athenaeum* (November 23, 1895) identifies the theme of fate as a growing concern in Hardy's novels and concludes that "in its latest development in this book it becomes almost grotesque,"[17] while William Dean Howells claims that in *Jude* Hardy has made him "feel our unity with that [pre-Christian] world in the very essence of his art. He has given me the same pity and despair in view of the blind struggles of his modern English lower middle-class people that I experience from the destinies of the August figures of Greek fable."[18] Here again we see Hardy as the great tragedian, who has consciously infused all of his novels with classical elements that provide a coherent theme to all of his works. So, just as one strain of criticism has argued that *Jude* is entirely caught up in social concerns, another contends that the novel has loftier, more "humanistic" goals: specifically, that in *Jude,* Hardy employed classical elements that lend a coherent tragic theme to his oeuvre—and the "classicist Hardy," again, is one of his most popular cultural identities.[19]

None of these traditional ways of reading *Jude the Obscure* is wrong, and all shed a great deal of light on Hardy's novel. However, as a book made up of disparate strands, *Jude* generates many simultaneous readings: for nearly every reading the novel creates, it also creates a *counter-reading* that puts the matter of interpretation into question. Take, for example, the way "Fate" is presented. On the eve of Jude's and Sue's planned wedding, Widow Edlin tells the couple the grim tale of their supposed ancestor's bad marriage, which culminates in his being gibbeted for stealing his child's coffin and his wife going mad. The narrator spoofs the tale as an "exhilarating tradition from the widow on the eve of the solemnization" (p. 350), but it resonates with Sue and Jude—and especially with Little Father Time, who, like the voice of doom, declares, "If I was you, Mother, I wouldn't marry Father!" (p. 350). The couple end up casting their own relatively small and insignificant planned marriage in the light of the grandest Greek and biblical tragedies. Sue says,

> "...How horrid that story was last night! It spoilt my thoughts of to-day. It makes me feel as if a tragic doom overhung our family, as it did the house of Atreus."
> "Or the house of Jeroboam," said the quondam theologian [p. 350].

The way this sequence is narrated is representative of Hardy's technique in the novel as a whole. Surrounding the Antigone-like story of the Fawleys' ancestor are multiple interpretive lenses: the satirical voice of the narrator, Widow Edlin's belief that it all may be legend, Little Father Time's grim pronouncement, Jude and Sue's referencing of Greek and biblical tragedies to give the story personal resonance. Four separate ways of reading the incident are brought into play, so it is difficult to determine what, exactly, is the story's significance. Hardy calls into question the characters'—as well as his and our own—understanding of how words relate to their referents, and how our perception of words shapes events.

While the dialogism of Hardy's novel calls into question the workings of fate, so too does it undercut the role society plays in Jude's and Sue's troubles. The characters often express the view that society has rejected them for their unconventionality, and at times the characters *do* suffer at society's hands—but the *novel's* treatment of society is problematic. David Lodge observes, "There *were* very real social and economic forces working against a man in [Jude's] position and with his aspirations, but they are only portrayed in the margins, so to speak, of the story; and Jude never puts them seriously to the test."[20] This is true. Jude immediately abandons his dream of becoming a don once he receives the discouraging letter from Biblioll College; similarly, he discards his plan to become a country parson almost as soon as he conceives it. It appears that Jude—and, it will be revealed, Sue—adheres to rigid principles that causes him to rule out compromise with the world he lives in. Jude and Sue both commit themselves to a kind of orthodoxy, a way of "living by the letter" that is manifested in their attempts to order their lives according to the written and spoken word. Throughout the novel, Jude and Sue rely upon older forms, uses, and expressions of language—Latin, the Bible, Greek mythology—to help them define themselves and the world that surrounds them; but in deferring to language, their sense of self eventually collapses. Similarly, the narrator of *Jude* is constantly deferring to earlier writers, to other genres, and to more exalted forms of expression in order to shape how the story is to be read; but all too often these forms reveal Hardy's own distrust of the power and authority of the Word to create a kind of reality.

Since *Jude the Obscure* constantly questions its own use of the Word, this raises a problem: Can this same novel be adapted to cinematic form and still be considered a faithful and accurate rendering of that novel? To put it bluntly, no. The novel's plot functions are so thoroughly catalyzed by literary referents that the story cannot be brought to the screen as Hardy wrote it. However, the novel has become so encrusted with popular critical interpretations that it *can* be filmed by basing the adaptation not so much on Hardy's *text* as on dominant modes of *reading* that text. This seems to be the approach taken in Michael Winterbottom's 1996 motion picture, simply titled *Jude*. When examined, it can be seen that though he changes Hardy's novel a great deal, Winterbottom remains faithful to one dominant cultural way of interpreting *Jude*—as a form of social protest. Winterbottom's approach is revealed in an interview with *Films in Review*, in which he says, "In any society there are always going to be those who are outside what's accepted, for political reasons or moral reasons, reasons of their behaviour or their ideas ... [You can] see that Jude is not able to fulfill the ambitions and dreams that he has because of economic and cultural problems."[21] The film does focus on "economic" problems, bringing the sordid living conditions of the characters to life in grimy detail; and the "cultural" problems Winterbottom identifies seem to be based on the original controversy that *Jude the Obscure* stirred up: how society responds to sexual relationships. Basically, the film replaces Hardy's admittedly difficult-to-translate booby-trap of a text with a highly visual story that focuses on love and sex; and it creates a dialectic that suggests that it is Jude and Sue's rejection of socially approved sexual relationships that drives the two characters to continued ostracization and eventual tragedy. The film also tries to reinterpret the story in more or less "feminist" terms, and it is here that it truly runs into trouble: for in trying to reproduce two dominant critical discourses that shape a reading of *Jude the Obscure*, the film begins to argue against itself, creating not so much a kind of dialogism akin to what marks the novel, but a kind of cinematic schizophrenia. Winterbottom's *Jude* blames society for sexual repression while it ultimately and unwittingly endorses that repression; so it is unclear what kind of cultural "Hardy" this film creates.

II

Jude the Obscure is a novel that is in perpetual motion: people continually move from location to location, incident to incident, creating a pattern that Richard Carpenter says is "equivalent to the rootlessness and confusion in the lives of the characters."[22] True enough, but rather than simply *mirroring* the characters' mental and physical states, *Jude*'s movements are brought into being by what the characters *see*. At just about every stage in the novel, the major characters must interpret something in the world around them, and how they interpret individual signs determines the courses they take. However, Hardy continually points out that there are no fixed, immutable meanings: no sooner does someone assign a value to what he or she sees, other values become possible. Jude sees masonry as a craft that will lead him to Christminster—"They built in a city; therefore he would learn to build" (pp. 76–7)—and he believes that *Gothic* masonry will be doubly useful to him because a church city needs such masons, and because Sue's father had succeeded as "an ecclesiastical worker in metal" (p. 77). However, when Jude arrives at a Christminster workyard, he comes to a realization that could destroy his plans:

> [He] perceived that at best only copying, patching and imitating went on here; which he fancied to be owing to some temporary and local cause. He did not at that time see that mediævalism was as dead as a fern-leaf in a lump of coal; that other developments were shaping in the world around him, in which Gothic architecture and its associations had no place. The deadly animosity of contemporary logic and vision towards so much of what he held in reverence was not yet revealed to him [p. 131].

This is a cardinal moment: Jude will either realize the folly of his plan and turn back, or adapt and go forward. Jude chooses to interpret the decline in Gothic architecture as a "temporary" problem, and his plans are not changed. He recommits himself to his original interpretation of the value of Gothic architecture and of what it will lead him to. However,

Hardy's narrator *also* commits to a particular interpretation of the scene: a belief that "contemporary logic and vision" will eventually crush Jude's dreams, and that Jude is blind to this. What to Jude isn't so much as a minor setback becomes for the narrator the source of tragedy, but is the narrator's perception automatically the correct one? Many critics believe the narrator purposely shapes the story as a tragedy[23]; but if this is so, the language the narrator uses to craft the tragedy is so loaded that it constantly undercuts his enterprise. Here, the narrator alludes to "other developments" that are shaping the world, but there is no evidence that, though they may be hostile to the Gothic, they are in *themselves* destructive; and given the popularity of the Gothic Revival and the influence of Ruskin's theories on Gothic art during the late Victorian period, the narrator's authority to pronounce medievalism dead is suspect. Ultimately, a reader may wonder *why* Jude pushes himself forward on his quest and *why* the narrator pushes his story toward tragedy.

Another aspect of the narrative voice is that, while it is determined to show that Jude is headed for tragedy, it is equally determined to undercut Jude's position as a tragic character. Hardy's narrator apparently believes that Jude has inadequately prepared himself to face the world, and that he allows himself to fall in love with visions and ideals that have little place in the world of "reality." To the narrator, these flaws make Jude not only tragic, but *absurd*—Jude's story is treated with elements of pathos and farce, and at times farce wins out.[24] Hardy undercuts Jude's status as a tragic character almost from his first appearance, when, as a lonely and orphaned child, and already pining over the imminent departure of Phillotson from Marygreen, Jude is sent to draw water from the well:

> He said to himself, in the melodramatic tones of a whimsical boy, that the schoolmaster had drawn at that well scores of times on a morning like this, and would never draw there any more. "I've seen him look down into it, when he was tired with his drawing, just as I do now, and when he rested a bit before carrying the buckets home! But he was too clever to bide here any longer—a small sleepy place like this!" [p. 49].

Hardy's exposition of Jude's "melodrama" and his fetishizing of the well, indicates what the narrator feels is a problematic trait in the character—one that will eventually have fatal consequences. Jude is a dreamer who turns objects and people into idols, and who allows his dreams to lead him into melodramatic behavior and poor decision making. Barbara DeMille suggests that Jude's idealism stems largely from his desire to escape the "ugliness and stasis" of Marygreen,[25] but it would also appear that his dreams reflect the way Jude has interpreted what he has been *told*. It is popularly thought that Jude's academic dreams are put into his head by Phillotson, but the schoolmaster's plans actually have nothing to do with Jude:

> "My scheme, or dream, is to be a university graduate, and then to be ordained. By going to live at Christminster, or near it, I shall be at head-quarters, so to speak, and if my scheme is practicable at all, I consider that being on the spot will afford me a better chance of carrying it out than I should have elsewhere" [p. 48].

Phillotson does not suggest that Jude should or even can follow in his footsteps: the schoolmaster's only advice is a banal "be kind to ani-mals and birds, and read all you can" (p. 49). Jude's desire for a Christ-minster education is put into his head by Aunt Drusilla, who scolds him by saying, "Why didn't ye get the schoolmaster to take 'ee to Christmin-ster wi' un, and make a scholar of 'ee. ...I'm sure he couldn't ha' took a better one" (p. 52). Drusilla's pronouncement carries tremendous weight with the boy; and it feeds into Jude's hero-worship of Phillotson to cre-ate an idealized version of the city to which Phillotson moves, a city that in turn becomes a place to which Jude can escape from his own unhap-piness:

> "You," [Jude] said, addressing the breeze caressingly, "were in Christmin-ster city between one and two hours ago, floating along the streets, pulling round the weather-cocks, touching Mr. Phillotson's face, being breathed by him; and now you are here, breathed by me—you, the very same."
> Suddenly there came along this wind something towards him—a mes-sage from the place—from some soul residing there, it seemed. Surely it was the sound of bells, the voice of the city, faint and musical, calling to him, "We are happy here!" [p. 63].

Jude's addressing of his feelings to the intangible breeze, which he transfers to the equally intangible city of Christminster, and the overly romanticized tone of his dialogue, serve to indicate that his vision belongs to the realm of fantasy.[26]

Hardy's narrator further attacks the stability of Jude's image of Christ-minster by deploying other points of view. Jude's visions of the city as "the heavenly Jerusalem" (p. 60), "a city of light" (p. 65), and "a castle, manned by scholarship and religion" (p. 65), is offset by the old carter, who tells Jude that Christminster is indeed "a serious-minded place. Not but there's wenches in the streets o' nights" (p. 64). But the dominant "alternate" voice is that of the narrator himself; for instance, Hardy treats Jude's blind, stumbling journey through Christminster at night as something out of a nightmare—Jude is sent down lonely alleyways, locked out of decrepit buildings, and seemingly pursued by ghosts—but when Jude goes to bed that night, his dark journey has made no impression on him: he dreams of the scholars from Christminster's romantic past. Hardy tends to show Jude as nearly struck deaf and blind by his ideals, and whenever he awakens from one dream he is always met with a shock. It is relatively late in the novel—by the time he has been in Christminster for some time—that Jude realizes he has no idea how he should apply for admission to the university. "It would have been better never to have embarked in the scheme at all than to do it without seeing clearly where I am going, or what I am aiming at...," he says. "This hovering outside the walls of the colleges, as if expecting some arm to be stretched out from them to lift me inside, won't do!" (pp. 163–4). But despite this moment of realization, Jude always does expect to be "lifted" into the bosoms of people he wants or into the midst of social arenas to which he aspires.

Hardy's farcical treatment of Jude is nowhere better seen than in the ways Jude deals with setbacks. Hardy brands Jude's behavior "melodramatic," and we can see that Jude's poor decisions are usually followed by personal actions that would be better suited to a romance novel or to a stage show. When Jude realizes that his marriage to Arabella is a mistake, he attempts suicide by trying to jump through a frozen-over pond. When the attempt fails, he hits upon a new idea:

> What could he do of a lower kind than self-extermination; what was there less noble, more in keeping with his present degraded position? He could get drunk. Of course that was it; he had forgotten. Drinking was the regular, stereotyped resource of the despairing worthless. He began to see now why some men boozed at inns. He struck down the hill northwards and came to an obscure public-house. On entering and sitting down the sight of the picture of Samson and Delilah on the wall caused him to recognize the place as that he had visited with Arabella on that first Sunday evening of their courtship. He called for liquor and drank briskly for an hour or more [p. 117].

Jude sees himself as performing certain roles, and that he must conform to what is expected of those roles. If he is not meant to commit suicide, then he must become the only thing he can possibly be—a stereotypical drunk. In a different novel, this scene would play as comic; as it is, the picture of Samson and Delilah is so obvious that the scene borders on parody. This passage also demonstrates how much Jude defers to other authorities: he has read Latin, Greek, and the craft of masonry as the words of a kind of "text" that will open the way to scholarship for him[27]; and he here reads his failed marriage and his family "history" of bad marriages as a text that gives him the authority to recast his life as a drunken, self-destructive wretch. Later, the letter from Tetuphenay will serve as a tangible *written* authority that allows Jude to become drunk and to take actions that result in his dismissal from work.

If Jude allows his actions to be shaped by the figurative texts he sees around him, he also uses actual literary texts to shape how he *perceives* his experiences. Jude often contextualizes his experiences through passages from the Bible in order to magnify and exalt what has happened to him. He rewrites a passage from Matthew to provide divine sanction to his scholarly enterprise: "Yes, Christminster shall be my Alma Mater; and I'll be her beloved son, in whom she shall be well pleased" (p. 80); and he provides a "cosmic" meaning to his rejection by Tetuphenay when he scribbles a passage from Job outside the gates of Biblioll College (p. 169). When at the end of the novel Sue refuses his entreaties to return to him, Jude cries, "Then let the veil of our temple be rent in two from this hour!" (p. 430), apparently forgetting that the passage he relies upon has traditionally been interpreted as signaling God's new *openness* to his creatures, not His separation from them. Finally, Jude decides to adopt and care for Little Father Time so the boy will never have to say as did Job, "Let the day perish wherein I was born" (p. 341); but on his deathbed Jude quotes the same verses, each one punctuated by the parodic "Hurrahs!" from the revelers at the Remembrance games outside. In all of these instances, Jude tries to shape his life along biblical lines, first casting himself as God's anointed, and then as a Job-like figure who suffers at the hands of God. But just as Jude's attempts to read the texts around him lead him to failure and turn him into something of a fool, his attempts to read his life *as* a text comes across as desperate—as if by expressing his experience in biblical terms Jude will give it the grandeur and importance that it lacks. Jude's experiences and the words that signify them do not mesh, and what emerges is an undermining of the meaning of the value that is placed upon language.[28] Effectively, Jude lives by his own particular Word, and, to the narrator, this results in a kind of orthodox thinking that more than anything else dooms Jude to tragedy. Likewise, Sue is bound by her own form of orthodoxy; but while Jude's orthodoxy stems from his reading his life as a biblical text, Sue's is grounded in a commitment to art.

Many have analyzed *Jude* as something of a dramatization of Arnold's theory in *Culture and Anarchy* (1869) that western ideology is divided between a self-disciplining dedication to duty that he identified as "Hebraism," and an idealistic pursuit of intellectualism Arnold called "Hellenism"—with Jude usually considered the Hebrew and Sue the Hellene, and with Hardy showing that in society as a whole a particularly repressive brand of Hebraism is on the ascendent.[29] Such readings do a great deal to explain Jude's consciousness of sin, his devotion to doing the right thing, and especially his reading his life as a biblical tragedy; but Sue's embracing of Hellenism is far more problematic. Sue is indeed the more intellectual of the two, but it would appear that Hardy meant for Sue to be more than simply an "intellectualized" woman: he intended her to strike a chord that his readers would recognize as contemporary radical thinking—specifically, from the Art for Art's Sake movement. In a key scene, Sue tells Phillotson that Jerusalem is a historically unimportant city since "we are not descended from the Jews. There was nothing first-rate about the place, or people, after all—as there was about Athens, Rome, Alexandria, and other old cities" (p. 156). Sue's opinion could be derived from Oscar Wilde's 1891 essay "The Critic as Artist," especially in the view that modern culture can be traced to the Greek "spirit" of ancient Alexandria.[30] Culture, in Wildean terms, is measured by the production and reproduction of art; and aestheticism is a kind of imperative for the survival of civilization, much as sexual selection is an imperative for the survival of the species: "Ethics, like natural selection, make existence possible. Æsthetics, like sexual selection, make life lovely and wonderful, fill it with new forms, give it progress, and variety and change."[31] Whether Hardy was influenced by this passage may never be known, nor is it particularly important,[32] but Sue does seem to share with Wilde an almost Darwinian concern with the cultural evolution of the species. Her personal complaint against Christminster is that the university's unquestioning devotion to medievalism in its theology, pedagogy, and curriculum mire the school in a kind of stasis that will eventually lead to its extinction: "The mediævalism of Christminster must go, be sloughed off, or Christminster itself will have to go" (p. 204). Short of saying that the university should be opened to poor but intelligent men like Jude (p. 205), Sue offers no plans for how the university should be changed after it rids itself of medievalism; but she plainly believes that classicism is a kind of rejuvenating force. She tells Jude that she is "more ancient than mediævalism" (p. 187)—or modern, for that matter—and that her greatest desire is to "get back to the life of my infancy and its freedom" (p. 191), meaning, of course, to the infancy of civilization, to classicism.

Like Jude, Sue also desires to shape both her life and the world around her according to the dictates of a particular Word: in this case, the language of classicism and art. This is nowhere truer than in her approach to sex, which she seeks to place on a "higher" level, one that she defines through allusion to the Greek goddess of spiritual, rather than physical, love:

"Their views [i.e., other peoples'] of the relations of man and woman are limited, as is proved by their expelling me from the school. Their philosophy only recognizes relations based on animal desire. The wide field of strong attachment where desire plays, at least, only a secondary part, is ignored by them—the part of—who is it?—Venus Urania" [p. 223].

Sue says this right after she has learned that Jude is married; and Hardy's suspicion of Sue's belief system is revealed in his terse comment, "Her being able to talk learnedly showed that she was mistress of herself again" (pp. 223–4). Sue's deference to classical mythology is defensive, and it actually creates more pain than it guards against. Her desire to elevate human love to a spiritual plain has the effect of turning love into a kind of art object that is meaningful only if it is approached in a spirit of joyful contemplation. She tells Jude that her feelings for him take the form of a "delight in being with you, of a supremely delicate kind, and I don't want to go further and risk it by—an attempt to intensify it! ...I resolved to trust you to set my wishes above your gratification" (p. 304). This, in a nutshell, is precisely the problem between Sue and Jude: Sue expects Jude to defer to her way of reading the world, and to join him in making love an object of contemplation. Jude for a while is happy to respect her wishes, but he places Sue on a pedestal so high that he cannot reach her. He calls her "you spirit, you disembodied creature, you dear, sweet, tantalizing phantom—hardly flesh at all; so that when I put my arms round you I almost expect them to pass through you as through air" (p. 309); and Sue also succumbs to this vision, insisting that Jude define her as the disembodied spirit of woman from Shelley's "Epipsychidion" (p. 309).

By turning their relationship into a kind of art object, Jude and Sue divorce themselves from meaningful experience. The early days of their relationship are basically arid, with Sue making increasingly intellectualized arguments to keep Jude at bay, and with Jude's growing sexual frustration leaving him more open to the advances of the returned Arabella. But even when Sue gives in to Jude's demands and they turn their relationship from an idealized union into a sexual one, it emerges that, deep down, the couple feels that they have each broken faith with some higher order, and that order acts through Little Father Time to kill the children. Sue's response to the childrens' deaths is to atone through religious orthodoxy, and Jude's is to brand himself a seducer (p. 418). Marjorie Garson has written on *Jude*'s theme of the danger of turning the Word into flesh, and though she attributes these opinions to Hardy, they better fit Sue's feelings about making her artistic relationship into a physical one: "...real danger lies in inscribing the word, giving it a material body. The incarnate word takes the place of what it signifies, precludes its fulfilment.

Incarnation means betrayal in this novel: to give or to take a body is to fall away from reality, to be involved in death."[33] By trading her spiritual relationship for a physical one, Sue feels the ideal has been destroyed.[34]

Sue's project to create for herself an existence along artistic lines is further undermined— and eventually destroyed—by her susceptibility to other discourses; specifically, she is in constant danger of succumbing to the religious orthodoxy she claims to oppose. Immediately after she tells Jude that she wishes to return to her Hellenic "infancy," she also confesses, "You don't know what's inside me. ...The Ishmaelite" (p. 192). That a person who associates herself with Hellenic idealism should see herself as a biblical outcast is odd, as are her violently mixed feelings about her plan to live with Jude a daringly new kind of lifestyle that will eventually benefit humanity. In a letter to Phillotson, Sue sounds very much like Wilde where she writes, "I don't want to be respectable! To produce 'Human development in its richest diversity' (to quote your Humboldt) is to my mind far above respectability" (p. 287); however, when Phillotson fails to respond, Sue resorts to orthodoxy: "No poor woman has ever wished more than I that Eve had not fallen, so that (as the primitive Christians believed) some harmless mode of vegetation might have peopled Paradise" (p. 287). If the novel deals with the clash between Hebraism and Hellenism, it is Sue who illustrates this division[35]: she is caught between two modes of being. After Little Father Time kills her children and she suffers a miscarriage, Sue rejects her Hellenism and lives a particularly grotesque and self-flagellating life of Hebraic renunciation.

Even though Jude's and Sue's tragedies are largely the result of how they read the world, it can still be argued that they are "unconventional" and are therefore punished by an extremely conventional society. This is certainly true in the scenes where Jude is fired by Willis and where his family is threatened with eviction from the Christminster boarding house; but, on the whole, society's reaction to Jude and Sue remains mixed—or even indifferent. Jude himself recognizes this when he tells Sue that, even though their divorces were granted on false charges of adultery, the law would never have taken the time to investigate whether charges against "poor obscure people" like themselves were true or not (p. 322).[36] To be noticed by society, one must be a "somebody," which neither Jude nor Sue is. When they do run into trouble it is at Aldbrickham; and here they suffer not so much because they flout society's laws or ignore established codes of morality, but because they inadequately define their relationship to a group of small-town busybodies. The couple is the subject of rumors that are only intensified by their running off for several days and then, upon returning, "let[ting] it be understood indirectly, and with total indifference and weariness of mien, that they were legally married at last" (p. 367). This public act, instead of putting rumors to rest, only make things worse. By living their lives so publicly yet so privately—refusing to confirm things one way or another—Jude and Sue are scorned, and Jude's headstone-carving business suffers. Yet Hardy indicates things needn't be hard for the couple: it is only that "their temperaments were precisely of a kind to suffer from this atmosphere, and to be indisposed to lighten it by vigorous and open statements" (p. 368). The suggestion is that things would go better for the couple if they'd simply be *open* about their relationship, or if they'd at least tell their neighbors to mind their own business.

In short, society in *Jude* is not monolithic, and individual actions within society produce varied reactions. This is nicely illustrated by what happens to Phillotson. Certainly if there is anything more shocking than an unmarried couple living together, it is a husband who willingly lets his wife live with another man ("What will Shaston say!" a flabbergasted Gillingham demands [p. 295]); but Phillotson refuses to resign his position as schoolmaster, which he feels would be an admission of his "having acted wrongly" by Sue (p. 312). At a public meeting, Phillotson defends his actions, which does not restore his job, but which does earn him the admiration of several in the audience—even if these admirers are largely "a curious and interesting group of itinerants" (p. 312) who spark the uproarious scuffle in the schoolroom between Phillotson's foes and supporters. Despite the farce of this sequence, Phillotson emerges as a somewhat admirable figure: he presents his case *before* society and defends himself, whereas Jude and Sue shy away from conflict with society. Significantly, though Phillotson does become something of a pariah among the educational establishment, he is able to return to Marygreen to teach, while Jude, Sue, and their ever-growing family are continually fleeing the cloud they perceive to be overhead.

What should be evident by this point is that *Jude the Obscure* is, as Hardy stated, a book that is "all contrasts"; but while he saw those contrasts in terms of "Sue & her heathen gods set against Jude's reading the Greek Test[ament]; Christminster academical, Chr in the slums; Jude the saint, Jude the sinner; Sue the Pagan, Sue the saint; marriage, no marriage; &c. &c.,"[37] the greatest contrasts are actually between and among the various discourses the characters use: Jude's reading the world with kindness and sympathy is mocked by Arabella's vulgarity and practicality; and Jude's attempts to reach idealistic and unobtainable goals are contrasted with the successful opportunism of Arabella, Vilbert, and even the Kennetbridge musician who gives up writing beautiful hymns to sell wine. Similarly, Sue's artistic enterprise is subverted by her own latent weakness to religious discourse. Jude and Sue both make their sexual nonconformity a sign of their ostracization, while Arabella and Phillotson—themselves sexual "rebels"—are left relatively unscarred, and Arabella certainly prospers. Even individual points of view are constantly being challenged: for Phillotson's belief that Sue should be set at liberty, there is Gillingham telling Phillotson he should repress Sue; for Aunt Drusilla's dire warnings against Fawleys getting married, there is Widow Edlin's parodic depiction of bad Fawley marriages; for the extinguishing of the lives of Jude and his children, and for Sue's grotesque return to religion and to Phillotson, there is Arabella and Vilbert creating a profitable union. And for the characters who read their lives as tragedies, there is a narrator who often reads their lives as farces and missed opportunities.

What ties these sets of oppositions together is the failure of language to create an acceptable reality, and this concern is embedded in the very structure of the book itself. At times it seems that Hardy is working at cross-purposes. In the preface to the first edition, Hardy wrote that one of his intentions was to "tell, without a mincing of words, of a deadly war waged between flesh and spirit" (p. 39), but at times a reader must wonder what words Hardy *wasn't* mincing. Beyond parodying and undermining the characters and their points of view, Hardy's language at times obscures his own narrative enterprise. Frequently the novel relies on exalted language and allusion to refer to the characters, their actions, and their surroundings; and, again, a strong dissonance is created between the word and its referent. The first part of the novel, "At Marygreen," is thick with such elevated language. For instance, when Farmer Troutham beats Jude, the narrator says that the sounds of the clacker as it hits the boy's buttocks reach only "the ears of distant workers," but that they echo "from the brand-new church tower just behind the mist, towards the building of which structure the farmer had largely subscribed, to testify his love for God and man" (p. 55). Hardy's magnification of the beating to indict Troutham's hypocrisy and the complicity of organized religion in Jude's punishment is impressive, but it also seems a case of overkill, as if the narrator is so blatantly stacking the deck against Jude that a reader cannot escape the conclusion that Jude's life is fated to be one of misery and tragedy. It is also hard to escape feeling that, in his zeal to create a tragedy for Jude, the narrator is often grossly unfair to the character. To Hardy, "every clod and stone" of the "utilitarian" field Jude works comes equipped with a rich history of both fertile harvests and sexual couplings; but "this neither Jude nor the rooks around him considered. For them it was a lonely place, possessing, in the one view, only the quality of a work-ground, and in the other that of a granary good to feed in" (p. 53). Does Hardy somehow expect the child Jude—and, strangely enough, the *rooks*—to have access to this incredibly idiosyncratic knowledge?[38] In another odd passage, young Jude looks out toward Christminster, and the narrator says that, "In the glow he seemed to see Phillotson promenading at ease, like one of the forms in Nebuchadnezzar's furnace" (p. 63). The question here is, *whose* point of view are we receiving? Is the boy Jude so well-read that he is already employing biblical allusions to shape his perceptions, or is Hardy reading the Bible ironically into Jude's point of view? Such questions of perspective abound in *Jude*, and in places the allusions are so heavy-handed that, rather than achieving clarity, Hardy seems to be questioning or even concealing the meaning of what he has just presented.

In one of the strangest authorial gestures in the novel, Hardy opens Part V, Chapter 5, by distancing himself from Jude's and Sue's decision to not marry: "The purpose of a chronicler of moods and deeds does not require him to express his personal views upon the grave controversy above given" (p. 357). *Why* does the narrator choose to be silent on this one issue, where elsewhere he indicts the Melchester Training-School for cooperating in a social system that brands women "The Weaker" in nature (p. 194), and where he condemns the university with the searing line, "the outer walls of Sarcophagus College—silent, black, and windowless—threw their four centuries of gloom, bigotry, and decay into the room [Sue] occupied" (p. 406)? Hardy says that he is not *required* to comment on the marriage issue, so, perhaps, like Bartleby, he "prefers not to," but it could simply be that Hardy felt he had already given that narrative function over to the *characters*. With the possible exception of the stonemasons, just about every character has *something* to say about why people marry, what the purpose of marriage is, and how marriage serves society's needs. Enormous stretches of Parts IV, V, and VI contain nothing but dialogue, and much of it concerns living together as a family and social unit. Hardy basically lets the characters have their say, offering little or no support to any of their viewpoints. The arguments are left to stand *as* arguments; the guiding narrative voice grows increasingly silent starting with Part IV.

Hardy also leaves quite a lot of detail in the margins of the narrative, or deals with things so elliptically that the reader is forced to *infer* what is going on. The passages leading up to Sue's eventual "surrender" to Jude make no mention of the issue dividing the pair; but Jude's dialogue is often so similar to that of the stereotypical seducer that at times he sounds like Alec d'Urberville ("It is all very well to preach about self-control, and the wickedness of coercing a woman. But I should just like a few virtuous people who have condemned me in the past ... to have been in my tantalizing position with you through these late weeks!" [pp. 331–2]), and

Sue sounds so much like the helpless victim ("I have nobody but you, Jude, and you are deserting me!" [p. 332]) that the reader certainly *knows* what is going on. It is interesting that in both of these sexually charged scenes, the narrator is all but absent: he relies on the characters' *words* to convey meaning, and the words never in fact *specify* what is happening. Rather than *showing* the "deadly war between flesh and spirit," Hardy lets his characters talk around it, and the reader must rely upon his or her store of cultural knowledge to fill in the blanks. In this way, both the characters and the reader—perhaps even the narrator—are shielded from naming the act itself.

Even what is usually considered one of the novel's most outrageous sequences, the "pizzle" scene, is highly elliptical and more suggestive than explicit. It is amusing that the word "pizzle" is so commonly employed by critics to define "the offending object," since the word is never used in the text: it comes to us only from a letter Hardy wrote to Edmund Gosse. In the text, the organ is simply "a piece of flesh, the characteristic part of a barrow-pig, which the country-men used for greasing their boots, as it was useless for any other purpose" (p. 80). Not very revealing, when it comes right down to it; and John Sutherland suggests that Hardy's reference to a barrow-pig is itself so obscure that it is easy to misunderstand just *what* the "characteristic part" is. To Sutherland, Hardy "continues to snare the readers into doing what he might otherwise criticize the novelist for—naming the pig's organ. Tactically, it is a devious and effective omission of frankness in a novel whose proclaimed boast is to eschew equivocation."[39] It is a bit of deviousness that Hardy also *worked* to attain; for, as is generally known, the pizzle sequence was far more explicit in the original magazine version of *Jude*, and over the years Hardy revised and softened the sequence.[40] Of course, for years Hardy struggled first with the manuscript and then with the published version of *Jude*, trying to force it into shape and eventually turning it into something of palimpsest. Patricia Ingham has shown that, when Hardy began writing the novel, there was no Phillotson: Jude wanted to go to Christminster only to be with *Sue*. Phillotson and Jude's academic ambitions are a late addition, which perhaps explains why the separate pursuits of Sue and Christminster seem to be so raggedly stitched together. The effect of Hardy's revisions is that *Jude* is less open and communicative than he meant it to be, as if Hardy could not find the right words to express what is at the heart of the novel. In the end, *Jude the Obscure* registers a deep and abiding distrust of the Word: the characters fail to create an adequate reality for themselves along literary lines; and Hardy the novelist juggles to find the appropriate literary language by which he can tell the story of these characters. These discourses frequently mesh, frequently work against one another, so all forms of interpretations are made risky. *Jude* is largely incoherent, and perhaps Hardy realized it couldn't be anything other than incoherent; but over one hundred years of criticism have given us versions of the novel we can understand. And it is through the lenses of social and feminist criticism that Michael Winterbottom created his film called, simply, *Jude*.

III

In the previous two chapters, I examined Schlesinger's *Far from the Madding Crowd* and Polanski's *Tess* not just as "movie versions" of Hardy's novels, but as films that fit into specific cinematic movements and as representatives of the directors' work. This task is slightly more difficult when it comes to Michael Winterbottom's *Jude*, since it belongs to a movement in British cinema the impact of which is still being debated; and because, while Winterbottom's talent is widely acknowledged, he is a relative newcomer as a director (*Jude* is only the second of his theatrical films), and his output has been so varied that he is difficult to pin down. Added to this complication is that *Jude* still hasn't really registered either on moviegoers or on Hardy scholars. Before the film opened, Peter Widdowson expressed fear that the cinematic *Jude* would "forever [put] a frame round" the novel; but so far this frame has not been constructed, and Widdowson is to date the *only* Hardy critic to write extensively on the film.[41] *Jude* performed poorly in England and America,[42] and it is not widely discussed in film studies. Time may prove *Jude* to be as important to a cultural construction of Hardy as are the films of *Far from the Madding Crowd* and *Tess*, but currently it is generally known as a seldom-seen Brit flick that highbrow critics tended to love, and which offers another fine performance of a "period" character by Kate Winslet. Still, Winterbottom's *Jude* raises two immediate questions: Why make a film of *Jude the Obscure*, and why was it made when it was?

One possible reason is the prospect of a big success on both sides of the Atlantic. Since the mid–1980s, many film adaptations of literary "greats" such as E. M. Forster, Jane Austen, and Henry James have been hits in England and especially in America, and BBC Films may have hoped that Hardy had the same box office potential as Austen and company. Certainly the casting of Winslet as Sue represents the producers' desire to cash in on a proven commodity, since she had won both critical acclaim and wide popularity for playing characters from the past (e.g., Peter Jackson's *Heavenly Creatures* [1994], set in 1950s New Zealand) and especially for appearing in "period" adaptations of literary "classics" (e.g., Ang Lee's

Sense and Sensibility [1995] and—almost simultaneously with *Jude*—Kenneth Branagh's *Hamlet* [1996], set in the late nineteenth century).[43] In America at least, Winslet was the film's strongest selling point—in the film's poster, her face is placed right next to Christopher Eccleston's ("HIS WORLD COULD NEVER CHANGE ... UNTIL SHE BECAME HIS WORLD," the film's tag line reads)—and a good many reviews were focused primarily on Winslet's performance.[44]

Still, though the producers may have wished to market the film as another *Sense and Sensibility*, it is clear that Winterbottom and screenwriter Hossein Amini had no desire to create a stolid literary adaptation on the order of Merchant-Ivory.[45] Where so many of the "filmed books" of the eighties and early nineties are brightly lit, leisurely paced, and abounding in sumptuous period detail, Winterbottom's *Jude* is stark, spare, fast-paced, and deliberately vague as to its time setting—though the final sequence is labeled "Christmas 1889." *Jude* is also radically different from both the Forster and Austen adaptations and from the previous two Hardy films in that Winterbottom and Amini have no particular reverence for the text: several minor characters have been eliminated, the dialogue has been modernized, many plot functions have been deleted, and the ending has been completely changed. Any literary-minded filmgoer expecting to see an English literary masterpiece faithfully captured on celluloid is in for a shock with *Jude*.

The many changes in the story were made, I believe, for two reasons. First, of course, is because *Jude the Obscure* is not a novel that lends itself easily to cinematic transference: considerable adaptation would inevitably have been needed. Second, Winterbottom's film reflects a major change in British cinema and in the attitude of British filmmakers toward literary adaptations. As explained by Andrew Higson, many of the period or "heritage" films and literary adaptations that were produced in the 1980s can be seen as ironic reflections on the Thatcher era: at a time when the Conservative government was dismantling established socialist systems and championing private enterprise, and while Thatcher herself was advocating a return to "Victorian" family values, filmmakers were reacting against Thatcherism by turning to an earlier era—predominantly the Edwarian period—to present a nostalgic vision of a more stable past.[46] Representative heritage films are usually thought to be James Ivory's enormously popular and visually lush adaptations of Forster, *A Room with a View* (1986), *Maurice* (1987), and *Howards End* (1992), which all depict an idealized, pastoral version of England. Though all three films raise issues that are relevant to the 1980s and nineties—the position of women in society, the treatment of homosexuals by an intolerant and narrow-minded culture, the emergence of a suffocating capitalist class—they also, in the words of Cairns Craig, "situate us firmly in the barricaded room of an English identity from which the outside world is viewed from above and without, not engaged with."[47] By setting these films in the distant past, the social concerns they raise are made subservient to gorgeous location photography and impeccable period detail.

Such was not the case with the literary adaptations and costume dramas that emerged later in the nineties, which—for want of a better term— can be called the "Post-Thatcher" era. If the "heritage" films of the eighties sought to escape what was seen as the dismantling of cherished social institutions in the present, the heritage films of the nineties readily acknowledge life *after* these institutions have been disassembled, when the government is seen as a faceless entity that privileges the wealthy and leaves the poor to fend for themselves—unless the government wishes to punish or abuse them. This trend is part of a general movement that has been emerging in British cinema in recent years: the depiction of men and women cast adrift and left to find a place for themselves in a cold, materialistic society and in a landscape that often resembles a wasteland. Danny Boyle's *Shallow Grave* (1994) and *Trainspotting* (1995)—which have become touchstone films of the nineties—can almost be seen as dissections of life in the post-Thatcher era. *Shallow Grave*'s yuppies degenerate into murderous caricatures of capitalists, while *Trainspotting*'s Glasgow youths seem caught in stasis, moving through the slums in search of the next heroin hit. There is a sense of displacement to *Trainspotting* that is also present in such films as Mike Leigh's *Naked* (1993). Its drifter-hero sees apocalypse in the coming millennium, and he ruthlessly interrogates people from all class levels until they confess how tenuous their notions of stability are. In a parallel story, a rich yuppie gleefully, sadistically, and openly abuses and rapes almost every woman he comes across; that he is never made to pay for his acts suggests his crass and grotesque consumption of everything in sight is part of societal norms. Beneath the veneer of respectability is insatiable greed and violence—the harbingers in this film of social collapse.

Even many recent British comedies derive their force and humor from societal displacement. In popular films like *Brassed Off!* (Mark Herman, 1996) and *The Full Monty* (Peter Cattaneo, 1997), the alienating effect of Thatcherite policies on the working classes are most laid bare—*literally*, in the case of *Full Monty*. In both films, a blue collar industry has been shut down by Conservative budget-cutting measures, and those who have depended their whole lives on the local industry are forced to redefine themselves in parodic terms. One coal miner in *Brassed Off!* transforms himself into a clown who performs at children's parties, and it is in clown makeup that he curses Margaret Thatcher and attempts suicide, and in *The Full Monty*, the unemployed men find in stripping a kind of redemption through degradation.

Literary adaptations and costume dramas were also popular throughout the '90s, but the subject matter was often darker than what was seen in the '80s. Iain Softley's adaptation of James' *The Wings of the Dove* (1997), for instance, focuses on English men and women so desperate to reclaim their lost class and social status that they play on the emotions of a dying American woman in hopes of inheriting her money. And the Victorian era, once held up by Margaret Thatcher as the exemplar of "family values," was subject to a merciless attack from filmmakers who emphasized that Victoria's age was one of systematic marginalization of lower classes and ethnic and sexual minorities by an exploitative and degenerative bourgeoisie. *Angels and Insects* (Philip Haas, 1995), *Wilde* (Brian Gilbert, 1998), and *The Governess* (Sandra Goldbacher, 1998) all seem bent on knocking eminent Victorians from their pedestals. In Haas' film, the upper class is ostensibly concerned with maintaining the virtues of domesticity and championing scientific exploration and Darwinism, but these prove to be a mere façade for their own incestuous degeneracy, while the films of Gilbert and Goldbacher are concerned with the Victorians' persecution of the other—Oscar Wilde in the former for being homosexual, and Minnie Driver's governess character in the latter for being both Jewish and a woman. In these films, the Victorians publicly promote decency and propriety, which they use as excuses to shove into the margins of society those who don't fit, or as clubs against those who break convention. It is within this movement in British film to depict the outsider as victimized by uncaring, even brutal, social system that Winterbottom's *Jude* may be placed.

Winterbottom began his career on television, directing a pair of documentaries on Ingmar Bergman, and he made perhaps his biggest impression as the director of the first few episodes of "Cracker," the dark, probing crime drama that delves into the abnormal psychoses of criminals—as well as into the neuroses of its psychiatrist hero. Winterbottom's interest in the "darker" elements of society is played out in his first feature, *Butterfly Kiss* (1995). Focusing on the relationship between a seemingly deranged drifter, Eunice (Amanda Plummer), and the sweet but slow Miriam (Saskia Reeves), Winterbottom brings out the aimlessness of contemporary English life. The film's controlling metaphor—as it will be in *Jude*—is the road: Eunice and Miriam travel a series of impersonal highways, stopping for brief encounters with people that usually result in Eunice's murdering someone and stealing a car. Eunice's killings are never pointless: at one point she cries out, "God's forgotten me! I kill people and nothing happens! You'd think he'd smite me or take me into bondage!" Eunice *wishes* to be punished by a greater authority—she even scourges her flesh with barbed chains and painful piercings—but God *doesn't* make her accountable for her crimes; and, in contrast to a film like *Thelma and Louise*, the police are nowhere in sight to suggest she can atone on a purely temporal level. The police are presumably behind the camera in the scenes where Miriam faces the audience and relates the story, putting them on the same level as the viewers of the film—capable of seeing, but incapable of acting. In *Butterfly Kiss*, human activity has been reduced to a series of brief, violent moments carried out inside an indifferent and unresponsive social system.

Winterbottom's third film, and *Jude*'s successor, *Welcome to Sarajevo* (1997), also tackles the theme of societal indifference, but here the director turns his attention to a current crisis—the Bosnian war—and clearly blames geopolitical realities for allowing the war to continue. Winterbottom uses a great deal of actual news footage from Bosnia, ranging from shattered bodies in the streets to human skeletons in the concentration camps, to blur the lines between the movie he has created and the very real war in the Balkans, and the film is intercut with soundbites of politicians like the first George Bush and John Major publicly declaring their reluctance to involve themselves in the fighting. The message of the film is clear: the suffering of innocents—mostly children—in Bosnia exists because political leaders in the west don't care enough to put an end to it. Winterbottom's concern for society's marginalized people seems arbitrarily inserted into the noirish thriller *I Want You* (1998), in which two of the characters are war refugees; and since this film he has moved into other areas, directing the Altmanesque family drama *Wonderland* (1999), as well as *The Claim*, a western loosely based on *The Mayor of Casterbridge* (see Chapter 6).

Since—at the start of his career at least—Winterbottom was most concerned with those who are "outside" the societal mainstream and who suffer at the hands of cold and indifferent power structures, his attraction to *Jude the Obscure* should be clear. The novel, after all, has often been recast as an angry indictment of society, or as a passionate plea for acceptance of the outsider, or as a bleak depiction of lives buffeted by blind fate, and Winterbottom's *Jude* stays faithful to these assumptions. The director's focus is almost exclusively on the lives of Jude and Sue, and through the use of realism he shows that the couple is turned into outsiders by a hegemonic power structure that will not tolerate them. Though *Jude* is not exactly a "faithful" version of *Jude the Obscure*, it is in fact a *familiar*

Sue (Kate Winslet) and Jude (Christopher Eccleston) in one of *Jude's* few happy moments.

version of the novel, one that confirms our own cultural expectations of Hardy even though Winterbottom produces a version of Hardy that is, ironically, in itself repressive.

The film *does* try to follow the novel and to find adequate visual companions to Hardy's written word, most obviously in its use of the novel's original section headings—"At Marygreen," "At Christminster," etc.—as intertitles. Widdowson charges that these headings are meaningless to anyone unfamiliar with Hardy's map of Wessex,[48] but they *do* emphasize the film's rapid shifts in locale; and Winterbottom usually enhances their significance by prefacing the intertitles with shots of characters on the road or in trains. Just as Winterbottom captures the novel's sense of fitful wandering, he has managed to find locations that visually evoke the places Hardy wrote about. The Christminster sequences, for instance, were shot in Edinburgh, where the university, as Rosemary Ashton says, has "a starkness, a forbidding quality, which makes the point visually that Hardy makes verbally in his novel, namely that poor stonemasons like Jude need not apply to get learning within the thick imposing stone walls that he is seen to be restoring."[49] Other locations utilized are New Zealand for the landscapes and Northumberland for the village scenes, and Yorkshire for the winter sequences. Although Winterbottom succumbs to pastoralizing the scenes of Jude's and Arabella's courtship and wedding, he uses his locations to create a sense of barrenness and dislocation. If anything, this *seems* like what a film of *Jude the Obscure should* look like.

In spite of its visual fidelity, *Jude* truly sets itself apart from Hardy in terms of its tone. While Hardy's *Jude* is continually teetering between tragedy and farce, subverting its own use of words, Winterbottom's *Jude* remains a tragedy of strict and uncompromising realism. Hardy's treatment of the murder of the children is potent stuff, but it is still handled with a level of abstraction: the narrator remains flat and neutral, and Jude and Sue manage to insulate themselves from the killings by comparing them to the tragedy of *Agamemnon* (p. 413). It is an unpleasant scene, but also a patently unreal one. In *Jude*, though, the same sequence is unflinchingly real. Winterbottom uses a hand-held camera to follow Jude into the room where he discovers the corpses, and the camera rapidly scans the bodies like a news photographer would cover a recently unearthed crime scene. The childrens' faces are blue, and "Juey's" black tongue lolls grotesquely from his mouth. After Jude moves the bodies to the bed, he breaks down crying; and the camera mercilessly stays above Sue as she lies in a fetal position on the floor, gyrating, twisting, and shrieking in grief and agony. The whole sequence is painful and nearly unwatchable, but it underscores Winterbottom's point: these people are *real*, and the death of the children causes *real* suffering.

The film further differentiates itself from the novel in its approach to the characters, situations, and dialogue. Amini's script eliminates almost all of the secondary characters, leaving only the four principals, Aunt Drusilla, and the Christminster stonemasons. None of the characters who were cut are particularly crucial to the story's *plot*, but they are contributors to the novel's multiplicity of viewpoints. Each one offers his or her own perspective or use of dialogue, which usually undercuts or questions the perspectives of the leading characters, and sometimes that of the narrator. Winterbottom's film is far more "fixed" in terms of the viewpoints it presents: what the characters say all harmoniously support the director's social critique. Likewise, the situations are presented in a manner that is much less fluid and open to question than is Hardy's: Winterbottom's camera usually doesn't approximate the characters' points of view, so what we see is scrupulously controlled by the director. Finally, Hardy's dialogue has been modernized, simplified, and stripped of its allusiveness. If the characters in *Jude the Obscure* are rendered almost inarticulate by their devotion to allusion and to elevated speaking, the characters in *Jude* are unremarkably plain-spoken. Compare the way Jude rebukes Sue after she has embraced orthodoxy. In the novel, Jude declares,

"You make me hate Christianity, or mysticism, or Sacerdotalism, or whatever it may be called, if that's which has caused this deterioration in you. That a woman-poet, a woman-seer, a woman whose soul shone like a diamond—whom all the wise of the world would have been proud of, if they could have known you—should degrade herself like this! I am glad I had nothing to do with Divinity—damn glad—if it's going to ruin you in this way!" [p. 426].

In the film, Jude's remonstrance is a simple, "You make me hate Christianity and God and whatever else has reduced you to this state!" The difference isn't simply that Amini's dialogue telescopes Hardy's: Jude in the novel relies on the word "*or*" to indicate he doesn't know *what* has happened to Sue. The film Jude knows his targets: "Christianity *and* God" are responsible for Sue's change. Jude's concern in the novel isn't so much for Sue *herself*, but for what Sue means *to him:* he still wishes to cling to her as a transcendent vision. But the film Jude is not so deluded: his language, like that of everyone else in the film, is blunt and ordinary. And through the spoken word the characters help construct Winterbottom's vision of a society that arbitrarily deceives and punishes.

The first few scenes of *Jude*, shot in stark black and white, establish in no uncertain terms that it is society and not Jude's perceptions that lays the groundwork for his tragedy. The first three scenes are roughly analogous to the first two chapters of Hardy's novel, but they are re-arranged so as to establish the social hierarchy's role in oppressing Jude, and the false promise of hope it extends. The opening scene shows young Jude (James Daley) feeding the rooks he is supposed to be scaring away. Jude's action is prompted, perhaps, by the sight of a gibbet from which several rook carcasses dangle—a touch so Hardean it almost comes as a surprise to realize that this moment is *not* in the novel. Jude is caught and beaten by Troutham, and as the farmer strikes the boy, he taunts him by yelling, "You've gone up in the world!" Troutham's mockery is made significant in the next scene, when Jude limps into the bakery and Aunt Drusilla (June Whitfield) exclaims, "Did he hit you? Shame on you for letting him! His father was my father's journeyman!" Within its first five minutes, the film establishes that Jude and the Fawleys are alienated from their proper place within society. Through some unexplained disruption in the status quo, Jude is now on the bottom rung of the social ladder, and men like Troutham actively work to keep him there. Aunt Drusilla's harsh words are spoken less to encourage Jude to stand up for himself than they are a bleak acknowledgment of the Fawleys' loss of status. Winterbottom shows that, from the beginning, Jude is an alien, and he is in danger of being beaten down every time he tries to "go up" in the world.

Jude's connection to Phillotson (Liam Cunningham) is dramatized in a scene where the departing schoolmaster takes Jude to a rise in the road and points to Christminster in the distance. Phillotson explains,

> "If you want to do anything in life, Jude, that's where you have to go— even if it means giving up everything else for a while. You have to read your books while your friends are out playing, get out of bed early in the morning when it's freezing cold, study every chance you get. One day it will all pay off, I promise you. Once you're there, everything's open to you. You can become anything you want. You can choose your own future."

This is, of course, a direct change from the novel, where Phillotson does not so much as hint that Jude has a place at Christminster. However, Phillotson here puts Jude on the course he will follow for roughly the first half of the film: he *directly* holds out the promise of advancement in the world. Since Jude is not the originator of his own aspirations, there is no irony in Winterbottom's treatment of them—no sense that Jude has put himself on a course he is unprepared to follow, or that he pursues avenues that will prove to be dead-ends. After the scene on the road, the film jumps ahead in time some ten years (and shifts to color, which will remain until the end), and picks up the action with the adult Jude (Eccleston) taking a break from work as a stonemason to read Latin under a shade tree. Since Jude rejects the society of the jovial stonemasons to study, we can safely assume that for years he has followed the clear course that Phillotson laid out for him. During his courtship of Arabella (Rachel Griffiths), Jude tells her, "I'm going to be a scholar. Maybe even a professor one day." When he makes it to Christminster, Jude sends a letter of application to the "Dean of Admissions" of Biblioll College, showing that he is ready to join it. What is never made entirely clear is whether Jude is self-taught, or if he has received additional schooling. Likewise, we are not told that Jude picks up masonry as part of his vaguely defined plan to get into Christminster. He appears to be pursuing an attainable goal, so when Jude fails to gain admission into the college, it truly seems that he has been betrayed by society— for it was society, in the form of the schoolteacher Phillotson, that put the desire to become a scholar into Jude's head in the first place, and which guaranteed him that his dream was entirely possible.

However, Winterbottom does show that society's treatment of Jude is not entirely arbitrary: Jude is treated as he is because of his class situation. The director's sympathy for the working class can be seen in his depiction of the stonemasons—both at Marygreen and at Christminster— who are always good-hearted, fun-loving, down-to-earth, and genial. The pub scene, in which Jude is challenged by an undergraduate to recite his

Apostle's Creed in Latin, is directed so that it clearly favors the proletariat: the well-dressed but effete—even campy—students occupy one side of the pub, and the ragged but amiable stonemasons are on the other. Jude is clearly at home with the masons—he drinks his disappointment away with *them*, instead of by himself—and, as the visual divide between the classes makes clear, Jude has been thwarted for trying to move from the place where he belongs to one where he is not wanted.

Just as Jude is made more understandable by making him into a marginalized alien, Sue is made more coherent by disentangling her ambitions from her artistic ideals and turning her into something of a modern feminist and a political radical. While Jude is tailing her throughout Christminster, she goes to a political meeting where a Scotsman advocates the overthrow of the class system; significantly, in the novel, Jude follows her into a *church*. Sue also boldly proclaims her "New Woman" status to Phillotson: "Please don't call me a 'clever girl,' Mr. Phillotson—there are too many of us about these days!" During the scenes of Jude's and Sue's developing friendship at Christminster (scenes that have been fleshed out from the novel), Winterbottom shows that Sue is, in fact, more a woman of the twentieth century than the nineteenth, and that she is every bit the equal of any man: Jude takes her to a pub with his fellow stonemasons, and Sue robustly drinks, shows off while smoking a cigarette, and laughs with the men over their jokes and good-natured flirting.[50] Amini's script adds several scenes to the "In Christminster" section in which Sue "banters" with Jude, which show that she is not only capable of matching Jude

Kate Winslet as a thoroughly modern Sue.

intellectually, but that she has evolved beyond Jude's childlike awe at and delight with the medieval university setting. Sue's comfort with men and her ability to stand with them on their own turf are all related to her own concept of how the sexes interact. After Sue runs from the Melchester teacher's college and finds shelter with Jude, the following exchange occurs:

> SUE: I'm not afraid of any man.
> JUDE: Why not?
> SUE: Because no man will touch a woman unless she invites him to. Until she says with a nod or a smile, "Come on," he's always afraid. If you never say it or look it, he'll never come. *You're* the timid sex.

The dialogue is derived from Hardy, but it is put into a context that fits the director's purposes. In the novel, Sue is speaking of how she obtained her education by blurring her own sexual identity:

> "I have no fear of men, as such, nor of their books. I have mixed with them—one or two of them particularly—almost as one of their own sex. I mean I have not felt about them as most women are taught to feel—to be on guard against attacks on their virtue, for no average man—no man short of a sensual savage—will molest a woman by day or night, at home or abroad, unless she invites him. Until she says by a look 'Come on' he is always afraid to, and if you never say it, or look it, he never comes" [pp. 201–2].

As Kathleen Blake explains, Sue in the novel strives *not* to look, say or *feel* "Come on": in this way she can escape being sexually objectified.[51] In addition, I feel it allows her to enter into an intellectual relationship with a man without fear of sex interfering. Of course, Sue remains oblivious to the fact she *is* sending signals to "come on," for immediately after this passage she tells Jude of her unconsummated relationship with the frustrated Christminster undergraduate (omitted from the film), and certainly Jude remains confused for much of the book as to whether or not she is telling him to "come on." This ambiguity is entirely absent from Winslet's Sue: during this scene, she is curled up in Jude's armchair, in his clothes and under his cloak. The gas fire lights her face in a warm, romantic glow, and she never breaks eye contact with Jude as she speaks. The sensuality of the scene—and of Winslet's performance—say "come on" loud and clear; but, as if in a show of power, when she finishes speaking, Sue shuts her eyes and keeps them shut. Jude then sheepishly moves out of the scene. The whole sequence seems to prove Sue's point that men *are* the timid sex: she has intimated to Jude that he is welcome to "come on," and then abruptly revokes the promise, keeping him at bay.

The film Sue, unlike her literary counterpart, is a *true* rebel, a woman who uses her sexuality for power. With her outspokenness and her ideological opposition to marriage (which she calls "a government stamp. A license to love!") she is a clear danger to established society. Winterbottom, then, perpetuates a view of Jude and Sue that has been common for about a century: Jude is a poor innocent who is cruelly rejected by the workings of the establishment that first gave him reason to hope, while Sue is a threat because she subverts traditional gender roles and is proud to do so. After Jude scolds Sue for revealing their unmarried state to the Christminster landlady, Sue declares that she will not "live a lie." In the novel, Sue's decision to admit her marital status to the landlady is largely "impulse" (p. 403), but in the film her admission is in keeping with her re-interpretation as a sexual threat. When the family's eviction from the lodging causes the child "Juey" (Ross Colvin Turnbull; the appellation "Little Father Time" has been dropped, for reasons I examine below) to murder the other children and to hang himself, it can be assumed that he is acting in response to society's rejection of his rebellious stepmother and unconventional family.

However, when one carefully examines how the film Sue has been rewritten by Amini, presented by Winterbottom, and played by Winslet—and especially when her character is compared to that of Arabella—it can be seen that the film ultimately presents a dialectic that favors traditional gender roles: thus the film's use of Hardy to champion the cause of the oppressed and marginalized becomes destabilized. The chief problem with the film's Sue is that she is caught between the filmmakers' apparent desire to make Sue more relevant to the 1990s, and their desire to be faithful to Hardy. Winterbottom/Amini's Sue is both extremely self-aware and not innocent about sexual relations; however, she is *also* the sexually repressed neurotic of Hardy's vision. One moment where Hardy's Sue is rewritten occurs when Jude observes Phillotson put his arm around Sue. In the book, Sue removes Phillotson's arm, but he promptly returns it; and Sue merely "let[s] it remain, looking quickly round her with an air of misgiving" (p. 159). However, in the film, Sue *also puts her arm around Phillotson*. She does not complacently accept Phillotson's attentions: she returns them.

Had the film consistently presented this "new Sue," that would have been one thing, but there are times when she reverts to Hardy's Sue—especially in regard to her horror of the sex act. The film faithfully recreates the novel's presentation of Sue and Phillotson's married life—with the chief difference being that it is Jude, rather than Hardy's omniscient narrator, who observes the goings-on. During the "At Shaston" sequence, Jude overhears the couple quarreling and later goes downstairs to find Sue curled up on the floor of a closet. She looks up at him with tearful eyes and cries, "What's wrong with me, Jude?" They then embrace and share a long, passionate kiss—the first physical contact between them. "What's wrong" with Sue appears to be that she has chosen the wrong man. Liam Cunningham's Phillotson is far from physically repulsive—in fact, he hasn't aged at all since he was on the road to Christminster—and he plays the character as kind and considerate. It simply appears that Sue just doesn't respond to Phillotson, while she *does* respond to Jude. It is strange, then, that once Phillotson sets Sue free to live with Jude, she is *still* repulsed by the sex act. During some mild sexual rough-housing, Sue abruptly pulls away from Jude and stiffly tells him, "Don't touch me like that, Jude.... It's a prelude to something else." The moment is jarring in light of the fact Sue had previously informed Jude that a man will "come" to a woman only if she has let him (don't Sue's actions tell Jude he is welcome to touch her?), and because she surrendered to a passionate kiss with Jude in the closet. Sue here is sexually knowledgeable and is lacking the Romantic desire for sexless love that characterizes her counterpart in the novel, so how are we to understand her rejection of Jude's sexual advances?

The answer is to be found in the film's treatment of the theme of marriage, and it is here that Arabella becomes important. Through Arabella's character, we can see that the film initially criticizes marriage as a cruel and artificial means of societal repression; yet, in the end, marriage is upheld as the only legitimate means by which a couple may stay together. The duality that informs Winslet's Sue becomes a major part of the film's dialectic as a whole.

Arabella is introduced in the film much as she is in the novel, though as is often the case with *Jude*, the cardinal function of the scene is intact, while the catalyzers are entirely different. In the novel, of course, Jude meets Arabella when she flings the pig's pizzle at his head, waking him from an absurd fantasy about his own eventual successes. Here, Arabella ensnares Jude while he is under a tree, reciting from a Latin book. Once he reaches the end of a line (a note of triumph in his voice), an object flies out from out of nowhere and lands with a moist splat in the middle of a page. He picks up the object, and in close-up it is revealed to be not a pig's pizzle—but its *heart*. This change from Hardy's crudely sexual image to one associated with love, or at least with the vitality of the being, also results in a change in Arabella's motives—rather than sending Jude a grotesque symbol of her own desire for him, she has sent him the butcher-shop equivalent of a Valentine. What's more, by throwing the heart not at Jude's head but at the scholarly book, Arabella makes a statement that could serve as a motto for the film itself: love conquers scholarship. The film even shows its awareness of its reversal of Hardy's imagery when, after Arabella encourages Jude to meet her again, she returns to her friends who are cleaning chitterlings in the creek. "Did you catch anything?" one of them asks Arabella. "Nah," she replies. "I should have thrown *something else* at him" (my emphasis).

While this change from the pizzle to the heart might seem trifling or even amusing, it actually serves as the film's symbol for Arabella's feelings for Jude. The heart is a gross piece of flesh, but it is also the symbol of love, and for the first part of the film, Arabella embodies the carnal side of love. To impress Jude she climbs a tree, she seduces him in a sty surrounded by grunting pigs, and on their wedding night she aggressively bites Jude on the chest. The animal imagery used to characterize Arabella also becomes a symbol for her marriage to Jude. At the springtime marriage feast, the couple is presented a pig, which a group of children later chase and capture. The wedding scene soon shifts to bleak winter, and the pig has become a hog. As in the novel, Jude and Arabella are forced to chase the pig around in its pen— almost a mockery of the children chasing the young pig—capture it, and slit its throat. But it is Arabella who does the actual butchering of the carcass, and as she guts it, Jude sadly leaves their house to visit with Aunt Drusilla. The meaning is clear: Arabella has disemboweled the marriage, and—by implication— Jude. As if to hammer this point home, when Jude returns he finds Arabella is gone; in her place is the butchered hog carcass on which she has pinned a good-bye note.

By this point in the film, Arabella has more or less been presented as Hardy wrote her, and Rachel Griffiths is extremely well-cast. Winterbottom also succeeds at turning the audience's sympathies away from the character—her coldness in killing the hog and her cruelty to Jude come through clearly. In Jude's scene with Aunt Drusilla, the audience is given further reason to dislike Arabella when Drusilla observes that "it's been months" and Arabella shows no signs of pregnancy. As with the novel, then, Jude must have been "trapped" into marriage—though the scene of his entrapment is nowhere in sight, and there was no mention of any pregnancy between the pig sty seduction and the wedding. But no sooner does the film bring up this information than it throws it all into doubt. As Jude reads the good-bye note that Arabella has left him, she is heard in voice-over:

> "I know you think I tricked you into marrying me, but I swear I really believed I was pregnant. I'm going to Australia to start again. Perhaps now you'll be free to go to Christminster and be a university man. Good luck."

The scene transforms from Jude reading the letter in his home to his sitting in a train car; and as soon as the voice-over stops, the intertitle card appears: "At Christminster." Arabella's plea for vindication, and her gesture of setting Jude free to pursue his goal, cast the character in an entirely new and favorable light. When one considers the "Valentine" she sent Jude to initiate the relationship, it is hard not to wonder—did Arabella act out of a simple and cynical desire to "get" a man, or did she act entirely out of love; and does she leave Jude out of a selfless desire to take herself out of the way and allow him to pursue his life-long ambition?

The film further suggests that Arabella is motivated by love when, after Sue's wedding, Jude finds Arabella tending bar. They have sex, after which Jude falls asleep on Arabella's naked breast—a tableau that is remarkably maternal, and which fits in with the film's infantalizing of Jude. Arabella lovingly strokes his hair, and quietly muses, "You know how I said I was pregnant when we got married? Jude? ... Jude? ... I met someone in Sydney and didn't tell him about us.... It wasn't as nice as how we did it." The scene then fades to black. Arabella's halting speech is indicative of two things: she seems on the verge of confessing something about the supposed false pregnancy—which may, in fact, be that she really *was* pregnant, since Jude's child will shortly appear in the film—and that she feels that Jude is the superior of the two men she's had. In the novel, Arabella seeks to get Jude back, but her motives are entirely cynical and satirical—here, it is hard to conclude that Arabella's feelings are anything other than warm and loving.

The rehabilitation of Arabella continues to show that she is also a loving mother to her child. Interestingly, Arabella chooses to name the boy Jude Fawley, or "Juey," as he's usually called; and this is a direct reversal of her attitude toward Jude as expressed in the novel—Sue realizes Arabella would never have given the child Jude's name, since "she was hating [him] all the time" (p. 347). By naming her child after her estranged husband, the film's Arabella shows her lasting commitment to Jude—a desire to see a part of him carry on. Furthermore, in this highly realistic film, Juey is not a satire of his father: though Winterbottom associates the boy with death, Juey is primarily a solemn-faced child for whom his mother has the greatest sympathy and affection. In the voice-over that announces the existence of Juey, Arabella explains that she is giving up the child simply because neither she nor her parents can afford to take care of him. Later, at a fair, Arabella dotes on the boy and calls him "a good boy." Finally, at the funeral of the children, Arabella is seen deeply in mourning. "I should have kept him myself," she tells Jude. "None of this would ever have happened. If I'd come back to you—!" Then, when Jude moves away, Arabella tries to comfort him by saying, "It wasn't your fault, Jude."

This is an enormously sympathetic Arabella: she is a loving mother and she shows every indication of being a good wife. In the cemetery she even recognizes that she has wronged Jude and destroyed the possibility of their having a happy marriage. It would seem that the film is arguing *against* this point of view, since we are to believe that Jude and Sue are meant for each other, but this notion is difficult to accept when Arabella is compared to Sue. Arabella is not only the more sympathetic character, but she has the stronger legal and moral claim on Jude. Significantly, there is no mention of divorce in this film: once Sue is set free to live with Jude, we are treated to scenes of the happy couple riding bicycles and playing on the beach, and so we can't conclude that they are *not* still married to their original spouses. Perhaps they are even legally barred from getting divorces. The closest the film comes to addressing the issue is when Jude asks Sue if she would consider marrying again, and she declares, "I'd run a mile if you had a piece of paper that forced me to love you!" The viewer is left either to ponder the couple's legal standing or gloss over it—something the film clearly does. That society views the couple as living in sin, however, is never in doubt: as in the novel, Jude obtains a position repairing the Ten Commandments in a church, and Sue assists him. With them are Juey and a squalling infant. As they work, a cadre of grim-faced, black-clad old women glide past the family, their expressions displaying stony disapproval. Jude is sacked in the next scene. Coming on the heels of this sequence, the family is shown at their apartment window, watching the auction of their household goods in the grimy courtyard below. The dialogue makes it clear that Jude and Sue have been brought to this state not by poverty in general, but by the workings of a disapproving society:

> SUE: It's going to be like this everywhere we go, as soon as people find out we're not married.
>
> JUDE: We'll move on. Move somewhere where nobody knows us. And if they find out, we'll move on. And again. And again. As long as it takes the world to change. We've done nothing wrong, Sue. You're the one who taught me that.

Winterbottom's Jude and Sue are victims of an unchanging world, one that drives them into the streets and forces them, like Dickens's Jo, to "move on." What's more, they are on an ideological mission to change the world—to force society to accept their unconventionality. This desire to change the world has a certain religious quality, for when the family returns to Christminster, they trudge from lodging to lodging in the pouring rain, only to be told—like the Holy Family—"no room."

However, the film undermines its own argument and actually endorses the view of this "unchanging" society in the sequences that depict Sue losing her virginity to Jude, and its immediate after-effects. Sue realizes the only way she can keep Jude from visiting Arabella is by giving him what he wants. She strips off her nightgown and lies down on the bed, completely naked. The way the scene is shot is unabashedly erotic: Winslet's nude frame occupies two-thirds of the right half of the screen and is softly lit by the gas lamp, while Eccleston, his back to the camera and partially in the shadows, undresses in the left one-third. This positioning makes Winslet's body the focus of the entire scene,[52] and as she lies woodenly and supine, her hands awkwardly placed just above her breasts, she exudes erotic vulnerability. Her vulnerable position is enhanced by her nervous, oddly charming dialogue: "Do I talk too much? I'm doing it wrong! I'm intellectualizing!" Jude climbs atop her, and the scene earns the film its R rating, with Jude kissing Sue all over her body, and finally slipping between her legs. The scene fades out, and next we see Sue preparing breakfast. She and Jude are happy and contented, kissing and nuzzling each other: the well-adjusted couple after a night of satisfying love-making. But the happiness of this scene is cut short when Jude picks up the letter Arabella has left for him, and, in voice-over, we learn of the existence of Juey and the fact that Arabella is sending the boy to live with his father.

After the eroticism of the sex scene—which is calculated to deliberately excite the viewer and reward him or her for waiting to see Jude and Sue consummate their love (the filmmakers apparently hoped to reward curious viewers in other ways, too, as it was publicized before the film's release that Winslet would be doing her first nude scene; this was, remember, a year before *Titanic*, and her much more celebrated foray into onscreen nudity)—the arrival of Juey is like a douche of cold water. The boy is associated with dreariness—he is first seen on the deck of a ship surrounded by dark waves and gray sky, and he appears in the train station dressed in drab colors. Sue tries to be a mother to Juey, but her resentment of the boy is revealed when she tells Jude she can see half of him in the child, "but the other half is her." The scorn in Sue's voice is echoed later, at the lodging in Christminster, when she sharply orders Juey to "go to bed!" Juey is filled with remorse, and it is Jude who comforts him, becoming in effect a maternal figure.

Shortly after Juey's arrival, the small, manufactured family attend a magic-lantern show (a scene that is not in the novel), and during the time spent under the tent, Juey watches enthralled as an image of an old man turns into a skeleton, and as sheeted "ghosts" run through the crowd. His wide eyes are important in the next scene, where Juey is crouched in a corner, watching Sue give birth. Winslet has been directed to howl piteously (though her howls are strangely orgasmic), and in one instant, she is revealed to have her legs spread wide open, with blood and gore emitting from her crotch. The childbirth, perhaps, is meant to presage Juey's murder of the other two children—he has seen the agony a woman endures in giving birth, and might naturally conclude that life itself is agony—and Winterbottom's focus on the boy's eyes during the entire sequence would seem to prove this. However, the entire sequence of events works to undermine what the film wishes to convey. The arrival of Juey almost immediately after the sensual love-making scene, in effect, displays the immediate consequences of sex: children. That the boy is almost immediately associated with images of death casts him in the role of executioner—is he, perhaps, Arabella's retribution for Sue's stealing her husband? If anything, the bloody childbirth scene brings to mind Laura Mulvey's comment that, in cinema, "Woman's desire is subjected to her image as bearer of the bleeding wound, she can resist only in relation to castration and cannot transcend it."[53] Here, the "bleeding wound" is made the subject of the shot, horrifying both Juey and the audience. The viewer therefore becomes complicit in Juey's desire to contain the threat of the feminine by destroying its product.

I do not believe that this repressive attitude toward sex is intentional; rather, it springs from the filmmakers' twin desire to appropriate femininity as a means of contextualizing the past and to show the characters as victims of forces beyond their control. Marcia Landy has argued that many of the films from the 1980s and 1990s that dramatize British history are also deeply concerned with the roles women play in reproducing national culture. Landy claims that women in these films fall into two general categories: maternal figures, who are "positioned as the guarantor of identity, authenticity, and wholeness, an antidote to nationalism, racism, and violence"[54] and who also can invest men with the much-needed values of compassion and empathy[55]; and women who, like the "imperialist Other," are associated with social disruption, decomposition, and death. To Landy, these twin images represent "not only a crisis of historicizing but a crisis of representation in contemporary British cinema"[56]—in short, femininity becomes the locus for a study of Britain's own divided feelings about *itself*. The film's depiction of Sue and Arabella seems to bear out Landy's theory. Sue, associated with rebellion, pain, blood, and madness, disrupts the social order, while Arabella, who transforms from animal into a sympathetic mother-figure, represents a kind of recuperation of social identity. When Jude rejects her at the children's funeral, he is rejecting an offer to reclaim stability in his own life.

Moreover, the film seems to come out on the side of Arabella—and of traditional marital roles—because it is clear that Winterbottom wishes to turn everyone into a victim of society: Arabella *had* to be made more sympathetic. In a film that champions the working class, a working-class Arabella who consciously victimizes Jude would undermine the director's intentions. Arabella's "deceiving" Jude about the pregnancy is therefore cast into doubt; she willingly sets Jude free to pursue his academic career; and she does not get Jude drunk and force him to remarry her after Sue has left him. Arabella disappears from the film after the funeral, as traumatized by the death of her child as Sue is by the deaths of hers. By making Arabella into a "good" character, the appeal of Sue in contrast is utterly lost. In Hardy, there is always the knowledge that no matter how difficult Sue may be, she is always superior to the scheming and manipulative Arabella; but in the Winterbottom version, Jude has the choice between a callous sexual glutton who metamorphoses into a loving maternal figure, and a fun-loving free spirit who becomes more sexually repressed and neurotic as the film goes on ... and it's hard to understand why he chooses the latter over the former.

Just as Arabella is redeemed by Winterbottom's sympathetic treatment, so too is Phillotson. Liam Cunningham is both far too young and robust to be the Phillotson who fills Sue with sexual revulsion; and he, like Arabella, is not allowed to be a victimizer. There is no Gillingham to make him question his rationale in letting Sue go: in fact, when Jude tells him that he wishes to live with Sue, Phillotson admits that the marriage was a mistake from the beginning. Phillotson is sent off midway; what becomes of him we are not told. After the children's deaths Sue mentions that she plans on returning to him, but it is not clear if she does do it; and certainly Phillotson does not collaborate with Arabella in a scheme to win back their spouses—for to make Phillotson a victimizer would deprive him of his status as hard-luck loser in the romantic stakes, and as victim of the same false promise of advancement in society that he had shared with Jude.

In place of Hardy's ironic, patently artificial ending, in which Jude and Sue remarry their original spouses and Jude dies alone, mocked by the revelry at the Remembrance games outside, Winterbottom has created the "Christmas 1889" scenario, shot in muted grays that recall the film's opening black-and-white section. A cadaverous-looking Jude discovers Sue in the cemetery, kneeling over the graves of the children. After Jude makes a plea for Sue to return to him and after they share a long kiss, Sue retreats, leaving a solitary Jude to cry out, "We are man and wife, if ever two people were on this earth!" The End. Strange that a film that has been so unflinching in its imagery—a disemboweled pig, gory childbirth, dead children—should stop short of showing Jude's death; but by keeping Jude alive, Winterbottom denies society a *total* victory. So long as Jude lives, there is the possibility that society will be brought to justice. Modern viewers of course know that today a poor kid can get a college education, and that the definition of a legal marriage has become somewhat flexible since 1895: there is a certain comfort in knowing that Jude's impossible dreams are today's realities.

In the final analysis, *Jude* is so different from *Jude the Obscure* that at times the novel seems like an afterthought. Yet, like Schlesinger's *Far from the Madding Crowd* and Polanski's *Tess*, *Jude* received a number of reviews that praised it precisely *for* its fidelity to Hardy. Michael Wilmington claims that "the movie, like the novel, has a consistent vision, a tragic trajectory. There's a harrowing, crystalline quality to the images in *Jude* ... that suggest the chill and fascination of reading Hardy—one of the British novel's masters of mood and atmosphere"[57]; and James M. Welsh writes that *Jude* is not meant for the general public at all: instead, it is "a film conceived for the readers of Thomas Hardy who know the novel and will be willing and able to fill in the gaps in the screenplay."[58] Winterbottom's *Jude* no doubt captures what we *expect* of Hardy and *Jude the Obscure:* an angry indictment of society for its treatment of the poor, the alienated, and the outsider. Yet in trying to make Hardy's story more relevant to the '90s— and more *real* in terms of how it depicts women and how it treats the deaths of the children—the film delivers mixed messages. What kind of Hardy is created by Winterbottom's *Jude?* One that at times is on the side of a repressive social order, and somehow this seems to be a much more drastic change than any the film made to Hardy's novel.

Part Three

Hardy in Other Forms

6

The Lesser Known Hardy Adaptations: *The Woodlanders,* *The Scarlet Tunic,* and *The Claim*

When *Far from the Madding Crowd* was released in 1967, it was the first major film version of a Hardy novel in nearly forty years. Between *Crowd* and *Tess,* twelve years elapsed; and between *Tess* and *Jude,* seventeen years went by. This paucity of adaptations, and the fact decades if not generations separate the films, has helped lead to the possibly justified claim that Hardy's fiction is not suitable to cinematic transformation—or that audiences simply have no real interest in seeing Hardy on film. However, not two years after *Jude* was released, two more films based on Hardy works—*The Woodlanders* and *The Scarlet Tunic*—appeared in British theaters; and at the end of 2000, Michael Winterbottom unveiled his second film derived from a Hardy novel. Not since the silent era has Hardy been so well-represented on the screen.

This revival of interest in Hardy on the part of filmmakers no doubt owes something to the continued popularity of "heritage" melodramas in both Britain and the U. S., and certainly *The Woodlanders* and *The Scarlet Tunic* demand to be seen *as* heritage films. *The Woodlanders* was produced in cooperation with the Arts Council of England, and a good deal of its funding was provided for out of the National Lottery, so it comes readily encrusted with the label of a film based on a British literary treasure. However, *The Scarlet Tunic,* based on Hardy's popular 1888 story

"The Melancholy Hussar of the German Legion," derives its "heritage" status not just from its association with one great author, but from its
exploitation of heritage films based on the works of *another* canonized
British writer—Jane Austen. Neither film was a great success at home, and
both are practically unknown in the U. S., two facts that call into question the suitability of Hardy materials to the heritage industry. Then again,
the fate of Winterbottom's *The Claim*, a post–Gold Rush era saga "inspired"
by *The Mayor of Casterbridge*—which played at film festivals and in large
American markets, but was given an otherwise anemic distribution and a
low-key publicity campaign—suggests an audience does not yet exist for
films that remove Hardy from his traditional Wessex locale. The pity of it
all is that, while *Woodlanders* and *Scarlet Tunic* perhaps deserve their
obscurity—delivering in the former case an ossified version of Hardy, and
in the latter a campy distortion—*The Claim* actually opens new and exciting ways of seeing Hardy and *The Mayor*, and deserves a wider and more
appreciative audience.

The Woodlanders, directed by documentary filmmaker Phil Agland and
scripted by David Rudkin, was shot in Dorset over an extended period to
capture the seasons,[1] and released in Britain in February 1998. As of this writing, it has never appeared in the United States either in theaters or on television, although Miramax owns the American distribution rights. The film's
absence from U. S. screens is easy to understand: *The Woodlanders* is not one
of Hardy's better-known novels to Americans; and even though the film has
a talented cast, led by Rufus Sewell as Giles Winterborne, its lack of top-
drawer stars no doubt also hurts its chances for stateside distribution. It also
can't be denied that the *Woodlanders* film is, for the most part, agonizingly
dull, and those who know Hardy's novel are likely to be dissatisfied with the
cuts Rudkin made in the story. Americans are missing out on very little.

The film, which runs just over ninety minutes, is one of the most
scaled-down of any of the Hardy adaptations. Normally, cuts in the text
may not be noticeable to people who haven't read the source novel, but
the excisions in *The Woodlanders* are glaring. For instance, an early portion of the novel is devoted to the blooming friendship between Grace Melbury and Felice Charmond and to Grace's distress when Felice breaks her
promise to take Grace with her to the Continent. However, in the film,
Grace (Emily Woof) and Felice (Polly Walker) don't lay eyes on each other
until late in the film, and there is no mention of Felice taking Grace with
her to the Continent—yet Grace is *still* distressed because she has been
left behind. Such lacunae abound in this film; whether they are the result
of the script or the editing, *The Woodlanders* comes across as disjointed
and the relationships between the characters are superficial in the extreme.

Even more damaging are the deliberate omissions made by Rudkin and Agland. Most notably, all of the humor has been drained from the story. Fitzpiers's Fieldingesque sexual exploits are minimized and glimpsed only in so far as they show the emotional pain he inflicts upon Grace. Grace and Felice do not bumble into the woods, leading to Grace's discovery that Fitzpiers has "had" Felice (*Woodlanders*, p. 272); Fitzpiers's wife and two lovers do not gather in frenzied excitement around his sickbed; and the cuckolded Tim Damson does not lay a man-trap to avenge himself on Fitzpiers. Ironically, all of these sequences are very vivid and would probably film very well; however, they are all blatantly comedic in nature, and—as many critics of the novel have complained—the comedy detracts from the romantic and tragic elements of the story.[2] With the humor removed, what remains is the usual pastoral virtues, some melodrama and tragedy, and—because Grace cannot get a divorce—a sense of outrage against society. As we have seen, all of these elements are part and parcel of Hardy's received cultural identity.

The cuts made to the story also take from Hardy's fiction one of its best-known traits: a reliance on coincidence. Admittedly, earlier filmmakers were often hostile to Hardy's coincidences, and everyone from Schlesinger in the '60s to Winterbottom in the '90s attempted to make his stories more "realistic," but the coincidences in *The Woodlanders* are crucial, and they occur because the characters' lives are deeply intertwined with one another and with the history of the region. A key cardinal plot function in the novel is Giles's cutting down of Old South's tree—an act that so terrifies the old man that his death is hastened. It is later revealed that Giles's father had entailed the family's house upon Old South's life; and when Giles attempts to renew the lease with Felice—whom he had offended when he refused to move his cart out of her way—he has no more legal standing, and she evicts him. The whole series of plot functions is highly convoluted, but through it Hardy illustrates how bound up in each others' lives these woodland characters are. South's death results immediately in Marty losing her house, and it also puts into effect an ancient law through which Giles is denied his suit. An entire system of landholding—a way of life for the Little Hintock community—is thus implicated in Giles's fate. In the film, however, there is no tree and Old South himself has been removed from the story. As a result, there is no explanation for how Felice gains control over Giles's land—and over his fate. She is merely a two-dimensional villainess who, in her brief scenes, voices her dislike of the community, evicts Giles, and takes up with Fitzpiers—all with heartless abandon and often while wearing the crimson dress of a wanton woman. Felice here is a foreign interloper, a sexual threat, and an economic tyrant. Through her character, Agland's film creates simple dichotomies between woodland values and city glitz, honest poverty and heartless capitalism.[3]

Just as the act of cutting down Old South's tree and its repercussions are gone, so too is the information surrounding Mr. Melbury's original decision to "give" Grace to Giles. In the novel Mr. Melbury won away the fiancée of Giles's father by a "trick," and he is resolved to atone for his "wrong-doing" by uniting his daughter with the son of the man he injured (*Woodlanders*, p. 49). In his attempt to make Grace a suitable prize for Giles, he provides for her education, but, of course, he fears that he has now made her "too good" for a simple woodsman. In the film, Melbury (Tony Haygarth) makes no mention of any obligation to Giles's father; in fact, his reasons for educating Grace have nothing to do with Giles and everything to do with *himself* and his own past as a poor and apparently dim-witted laborer. As Melbury explains to Grace, when he was a schoolboy, "They laughed at me for my ignorance. Well, I vowed then and I vow now no one shall ever look down on a child of mine for ignorance." Emphasizing Melbury's personal ambitions over his sense of duty to the past and to his fellow woodlander is one example of how Agland and Rudkin turn Hardy's story into a straightforward and simple critique of the British class system. While Melbury may be able to work himself into a position of bourgeois respectability and even transform his daughter into something better than he could have been, he still cannot erase the stigma of being born into the laboring class. The gentleman Dr. Fitzpiers (Cal MacAninch) treats Melbury with ill-disguised contempt, even going so far as to call him—in very un-Hardean terms—a "God-damned timber merchant." Fitzpiers's disgust for Melbury's social station extends to Grace, whom he will not allow to associate with her old friends, and to whom he deals the greatest insult by running away with Felice, a woman more from his own class.

The film story, devoid of Hardy's comedy and sense of connectedness, is chiefly interested in economic relationships and the problems of class and gender divisions. Giles is victimized on two fronts: by Felice's disdain for a poor man who defied her will, and by Melbury's snobbish desire to get a better husband for his daughter. Likewise, Grace suffers from her husband's snobbery, and she is further victimized by the government's inability to see the cruelty in her husband's treatment of her. Effectively, the film replicates a popular image of Hardy as a writer who cried out against the economic and social plight of England's poor and marginalized, but it transforms Hardy into someone who wrung his hands over society's wrongs instead of showing him perhaps more accurately as a launcher of satirical volleys. The novel continues for several chapters after Giles's death, documenting both Grace's self-abnegating reconciliation with Fitzpiers—who, the reader is assured, will not be faithful—and Marty's pathetic devotion to the dead Giles, who is now hers alone (*Woodlanders*, p. 393). The lonely death of Giles, defeated by societal forces beyond his control, becomes the climax of the film, but a brief denouement indicates that society is losing its power over marginalized people like Giles and Grace. In fact, the final scene of *The Woodlanders* anticipates modern feminism, as Grace chooses to rid *herself* of Fitzpiers. The estranged husband asks for a reconciliation and then demands of Grace, "What do you feel for me?" Grace replies, "Nothing," and walks away, leaving Fitzpiers alone on a wind-swept heath. The music swells, the credits roll, the wronged woman revenges herself upon the man who wronged her. This moment perhaps capitalizes on the none-too-accurate image of Hardy as an early feminist, but it is entirely un-Hardean. The novel's bitterly comic depiction of Grace's inability to rid herself of Fitzpiers and her acceptance of her lot speaks more tellingly of how Hardy saw the fate of women in Victorian England than does Grace's triumphant exit in the film. In fact, Grace's tragicomic return to her husband anticipates Sue Bridehead's bleak return to Phillotson in *Jude the Obscure*.

Ultimately, the desire of the filmmakers to replicate a Hardy we "know"—a pastoralist, tragedian, social critic, and even feminist—turns *The Woodlanders* into a static, lifeless film. Even so, it still delivers a version of Thomas Hardy that many people will recognize and be comfortable with, which is not necessarily the case with the second "Hardy film" of 1998. *The Scarlet Tunic*, directed by Stuart St. Paul and released in Britain in June, is a true oddity among the Hardy adaptations in that it is the only full-length motion picture based on one of Hardy's historical works; and it is the only film to promote Hardy's name while apparently trying to capitalize on films based upon the works of another, if earlier, nineteenth-century author.

The Scarlet Tunic was released toward the end of a period that saw a number of popular and profitable films based on the novels of Jane Austen. Both Ang Lee's *Sense and Sensibility* (1995) and Douglas McGrath's *Emma* (1996) were hits with filmgoers and critics; and on television new versions of *Pride and Prejudice, Persuasion,* and *Northanger Abbey* were well-received. Though Hardy's fiction is radically different from Austen's, he was interested in the era in which she lived and he set not only "The Melancholy Hussar" but *The Trumpet-Major* and portions of *The Dynasts* in Wessex during the period of the Napoleonic Wars.[4] In fact, with its plot involving soldiers encamped near a house containing an impressionable young woman, "The Melancholy Hussar" bears a superficial resemblance to *Pride and Prejudice,* and it is perhaps this element of the story that attracted the filmmakers. The look of the film also closely hews to that of many of the Austen adaptations, with much of the action occurring on rolling green lawns and in the shade of arboretums, and a great deal of dialogue is dedicated to that most Austenian subject—*manners.* It also cannot be an accident that Emma Fielding, who plays Frances Grove, bears an astonishing resemblance to Emma Thompson, who starred in Lee's *Sense and Sensibility.* While the screen story ultimately emerges as something entirely different from Austen (and from Hardy, for that matter), Austen is nevertheless a phantom-like presence in the film.

Despite its resemblance to the Austen adaptations, *The Scarlet Tunic*'s basic storyline is clearly derived from "The Melancholy Hussar," and the film's advertising played upon its Hardean associations. The theatrical trailer opens on a dramatic shot of the cliffs near Bournemouth, and a narrator boasts that the movie was "filmed in Thomas Hardy's Dorset, where the story truly belongs." The film was later released on video in both Britain and America (where it did not receive a theatrical release, but did appear on the cable "Romance Classics" network) in an absurd "gift set" that divides the 88-minute film into two cassettes, the second of which contains both the trailer and behind-the-scenes interviews with the cast and crew. These interviews are illuminating largely because they reveal how the actors felt about Hardy and the task of bringing him to the screen. Jack Shepherd, who plays Dr. Grove, says that, in Hardy's stories, "You sense fate or society or capitalism or religion or morality like a great engine crushing the heroes and heroines of his books." John Sessions, the film's Humphrey Gould, says that an "essential feature" of Hardy's fiction is that "it's very bleak and one is controlled by the gods." Given these views, it can be assumed that the actors approached the material as if they were in a "typical" Hardean tragedy of Fate. However, the film emerges as something close to burlesque comedy—and this may not have been the intention.

While earlier filmmakers had to deal with the problem of reducing fairly hefty novels down to fit acceptable running times for movies, St. Paul and his co-screenwriters had to deal with the *opposite* problem of *adding* material to Hardy's story in order to create a feature-length film. Many of the additions to the story flesh out the characters and provide them lives beyond the narrow limits of Hardy's short tale. The script develops Frances's relationships with her father and with the household servants; it further tightens the bond between Matthaus (Jean-Marc Barr) and Christoph by making them brothers rather than friends; and it gives

Christoph (Thomas Lockyer) a love interest to complement the romance between Matthaus and Frances. A few names and character details were also changed: Hardy's Phyllis becomes Frances, and she is equipped with a suitably Gallic background; and Corporal Matthäus Tina is given the more poetic surname of Singer and raised in rank to sergeant. So far, so good; unfortunately, the rest of the new material seems designed to graft to Hardy's story a theme of unfettered sexuality trying to assert itself in the teeth of brutal sexual repression, and the result, frankly, is ridiculous.

Much of the dramatic action involves Matthaus and Christoph's need to sneak away from the tightly restricted camp to meet their lovers; and in the love scenes there is an enormous amount of discreet bodice-ripping. There are couplings in the woods, in a barn, and on a beach. Even crusty old Dr. Grove has a healthy libido, as we learn the housekeeper Emily Marlowe (Lynda Bellingham) is Grove's lover, and there is the hint that Grove is the father of Emily's daughter. All of this sexiness, of course, owes nothing to the strait-laced Austen adaptations *The Scarlet Tunic* resembles, but it *does* capitalize on Hardy's image as a writer who delved into issues of sexual freedom. All of the couplings in the film are, in the eyes of polite society, inappropriate: Frances crosses boundaries of class and ethnicity—and risks ruining her reputation, since she is engaged—to take up with her German soldier; Matthaus and Christoph defy army rules and codes of conduct to pursue their relationships with Frances and Amy; and for years Dr. Grove has been carrying on a long-term affair with a lower-class woman. The consequences of these couplings are not dealt with in any detail or seriousness; in fact, the characters seem blissfully defiant of convention. When Frances is asked to arrange a clandestine meeting between Christoph and Amy (Lisa Faulkner), she responds with cheerful pluckiness, "It's not proper, but I'll try." It seems as if St. Paul is trying to *subvert* the Austen films with their emphasis on propriety, and that he is using Hardy's reputation as a "sexy" writer to do it. However, a reading of such novels as *Tess* and *Jude* show Hardy believed that those who act on their passions are more than likely to be enslaved by them and condemned for them; championing unrestrained sexual freedom is more in the territory of D. H. Lawrence.

The element of societal repression the characters are rebelling against is most strongly embodied by Captain Fairfax, a sadistic martinet who is entirely a creation of the screenwriters. In Hardy's story, the soldiers' main complaints are boredom and homesickness, but in the film they are chafing under Fairfax's strict adherence to military duty and his gulag-like governance of the camp. Fairfax also becomes a symbol of mindless warmongering to both the soldiers and the audience. When he learns that the unit will be deployed to the East Indies if peace is reached with Napoleon, Christoph grumbles against fighting a "stupid captain's war." Christoph is later personally whipped by Fairfax for concealing his brother's unauthorized use of a horse, and Fairfax also suspends the men's beer rations and supervises the execution of a soldier, which he announces as a warning to everyone in the camp.

As played by Simon Callow, Fairfax is both brutally repressive and deeply repressed, but the character is so outlandish that he can never be taken seriously. Callow is a gifted performer, but too often he tends toward hamminess and camp, and those elements are pushed to the hilt here. Callow's Fairfax just barely manages to keep his homosexuality under control: he makes bedroom eyes at Matthaus and his flogging of Christoph is done in a near-sexual frenzy. Callow is at his campiest, however, when he confiscates a volume of Wordsworth from Matthaus and drawls, "It would be a bitter disappointment to me to have you lose the stripes from your tunic only to gain stripes on your skin!" Poets, he says as he grabs Matthaus from behind and begins thrusting against him, are "precursors of revolution" who only keep soldiers from their duty of "defend[ing] the realm from sedition." The scene is laughable, but it underscores the theme of the film: sexual repression results in war, tyranny, and—God forbid!—lack of appreciation for poetry.

As should be evident, by expanding upon Hardy's story and trying to make it somehow both more Hardean and subversive of Austen, the filmmakers have created a film that is totally bizarre. *The Scarlet Tunic* also—and perhaps inadvertently—distorts and ultimately spoofs Hardy's original story. The confines of "The Melancholy Hussar" are so small that the romance between Phyllis and Matthäus covers only about eight pages. This does not leave much room for character development and logically thought-out motivations, so it is a fairly simple thing for Hardy to write that Phyllis decides to reject Matthäus for the wayward Humphrey because she is "conscience-stricken" ("Hussar," p. 51). The film, however, spends more than an hour establishing both Humphrey's faithlessness and the genuine love between Frances and Matthaus. Frances's decision to go back to Humphrey because he has brought her gifts and has admitted to treating her badly may be true to Hardy, but it simply doesn't wash in the context of the film; and the cartoonish way Frances deals with Humphrey's news that he is married—smashing a mirror over his head—just underscores the silliness of the situation. It was also apparently felt that Hardy's original ending—with Matthäus and Christoph executed by firing squad, and Phyllis spending the rest of her long life in solitary regret—was not suitably tragic; so the filmmakers devised a scene where Frances arrives at the site of Matthaus's execution (Christoph escapes, leaving a pregnant Amy behind) just as he is shot. In a rage, Frances grabs a rifle and aims it at Humphrey, but she is shot dead by Fairfax. The tragedy is so piled on and the scene is so over-acted by everyone involved that it actually lampoons the tragic ending that is usually expected from Hardy. Ultimately, *The Scarlet Tunic*, in its attempt to both exploit Hardy for his reputation as a romantic or even "sexy" writer and to use Hardy as sort of a counterstrike to Jane Austen, should be regarded for what it is: an experiment.

Still, as far removed in tone and spirit from Hardy as *The Scarlet Tunic* may be, it is nevertheless set in a *place* that is recognizably "Hardean." To many, the very fact the film was shot in Dorset and has the requisite scenes of grazing sheep and rolling heaths is probably enough to establish its literary fidelity. Again, the importance of "Wessex" to Hardy's reputation — and to moviemakers — cannot be overemphasized. Wessex is so identified with Hardy that prior to 2000 only one filmmaker had ever brought a Hardy novel to the screen without using Wessex as a backdrop: Dharm Dev Kashyap, whose *Dulhanek raat ki (Bride for a Single Night,* 1967) moved the basic story of *Tess* to India.[5] The fact moviemakers have striven to keep Hardy in Wessex made Michael Winterbottom's announced project for 2000 sound particularly intriguing — if not foolhardy. The film, originally to be called *Kingdom Come* but later changed to *The Claim*

Far from Casterbridge: *The Claim's* Kingdom Come set.

(presumably to avoid confusion with a video game and comic book of the same title, as well as an American film comedy that would be released in 2001), would be adapted from *The Mayor of Casterbridge,* but the setting would not be Casterbridge or any other place Hardy wrote about; instead, it would be set in the Sierra Nevada mountains of California in the years following the Gold Rush of 1849. With the change in locale would come changes in characters, motivations, and situations; and so the film raises an obvious question: if you take a Hardy story out of its "native" environment, what happens to Hardy?

According to Frank Cotrell Boyce, who wrote both *The Claim* and Winterbottom's *Welcome to Sarajevo,* this is actually a non-issue. Boyce argues *The Claim*'s connections to Hardy are actually very tenuous, and the end titles duly credit Hardy's novel only with "inspiring" the film story. In an interview posted on the film's official website, Boyce says that his script began as a straightforward version of *Mayor,* only with the location changed to California, but as he revised and rewrote the story it moved so far from the Hardy original that "now I would probably would say it was adapted from the same newspaper story that Thomas Hardy used for *The Mayor of Casterbridge.* They're both based on the same story but they've got nothing in common in terms of treatment and everything."[6] Boyce's claim that both he and Hardy delved into the same intertextual space to create very distinctive fictional works is downright Barthesian; but it is belied by other material on the website, which invites users to see the film as an extension of the novel— and of Hardy himself. From the site, a user can link to an astonishingly inaccurate biography of Hardy (which says *Jude the Obscure* was condemned for its depiction of "incest"), download the entire text of *The Mayor of Casterbridge* from Project Gutenberg, and view a photo of Hardy wearing a long handlebar mustache, looking for all the world like Wyatt Earp. And even though Boyce argues his script really isn't based on Hardy's novel, he still credits Hardy with writing on themes that lend themselves to film westerns like *The Claim:* specifically, "Landscape, big men, big landscapes, big passages of time, old crimes, retribution, revenge."[7] Such images really bring to mind John Wayne riding through the Red River Valley more than they do Tess's lonely journey into the Valley of the Little Dairies; but at the same time Boyce's interpretation of Hardy—and the presence of Hardy on the website— recreates a figure we know very well: a man who wrote about the past, about a way of life that is long gone, and about people who are unmatched by anyone you're likely to see walking down the street today. The Web has become the latest tool in continuing some very familiar images.

The Claim also promotes an identification with Hardy through the presence of two people who were involved with earlier Hardy adaptations:

Michael Winterbottom and Nastassja Kinski (as she is now billed). Many authors have become identified with particular filmmakers and performers: we need think only of David Lean's adaptations of Dickens or Alec Guinness's many roles as Dickens characters. In more recent years, the Merchant Ivory producing and directing team—along with their "stock company" of actors—became largely identified with E. M. Forster, so that the Merchant Ivory name became for many a guarantee of fidelity to—or reverence for— Forster's source novels. Winterbottom will probably never be to Hardy what James Ivory has become to Forster or what Lean was to Dickens, but he still came into *The Claim* already experienced with translating Hardean themes, plots, and concerns to the screen. The participation of Kinski, however, belongs to an altogether different order. Although she has had many other roles since *Tess,* Nastassja Kinski's signature role remains Tess Durbeyfield; and to many readers who came to the novel after the film was released, Hardy's heroine wears Kinski's face. Just as Helena Bonham Carter has largely become identified in the public's mind as the personification of the Forsterian heroine, Nastassja Kinski is often viewed as personifying the Hardy heroine. Her presence in *The Claim* is a reminder of *Tess,* and to her performance as Elena—who, like Susan in *The Mayor of Casterbridge,* is sold along with her infant daughter by her drunken husband—Kinski brings much of the stoicism and quiet dignity she brought to Tess.

However, it is in Winterbottom's and Boyce's understanding of the importance of place that *The Claim,* this least-likely of all Hardy adaptations, manages to best succeed at evoking Hardean themes and ideas. *The Mayor of Casterbridge* is the only one of Hardy's novels to be specifically concerned with a single city, and the history of this city is tied up in the fate of the man who becomes its mayor. Casterbridge is something like the city of Troy: it is an ancient area that has been continually occupied, with layers of inhabitation piled on top of earlier layers, and with remnants from ancient periods sticking up in odd places. Elizabeth-Jane observes that the city is "shut in by a square wall of trees, like a plot of garden ground by a box-edging" (*Mayor,* p. 94); and Hardy's narrator goes on to describe the city's squareness as its primary characteristic. The city is square because Casterbridge has not exceeded the dimensions of its medieval walls; and in fact the earlier fortification has been reclaimed as part of the town's modern identity as a mercantile capital: "Within the avenue and bank was a wall more or less discontinuous, and within the wall were packed the abodes of the burghers" (*Mayor,* p. 95). Casterbridge's history as a fortification goes all the way back to the era of the Romans (the city retains in its name the Latin word for camp); and, as Hardy illustrates, the presence of the Romans in Casterbridge is inescapable:

> Casterbridge announced old Rome in every street, alley, and precinct. It
> looked Roman, bespoke the art of Rome, concealed dead men of Rome.
> It was impossible to dig more than a foot or two deep about the town fields
> and gardens without coming upon some tall soldier or other of the
> Empire, who had lain there in his silent unobtrusive rest for a space of
> fifteen hundred years [*Mayor*, p. 140].

This is quite different from what is likely to be disinterred from the
Egdon Heath barrows in *The Return of the Native*—remains of ancient
Celts. The difference is significant, for while Hardy's heaths and woodlands
are likely to reverberate with the spirits of ancient and mysterious Britons,
Casterbridge bears the imprint of order and civilization, which were the
by-products of Rome's imperial domination of Britannia. Though its modern role is as an agrarian capital, Casterbridge's history is tied up with
conquest, subjugation, and control over "native" elements[8]—and it hasn't
always been successful at containing them. Buzzford the dealer reports
that Casterbridge's history has been tainted by rebellion (*Mayor*, p. 121);
and the presence of Mixen Lane—a place of slums and illegal commerce—
just inside Casterbridge proper is a reminder that uncivilized forces are
in constant danger of breaking free from their civilized boundaries.

Just as Casterbridge is a place of shaky respectability built atop a
foundation of anti-social or even primitive elements, Michael Henchard's
outward respectability and successes as merchant farmer and local politician precariously cover a shameful and even "savage" past. The first chapter establishes this "man of character" as a small-time journeyman and an
alcoholic, who commits what by any measure should be a great crime
against civilized behavior: he sells his wife and daughter for five guineas.
Hardy glosses over what Henchard does to attain his position of power
and respectability and picks up the story some twenty years after the event,
when Susan and Elizabeth-Jane (who is actually not Henchard's daughter) return and demand support. To Henchard, the return of his wife is a
chance to finally set things straight: he believes that by remarrying Susan,
he will shore up any cracks in his image as a respectable man about town
and also make things right with a greater power he cannot define. Critics
of the novel tend to be divided as to whether the calamities that befall Henchard after the return of his wife and her daughter—the failure of his business, the exposure of his past, his loss of Elizabeth-Jane—are the result of
his original crime against society, or if he simply loses his touch as a busi-
nessman and blames fate for what happens to him[9]; but the fact cannot
be escaped that Henchard *himself* feels that his misfortunes are the price
for committing a crime against the community. Ultimately, Henchard
acknowledges the power of civilization by exiling himself from it.

The novel's focus on civilization vs. savagery—and Henchard's position within this battle—point to just how class-conscious, and how ultimately *British, The Mayor of Casterbridge* is. Henchard's actions largely go toward burying his past in order to sustain his class position and image, and his reliance on "traditional" means of farming and doing business indicate how much he respects belonging to an established culture and civilization. However, once Henchard's past is laid bare and he realizes he cannot compete with Farfrae's innovations, his sense of identity collapses and his public persona crumbles along with it. What Henchard has attained means very little as the class he was born into and the crimes he committed long ago become apparent. Henchard, to a degree, is a more tragic rewriting of Dickens's Pip, whose pride at having risen in society is destroyed when he realizes his money comes from a convict. In both cases, neither character can sustain himself in the class situation he has attained: a background in poverty, crime, and humiliation reasserts itself. In class-conscious Britain of the nineteenth century, social class always will out.

Since *The Mayor* is so tightly connected to the politics of both place and class, it would seem that removing the action to the American West would be a pointless enterprise. After all, one of the tenets of the Western myth is that the land is not burdened by history—it is open and empty, a blank space on which any man with enough determination and will can write his own story. *The Claim* even pays homage to this myth, as at the end Dalglish (Wes Bentley) eulogizes Dillon (Peter Mullan) and men like him as kings and pioneers: "They came out when there was nothing, built these towns, and ruled them—like kings." The very same class and historical factors that ultimately make Henchard a failure in Britain really play no part in the fate of his counterpart, Daniel Dillon. Though Dillon also sells his wife and daughter, this is never exposed before the public, and the only suffering he does over this original crime is of a personal nature. Dillon also does not need to cultivate a "civilized" exterior for himself: the film makes it clear that he has risen to a position of financial power by catering to the needs of miners, providing them with whores, liquor, and tobacco. While Henchard has to hide his affair with Lucetta, a woman of questionable character, Dillon openly lives with Lucia (Milla Jovovich), a chanteuse and madam. Henchard's past is a constant threat to him because he has established himself in an ancient society bound up in history and tradition; but Dillon's past cannot threaten him because in the town of Kingdom Come—and in the American West—there is no history, no traditions, no time-honored standards of right behavior. Or so it would seem.

The myth of the West—and, by extension, the myth of the founding of America—is built on a fallacy: the land was never empty, and it is rich with the history of native peoples, although that history was largely erased by the arrival of Europeans. Significantly, the only Native Americans seen in *The Claim* are in the margins of the story—one is Lucia's servant, and another is a drunk who complains he's been waiting too long for the services of a whore. As these minor characters—and as the lack of any other native characters—suggest, the Native American population has been deracinated and pushed into the margins,[10] much like the native Celts who lived in Britain before the invasion of the Romans. This comparison is not made casually: whether this effect was intentional or not, by moving the story of *The Mayor of Casterbridge* to the American West during its "opening," Winterbottom and Boyce have asked us to reexamine the origins of *European* culture, the effects of which play such an important role in Hardy's novel. The "Wild West" of the late 1860s and Britannia in the first century are comparable places: both are hostile frontiers populated by fierce natives who follow strange gods, and both land and people must be subjugated in order for civilization to take root. However, civilization on the American continent acts at an accelerated pace: the same civilizing forces that take 1800 years to grind Michael Henchard under heel manage to destroy Daniel Dillon in just a generation—and for reasons that have more to do with economy than morality.

The Americans and Europeans who poured into California in search of gold were, like ancient Roman soldiers, the first wave of foreigners from the east who would bring "civilization." As if to underscore the foreignness of the people who have come to this "empty" space, all of the characters in *The Claim* are immigrants or second-generation Americans. Dillon comes from Ireland, perhaps a refugee from the Potato Famine; Elena is a Pole; Lucia is Portugese; and Dalglish is of Scottish descent. Even the whores, with their mixture of accents, come from all parts of the world. Typically, the first thing both Romans and Americans did to protect early settlers and the nascent civilization they brought was to build a fortress. There is no fort in *The Claim*, but Dillon recognizes the need for defense, and he accordingly runs Kingdom Come much like a medieval fiefdom. Dillon refuses to allow anyone to carry firearms, and in criminal matters he serves as judge, jury, and executioner. In a key scene, a man is found to have stolen some gold, and his punishment is to confess his crime before the city and to then endure 25 lashes administered by Dillon. Dalglish, who is observing the scene, notes that Dillon's treatment of the man is "generous"—in most places, mob mentality would rule and the man would have been lynched. Basically, the first few years of Kingdom Come's existence encapsulate one thousand years of English and European history, from settlement by invaders to barony where all agree to live under the

Nastassja Kinski as Elena and Peter Mullan as Dillon in *The Claim*.

law of the local lord. However, Dillon's autocratic rule is about to end: Dalglish is in town because he is scouting the route for the Central Pacific railway; if he determines that it should run through Kingdom Come, the town will receive a school, a church, a city government, and new businesses—practically overnight it will be transformed from medieval village, cut off from the rest of the country, to modern, industrialized city.

In keeping with moving the location to a place where "civilization" is still being formed, the storyline and characters have been made into more basic, perhaps even less civilized, versions of what Hardy originally created. Boyce's screenplay divests Hardy's novel of much of its Victorian trappings: once again, there is no reason for Dillon to hide his relationship with Lucia, as Henchard hides his affair with Lucetta, so there is no business of stolen letters to emerge; the Elizabeth-Jane character, Hope (Sarah Polley), is in fact Dillon's biological daughter, and the revelation of her origins is saved for the end of the film; Hope's adopted father, Burn, does not miraculously reappear after being thought dead; Dalglish and Lucia have an affair, but there is no marriage; and there is no rise of Dalglish into Dillon's old position of power and authority to parallel Dillon's fall into disgrace—in fact, Dillon is *never* disgraced; he is simply the only person left in town after the Central Pacific decides to bypass Kingdom Come and invest in the building of a new city. Boyce's script most clearly resembles only the first eighteen chapters of Hardy's *Mayor:* the film begins as Elena and Hope arrive in the town to ask for help from Dillon, right at the time Dalglish and his surveyors also appear; and it goes on to chronicle Dillon's remarriage to Elena, her protracted death, Dillon's disenchantment with Dalglish (because it looks as though the younger man won't bring the railroad to town), and Dillon's revelation to Hope about her origins. The end of Dillon's relationship with Lucia, and Dalglish's romances with Lucia and finally with Hope, which have parallel sequences in the second half of Hardy's novel, form a subplot to the main story of the film. The film story is far simpler, less labyrinthian and more basic than is Hardy's story, and since *The Claim* is not a "straight" adaptation it does not seem to be a reduction of Hardy's work. If anything, it is more focused than is Hardy on the consequences that a single act has on an individual's consciousness. Everything Dillon has done, from building a city to running it by his own sense of order and justice, is to atone for his crime against his wife and daughter. When Hope abandons him at the end, Dillon burns down the empty town, an admission of his failure to set the past aright.

In keeping with the "basic" nature of the storyline, the characters can all be seen as types who are motivated by essential or even primitive needs. Underlying Dillon's sense of sin and his desire for order is his almost childlike devotion to Catholicism: in a flashback scene he dangles a crucifix over the crying infant Hope to soothe her, and the first thing he does after Elena's death is to seek a priest. Henchard can never name the force that seems to be controlling his life—he only confesses to believing he is in "Somebody's hand" (*Mayor,* p. 374)—but Dillon clearly believes his life is controlled, and judged, by an omnipotent deity whom he has offended. When Dillon announces his wedding plans to an enraged Lucia, she accuses him of marrying Elena because he really wants to sleep with Hope—an "uncivilized" desire that may in fact underlie Henchard's decision to keep Elizabeth-Jane with him even after he realizes she isn't his real daughter. Elena candidly admits to Dillon that she has come back to him looking for money, which brings to the surface the secret that Susan Henchard recorded in a letter to be read only after her death. And Lucia is really an elemental version of Hardy's Lucetta: while Lucetta is cloaked in mystery and there is gossip about her apparently shady past (her surname, Templeman, also suggests a foreign—specifically Jewish—background), Lucia openly worked as a whore. Interestingly, when Dillon gives her title to the whorehouse, tobacco shop and liquor supplies, he turns her into the most powerful person in town: Kingdom Come is abandoned after Lucia moves the women and liquor to the new site the railroad will pass through. In this new town, it is Lucia who takes on the mantle of civic power Dillon possessed in Kingdom Come—she is the de facto mayor, and she even names the new city Lisboa in honor of the city her father came from. Civilization, in this film, is built upon land that has been cleared of natives, and on the bones of demigods like Dillon, and its building blocks are commerce—supplied by the railroads and by madams. The "new" American civilization that has been carved out of the West is the same kind of civilization the Romans forged in the wilds of Britannia during the reign of Claudius. By moving Hardy's storyline to the American West, Winterbottom and Boyce have not so much adapted *The Mayor of Casterbridge* itself as they have exposed the meaning of "civilization" that lurks beneath the surface of Hardy's novel.

Sadly, like most of Winterbottom's films, *The Claim* played mostly in art houses and its progress through America was slower than a wagon train's. In some areas, it reached the theaters in mid 2001, just weeks before its video and DVD release. Reviews were mixed, with some critics calling the film a masterpiece and others dismissing it as a plodding dud or even as a retread of Robert Altman's *McCabe and Mrs. Miller* (1971)—to which *The Claim* does bear a certain stylistic resemblance. Still, *The Claim* is clearly one of Winterbottom's best films, and it displays his continued growth and mastery of diverse subject materials. Like his previous film, *Wonderland* (1999), *The Claim* is a profoundly compassionate film that demonstrates sympathy and affection toward its disaffected characters. This quality of compassion makes *The Claim* more accessible than Winterbottom's earlier films—and this is certainly true of the bleak *Jude*. Furthermore, this time out Winterbottom has crafted a film version of Hardy that perhaps adds depth to a reading of the novel, for what Winterbottom does is probe under the surface of *The Mayor,* bringing to the fore Hardy's feelings about the instability of civilization and the forms of government that are created to keep "savage" elements in check. Unlike *The Woodlanders, The Scarlet Tunic,* and some of the more high-profile Hardy adaptations, *The Claim* complements Hardy's work and doesn't merely mine it for its most familiar elements.

7

"Moments of Television"; or, Thomas Hardy Is Brought to You By...

Thomas Hardy is so readily identified as a Victorian that it is hard to believe television was in development over the last twenty years of his life, and that, in 1926, two years before he died, TV was given its first practical demonstration in London. Some ten years after Hardy's death, television was a small industry in pockets of Europe and America, and within a generation TV sets would become standard appliances in many living rooms and aerials would appear on the roofs of the same Dorset houses Hardy had known since he was a boy. That one of the most ubiquitous symbols of the present age came into being during Hardy's lifetime makes him all the more modern, and reminds us that Hardy deserves to be seen as someone who reflected on a world we can still recognize. Perhaps not insignificantly, television—the same medium that so defines modern society and which brings the world together, in Marshall McLuhan's over-used but increasingly accurate phrase, into a "global village"—has been highly instrumental in allowing people to see Hardy and his works. In fact, TV adaptations of his fiction have even been credited with sparking today's interest in Hardy.[1]

One of the most telling things about the made-for-TV movies and episodic serials based on Hardy's novels and stories is that they were all produced under circumstances that demanded Hardy be viewed as the author of "classic" works of literature. The first TV adaptations of Hardy were made by and for the BBC, which, from its earliest days of telecasting, has maintained a tradition of creating dramatized versions of "The Classics," usually in the form of weekly serial installments that can run anywhere from two weeks to several months. The serialization of "Classics" actually began on BBC radio—on which, Peter Widdowson reports, Hardy's works have been well-represented[2]—and it was fairly natural for BBC-TV to continue the tradition when it began regular service. Classic Serials were in part born out of the BBC's public service policy, which dictated that it air a number of artistic, literary, and cultural programs to the populace—a substantial portion of which, before World War II, ended all formal education at the age of 14.[3] By serializing canonical works from British, European, and, occasionally, American literature, the BBC could air programs that were both educational and which succeeded as drama. That the BBC didn't simply deliver educational pap is demonstrated by the lasting popularity and durability of the Classic Serials, and by the fact that after the British government ended the BBC's monopoly in the 1950s, the new rival networks also included serials based on the classics as part of their own programming. By 1982, the Classic Serial had become such an institution on British TV that Paul Kerr claimed that "any serial scheduled in an associated slot and accorded similar special treatment by the [television] company concerned has been automatically designated a classic. And that status refers both to the prestige of the original novel in the literary canon and to the standing of the specific serial in the television canon."[4] Kerr argues that the titles chosen for dramatization as Classic Serials differ little from those included in Leavis's "Great Tradition" and printed in paperback as "Penguin Classics"; therefore, Classic Serials transform canonized literature into a kind of cultural commodity that preserves for British audiences a sense of themselves.[5]

Classic Serials have also allowed those outside Great Britain—most notably, Americans—to develop their own sense not only of what Britishness is, but for what classic literature and "quality television" are. British programs made very little impact on the American television market until the early 1970s and the creation of the PBS program *Masterpiece Theatre.*[6] Laurence Jarvik has shown that this now-venerable program came into being largely because of three reasons: the successful airing in 1969 of *The Forsyte Saga* on PBS, which demonstrated the appeal of British "period" serials; the desire on the part of the Mobil Oil Corporation to sponsor a quality television show that would boost the company's prestige; and the pressure put on PBS by the Nixon Administration to move away from "left-leaning" community affairs broadcasting and to focus more on educational programming—and Nixon himself believed that the best education was attained through immersion in the classics.[7] *Masterpiece Theatre* quickly became—and has largely remained—established in many Americans' minds as High Culture: it showcases both adaptations of literary classics and sophisticated original "period" dramas, and provides a kind of cultural education through an erudite host (first Alistair Cooke and then Russell Baker) whose commentaries on the serials offer insight into authors, social customs and milieus of the time period, important and influential people of the day, and the like. Moreover, to Americans, *Masterpiece Theatre* became synonymous with "quality television." Americans tend to see the subjects of British TV as high-minded and based in solid British customs and traditions; the scripts as polished and literary; and the performers as the cream of the stage and screen.

Many Americans believe that the serials shown on *Masterpiece Theatre* are made specifically for this program, but this is not the case—or at least it wasn't at the beginning. *Masterpiece Theatre* is produced by Boston's PBS station WGBH, which, using the funds provided by Mobil, originally just purchased existing serials from the BBC—and, later, from Britain's other networks—and then aired them on the program. As *Masterpiece Theatre* increased in popularity and as it became clearer to the producers what "kind" of serial went over best with its viewers, WGBH began funneling American money into British serials while they were still at the production stage, thus ensuring an output of quality British material to American consumers.[8] That Americans have been involved with the television productions of Hardy's novels is critical to this chapter, since only one of the productions considered here—the 1971 *Jude*—was made entirely by British hands. The 1994 TV movie of *The Return of the Native* was made in Dorset with a British cast and crew, but it was produced by the Hallmark greeting card company of Kansas City as part of the *Hallmark Hall of Fame*, a series of movies and specials that are meant to provide quality entertainment for American families. The 1998 serial of *Far from the Madding Crowd* is a coproduction of WGBH and Britain's Granada Television and ran as part of *Masterpiece Theatre*. Finally, the 1998 serial *Tess of the D'Urbervilles* was co-produced by London Weekend Television and the American Arts and Entertainment cable network, which emerged in the 1990s as a serious rival to PBS in airing, and, in part, funding, quality British programming. The investment of U.S. dollars in these productions suggests that Americans have their own interest in seeing Hardy—if only as the creator of colorful "period" entertainments that provide access to another time and another place.

As was the case in the previous chapters, my interest here is to consider the "kinds" of Hardy that are created through the serials and TV movies. Although cinema production and television production are very different, I do not feel it is necessary to go into considerable detail about *how* they are different or what *makes* them different. However, I do feel it is necessary to address the popular assumption that serial (or "miniseries") form is ideal for adaptations—especially of lengthy Victorian novels—since the longer running time of the serial allows the scriptwriter to include more material from the novel than would be the case if the novel were being adapted for a two-hour film. It has even been suggested that, since most Victorian novels originally appeared serially in chapbooks or in magazines, the miniseries replicates the structure of the Victorian novel and allows viewers to experience the same kind of anticipation that the novel's original readers felt while waiting for the next installment. Personally, I am not convinced that serialization *itself* has resulted in "more faithful" adaptations of Hardy's novels. Granted, the serial version of *Jude the Obscure* is about twice as long as Michael Winterbottom's 1996 film of *Jude*, and it includes a great deal of material that would be left out in Winterbottom's version; but the serial still excludes some of the novel's characters and events, and some sequences are created by the scriptwriter. Then again, the 1998 serial of *Far from the Madding Crowd* is in total only about half an hour longer than John Schlesinger's 1967 film, and the 1998 *Tess* serial is actually *shorter* than Polanski's 1979 film. So can it be said that these serials contain markedly "more Hardy" than the earlier film versions? As is the case of cinematic adaptations, TV adaptations of novels will naturally reflect conscious choices in how to transform the stuff of the novel into visual form, as well as compromises and changes in the original material.

This chapter does not analyze all of the TV versions of Hardy that have been made, for the simple reason that some of them are not readily available—and two of them perhaps no longer exist.[9] The first known TV version of a Hardy prose work was apparently BBC-2's 49-minute adaptation of the short story *The Distracted Preacher*, which aired late in 1969. This production was followed by three serials that also ran on BBC-2: *The Woodlanders* (1970), *Jude* (1971), and *Wessex Tales* (1973), which was actually an anthology of six adaptations of Hardy's stories. *The Mayor of Casterbridge* aired in 1978, also on BBC-2 and later on *Masterpiece Theatre*. Of these five programs, only *Jude* is considered here. *The Distracted Preacher* and *The Woodlanders* are gone, no doubt casualties of the BBC's policy in the 1970s of "wiping" old programs it planned to never air again. All six of the *Wessex Tales* apparently survive—the series is listed in Britain's National Film and Television Archive—but none of the tales are available on video or DVD, and the series has not been on television in years. *The Mayor of Casterbridge* for years was missing two of its seven parts and the

Alan Bates as Henchard and Anne Stallybrass as Susan in *The Mayor of Casterbridge* (1978). The serial has long been unavailable in the U.S.

remaining episodes languished in the BBC vaults; the serial has since been restored and is now available on video in Britain. Unfortunately, at the time of this writing, *The Mayor* remains unavailable in the U. S.; this problem — and the fact the serial has been unseen in America for some twenty years — has kept me from giving it full consideration here. A future study will be devoted to both the 1978 *Mayor* and to a new serial based on the novel that is yet to air in America; and it can only be hoped that *Wessex Tales* will again be put before the public. While this chapter would no doubt be enhanced by the inclusion of *Wessex Tales* and *The Mayor*, the television productions considered here still provide many images of Hardy that are interesting and worthy of study, and two of the programs strike me as among the best adaptations of Hardy that have ever been made.

Jude the Obscure (BBC-2, 1971)

BBC's *Jude the Obscure,* which ran in six 45-minute episodes, is probably seldom watched today, and it has certainly been eclipsed in the popular memory by Winterbottom's cinematic *Jude* of 25 years later. The relative obscurity of this production may seem weirdly appropriate, but its status is a pity, for this *Jude* is a good drama in its own right and it makes an interesting companion piece to Hardy's novel. From a present-day perspective, there is much that is wrong with the serial: the script is very talky, as dramatist Harry Green retains the many philosophical discussions between Jude and Sue almost intact; most of the production is confined to interiors, with a good deal of the action happening "off-stage" (i.e., the beating of young Jude by Farmer Troutham; and the pig-killing sequence, which is overheard by the late-arriving butcher); the stationary camera and video format give the production a static look; there is no musical soundtrack to underscore the action; and beards, mustaches, and sidewhiskers often look pasted on the actors. It is also hard to overlook the fact that the sets for the most part look like sets. Unlike the pseudo-documentary realism of Winterbottom's *Jude*, the *Jude the Obscure* serial constantly advertises itself *as* a production; yet, in a perverse way, the program's artificiality is in accord with the novel on which it is based. For instance, the scene where Jude confronts the now-orthodox Sue inside the church is handled in a highly stylized way: Sue is in close-up, nearly facing the camera, while Jude stands in the background, in front of the altar. For several minutes, neither moves, and they do nothing but talk, speaking dialogue that has been lifted nearly unedited and unchanged from Hardy's novel. If this scene comes across as staged, static, and talky, it is nevertheless a reminder that Jude and Sue are ruled by their words, even going so far as to use words to defer their emotions. Now their words fail to close the very visible gap between them.

A crucial aspect of Hardy's novel is that the characters suffer for misreading things that are false and mutable as things that are true and permanent. In the televised *Jude*, we are clearly in a world of make-believe: the artificiality of this world is so apparent to the viewer that the characters' inability to see it automatically calls into question their perceptions and desires. The artifice of the production extends to the characters and how the actors portray them. The acting is often florid and even hammy: all too often it seems the performers are acting for the back row and not for a camera less than ten feet away. It also seems that while Robert Powell, with his thin face and large, child-like blue eyes, makes a perfectly befuddled Jude, Fiona Walker strikes a false note as Sue. In the first four parts, Walker's patrician looks and lofty manner belie the girlish enthusiasm that is part of the character she plays—though, to be fair, Walker's looks and performance are perfectly suited to the sobered and tragic Sue of parts five and six; but even in the miscasting of Sue the viewer is reminded that we are witnessing a performance, and performance is central to Sue's character. A particularly good example of Sue's "acting" occurs after Jude and Sue have arrived at the hotel room in Aldbrickham. In a moment drawn straight from Part IV, Chapter 5 of the novel, Sue insists that Jude recite some lines from Shelley's "Episychidion" and apply them to her; but, unlike in the novel, Jude does not already know the poem, and so Sue must say each line and have Jude repeat the lines after her. Sue appears to be in the grip of self-delusion, and she is using Jude to ratify her false self-image. For his part, Jude declares Sue to be a "dear, sweet, tantalizing phantom," a line of dialogue that refers the viewer back to a scene that occurred after Jude has just arrived in Christminster, where he stands in the middle of the campus square, looking about with wonder on his face. A passing constable demands to know Jude's business, and the young stonemason tells him he is "looking at phantoms"—the spirits of dead scholars. The script subtly indicates that Jude's two main pursuits—education and Sue—may simply be a long chase after phantoms.

The presentation of Jude and Sue as being in the grip of self-delusion is part of the general theme of the serial, which seems to be to call into question the reality each character experiences. This approach is, I believe, entirely in keeping with the spirit of Hardy's novel; moreover, by developing and expanding this theme beyond even Hardy's original conception, dramatist Green and director Hugh David have brought to the surface much of the comedy and satire that too often goes unnoticed in Hardy's novel. This *Jude* is frequently very funny, a fact which in and of itself may come as a shock to those whose conception of the novel is of a bleak, grim, deterministic tragedy, and who believe Hardy himself to have been a writer who constantly wept in sorrow or shook his fists in anger over the fates suffered by his characters. The serial opens up the possibility that Hardy envisioned his novel not as the stuff of great tragedy, but as a cutting parody of the illusions upon which too many people build their lives.

One of Green's wisest choices was to expand the role of Phillotson to emphasize this character's own self-delusions and his (unwitting) role in feeding those of Jude. The script establishes that Phillotson has lodged with Jude and Aunt Drusilla throughout his stay in Marygreen. This intimate connection with the Fawleys makes Phillotson's failure to remember Jude at Christminster seem particularly obnoxious; that Jude continues to admire Phillotson in spite of this snub indicts his idealization of the old schoolmaster. However, Green's script does free Phillotson from any blame for *directly* sparking Jude's academic ambitions. Phillotson *accidentally* leaves his Greek and Latin grammars at the Fawleys' house, and his cart passes Jude by as the boy tries to return them. Jude takes this to mean he has been given the books and that Phillotson has blessed Jude's course of study. In fact, before he had left the house, the schoolmaster expressly warned the boy against following in his footsteps, even providing Jude with a maxim paraphrased from Hardy's narrator: "There is a flaw in the terrestrial scheme, where what is good for God's birds is not good for God's gardener."

As Phillotson, John Franklyn-Robbins succeeds in undermining for the viewer the faith Jude instills in him. With his strange bouffant hairdo and waxed handlebar mustache, this Phillotson resembles a rather sad rake past his prime (imagine Alec d'Urberville reaching middle age), and both the script and Franklyn-Robbins's performance hint that Phillotson may be actually something of a pervert. In the novel, Phillotson and Sue do not meet until Jude introduces them, but in this serial, Phillotson has been watching Sue at work for a long while before he finally introduces himself to her. In many of his scenes with Sue, Phillotson hovers over her shoulders, his hands just inches from caressing her; and in one scene drawn from the novel, Phillotson removes a stack of photos of Sue from his desk drawer and peruses them with what looks like the kind of appreciation only a pornophile could have. Phillotson too has his illusions, which possibly stem from twisted desire.

Green's script further expands on the theme of misapprehension by dramatizing elements that are only in the margins of Hardy's novel. Jude's failure to gain admittance into a college is handled in such a way that the viewer can understand both the short-sightedness of Jude and the narrow-minded prejudices of the college that rejects him. Green invents a sequence in which Jude presents himself to Dean Tetuphar (Charleton Hobbes; the character is named Teutephany in the novel and is never seen), who turns out to be the epitome of a doddering academic. Jude, wearing his work clothes in the dean's office, looks ridiculous, and Tetuphar tries to turn him out. This leads to a comic shouting match, topped by Jude's cry from Job: "I have understanding as well as you!" While this sequence seemingly distorts and even burlesques Hardy's novel, it also succeeds in conveying the theme of mutual misapprehension that is so crucial to Hardy's *Jude*. As the only academic to actually appear in the serial, the stuffy, spluttering, and possibly senile Tetuphar becomes for the viewer the embodiment of Christminster itself. As such, we see that the object of Jude's quest has scarcely been worth his effort (in some respects, Tetuphar takes the place of a minor character from Hardy's novel, the composer of the hymn "The Foot of the Cross," a man Jude earnestly seeks out for spiritual enlightenment, and who turns out to have given up music for the lucrative wine trade (*Jude*, pp. 253–4), while the old Dean's realization that Jude can quote scripture is a sign that Tetuphar has misjudged Jude on the bases of class, age, and occupation.

Another character fleshed out from the margins of Hardy's novel is Miss Fontover (Sylvia Coleridge), Sue's Christminster landlady, who has also been made Sue's employer and supervisor at the ecclesiastical warehouse ("*Much* is expected from those who deal in ecclesiastical objets d'art!" she tells Sue with arch seriousness). Miss Fontover is essentially Mrs. Grundy made flesh, and while her self-righteousness and prudishness make her comic, they also make her a formidable adversary to Sue. Green's script dramatizes Miss Fontover's discovery of Sue's "naked pagan deities," and shows her smashing the statuettes. As Sue picks up the pieces she looks to a painting of the crucifixion on her wall, and recites from Swinburne, "Thou hast conquered, O pale Galilean!" Miss Fontover is, then, a representative of the powers of Christian dogma, the same powers with which Sue and—later on—Jude will presumably be at war. This presentation of Miss Fontover would seem to be in keeping with a popular view of how Hardy felt about religion; but the serial also shows that there is a "good side" to organized religion in the character of Rev. Dawlish (Michael Rothwell), who suggests that Jude put his mind to use as a country parson (but Jude abandons this idea almost immediately after Dawlish proposes it), and who chides Jude for burning his books. There is a definite sense in this version of *Jude the Obscure* that Dawlish lays out a viable path in life for Jude, but Jude refuses to compromise his vision in order to follow that path.

Without doubt, the serial's most successful—and funniest—character is Arabella (Alex Marshall). As with Phillotson and Miss Fontover, Arabella's role has been expanded from the novel, so that her scenes create a parodic counterpoint to the story of Jude and Sue. Hardy once remarked that Arabella owes a good deal to Fielding,[10] and Marshall's lusty performance seems almost to be modeled after Diane Cilento's portrayal of Molly Seagrim in Tony Richardson's film of *Tom Jones* (1963). Arabella's sensuality, however, has a malicious side to it that is largely absent in Molly. On their wedding night, Jude is shocked to learn both that Arabella has extensions in her hair and that her pregnancy was a lie, and he proceeds to berate her for her deceptions. Arabella's response is to bare her breasts—first for the camera and then for Jude. "You wanted me, now you got me," she exclaims. "What more do you want?" This scene has its shock value (especially for Americans), but it perfectly illustrates Jude's dilemma: on one hand he wants education and spirituality, while on the other he wants sensual pleasure. Arabella's question seems to say that Jude can have the latter only at the expense of the former: she positions herself as the fleshy text to Jude's spiritual one.

The parodic nature of Arabella's character is emphasized most strongly in the final two episodes. As Jude and Sue sink deeper into poverty and ill health, Arabella seems to *rise* in prestige. How she managed to rise in the world is not explained—though it is not difficult to conclude from her dress and from Sue's discovery of Arabella in a hungover, disheveled condition, that she has become a prostitute. Arabella in the serial is akin to the main character in Hardy's poem "The Ruined Maid"—a woman whose finery and comforts in life all spring from allowing herself to be "ruined" by men—while Jude and Sue's chaste relationship makes them suspect to others and results in their continual degradation. While Arabella's overt sexuality stands in contrast to the ultimately limited and limiting idealism and physical purity by which Jude and Sue live their lives, the child "Juey" (as would be the case in Winterbottom's film, "Little Father Time" is not used: perhaps Hardy's sense of humor in regard to this character is just too perverse for most tastes) is apparently used to parody Jude's spiritual and humanistic traits. Pale, dressed as an undertaker, covered with ugly warts on his face, and bursting into hysterical tears at every mishap, Juey (Gary Rich) seems to be a grotesque embodiment of his father's high-minded seriousness. Jude's remorse over slaughtering the pig and his refusal to eat the rabbit he killed to end its suffering are parodied by Juey's shrieks when Jude releases the boy's pigeons to save them from the butcher, and by his weeping over the sight of flowers because he knows they'll soon be dead. Arabella and Juey are both mockeries of Sue and Jude: Arabella thrives by exploiting her sexuality, while Sue clings to chastity and sinks into degradation; and Jude tries to live by his ideals which, in the form of his son, turn into fanaticism and murder.

The final episode of *Jude the Obscure* stops just short of all-out satire. Sue mourns her dead children and resists Jude's attempts to comfort her; but the pathos of this scene is destroyed by the entrance of Arabella, who dabs at her eyes in an exaggerated gesture of her own grief, crassly tells Sue she can't feel anything for the children Juey killed, and then casually nibbles at Sue's untouched breakfast and noses through the flat after Sue runs out in despair. After Sue begs Phillotson to be allowed back into his bed, she falls into his arms and he carries her over the threshold like the mummy carrying off the heroine in a Universal horror film of the 1940s. As Jude lies dead in his bed, Arabella saunters out of the room with Tinker Taylor. These are all scenes that deal with ugly subject matter, but they are not handled realistically or even sympathetically. Instead, they are handled grotesquely: as pathetic and tragic as are the deaths of the children and the fates of Sue and Jude, these elements are mitigated by comedy, burlesque, and sensuality. Like all grotesqueries, this *Jude the Obscure* isn't supposed to edify us by showing a grand tragedy or make us contemplate the workings of Fate: instead, it shocks us and unnerves us by distorting reality and undercutting our expectations.

If this *Jude the Obscure* is representative of how the BBC adapted Hardy's novels in the early 1970s, then he was well served. The very limitations imposed by the BBC—mostly indoor shooting, video cameras, and the like—forced Harry Green to take the emphasis off the physical locations, which have perhaps been relied on too greatly by others who have adapted Hardy's novels, and instead bring to the surface those elements of Hardy's novel that had been subsumed in order to flesh out the characters and the actions they take. Likewise, Hugh David's direction is limited to the studio settings, and by its very nature it is theatrical and affected. But Hardy's *Jude the Obscure* is a novel that advertises its own artificiality so as to question the nature of reality. The BBC *Jude*, of course, is not Hardy's *Jude*, but it serves many of the same ends as does the original novel, and it perhaps deepens our understanding of Hardy by showing that he was capable of creating farce and parody.

The Return of the Native (Hallmark Hall of Fame, 1994)

The 1994 TV movie *Thomas Hardy's The Return of the Native*—to use its full onscreen title—is significant because it is the first film or television adaptation of a Hardy novel in 15 years,[11] and because it signaled the coming of more films and TV productions derived from Hardy's fiction. This *Native* is also the only adaptation of a Hardy novel that is entirely produced by Americans; and the public identity of the American company behind the production largely explains why *The Return of the Native* was chosen as a TV movie property, and sheds a good deal of light on the choices that the screenwriter and director made in adapting the novel.

Native was produced by the Hallmark greeting card company to air as part of the *Hallmark Hall of Fame*, a series that began in 1951 to showcase made-for-TV specials—usually adaptations of stories, plays, and novels. There is no weekly spot for the *Hall of Fame* productions, but, as John Kiesewetter reports, the movies usually air "during February, May and November ratings' sweep periods—which coincidentally fall during the peak greeting card sales for Valentine's Day, Mother's Day and Christmas." Hallmark reportedly invests more than $30 million a year in the *Hall of Fame*, and since the corporation entirely sponsors each movie there are few commercial breaks—and then the commercials that do appear are, of course, for Hallmark cards and products. The president of Hallmark Hall of Fame Productions, Brad R. Moore, has even been quoted as saying that the whole purpose of the movies "is to equate Hallmark Cards with quality and good taste. So when the audience is finished watching for two hours, they feel better about Hallmark than before."[12] Interestingly, the *Hall of Fame* movies may serve the initial purpose of selling Hallmark products, but usually within a few months of their original airdates the movies are mass-produced as home videos for sale in Hallmark's retail stores, becoming themselves Hallmark products.

It would be an easy thing to carp that the Hallmark adaptation of *Native* is a particularly egregious example of the commodification of Thomas Hardy—after all, greeting cards, wrapping paper, and Christmas ornaments are being sold on the back of one of Hardy's greatest and most popular novels—but I am not convinced that what Hallmark does to Hardy is any worse than what other producers have done to him. However, Hallmark's stated goal to produce movies of "quality and good taste" says a great deal about the way the corporation perceived both the novel *The Return of the Native* and the man who wrote it. *Native* (1878) is one of Hardy's five or six "greatest" novels, and it is popularly read and widely taught on both sides of the Atlantic. *Native* was a fairly safe bet for Hallmark: its quality is proved, more or less, by its canonicity, and its story is one that would be familiar to many viewers.

In addition to wanting to make a "quality" movie based on a classic, it is clear that the producers also wished to make a movie that would be "authentically Hardy." The home video of *Native* ends with a short "Making of" documentary that does a great deal to explain how both the cast and crew interpreted Hardy's material and how they sought to reproduce their visions of Hardy on the screen. Joan Plowright (Mrs. Yeobright) calls Hardy's novels "a part of our heritage" and says, "One feels a great deal of patriotic pride in being part of something so English." Catherine Zeta Jones, who as Eustacia Vye had one of her first major roles, recalls that she had read *Native* as part of her high school curriculum and that she had long dreamed of playing Eustacia. Executive Producer Craig Anderson, an American, stresses to the viewer that, although U.S. dollars entirely funded the movie, it was important to make everything truly *English:* to this effect, the production utilized a British cast and crew, and the movie was shot "in Thomas Hardy's back yard." The documentary also interviews James Gibson, at the time the president of the Thomas Hardy Society, who served as an advisor on the production and whose function—presumably—was to ensure the movie maintained fidelity to Hardy's novel. "The Making of

The Return of the Native" has the effect of confirming for the viewer that the movie is, in all respects, authentic: authentically English, authentically historical, and authentic to Hardy both in terms of themes and locations. But how much "Hardy" is really *in* this production?

It seems to me that *The Return of the Native* largely suffers from the old problem that locations, period details, and atmosphere are played up to the expense of the story. Added to this is the greater problem that the running time of the movie is held to around 100 minutes, necessitating drastic simplification of the characters and situations. Unlike David Rudkin's screenplay for the later film of *The Woodlanders,* which removed a good deal of the novel's crucial material, Robert W. Lenski's script for *Native* retains many plot functions and some of Hardy's dialogue, but these elements are crammed into a tiny space. *Native* is extremely fast-moving and most of the dramatic scenes last no more than two or three minutes; as a result, the movie plays like a series of filmed highlights from the novel—the most memorable moments are on view, but they seem divorced from a larger context.

Even if the movie is viewed simply as a series of highlights, there is the problem that—even to a person who has never read the novel—many of the dramatized moments are inexplicable without Hardy's narrative voice to provide meaning. For instance, the action begins with a group of heath dwellers gathered around an enormous bonfire. A caption at the bottom of the screen reads "EGDON HEATH 1842—NOVEMBER 5—BONFIRE NIGHT." A British viewer—and even some Americans— would recognize November 5 as Guy Fawkes' Day; but to the vast number of Americans for whom this program was made, the date is essentially meaningless, and no explanation is provided for what the heath dwellers are commemorating. Then again, knowing the significance of the date certainly doesn't explain the complex meaning of the bonfire celebration in Hardy's novel, which is bound up in history, culture, and collective memory:

> It was as if these men and boys had suddenly dived into past ages, and fetched therefrom an hour and deed which had before been familiar with this spot. The ashes of the original British pyre which blazed from that summit lay fresh and undisturbed in the barrow beneath their tread. The flames from funeral piles long ago kindled there had shone down upon the lowlands as these were shining now. Festival fires to Thor and Woden had followed on the same ground and duly had their day. Indeed, it is pretty well known that such blazes as this the heathmen were now enjoying are rather the lineal descendants from jumbled Druidical rites and Saxon ceremonies than the invention of popular feeling about Gunpowder Plot [*Native*, p. 67].

The bonfire ritual may be ancient, but its forms and rites have not been static—it has changed and evolved, becoming something new while never losing the trappings of its origins.[13] Granted, it would be difficult for any film or TV movie to convey this sense of a rite that remains continuous but which is constantly evolving, but Lenski's script doesn't even try. The "Bonfire Night" scene shows the heath dwellers dancing and singing, gossiping about the presumed marriage between Thomasin and Wildeve, and speculating that Eustacia may be a witch, all of which only makes them out to be colorful—and very typical—"Hardean" rustics.

The concept of evolving history, in many respects, is the animating force of Hardy's novel. Egdon Heath abounds with history: many of its locations are identified with Druid and Saxon legends, and Hardy mentions that the only enduring signs of human inhabitation are, significantly, "an aged highway, and a still more aged barrow ... themselves almost crystallized to natural products by long continuance" (*Native*, p. 56). The road connects the inhabitants literally to different places on the heath and figuratively to the Romans who first built it; and the barrow is of even greater significance: it is the most ideal location to observe the goings-on, and later it will be excavated to reveal the burial urn of an ancient inhabitant. While Hardy depicts the geographical history of Egdon as unchanging and resistant to "Civilization," he also shows that the heath has a *social* history that human evolution is beginning to reflect: "The time seems near, if it has not actually arrived, when the chastened sublimity of a moor, a sea, or a mountain will be all of nature that is absolutely in keeping with the moods of the more thinking among mankind" (p. 55). Just as ancient rituals have evolved into present-day traditions and Roman roads have become modern thoroughfares, people change and evolve, transforming— in Hardy's view—to something more intelligent and more tragically self-aware.

Appropriately, Hardy places the novel at a time when the lifestyles of the heath people are in the process of transformation and evolution. He explains, for instance, that reddlemen such as Diggory Venn are—as of 1878—nearly extinct, since the coming of the railway largely put an end to their trade routes (p. 131) and that the people's conceptions of themselves and their roles in life are being transformed by the spread of national schools.[14] The main characters are all literate and reasonably well-educated: Wildeve and Clym, in fact, are mirror-images of one another in terms of the uses to which they've put their educations. Where Wildeve wastes his training as an engineer, Clym puts his education to use abroad in the diamond trade. Though education is viewed suspiciously by the "folk" characters, there is a strong sense that the changes brought to Egdon society by the schools were inevitable. One of Mrs. Yeobright's objections to Clym's plan to become a teacher, in fact, is that "The place is overrun with schoolmasters" (p. 261). Hardy also makes Clym into a kind of evolved "type": his physical appearance represents a step up in the human conception of attractiveness, as physically beautiful men were "the glory of the race when it was young," and are "almost an anachronism now" (p. 225); but Clym's *mind* has evolved to a point where, ironically, he has surpassed the needs of the Egdon community, and there is little he can bring to it. Clym wishes to establish a school that teaches a curriculum that is far in advance of what the community can now handle—in effect, he wishes to *force* the inhabitants to evolve into a new way of thinking; but he misses the fact that it is impossible for people to "rise to a serene comprehensiveness without going through the process of enriching themselves" (p. 231). Clym fails because he believes in immediate, as opposed to gradual, advancement: he cannot see—and literally becomes blind to— the truth that the inhabitants of Egdon are already evolving, and that they don't need Clym to speed them along.[15] In contrast, Eustacia, who sees herself—and is often seen by the narrator—as a figure who springs from the remote, mythical past, is so enraptured by time-worn images of romance that she is never a functioning, integral part of the *present* community: she stays tied to the past, unwilling to move forward, and desperate to escape a place she finds oppressive. Clym and Eustacia stand at the opposite poles of evolution; small wonder their marriage is a failure in the *present*.

The most "balanced" character in the novel is Diggory, who, after he has been rejected by Thomasin, abandons farming and takes up the reddle trade; for, to "be in Thomasin's heath, and near her, yet unseen, was the one ewe-lamb of pleasure left to him" (p. 134). Diggory puts himself into a position where he is constantly watching over Thomasin to ensure she is spared disgrace and pain; and—perhaps inadvertently—he becomes a kind of guardian of the community. Diggory is perhaps the supreme watcher in a novel that is filled with watchers: very few of the novel's incidents occur without someone overseeing or overhearing what is happening; and, frequently, significant actions are not dramatized by Hardy—they are related second-hand through another character. Though a system wherein people are constantly being scrutinized may strike our postmodern imaginations as sinister—and in later Hardy novels the overseeing eye *will* become sinister—in *Native*, the quality of watching serves to reinforce the importance of the community. There is a sense in which the heath dwellers are watching out for one another—not to exert power over the other, but to ensure survival of the community, in whatever form the community takes. Interestingly, when the heath dwellers scrutinize Eustacia's lone bonfire at the beginning of the novel, they are critical of her not so much because of her strange ways or because they believe she's a witch—the implications in the TV movie—but because she has made a fire inside her "own bank and ditch, that nobody else may enjoy it or come anigh it" (p. 79). Eustacia is considered suspicious by the community because she takes herself *outside* of the community.

As noted before, it would be difficult for any motion picture to capture the themes of Hardy's novel in all their complexity, but there are ways that the production could have conveyed a sense of evolving history and of the importance of safeguarding the community, and neither Lenski's script nor Jack Gold's direction bother. Simplification and splendor are the rules of this production. One particular scene that is brimming with potential is the excavation of the barrow. Clym (Ray Stevenson) removes a funeral urn from a pit, and after he speculates as to the identity of the cremated inhabitant, he hands the relic to Eustacia. "It was a maiden who wanted to escape the heath," Eustacia declares, and she holds the urn up

Ray Stevenson as Clym and Catherine Zeta Jones as Eustacia in Hallmark's *The Return of the Native*. This operatic pose is not in the actual production, but it embodies the moviemakers' glossy approach to the material.

to the sky. Gold's camera captures Zeta Jones's figure in full profile, urn thrust forward and above her head, her cloak flapping dramatically behind her, the billowing clouds and soft grasses of the heath creating a majestic backdrop to her classical form. Certainly, the moment captures Eustacia's egotism, but by tying the history of the urn in with Eustacia's desire to escape, the object ceases to convey any sense of communal history functioning *within* the heath. Moreover, both Eustacia's vanity and the significance of the urn largely become meaningless as soon as Eustacia raises the urn over her head. What is ultimately important in this scene is *beauty:* the camerawork, the setting, Catherine Zeta Jones and the pose she holds, are all gorgeous. It is as if the barrow were excavated just for the sake of the shot.

The dramatic image of Eustacia on the barrow is highly typical of this production: it is a glossy, often beautiful movie that derives its visual appeal from two sources—the location and from Catherine Zeta Jones herself. Zeta Jones is as much an object of Gold's camera as Nastassia Kinski was of Polanski's. She is most often photographed in closeup, and in scenes where she appears with another character, she is usually positioned so that she is in the foreground, or so that her face is fully visible while the other actor's is partly obscured. We never forget that Eustacia is the subject of Clym's and Wildeve's admiration—and that we are welcome to admire her, too. Similarly, the Exmoor locations are photographed in such a way as to maximize the exotic beauty of the area. Though the documentary shows that the movie was shot during cold and wet March weather, the photography is bright, the heath is in bloom, and the houses and cottages are uniformly charming. The Exmoor location is indeed lovely, and it is usually made lovelier by Eustacia's presence in it. This quality is best illustrated during the opening credits, in which the action of the movie begins—somewhat like Hardy's novel—by showing the heath absent of human habitation; but soon the camera spots a female figure clad in a blue cloak, and as it follows her, the viewer passes a pair of Hardean clichés: a sheepshearer and a man carrying a furze bundle on his back. Finally, the figure stops at a high point on the heath, and the camera reveals the face of Eustacia. As the camera pulls back in a dramatic overhead shot that puts Eustacia at the center of the vast, rolling expanses of the heath, she is heard in voice-over, declaring, "Deliver my heart from this fearful, lonely place. Send me a great love from somewhere, or I shall die. Truly, I shall die!"[16] Hardy says that "the subtle beauties of the heath were lost to Eustacia; she only caught its vapours," and that the environment makes Eustacia's natural rebelliousness become "saturnine" (p. 123). We can certainly see the "subtle beauty" of the heath, but there is no shot that corresponds to

Eustacia's "negative" point of view and which would indicate why she finds the location so oppressive. Further, she seems such a natural part of the landscape—like the heath around her, Eustacia is both beautiful and exotic—that she appears to be right at home. Everything is so breathtaking and dramatic it's hard to understand what Eustacia is complaining about.

In all fairness, it should be noted that although Eustacia is clearly adored and idealized by the camera, she isn't turned into a passive subject by it; in fact, the most successful—and most "Hardean"—moments in the movie are those in which the camera is used to provide some insight into Eustacia's vanity and romanticism. A particularly good sequence shows Eustacia in her room, holding a book and lovingly running her hand over an engraving of a woman greeting her lover, when she overhears a group of men outside discussing the imminent return of Clym from Paris and speculating that he and Eustacia would make a good match. Eustacia, clearly enchanted by the possibilities represented by the unseen Clym, begins dancing around the room. Another good sequence occurs when Eustacia bares her arm to show Clym the wound made by Susan Nunsuch. In a movie where everyone is covered from neck to toe, this is a surprisingly erotic moment, and it shows Eustacia's ability to control her own image—to show what she wants to show—in order to get the desired response from a man. However, while Eustacia can clearly deploy an image of herself, she can also become misled and even deluded by the images she creates. Toward the end of the movie, she admits to Clym, "I lived on promises you never made," and it is at moments like this that we can understand that Eustacia might be a victim of her own illusions.

Sadly, the same care that went into Eustacia's characterization and into the handling of her point of view is entirely absent in the presentation of the other characters. From the moment Clym first sees Eustacia through a clearing in the fog (a singularly corny moment), he becomes a love-struck dope. As soon as Mrs. Yeobright notices her son's infatuation she does little more than warn him against Eustacia and cluck over his preferring Eustacia to her, but the scenes of mother and son together are so few and peripheral that the rift between them seems to develop almost instantaneously. Wildeve (Clive Owen), often seen wearing open-necked collars and sporting a stubbly beard that is more *Miami Vice* than Egdon Heath, spends most of his screen time mooning after Eustacia. He fulfills the purposes of the plot, and little else. Thomasin (Claire Skinner) all but disappears from the movie after she marries Wildeve. Diggory Venn (Steven Mackintosh) fares worst of all: very little time is given to explaining his history with Thomasin, the sacrifice he made in taking up the reddle trade (and no explanation is provided for what a reddleman is), or how his self-imposed duties as watcher play a role in the community.

The movie does try to retain some sense of the heath dwellers' watching out for others, but there is no sense that they are looking out for the good of the community. In fact, the heath dwellers seem to be a suspicious, petty lot who dislike anything that is "different" from themselves. Not only do the heath folk come across as small-minded snoops and gossips, but when Eustacia bares her arm for Clym, she is watched by a disapproving furze-cutter. The supreme "watcher" in the movie, however, is Susan Nunsuch (Celia Imrie), whose role here is far more important than it is in the novel. As soon as Susan learns her son has been tending Eustacia's bonfire, she suspects that he has been "bewitched" (why?), and she begins following Eustacia with the intensity of a stalker. The scene where Susan stabs Eustacia with her hat pin is dramatized in the movie, giving Clym an opportunity to denounce the "superstition" that is rampant on the heath, and to prove to him that his proposed school is necessary. Susan is the only character outside the Yeobright circle who is given any real screen time, and as a result she seems to be the "typical" heath dweller— a "peasant" who is backwards, superstitious, and in need of enlightenment. All told, the heath dwellers in this movie are the kinds of rustics Hardy is commonly believed to have created, filled with folklore and brimming with color, but incapable of advancing in the world.

In the final assessment, *The Return of the Native* raises countless questions that it does not—or cannot—answer. Why does Clym go partially blind? Everything around him is bright and airy, so is his blindness symbolic, or perhaps owing to a mysterious eye disease? What, exactly, causes the death of Mrs. Yeobright? Her journey across the heath doesn't seem particularly arduous—is she done in by exhaustion, a heart attack, or, in fact, by seeing Eustacia's face at the window? (For that matter, why does Eustacia stay at the window so long that the camera is again allowed to devour her beautiful features?) If the reddle on Diggory's skin stays there for months—as he clearly says it does—why does it wash off as soon as he jumps in the river to save Clym, Eustacia, and Wildeve? And was there any build-up to that climactic storm, or did it just appear literally out of the blue? Finally, what is the meaning of Clym's "rebirth" as a preacher of "no creed," who is last seen testifying before a crowd on the heath, as if he is Christ preaching on the Mount?[17] These questions point to a central problem with the script: it seems that as much of Hardy's novel as possible was retained for the movie, but since it all had to fit into a 100-minute time frame, some much-needed expository material and linking scenes were cut out; and the remaining scenes and actions were reduced and simplified.

The resulting story makes little sense, and with Gold's camera focused more on the locations and on Catherine Zeta Jones than on the dramatic sequences, it all seems glossy and superficial to boot.

Still and all, this *Native* delivers an image of Hardy we can recognize: it is the Hardy who wrote of people falling in love in the middle of picturesque settings; the Hardy who painted loving pictures of peasants wedded to their stations in the earth; and especially the Hardy who wrote timeless works of English literature. Certainly, these are the ways that the Hallmark corporation perceived Thomas Hardy, and this is the Hardy they have packaged, wrapped, and delivered.

Far from the Madding Crowd (Granada/WGBH, 1998)

The year 1998 saw the airing of the first serials in 20 years that were based on Hardy novels, and both productions were also the first "TV versions" of Hardy novels that had previously been filmed.[18] These facts are significant, for the new *Far from the Madding Crowd* in some respects appears to be a remake—or at least a rethinking—of John Schlesinger's 1967 film. Nicholas Renton's direction at times seems to mirror that of Schlesinger, and Philomena MacDonagh's script replicates a few of the dramatic choices that Frederick Raphael made in his screenplay for the earlier film; for instance, dramatizing Fanny's going to the wrong church, and in leaving the audience to wonder if Troy has drowned after he throws himself into the ocean. Yet, in spite of the familiarity of the production, this version of *Far from the Madding Crowd* far surpasses the Schlesinger film (in my view, at least) and stands next to the serial of *Jude* as the best of the existing television adaptations of Hardy's novels.

An initial drawback to the serial is that, at first glance, some of its visual qualities are highly reminiscent of Schlesinger's film: many of the locations are similar to—and perhaps the same as—the ones where the 1967 *Crowd* was shot; and a few sequences almost seem to be patterned after Schlesinger's direction. What, then, makes this 1998 serial markedly different from the 1967 film? For a start, there is little to no lingering over "quaint" and "colorful" aspects of the story. For instance, in the Schlesinger film, after Gabriel fails to find work at the Casterbridge market, he is seen playing his flute for money while a group of townsfolk begin an impromptu jig—a moment that *is* in the novel, but which seems included in the film largely for the sake of charm. In the serial, however, after Gabriel is not hired he is simply forced to move on to another place where work is likely to be found. Another sequence, Troy's performance as Dick Turpin,

The cast of the 1998 *Far from the Madding Crowd. Left to right:* Nathaniel Parker (Gabriel), Paloma Baeza (Bathsheba), Jonathan Firth (Troy), Nigel Terry (Boldwood).

takes up several minutes in Schlesinger's film and is handled like a moment out of Cecil B. DeMille's circus epic *The Greatest Show on Earth*; but in the serial, the most that is established is that Troy's true identity is in jeopardy of being discovered, and that he must further disguise himself to prevent Bathsheba from recognizing him. In 1967, moments such as these seemed to be offered solely for their escapist values, while in 1998 there is an acknowledgment of the *drama* in the sequences.

One of the biggest differences between the two productions is that, in the serial, "Nature" is never allowed to be the star of the show. The glossy, pastoral splendor of Schlesinger's film is not a part of this production: the Dorset locations are often attractive, but they are never idealized. The first episode takes place during winter, when the skies are overcast, the weather is visibly cold, and the topography is brown and muddy. The weather and location make clear hardships for Gabriel (Nathaniel Parker), who cannot water his sheep without first breaking the ice that covers the trough, and who closes off all the ventilation in his hut to keep warm—and nearly gases himself to death as a result. Although later episodes are set during the spring and summer, when the locations grow more inviting and become seemingly more hospitable to humanity, director Renton does not allow the camera to linger on rolling meadows and on the sight of wildflowers in bloom. What is usually most important to Renton—and this is what completely differentiates his version from Schlesinger's—is the *work* that is being done outdoors. When the characters are outside, they are almost always laboring—harvesting grain, washing sheep, performing any number of farm chores—and all of it looks hard, and some of it even looks like drudgery. No one in the serial seems to be in "communion" with Nature: if the people are part of the land it is because they *work* it, and the land is not always cooperative with their efforts. This approach to Nature strikes me as being somewhat in accord with Hardy. After all, in the novel, the characters who try to live according to the "dictates" of Nature become misled; it is the characters who learn that Nature is *not* in accord with their actions who are most likely to survive and prosper.

Even though this new *Crowd* does not idealize Nature and rural life, neither does it embrace a view that people blindly suffer at the hands of Nature or—that other old Hardean saw—Fate; in fact, the serial clearly argues that people can pull together in order to improve the collective lot of the community. Both Gabriel and Bathsheba (Paloma Baeza) are "outsiders" to Weatherbury, but instead of bringing harm to "traditional" ways of life, they bring with them new ideas that can and will revitalize communal life. When Bathsheba first takes possession of her uncle's farm, the work folk treat her with distrust, both because of her sex—"What would a young girl do with a farm?" one of the house servants asks—and out of fear of the changes she's likely to bring. At Warren's Malthouse, the workers discuss Bathsheba in entirely contemptuous terms: "She doesn't know her pretty arse from her elbow," one grumbles, while another says, "We'll know her fancy come payday—who's to stay and who's to go." These characters aren't simply colorful "rustics," but men and women who have an active stake in the economy of Weatherbury—and that economy is largely managed by Bathsheba.

The fears and concerns of the working community are most often voiced by Henery Fray, who in MacDonagh's script is given a larger role than he has in the novel. In the serial, Henery (Robin Soans) anticipates being named bailiff, and he becomes resentful when Bathsheba does away with the position altogether. Later, when Gabriel begins to exert control over the farm, Henery complains that Gabriel is bringing in "newfangled machines that can do the work of twenty men"—and which, he fears, will put the laborers out of work. In the novel, Pennyways discovers Troy has faked his own death, and the old bailiff uses this knowledge for simple monetary gain; but MacDonagh makes an interesting change to the story by having Henery discover the secret about Troy (Jonathan Firth), who buys Henery's silence by promising that, after he resumes control of Bathsheba's farm, he will fire Gabriel and elevate Henery to his place, thus restoring the old system on the farm. The last time Henery is seen, he is gathering the wheat that has been mown down by a stream-driven thresher. "We shouldn't be welcoming this!" Henery mourns. "Soon they won't need none of us!" But this is not the impression that the viewer is left with: by this time, Gabriel has combined two farms, he is on the verge of winning Bathsheba, and he has brought technological progress. He is a man who has ushered in a new era for Weatherbury—without firing anyone.

In some respects, the positioning of Gabriel as a character who modernizes the farm in order to improve it seems to be very much a product of late 1990s ideology, where economic success is often heralded as the greatest of all possible values.[19] However, despite the serial's championing the changes and improvements that are brought about by Gabriel, it should not be thought that this *Crowd* blindly embraces capitalism or industrialism. What the serial *does* embrace is a strong sense of community, and Gabriel's actions constantly go toward making the community thrive. The importance of community is perhaps best emphasized by the development of the role of Fanny Robin (Natasha Little) to show that she isn't simply the woman who was "wronged" by Troy, but that she is a vital part of Weatherbury society.[20] Shortly after Fanny leaves the Everdene farm to elope with Troy, we learn that Boldwood (Nigel Terry) took Fanny under his wing and found her a position with old Farmer Everdene. Boldwood, fearing that Fanny is dead, heads the search for her body, and it is their shared concern for Fanny that brings him and Gabriel together in a trusting and friendly relationship. It is this concern over the well-being of a single person that indicates just how closely knit the community is, and how dependent these people are on one another. Boldwood himself will be the recipient of the kind of concern he showed for Fanny: after Boldwood murders Troy—perhaps ridding the community of a destructive force—Gabriel gathers the evidence that proves Boldwood insane, thus sparing his life. Gabriel becomes a literal *savior*—he saves crops, sheep, and human lives—but he is also a guide who will bring who and what he saves into a new era. The serial is perhaps much more optimistic than is Hardy's novel, but the emphasis on communal cooperation is certainly a part of the book, and it is a theme that Hardy touches upon in much of his early to mid-career fiction.

A further benefit to the expansion of Fanny's role is that it allows the viewer to glimpse societies that are outside of—but not entirely divorced from—Weatherbury. After Troy calls off the wedding, the serial devotes a few scenes to illustrating Fanny's progress from the church door to the Casterbridge workhouse. These scenes of Fanny's degradation through physical labor perhaps owe something to *Tess*, but they are also reminders that Weatherbury does not exist in a vacuum: just outside its limits is a world of workhouses and often backbreaking toil, and where the values of community perhaps have little meaning. And, since it is the places outside of Weatherbury that purchase the wool and grain that the community produces, Weatherbury cannot exist without that outside world. The distance between the community and the madding crowd may not, in fact, be as far as is usually thought.

Finally, while the Schlesinger film boasted major stars of the 1960s, this *Crowd* features a fairly young cast of actors who are essentially unknown outside of Britain. Julie Christie's Bathsheba seems always to be acting out of cocky self-confidence, which gave rise to numerous complaints that hers was a character who belonged more to the 1960s than the 1860s; but Paloma Baeza's Bathsheba is, simply put, a girl who is trying to live up to her own expectations and down to the negative assumptions that others have of her. It is also apparent that Bathsheba believes that taking charge of the farm has elevated her to a position far above everyone else's, and that she is determined to play the role she's been assigned—even if she doesn't like it. In one scene, Bathsheba is on the verge of entering a room where the servants are gathered together and laughing merrily, but she stops herself and sadly walks away. Bathsheba even distances herself from Gabriel, although it is evident she does not want to. When Gabriel addresses her by her first name, she corrects him with a terse "Miss Everdene," but Baeza delivers the line sadly, as if Bathsheba regrets having to put a barrier between them. Gabriel also attempts to give her advice on her personal conduct, and she responds by trying to hold him to his lower station: "How dare you speak to me like that? I pay your damn wages!" The profanity is not from Hardy's novel, but the moment works, since Bathsheba's use of "damn" is pure bravado, a signal that she is really a girl who sees herself in the masculine role of landowner, and that she is willing to appropriate masculine discourse to prove her own power.

Bathsheba's girlish qualities also explain her reasons for sending the valentine to Boldwood—it is, to her, just a game to pass the time—and she rebuffs Boldwood's offer of marriage by pleading, "I'm only a girl!" It is clear that, from managing the farm to marrying Troy, Bathsheba is in over her head, and that all her mistakes are owing to her being too young, too vain, and too inexperienced. This treatment of Bathsheba may seem patronizing and sexist, but in many respects, so is Hardy's. In both the novel and the serial, Bathsheba at times is a wild, impetuous force who confesses that what she really needs is a man who will "tame" her; and, as it turns out, Gabriel, who cultivates the land and brings new innovations to the farm, is the perfect man to bring Bathsheba into maturity.

Another character who is well-served by this adaptation is Troy, whose status as illegitimate child of a local lord (which is essentially ignored in the 1967 film) is used to explain many of his motives in pursuing Bathsheba. On the morning after their wedding, Troy tells Bathsheba about his origins and admits, "This is what I am, Bathsheba: a bastard, destined to never belong anywhere." He then shows her his watch, the one thing his father gave him, and says, "If we should have a son, the watch shall go to him. He shall know who he is." Troy, then, is a social climber who by marrying Bathsheba is in a position to start a dynasty. However, in the dialectic of the serial (and, for that matter, in Hardy), Troy is a poor steward of the land, whose getting the men drunk nearly results in the loss of the ricks. Troy may come from the Weatherbury community, but he brings nothing to it, and he is, in fact, a figure who could ruin it.

In spite of Troy's status as ostensible "villain," Jonathan Firth still invests the character with a good deal of humanity. The serial does not gloss over Troy's womanizing—when he takes leave of his company to harvest grain, a fellow soldier asks him, "Wenching in the country again?"—but it also shows that Troy truly is in love with Fanny. When Troy first arrives in the fields, several women flock around him (old conquests?), but his first question is to whether Fanny is there—an indication that she is, perhaps, the reason for his return home. It is also evident that Bathsheba is, to Troy, first a distraction and then a means to obtain financial success. Even though Troy *lusts* after Bathsheba, he doesn't even seem to *like* her. During his sword demonstration, Troy stands just a few feet from Bathsheba, hacking and thrusting at her in a manner that suggests sublimated hatred.[21] His imagined abuse of Bathsheba perhaps becomes real on his wedding night, when Troy roughly shoves Bathsheba up against a wall and begins thrusting against her in a way that comes extremely close to violence. That Bathsheba is so taken by Troy's looks and his flattery that she cannot see the contempt he has for her creates a complete condemnation of Bathsheba's point of view.

The 1998 *Far from the Madding Crowd* serial, then, succeeds not just in replicating the plot of Hardy's novel, but also in conveying both Hardy's interest in the value of community and his concern with the illusions by which people tend to live their lives. Granted, at times the serial is as visually attractive as are other films based on Hardy's works, but it is clear that the producers were far more interested in what the characters are *doing* than in where the characters *are*. The serial retains the Hardean notion that mutual shared labor and concern for the community are the only safeguards for happiness—and it has been difficult in the past for filmmakers to show this side of Hardy without turning him into a cloying pastoralist. The *Madding Crowd* serial presents an honest and straightforward interpretation of Hardy and his novel—which would not be the case in the serial of *Tess of the d'Urbervilles,* shown in America later in the same year.

Tess of the D'Urbervilles (A & E/LWT, 1998)

The two-part, three-hour serial of *Tess of the D'Urbervilles* is, to date, the only adaptation of a Hardy novel produced in association with an American cable company. Significantly, that company is the Arts and Entertainment network, which, as its name announces, would seem to be dedicated to providing the best in cultural programming and thus be the ideal medium for an adaptation of Hardy. A & E often puts its emphasis on *entertainment,* and where it seems to lay claim to *art* is in its reliance on British television shows. During its early years, A & E simply re-ran the same British serials and TV movies that had previously been shown in America on *Masterpiece Theatre* and *Mystery!;* but, beginning around the mid–1990s, the network managed to bypass PBS and secured the exclusive rights to air original British programs. Where PBS had once been practically the sole vessel for British programs in the United States, A & E became a serious rival, and in short order it began to beat WGBH at its own game—teaming up with British television companies to create their own Classic Serials and TV movies.[22]

A & E announced its entry into the serial competition with the airing in late 1995 of a lavish, six-part adaptation of *Pride and Prejudice,* produced in cooperation with BBC-1. The program was a hit with both critics and viewers, and since that initial success, A & E has worked with the British networks to create more serials and movies, many of which originally aired as part of "A & E's Literary Collection"—a banner that now seems to have been dropped. Stylistically, A & E's serials and movies are little different from the ones that air on *Masterpiece Theatre* and they serve a similar ideological purpose: to preserve an image of British TV as "high-minded," informed by a literary sensibility, and impeccable in terms of acting, writing, and production values; and, more importantly, to present the novels on which these programs are based as capital-L literature.

A & E's *Tess* was put at an automatic disadvantage in having to not only be true to a classic novel, but in having to compete with the memory of a popular and respected film. By the time the TV version of *Madding Crowd* was shown, more than thirty years had passed since Schlesinger's film; and in America at least, the original had little impact on the popular consciousness. The makers of the new *Crowd* didn't have to worry about negative comparisons to a beloved film. Polanski's *Tess*, however, was a major hit with audiences in Europe and America, and the film has endured as something of a classic. In terms of film production, the nineteen years that separate *Tess* and *Tess of the D'Urbervilles* might as well be a century (the 1990s alone saw more than one version of *Hamlet, Jane Eyre, Wuthering Heights, Great Expectations,* and other classics); but the continuing popularity and acclaim of Polanski's *Tess*, and the fact it continues to be studied for its filmcraft, have given it a life that goes beyond the period in which it was made. The producers of the serial version of *Tess* therefore not only had to adapt Hardy's novel, but they had to differentiate their version of it from Polanski's.

The *Tess* link on A & E's website reveals a great deal about how the cast and crew went about making their adaptation of the story both separate from the Polanski film and "true" to the Hardy novel. Director Ian Sharp explains that the difference is in that "we exploit the passion in the novel much more. [Polanski's *Tess*] had a curious detachment to it, I felt. It was treated and shot as a series of tableaus, as opposed to really getting inside and under the skin of the characters and their relationships."[23] Scriptwriter Ted Whitehead admits to never having seen the earlier film, but he lays claim to having captured an essential Hardean theme that Polanski likely missed:

> I guess from the title, *Tess*, one major difference I've highlighted is the fact that this is *Tess of the D'Urbervilles*. Hardy does this very deliberately. Okay, the D'Urbervilles are a now extinct family, but Hardy has a great fondness for the old English families, even if they are extinct. He admires, you know, a certain sort of fighting warrior quality, as he sees it, and a certain haughtiness, if you like. Whereas, he has very little time for the nouveau riche. ...[The Stokes have] come down south and adopted the name of D'Urberville, which, for Hardy, is a travesty. You can't buy that kind of fineness. Now, Tess has inherited it. She's fine, she's noble, and you know money doesn't mean much to her. What matters to her is the truthfulness of her love.[24]

Of the three actors interviewed—Justine Waddell (Tess), Oliver Milburn (Angel), and Jason Flemyng (Alec)—only Jason Flemyng professes any familiarity with the Polanski film, and he credits it only for the eroticism of the strawberry sequence and for getting "the story firm in [his] head."[25] Otherwise, all three performers reminisce about reading Hardy in school, and they all profess admiration for the "classic" qualities of his characters. Reading all five interviews is a fascinating experience: it is difficult not to come away with the impression that all the principals involved in the production wish us to put the Polanski film aside; what they are offering on A & E is the authentic *Tess*.

Strangely, despite the producers' desire to distance their production from Polanski, at times the serial plays like a critique of the earlier film. Specifically, it almost seems that before he began writing his script, Ted Whitehead studied Jane Marcus's blistering attack on Polanski, "A Tess for Child Molestors," and set about to make sure the same charges couldn't be leveled against this adaptation. As was discussed in Chapter 4, Marcus accused Polanski of infantilizing Tess, and of making her nothing more than a passive victim. Marcus was especially offended because, in her eyes, Polanski "sides" with Tess's rapist and denies women the satisfaction of seeing Tess "punish" Alec by killing him.[26] Of course, Marcus misses the point that Hardy obscures the issue of whether Tess is raped or not—and, for that matter, he doesn't "show" the murder of Alec. It is clear in the serial, however, that Tess *is* the victim of rape. During the scene in The Chase, Tess clearly cries out "No! Stop!" while Alec is on top of her—absolute and incontestable proof that she is not submitting willingly. Immediately following this scene, we see Tess on the road to Marlott, followed by Alec. In the ensuing dialogue, there is no mention of the length of time that has elapsed since the night in The Chase: it could, for all we know, be the next morning. There is no sense that Tess may have cooperated with Alec; as a result, the viewer has no choice but to see Alec as rapist and Tess as victim.

Whitehead also shows that Tess is anything but accepting of what Alec has done to her, and he allows Tess a "victory" by dramatizing the events in the hotel room that lead to Alec's death. Whitehead makes a major change to the story by leaving Tess in the dark as to Alec's true identity: she learns the truth only in the hotel room, when he blurts it out during an argument. After Alec insults Angel, calling him a "spineless bastard," Tess erupts into a rage and graphically plunges a knife into Alec's chest. Tess is allowed the victory that Jane Marcus claims Polanski has denied her. Alec has raped, lied to, and manipulated Tess. He deserves everything he gets.

The kind of fury that Tess displays in the hotel room is not isolated to this one scene: Justine Waddell's characterization of Tess emphasizes her anger, her fierce pride, and even her ability to be a bit of a coquette. It cannot be argued that *this* Tess merely accepts what life hands her, or that the director turns her into the dumb object of his camera's admiration. Waddell is such a spitfire, in fact, that it is difficult to believe that she is as "tractable" as her mother (Lesley Dunlop) claims, or that she is as capable of being Alec's dupe as the script makes her out to be. In most of her scenes with Alec, Tess usually shows scorn and defiance—though there is a nice moment when Alec tries to teach her to whistle and she breaks into a wide grin; likewise, in her dealings with the other characters, Tess is often quick to anger and she usually seems capable of maintaining the upper hand. Her scenes with Joan almost invariably turn into shouting matches, with Tess loudly condemning her mother's scheming and her foolishness; and even during the scenes of her courtship with Angel, Tess tends to fly off the handle. In the "garden" sequence, Angel (who here plays the concertina and has just squeezed out a tune that resembles "How Much is that Doggie in the Window?") says to Tess, "I should call you Artemis, the goddess of purity." Tess, who has been coyly playing with some flowers, suddenly flashes her eyes at Angel. "Call me *Tess!*" she snaps, and begins

No shrinking violet: Tess (Justine Waddell) makes her interest in Angel (Oliver Milburn) clear in *Tess of the D'Urbervilles.*

to storm off. Waddell's emphasis on Tess's fiery qualities almost seem designed to erase the memory of Nastassia Kinski's quiet, subdued Tess; however, this aspect of Tess's character is played up at the expense of her other qualities. Waddell's Tess very seldom shows vulnerability or charm; she does, however, frequently burst into tears—over the dead horse, after Angel calls her "the most perfect woman I have ever met," after Angel comes to the hotel and admits his mistake in leaving her. Waddell bounces so often between fury and tears that her performance is frequently alienating.

Beyond answering the "charges" that have been leveled against the Polanski film, what else does this new *Tess of the D'Urbervilles* do, and, more importantly, how does it contribute to the process of seeing Hardy? The serial, as was mentioned before, is positioned as an "authentic" version of the Hardy novel. Like so many Hardy adaptations, it was filmed on location in Dorset (though many of the outdoor settings are oddly similar to those Polanski used in France, throwing into question the need to film in "real" places), and boasts the usual period detail and "Hardean" touches. Ted Whitehead claims that "the only alterations we've made to the novel really are in terms of omitting some material we just did not have time to include"; otherwise, his major task as screenwriter was to edit and condense Hardy's material.[27] The script does include some incidents from the novel that aren't in the 1979 film—the death of Prince, the midnight baptism, Alec's reappearance as an evangelist—but Whitehead also follows Polanski's lead in eliminating the sign painter, Angel's somnambulistic "burial" of Tess, and the scene of Tess's execution, followed by Angel's leaving with Liza-Lu. Whitehead's script even eliminates some Hardy material that Polanski's film retains—most of it relating to Angel. Mr. and Mrs. Clare, Mercy Chant, and the moment where Angel nearly asks Izz to accompany him to Brazil are all gone. As a result, Angel loses much of his background and many of the contexts by which we understand him. And, as we have already seen, Whitehead changes Hardy's novel by having Alec mislead Tess about his "kinship" to her all *throughout* the serial. Certainly, Whitehead does a bit more than simply edit, omit, and condense.

The essential problem with both the script and Sharp's direction is that they tend to radically simplify Hardy's story to the extent that it is dumbed down. The fact Tess will be raped could not be more apparent had Sharp included an intertitle card *announcing* the fact. When Joan proposes the scheme of claiming kin to Jack (John McEnery) at Rolliver's, an eavesdropper comments to a companion, "Joan Durbeyfield better be careful—she'll be getting that Tess into trouble." When Tess alights from the cart that has taken her to The Slopes, her first sight is of a man sharpening a scythe. As Alec leads Tess to other parts of the grounds, several washer-women watch them and exchange knowing grins; and Car Darch (Linda Armstrong) emerges from the same building Alec had just exited, buttoning her dress. Finally, after Tess has returned home, Whitehead includes a scene where Alec discusses with his blind mother (Rosalind Knight) the possibility of hiring Tess. Mrs. D'Urberville at first scolds her son for not revealing that their name is adopted, but presently she asks Alec, "Is she pretty?" Alec admits that Tess is, and Mrs. D'Urberville says with resignation, "Then I suppose you'd better go get her." Frankly, Sharp's manipulation of images and Whitehead's invented scene insult the intelligence. Isn't it enough to *hint* as to what might happen to Tess? And why make Mrs. D'Urberville complicit in Alec's scheme? The answer is that Sharp and Whitehead are narrowly invested in presenting Tess's tragedy as tied up in the workings of Fate. When Tess is hired to work at The Slopes, the voice-over narrator (Gerald James) solemnly intones, "So Tess had to abandon any hope for the future that she might become a teacher and instead accepted the role that Fate had decreed for her." If all the imagery and the scene between Alec and his mother haven't made it clear enough that Tess is destined to suffer at Alec's hands, the narrator removes all doubts.

The narrator, whose voice and general persona are those of a wise old man, is omnipresent. At times the voice is merely annoying. For instance, shortly after Tess leaves The Slopes, the narrator tells us, "Tess had run away from her past, hoping to escape it, but there was no escape— she was carrying a child." Apparently, someone involved in the production feared viewers might not understand where the baby that appears in subsequent scenes came from. In another instance—and in another moment entirely invented by Whitehead—Tess's decision to confess her past to Angel is sparked by Car Darch being hired on at Talbothays. This addition to the story in itself simplifies Tess's reasons for writing to Angel— she seems merely afraid that Car will reveal her past with Alec—but the implications of the moment when Tess first sees Car are needlessly spelled out for the viewer by the narrator: "The past would not go away, but appeared right there in front of her in the form of her old enemy, Car Darch, filling Tess with the dread of exposure."

Though it may seem that the narrator is a mere gadfly, he actually serves a clear ideological purpose of imposing a text upon the serial. The narrator *makes* the viewer see the story as a tragedy of fate. The narrator is first heard over the opening scene, when the camera picks up the sight of Jack Durbeyfield walking up a country lane: "It was on the day of the

May dance that Tess's father encountered the parson who revealed to him what would better have been left forgotten. A chance encounter—a chance remark—yet such things determine our fate." As we have already seen, the narrator also attributes to "fate" Tess's rape and the reappearance of Car Darch; yet, strangely enough, in his final pronouncement on the story, the narrator doesn't invoke fate at all: "Justice was done. Mankind in time-honored way had finished its sport with Tess." Does this mean that the narrator has shifted blame from fate to mankind, or does he suggest that mankind in persecuting Tess has acted as the *instrument* of fate? One would tend to suspect the latter, since the narrator's overall tendency is to make gloomy and "fateful" pronouncements on just about every significant action.

But who *is* this narrator? That he has been given a distinctive voice—that of an old man—would indicate that he is a definite character, but there is no one in the first half of the story to provide a face to the narrator's voice. However, the narrator's identity is revealed in the second half of the serial, during circumstances that are utterly bizarre. Tess has made her wedding night confession to Angel, and, as in the book, Angel walks out into the night air, with Tess meekly following. In the production, Angel and Tess walk in single-file down a public street, where they pass a small man—his back to the camera—who doffs his hat, revealing a bald head surrounded by a fringe of white hair. The narrator rasps, "I shall never forget those lovers, their faces blind to time and place, each isolated in their mutual despair." As the narrator speaks, the old man turns to watch the couple walk away. There is a closeup of his face, and the narrator is revealed to be—*Thomas Hardy himself!* Or at least that's what we are to think, as the old man in the serial bears an astonishing resemblance to the octogenarian Hardy.

The "author's" presence in the production raises numerous questions. For viewers who are unfamiliar with Hardy's physical appearance and with his works, the moment when the narrator's face is revealed is meaningless: they are left to wonder, who is this character, and how did one glance at Tess and Angel give him such intimate knowledge of the story? To those viewers who are in on the joke, Hardy's physical presence makes no sense at all: the serial is set around 1890, when Hardy was 50, so why is he depicted as a very old man? And why include Hardy as a character/narrator at all? It almost seems that Whitehead and Sharp are trying to pull off the same trick that was used to great effect in the A & E/BBC coproduction of *Tom Jones*, in which an actor playing Henry Fielding wandered in and out of the scenes, interacted with the characters, and made commentaries and observations directly to the camera.

This device proved to be the perfect way to dramatize Fielding's "intrusive" narrator, and it actually furthered the serial's spirit of freewheeling fun. In some respects, Hardy's narrator in *Tess* is every bit as intrusive as is Fielding's in *Tom Jones*; but, unlike Fielding, Hardy does not position his narrator as a flesh-and-blood character who can *interact* with other characters, and who is reporting what other characters have told him, and Hardy never lets the reader forget that his narrator's viewpoint is *one* perspective, and not a totalizing one. Perhaps Whitehead and Sharp felt that, by creating a Hardy figure who narrates the story, they would be recreating for the screen Hardy's narrative voice. Unfortunately, all they have delivered is a Hardy stereotype: he emerges as the grand old man of English literature, who saw life as material evidence of the tragic workings of Fate.

In another sense, it almost seems disingenuous that the makers of this serial are trying to give credit to Hardy for the authorship of the story, for it is clearly far removed from Hardy's original. Many of the plot functions are intact, but the story is presented in such a way that we *must* see Tess as a victim of rape and, in a larger sense, of fate. But it is the full-scale dumbing down of *everything* that makes *Tess of the D'Urbervilles* both a poor drama in its own right and an even poorer vehicle for seeing Hardy and his novel. One has to wonder why Whitehead had to spell out every detail, and why Sharp had to employ such heavy-handed images. Was it necessary to depict Izz, Marian, and Retty as comically unattractive, thus making Tess the only possible object of Angel's interest? Could Marian's descent into alcoholism be conveyed more poignantly than by having her lug a bottle around in every scene? Was it necessary to have a violinist scratching out "Beautiful Dreamer" over the scene in which Jack Durbeyfield drops dead? Certainly if the makers of *Tess of the D'Urbervilles* thought they were doing justice to Hardy, their vision of his novel is a simplistic one, and the serial has done nothing to dislodge Polanski's film from popular memory.[28]

These four television adaptations of Hardy's novels represent, I believe, both the best and the worst ways to bring Hardy to the screen—whether that screen is on a television or in the cineplex. Both 1971's *Jude the Obscure* and 1998's *Far from the Madding Crowd* succeed not by slavishly trying to reproduce everything that is in Hardy's novels, but by creating dramatic equivalents to themes and ideas that are often relegated to the margins of Hardy's prose. These two adaptations show the depth of

Hardy's thought, and they showcase the fact he was more than a pastoralist and tragedian. *The Return of the Native* and the 1998 *Tess of the D'Urbervilles* are, to my mind, failures because they try only to replicate the Hardy that we know. As a result, Hardy's stories become simplified, laden with clichés, and little more than a series of pretty sequences.

Postscript:
Hardy on the Horizon

It would be slightly inappropriate to label this closing section a "conclusion," since the process of visualizing Hardy on motion picture and television screens is an ongoing one. This particular study is really just a snapshot in time—a glimpse at how Hardy has been seen by filmmakers and TV producers up to this particular moment. More adaptations of Hardy will emerge, and with them will come images of the author that will demand critical scrutiny. In fact, at the time of this writing, a new television version of *The Mayor of Casterbridge* has already aired on Britain's ITV network, and is expected to run in America on A & E in the near future. The two-part serial comes from the same hands that created the 1998 *Tess of the D'Urbervilles* miniseries and features the superb character actor Ciarán Hinds as Henchard and *Woodlanders* veteran Jodhi May as Elizabeth-Jane. In related news, the video distributor Acorn Media has announced it is finalizing a deal to bring to America the long-unseen 1978 BBC series of *The Mayor*, starring Alan Bates. The program was expected to be released on video and DVD in late 2002.[1] That three filmed versions of *The Mayor of Casterbridge*—counting *The Claim*—should be released within a two-year period in a testament both to the popularity of Hardy's novel and to the interest we have in seeing that novel recreated on film. With this fact in mind, and operating under the assumption more adaptations of other Hardy novels will follow, it is worthwhile to consider the "kinds" of Hardy films are likely to come and to look back upon the versions of Hardy we've already received.

One of the most striking facts about the history of Hardy in the cinema is that most filmmakers apparently believe he wrote only five or six novels. *Tess, Far from the Madding Crowd*, and *The Mayor of Casterbridge* have all been filmed at least three times going back to the silent era; and *Jude the Obscure* and *The Woodlanders* have both been filmed for the movies and for TV. A few moviemakers and TV producers have tackled other Hardy titles—*Under the Greenwood Tree* was filmed in 1929, and, of course, *The Return of the Native* and the story "The Melancholy Hussar" made recent appearances on the screen—but even these are among Hardy's most recognizable titles. No doubt filmmakers will continue to adapt the works that people know best, but Hardy also wrote other novels, some of them highly experimental, which might actually work better as films than they did as prose fiction. One novel in particular springs to mind: *The Well-Beloved*. This odd fantasy, which Hardy published in two different versions in 1892 and 1897, tells the story of the sculptor Jocelyn Pierston, who over forty years has his love sparked by three generations of women, all named Avice Caro and all nearly physically identical. Each woman is for Pierston "The Well-Beloved," the embodiment of female beauty that manifests itself in human form only rarely. Though Pierston pursues all three generations of women—mother, daughter, and granddaughter—he marries only the third, by which time he realizes the emptiness of his ambition and the waste of his years. On the page, the story is flat and never becomes much more than a platform for Hardy's theories on art and idealism; however, the potential for a good film is here. Pierston's quest for physical beauty is an entirely *visual* one, and so his desire naturally lends itself to film. Other of Hardy's "lesser-known" novels—such as *The Trumpet-Major* (1880), with its reliance on visual humor, such as characters crashing through walls and people jumping out of windows; and *Two on a Tower* (1882), fascinated as it is with telescopes and other visual apparatuses—are about the importance of *watching* action, and in film, the importance of watching is paramount. Film versions of these novels could work and possibly work very well, but getting new productions greenlighted by major studios is no easy matter, and there are probably few producers willing to take on an oddball novel, no matter who the author is.

I am convinced that if Hardy's novels are to continue to be the subject of film adaptations, then filmmakers need to do more than simply recreate a safe and familiar version of the Hardy that we know and then hope that by evoking this particular image, the film will gain authenticity and be seen as something truly "Hardean." To my mind, the weakest of the existing Hardy adaptations—John Schlesinger's *Far from the Madding Crowd*, Hallmark Hall of Fame's *The Return of the Native*, A &

E's *Tess of the D'Urbervilles*, the British films of *The Woodlanders* and *The Scarlet Tunic*—are weak because their makers try to use period detail, authentic Dorset locations, and images associated with Hardy to make the films *seem* faithful, instead of developing screenplays that actually *dramatize* the ideas and issues with which Hardy was concerned. Winterbottom's *Jude* does away with familiar Hardean "imagery" and locations, but his film also takes a very narrow approach to the novel, replicating the most common and most popular cultural assumption about the "kind" of novel *Jude the Obscure* is; as a result, the source is diminished and Hardy's own art and thought have been contained and simplified. The best of the Hardy adaptations—Polanski's *Tess*, BBC's *Jude the Obscure*, WGBH/ Granada's *Far from the Madding Crowd*, and, in its own way, Winterbottom's *The Claim*—work so well because their adapters cull Hardy's themes and ideas from the margins of his novels and create dramatic equivalents for them. In the case of *Tess* and the *Jude* serial, the screenwriters and directors work to distort reality, to create a sense of the "artificiality" of life, with which Hardy himself was deeply concerned. Polanski's film and the *Jude* and *Crowd* serials are in fact faithful to Hardy in that they replicate his stories and characters as completely as possible; but, more importantly, they remain true to his themes and ideas, which is perhaps more important than literal fidelity to his texts.

I would like to see future adaptations of Hardy follow the lead of Polanski and of Winterbottom in *The Claim*, but the popularity of British period dramas remains so strong that it is difficult to believe most filmmakers would be willing to divorce Hardy from either his familiar time and place or from his "heritage" trappings. The irony is that many of Hardy's stories would actually work quite well in a modern context. One thing that perhaps accounts for filmmakers' continued interest in *The Mayor of Casterbridge* is that its central premise is still relevant. It isn't uncommon to read in today's newspapers of parents selling their own children for money or drugs, or pushing family members into prostitution. It is possible that *The Mayor* could either be relocated to the modern world, or, better yet, directed in such a way that Henchard's situation is made to shine a light on a very modern problem (which could be the approach taken in the 2001 TV version of the story). Furthermore, I've long felt that readers and critics do a disservice to *Jude the Obscure* when they approach it simply as a relic from the past. When I look at aspects of American society today—at how people of my generation and even those who are years younger than me have put pressure on themselves to attain instant fame, instant wealth, and instant success, and who've put aside the things they're good at in order to pursue unobtainable dreams—I've often thought, how sad, and how absurdly funny, it all is. How Hardean. How very *Jude*-like. When readers, critics, and filmmakers position Hardy's novels in the past, stressing that he wrote about a world that was fundamentally different from our own, they invariably manage to minimize and contain Hardy. Film can open people up to the knowledge that many of Hardy's concerns are our concerns, and that his novels do more than provide us with a glimpse into the past.

The problem with doing a modern-dress version of Hardy is that it is all too probable that such an effort would emerge as a stunt, and have little to offer beyond the novelty of seeing Hardy done in blue jeans. However, it has recently been shown—to me, at least—that a "historical" or "literary" film can be made that is both faithful to the period in which it is set, and which can shed light on our own times. Mike Leigh's *Topsy-Turvy* (1999) is ostensibly a straight biopic about Gilbert and Sullivan during the time *The Mikado* was conceived, written, rehearsed, and first performed. The film is slavishly attentive to period detail, and it is remarkably entertaining as a backstage drama qua musical: in fact, at the showing I attended, an elderly man seated behind me was enjoying the film so much he couldn't help but sing along with the songs. But beneath Leigh's seeming affection for Victoriana, there is a criticism both of the age and of the mentalities that led to the creation of our own era. Leigh focuses on a number of gadgets that were new to the Victorians but which we take for granted as parts of our daily lives–and which we have improved upon through technological advances: electric doorbells (from which Gilbert's father fears electrocution), telephones (over which Gilbert speaks in code, lest anyone be listening in), even fountain pens. Leigh also draws the viewer's attention to details that are outside the action of the film, such as the death of Gordon at Khartoum and the dawning importance of Ibsen's drama. Such moments as these are reminders to us that the Victorian era is drawing to an end: Khartoum was one of the first major cracks in the empire over which Victoria reigned; and the drama of Ibsen would revolutionize the theater, effectively driving entertainments like those of Gilbert and Sullivan off the stage. In several isolated moments, Leigh highlights small and fairly insignificant physical and emotional defects in the characters—Gilbert's bad teeth, Sullivan's sudden cough in the middle of a rehearsal, the performers' battles with alcoholism, skin diseases, and cocaine—and he creates the subtle suggestion that everyone in the film is slowly, bit by bit, dying. Of course, we all know that the historical characters being portrayed on film (there are, I believe, no fictional characters in the picture) really *are* dead—and so will we all be. The characters in the film do not know their own fates, but we know what happens to the

Victorian era, and we know about the world that supplanted it. It is our world, and the fact that we don't know what will become of our world makes *Topsy-Turvy* far more chilling than its comedy and bright musical numbers would suggest.

Whether Leigh himself would be interested in tackling an adaptation of Hardy is not in my realm of knowledge; however, his approach in *Topsy-Turvey* strikes me as one that would complement one of Hardy's novels. Ideally, a filmmaker shouldn't show us just the world as Hardy knew it; rather, the filmmaker should strive to show us both Hardy's world and what it was to become. Such an approach would create—as *Topsy-Turvey* creates—a sense of dissonance, a realization that the objects and images presented on the screen have more than one meaning. I believe that Hardy largely saw the world as a place where few things were certain and where words, images, and even nature itself were rife with multiple meanings and multiple interpretations. A filmmaker who wishes to faithfully dramatize Hardy should realize that transferring Hardy's plot functions to the screen is only half the battle: what that filmmaker must then do is question or even criticize the significance of the images he or she has brought to the screen. Hardy was a writer who was constantly asking questions, constantly throwing down challenges, and constantly undermining the authority of his readers' assumptions. To truly see Hardy on the screen is to see *as* Hardy—and that means that what is *seen* is only one possible interpretation of what *is*.

Appendix A

The "Lost" Hardy Adaptations, 1913–1953

The following is a list of the Hardy adaptations that were made before John Schlesinger's *Far from the Madding Crowd* in 1967. The word "lost" is used guardedly: while the 1913 *Tess* and the 1915 *Madding Crowd* have apparently disappeared without a trace, portions of the 1921 *Mayor of Casterbridge* and 1924 *Tess* are known or at least thought to exist. *Under the Greenwood Tree* (1929) and 1953's *The Secret Cave* are possibly not lost at all, but I have been unable to locate information on the availability of these films. In all cases, I have tried to provide as much information as possible about the circumstances of production of the individual films, and I have looked to contemporary reviews and, in some cases, Hardy's own reactions to the films in his correspondence, in order to give some sense of what each film was like.

Tess of the D'Urbervilles (United States). *Director:* J. Searle Dawley. *Presenter:* Daniel Frohman. Based on the novel by Thomas Hardy. *Production company:* Famous Players Film Co. *Distributor:* States Rights. *Length:* Five reels. *Premiere:* September 1, 1913.

Cast: Millie Maddern Fiske, billed as Mrs. Fiske (*Tess Durbeyfield*), David Torrence (*Alec D'Urberville*), Raymond Bond (*Angel Clare*), John Steppling (*John Durbeyfield*), Mary E. Barker (*Mrs. Durbeyfield*), Kate Griffith (*Mrs. D'Urberville*), Franklin Hall (*Parson Clare*), Camille Dalberg (*Mrs. Clare*), J. Liston (*Parson Tringham*), James Gordon (*Crick*), Maggie Weston (*Mrs. Crick*), Irma La Pierce (*Marian*), Boots Wall (*Reta*), Caroline Darling (*Izz*), Justina Huff (*Liza Lou*), John Troughton (*Jonathan*).

Tess of the D'Urbervilles was one of the earliest productions from Adolph Zukor's Famous Players Company, which was formed in 1912 and which would become the nucleus of Paramount. Negotiations for the film rights to the novel were conducted between Famous Players and Hardy's North American publisher, Harper Bros., during the first half of 1913. Hardy was concerned about the effects a film adaptation would have on his novel, and he gave instructions to F. A. Duneka, general manager of Harpers, to ensure that "the story ... not be vulgarized or treated lightly, so that all possibility of a farcical view of the tragedy is prevented."[1] On July 1, the *New York Times* announced both that Daniel Frohman had secured the rights to the book and that Frohman had arranged for Mrs. Fiske to appear as Tess—a role she had first played on the stage in 1895. The notice in the *Times* goes on to say that the "photo-play will be given in five reels and [will] constitute a complete evening's entertainment. It is intended to be shown as a feature film at first-class theatres only."[2]

Indications are that, for the time, this *Tess* was a lavish production. The making of the film was the subject of a two-page article in The *Moving Picture News*, which reveals both the status Hardy's 22-year-old novel had achieved in literature, and the status film was then trying to reach: "'Tess of the D'Urbervilles is one of the masterpieces of the English language, and its film dramatization certainly marks an epoch in the field besides auguring much for the future. The appearance of our foremost actress in the best known work of a famous English novelist bestows upon the camera drama an importance and a dignity that it has not heretofore possessed."[3] Location work was done in New England, and, according to Adolph Zukor's autobiography, much of the film was made at Mrs. Fiske's country home.[4]

The film apparently followed Hardy's novel fairly closely. A review by George Blaisdell references the Durbeyfield family learning of their descent from nobility, Tess's midnight baptism of her baby, and a variation on Angel's somnambulistic "burial" of Tess—here, he carries Tess downstairs, "lays her by the fire, [and] puts a candle at each side of her."[5] The two-page article in *Moving Picture News* contains an interesting pair of stills: one captioned "Crick's Story Pains Tess" and showing Tess cringing in the corner as the dairy folk share a laugh, a moment that recalls Tess's discomfort over the story of Jack Dollop in chapter 21 of the novel; another showing Tess being arrested on the steps of a ruined temple—which is apparently referred to as Stonehenge in the film. A review in *Motography* mentions that Tess is not condemned to hang, but that she is sent to prison, where she spends "the remaining years of her life with her broken heart and shattered hope, a martyr to man's wrong."[6]

The few existing reviews of the film are favorable, but one decidedly unimpressed—or perhaps just diffident—viewer was Thomas Hardy. On October 13, prior to the film's release in Britain, Hardy was treated to a special screening in the office of his publisher. Hardy called the movie a "curious production" and claimed that he could say nothing "as to its relation to, or rendering of, the story."[7] Later, in a December 10 letter to Edward Clodd, he jeered at the film's "Americanized Wessex Dairy."[8] *Tess*'s "Americanness" seemed to stick in Hardy's craw: in later letters, he stressed the importance of film adaptations of his works being made in authentic locales. At the time the 1924 film of *Tess* was in preparation, Hardy expressed (in a letter he apparently dictated to his wife, Florence) that its authentic location work "will be a great advantage to the pictures, the former [1913] film, being American made, having failed to carry conviction over here."[9]

No prints of the Famous Players *Tess* are known to have survived.

❖   ❖   ❖

Henry Edwards as Gabriel and Florence Turner as Bathsheba in *Far from the Madding Crowd* (1915).

Far from the Madding Crowd (Great Britain). *Director, Producer, Screenplay:* Larry Trimble, based on the novel by Thomas Hardy. *Cinematography:* Tom White. *Production company:* Turner Films, Ltd. *Distributors:* Ideal (GB), Mutual (US). *Length:* Five reels. *Premiere:* November 16, 1915, in London; *general release date:* February 28, 1916.

Cast: Florence Turner (*Bathsheba Everdene*), Henry Edwards (*Gabriel Oak*), Malcolm Cherry (*Farmer Boldwood*), Campbell Gullan (*Sergeant Troy*), Marion Grey (*Fanny Robin*), Dorothy Rowan (*Lyddie*), John MacAndrews (*Farmhand*), Johnny Butt (*Farmhand*), "Jean" (*Gabriel's dog*).

In 1913, the artist Hubert von Herkomer, who had illustrated *Tess of the d'Urbervilles* for its 1891 run in The *Graphic*, set up a movie studio in his own garden and began producing films in collaboration with his son, Siegfried. In November of that year, Herkomer secured the rights to *Far from the Madding Crowd* from Macmillan for £150 and picked up an option on *The Mayor of Casterbridge* for £25 in the bargain.[10] On December 21, Hardy reported to Florence Henniker that "young Herkomer [i.e., Siegfried] came here a few days ago to get local colour, & has photographed the *real* jug used in the malt house"[11]—the latter observation perhaps reflecting Hardy's irritation at the Famous Players film of *Tess* for its lack of "authenticity." How Herkomer would have realized Hardy on film after having illustrated his most famous novel is a matter of speculation; the artist died after beginning work on the production, and with him died his studio and his film projects.

The *Far from the Madding Crowd* project was picked up about a year after Herkomer's death by Turner Films, a company established in England by the American motion picture star Florence Turner and American filmmaker Larry Trimble. The production apparently followed Herkomer's lead by shooting in real Dorset locales; unfortunately, little else is known about the shoot—or about the resulting film. Hardy apparently never saw it, although he did write a synopsis of the novel that was printed in a souvenir program distributed to the press and various dignitaries at a private screening of *Madding Crowd* at the West End Cinema in London on November 16, 1915.[12] The following day, an anonymous reviewer in the *Times* remarked, "So many authors and dramatists have allowed their work to be filmed for the cinematograph of late that one can hardly be surprised to find that Mr. Thomas Hardy has followed the prevailing custom." However, the reviewer continues, Hardy "can have little reason to complain of the way in which his work has been handled.... One feels that the country in which the action is laid is really the Wessex of the novel and that the farm, the cattle, the sheep are the genuine ones over which Gabriel Oak watched with such care."[13] That same day, Hardy wrote in a letter to his publisher that he was "glad to hear that Far from the Madding Crowd comes out so well."[14]

Far from the Madding Crowd went into general release in Britain the following February, and by June it had been released in America. Interestingly, a review of the film in *Variety* (June 30, 1916) reveals that *Madding Crowd* was one of six films made in England by the Turner company, and that "one of the officials connected with the Mutual [the film's U.S. distributor] stated that 'Far From the Madding Crowd' was the most unsatisfactory of the six features and therefore it was being released first." The reviewer goes on to pan Florence Turner's performance, to complain that the film is hard to follow, and to dismiss the source novel as "intended primarily for consumption in the scullery and pantry by the maids and the cook and the picture carries the same atmosphere."[15]

There are no records as to how the film performed in either Britain or America, but in 1920 Hardy reflected that *Madding Crowd* "seems to have been a failure."[16] Both Florence Turner and Larry Trimble returned to the United States at the end of 1916, and their film company folded. It is not known what became of the Turner adaptation of Hardy's novel.

The Mayor of Casterbridge (Great Britain). *Director, Screenplay:* Sidney Morgan, based on the novel by Thomas Hardy. *Producer:* Frank Spring. *Cinematography:* S. J. Mumford. *Production company:* Progress Film Company. *Distributor:* Butcher. *Length:* Approximately 65 minutes. *Premiere:* November 1921.

The Furmity Woman (Nell Emerald, standing) reveals the past of Michael Henchard (Fred Groves, at the judge's bench) in *The Mayor of Casterbridge* (1921).

Cast: Fred Groves (*Michael Henchard*), Pauline Peters (*Susan Henchard*), Mavis Clare (*Elizabeth-Jane*), Warwick Ward (*Newson*), Nell Emerald (*The Furmity Woman*).

The Progress Film Company was a tiny, open-air studio established in Shoreham-by-the-Sea, Sussex, before World War I. After the war the studio was purchased by Sidney Morgan, and for a few years Progress flourished.[17] Early in 1921, Morgan began negotiations with Macmillan for the rights to *The Mayor of Casterbridge*, and on February 19 Hardy signed the contract with Progress—but only after insisting that a phrase be added that would obligate the producers to make no "alteration or adaptation being such as to burlesque or otherwise misrepresent the general character of the novel."[18] Morgan was apparently serious about earning Hardy's approval: he sent the scenario to Hardy, and the octogenarian novelist promised to "see to the dialect of the titles" and pronounced the "general arrangement" of the script to be "as good as is compatible with presentation by cinemas."[19] Much of the film was shot in Steyning, near Shoreham, but in early July Morgan shot for a day in Dorchester, capturing images of Maiden Castle, Hangman's Cottage, and other Hardean locales.[20] An important guest on the set was Thomas Hardy himself; at the end of the day, the actors went to Max Gate to say goodbye to the author.[21] Hardy apparently never saw the completed film.

The Mayor seems to have concentrated almost exclusively on Henchard's relationship with Elizabeth-Jane, who in the film is Henchard's real daughter.

Accordingly, the sale of the wife and child and the arrival of Susan and Elizabeth-Jane after their 15-year absence are all in the film, but Farfrae and Lucetta do not figure in Morgan's scenario. Elizabeth-Jane falls in love with a doctor, and for whatever reason she apparently decides to leave Casterbridge with her adopted father Newson. The exposure of Henchard's past occurs toward the end of the film, and he leaves the city a broken man. The film appears to have changed the 1840s time frame of Hardy's novel, since the clothing styles the actors wear places the action more in the late 1800s or early 1900s. The *Times* praised *The Mayor* for its fidelity to Hardy,[22] and the film did well enough to earn a re-release in 1926—four years after Progress burned to the ground and disappeared from British film history.

The Mayor of Casterbridge itself also vanished from history until 1995, when 15 minutes of the film were salvaged and shown at the Marlipins Museum in Sussex to mark the centenary of the film industry. Dennis L. Bird reported at the time that the man who restored the film had hopes of securing the services of a musician to score the piece and to put the material on home video,[23] but as of this writing I have no knowledge of what has become of the project.

Tess of the D'Urbervilles (United States). *Director:* Marshall Neilan. *Presenter:* Louis B. Mayer. *Screenplay:* Dorothy Farnum, based on the novel by Thomas Hardy. *Cinematography* (black and white with "Kinekrom" coloring): David Kesson. *Production company/Distributor:* Metro-Goldwyn Pictures. *Length:* 88 minutes. *Premiere:* July 27, 1924, in New York; *general release date:* August 11, 1924.

Cast: Blanche Sweet (*Tess Durbeyfield*), Conrad Nagel (*Angel Clare*), Stuart Holmes (*Alec D'Urberville*), George Fawcett (*John Durbeyfield*), Victory Bateman (*Joan Durbeyfield*), Courtenay Foote (*Dick*), Joseph J. Dowling (*The Priest*), Babe London.

Tess of the D'Urbervilles was the last of the silent adaptations of Hardy's novels and the last Hardy film made during the author's lifetime. *Tess* was also one of the first films produced by the newly formed Metro-Goldwyn Corporation—which would soon add Louis B. Mayer's name to its own—and it was one of the most ambitious and expensive films of its era. Its loss is reckoned by many film historians as nothing short of a tragedy.

The film rights to the novel were purchased by the original Metro Company from Macmillan in 1919, but plans to make the film apparently were not launched until late 1922. In September of that year Hardy received a document relating to the film rights of *Tess* that he was to sign only as a "formality." Hardy did so, but expressed fear that a clause in the contract would give Metro the "power to distort or burlesque the novel, to the possible injury of the book here in England as elsewhere."[24] The following month Hardy learned that the film was to be shot on location in England, which pleased him greatly.[25] Hardy expressed no further interest in the production, and he apparently did not see it.

Although the filmmakers were true to Hardy's locales—shooting much of the production in Dorset and capturing a local folk dance, and even staging Tess's arrest at the actual Stonehenge—they removed the novel from its 1880s setting and placed it squarely in the 1920s, with the characters driving cars and using

Angel (Conrad Nagel) and Tess (Blanche Sweet) on the verge of confessing their pasts in the modern-dress *Tess of the D'Urbervilles* (1924).

telephones. This change was particularly upsetting to a reviewer in *Variety*, who charged that modernizing the story showed a lack of respect to "the tradition[al] way in] which Hardy wrote about his native Wessex and Dorchester land."[26] Reviews indicate that, time frame aside, the film followed Hardy's story fairly closely—though *Variety* notes that the seduction of Tess "is barely hinted at" in order to conform to modern standards of morality—but MGM apparently blanched at Hardy's tragic ending. Two endings were shot: one with Tess being hanged, the other with Tess and Angel happily reunited. Exhibitors were given the choice of which ending to show, but in subsequent re-releases only the tragic ending was issued.[27]

The silent *Tess* was apparently consigned to the MGM vaults, but the studio remained interested in the property. David O. Selznick tried for years to have the film remade, and in the mid–1960s MGM attempted to persuade John Schlesinger to undertake a remake of *Tess* rather than embark upon *Far from the Madding Crowd*. A second MGM *Tess* would never be made, and it is doubtful the studio's original silent film will be seen again. There are reports that a few reels of the film survive, but that they are in such poor shape that restoration is nearly impossible; however, I have been unable to confirm this information.

Under the Greenwood Tree [US title: **The Greenwood Tree**] (Great Britain). *Director:* Harry Lachman. *Screenplay:* Sidney Gilliat, Monckton Hoffe, Harry Lachman, Frank Launder, and Rex Taylor; based on the novel by Thomas Hardy.

Fancy Day (Marguerite Allan) cradles Dick Dewey (John Batten) in a scene from the early talkie *Under the Greenwood Tree* (1929).

Cinematography (black and white): Claude Friese-Greene. *Editor:* Emile de Ruelle. *Art Director:* C. W. Arnold. *Production company:* British International Pictures. *Distributor:* Wardour (GB), British International (US). *Length:* 101 minutes. *Premiere:* September 1929; *US premiere:* December 30, 1930.

    Cast: Marguerite Allan (*Fancy Day*), John Batten (*Dick Dewey*), Nigel Barrie (*Shinar*), Maud Gill (*Old Maid*), Wilfred Shine (*Parson Maybold*), Roberta Abel (*Penny*), Antonia Brough (*Maid*), Tom Coventry (*Tranter Dewey*), Robison Page (*Grandfather Dewey*), Tubby Phillips (*Tubby*), Bill Shine (*Leaf*), *uncredited cast members:* Syd Ellery, Queenie Leighton, Harry Stafford, The Gotham Singers.

    Under the Greenwood Tree is not acknowledged as a significant film in the history of British cinema—in fact it has been largely forgotten—but it is actually the first all-talking motion picture made in England. (Hitchcock's *Blackmail*, released by British International earlier in 1929, is really a silent film with several sound sequences.) The producers obviously sought to exploit the new medium of sound by incorporating many country songs and musical numbers into the film, enough so that one contemporary reviewer grumbled that the film is "handicapped by being jammed up with singing sequences."[28] Some reference works even categorize *Under the Greenwood Tree* as a musical. Unfortunately, sound apparently revealed the limits of leading lady Marguerite Allan, whose lines were actually spoken by Peggie Robb-Smith. In all likelihood Harry Lachman used the same trick Hitchcock used to great advantage in *Blackmail:* that is, having Robb-Smith speak the lines off-camera while Allan mouthed them in front of the camera. The film was shot at BIP's Elstree Studios near London; it is not known if any scenes were shot on location in Dorset.

    Accounts indicate that the film follows Hardy's novel only up to a point. As described by the anonymous reviewer in the London *Times*, the film contains many "leisurely" sequences—dealing with "the grief of the Mellstock instrumental choir at its supersession by the 'new-fangled' organ, the singing of Christmas carols, and the choir's New Year's Eve celebrations"—which the critic feels capture the spirit of Hardy's novel; but the reviewer also complains that the filmmakers invent sequences where Dick Dewey kidnaps Fanny on her wedding day, and where Fanny in a runaway gig has to be rescued by Dick. The *Times* review concludes that "it is a disturbing thought that not even a Hardy film is not regarded as complete without a pictorial sensation of some description."[29]

Reviews were not kind. To the *Times* reviewer, the producers were guilty of "turning a literary masterpiece inside out" by focusing on action rather than Hardy's words.[30] Hugh Castle in *Close Up*, however, argued that Harry Lachman did a fine job with the material, considering the film was based on a book that no motion picture company "should have bought"; and Castle concedes that the use of sound "helps the so-called story."[31] But to Castle, the main problem was that "the Elstree cutters have methodically pulled the picture to pieces," a fact that proves the "imbecility of letting one man make a picture and another cut it."[32] The film would be edited again for its American release, where it appeared at the end of 1930 as *The Greenwood Tree* and at a running time of just sixty minutes. *Greenwood Tree* apparently attracted little business. In the U.S., *Variety* sniped that the filmmakers have "taken Hardy seriously for the screen, and that's why [the film] displays some undesired comedy";[33] another report has it that audiences roared with laughter over the "ill-fitting costumes and phony mustaches."[34]

The present status of *Under the Greenwood Tree* is uncertain.

The Secret Cave (Great Britain). *Director:* John Durst. *Producer:* Frank Hoare. *Screenplay:* Joe Mendoza, based on the novella "Our Exploits at West Poley" by Thomas Hardy. *Cinematography* (black and white): Martin Curtis. *Production companies:* Merton Park Studios, Ltd.; Children's Film Foundation. *Distributor:* Associated British Films. *Length:* 62 minutes. *Premiere:* 1953.

Cast: David Coote (*Steve Draycott*), Susan Ford (*Margaret Merriman*), Nicholas Emdett (*Lennie Hawkins*), Lewis Gedge (*Miller Griffin*), Johnny Morris (*Charlie Bassett*), Trevor Hill (*Job Tray*).

The Secret Cave is the only film derived from a Hardy source made between 1929 and 1967. A short movie intended for children, *Secret Cave* attracted little critical attention, and information on the production is hard to come by. The film is not listed as being available on video and its whereabouts are uncertain, but the editors of a 1987 publication apparently saw it and duly characterized the film as "boring."[35]

Appendix B

Film Adaptations
of Hardy, 1967–2000

Far from the Madding Crowd (Great Britain). *Director:* John Schlesinger. *Producer:* Joseph Janni. *Screenplay:* Frederic Raphael; based on the novel by Thomas Hardy. *Editor:* Malcolm Cooke. *Director of Photography:* Nicolas Roeg. *Art Director:* Roy Smith. *Set Decorator:* Peter James. *Production Designer:* Richard MacDonald. *Music:* Richard Rodney Bennett; conducted by Marcus Dods. *Associate Producer:* Edward Joseph. *Casting:* Miriam Brickman. *Costumes:* Alan Barrett. *Makeup:* Bob Lawrance and Phillip Leakey. *Hairstylist:* Ivy Emmerton. *Sound Recording:* Robin Gregory and John Alred. *Sound Editors:* Gordon Daniel and Alfred Cox. *Production Manager:* Frank Ernst. *Assistant Directors:* Kip Gowans and David Bracknell. *Special Effects:* Trading Post Ltd.; effects supervised by Malcolm King. *Folk Song Advisor:* Isla Cameron. *Horse Master:* Max Faulkner. *Sword Master:* Derek Ware. *Production companies:* Vic Films; Appia Films; Joseph Janni Productions. *Distributor:* MGM. Filmed on locations in Dorset and Wiltshire counties, U.K. Filmed in Panavision and Metrocolor. *Running time:* 169 minutes. *Premiere:* October 18, 1967, in New York.

Cast: Julie Christie (*Bathsheba Everdene*), Terence Stamp (*Sergeant Troy*), Peter Finch (*William Boldwood*), Alan Bates (*Gabriel Oak*), Fiona Walker (*Liddy*), Prunella Ransome (*Fanny Robin*), Alison Leggatt (*Mrs. Hurst*), Paul Dawkins (*Henery Fray*), Julian Somers (*Jan Coggan*), John Barrett (*Joseph Poorgrass*), Freddie Jones (*Cainy Ball*), Andrew Robertson (*Andrew Randle*), Brian Rawlinson (*Matthew Moon*), Vincent Harding (*Mark Clark*), Victor Stone (*Billy Smallbury*), Owen Berry (*Old Smallbury*), Lawrence Carter (*Laban Tall*), Pauline Melville (*Mrs. Tall*), Harriet Harper (*Temperance*), Denise Coffey (*Soberness*), Margaret Lacey (*Maryann Money*), Marie Hopps (*Mrs. Coggan*), Peter Stone (*Teddy Coggan*), Walter Gale (*Jacob Smallbury*), Leslie Anderson, Keith Hooper (*Boldwood's Laborers*), Jonathan Newth (*Gentleman at Cockfight*), Derek Ware (*Corporal*), John Donegal (*Sailor*), Peggyanne Clifford (*Fat Lady at Circus*), Bryan Mosley (*Barker*), David Swarbrick (*Fiddler at Barn Dance*), Julius Alba (*Gentleman at Party*), Frank Duncan, Hugh Walter (*Farmers at Corn Exchange*), Michael Beint (*Laborer*), John Garrie (*Pennyways*).

Tess (France/Great Britain). *Director:* Roman Polanski. *Producer:* Claude Berri. *Screenplay:* Gérard Brach, Roman Polanski, and John Brownjohn; based on the novel *Tess of the d'Urbervilles* by Thomas Hardy. *Editors:* Alastair McIntyre and Tom Priestly. *Directors of Photography:* Geoffrey Unsworth, B. S. C., and Ghislain Cloquet, A. S. C. *Art Direction:* Jack Stephens. *Production Designer:* Pierre Guffroy. *Music:* Philippe Sarde; conducted by Carlo Savina. *Executive Producer:* Pierre Grunstein. *Co-Producer:* Timothy Burrill. *Associate Producer:* Jean-Pierre Rassam. *Casting:* Mary Selway. *Costumes:* Anthony Powell. *Makeup:* Didier Lavergne; assisted by Paul Le Marinel. *Hairstylist:* Ludovic Paris; assisted by Alain Bernard. *Production Manager:* Paul Maigret. *Unit Manager:* Tadek Zietara. *Second Unit Director:* Hercules Bellville. *First Assistant Director:* Thierry Chabert. *Second Assistant Directors:* Romain Goupil and Hugues de Laugardière. *Sound Editors:* Peter Horrocks and Hervé de Luze. *Sound Mixer:* Jean-Pierre Ruh. *Dubbing Mixers:* Maurice Gilbert and Alex Pront. *Sound Effects:* Jean-Pierre Lelong. *Boom:* Louis Gimbel. *Dolby Stereo Sound Consultant:* David Watts. *Unit Manager:* Alain Depardieu. *Location Managers:* Patrick Bordier, Phillippe Desmoulins and Jérôme Jeannet. *Voice Teacher:* Catherine Fleming. *Dialogue Coach:* Jennifer Patrick. *Postsynchronization:* Robert Rietti. *Choreographer:* Sue Lefton. *Production companies:* Renn Productions (France); Société Française de Production (France); Burrill Productions (England). *U.S. Distributor:* Columbia. Filmed on locations in Normandy and Brittany, France. Filmed in Panavision and Eastmancolor. *Sound Mix:* Dolby 70 mm. 6-Track. *Running time:* 170 minutes. *Premiere:* October 25, 1979, in West Germany.

    Cast: Nastassia Kinski (*Tess Durbeyfield*), Peter Firth (*Angel Clare*), Leigh Lawson (*Alec d'Urberville*), John Collin (*John Durbeyfield*), Rosemary Martin (*Joan Durbeyfield*), Sylvia Coleridge (*Mrs. d'Urberville*), Richard Pearson (*Vicar of Marlott*), Fred Bryant (*Dairyman Crick*), Carolyn Pickles (*Marian*), Suzanna Hamilton (*Izz*), Caroline Embling (*Retty*), Josine Comellas (*Mrs. Crick*), Arielle Dombasle (*Mercy Chant*), David Markham (*Reverend Mr. Clare*), Pascale de Boysson (*Mrs. Clare*), John Bett (*Felix Clare*), Tom Chadbon (*Cuthbert Clare*), Dicken Ashworth (*Farmer Groby*), Patsy Smart (*Housekeeper*), Patsy Rowlands (*Landlady*), Tony Church (*Parson Tringham*), Brigid Erin Bates, Jeanne Biras (*Girls in meadow*), Géraldine Arzul, Stephanie Treille, Elodie Warnod, Ben Reeks (*Durbeyfield children*), Lesley Dunlop, Marilyne Even (*Girls in henhouse*), Jean-Jacques Daubin (*Bailiff*), Jacob Weisbluth (*Yokel at barn dance*), Jacques Mathou, Véronique Alain (*Harvesters*), John Barrett, Ann Tirard (*Old dairy band*), Gordon Richardson (*Parson at wedding*), Jimmy Gardner (*Pedler*), Forbes Collins (*New tenant*), Keith Buckley, John Moore (*Postmen*), Graham Weston (*Constable*), Reg Dent (*Carter*).

Jude (Great Britain/United States). *Director:* Michael Winterbottom. *Producer:* Andrew Eaton. *Screenplay:* Hossein Amini; based on the novel *Jude the Obscure* by Thomas Hardy. *Editor:* Trevor Waite. *Director of Photography (Color and black and white):* Eduardo Serra. *Art Direction:* Andrew Rothschild. *Production Design:* Joseph Bennett. *Music:* Adrian Johnston. *Associate Producer:* Sheila

Fraser Milne. *Executive Producers:* Mark Shivas and Stewart Till. *Casting:* Simone Ireland and Vanessa Pereira. *Costumes:* Janty Yates. *Hairstylists and Makeup:* Mel Gibson and Amanda Warburton. *Assistant Director:* Matthew Baker. *First Assistant Director:* Howard Arundel. *Second Assistant Director:* John Duthie. *Third Assistant Director:* Damian Wright. *Sound Editors:* Jeremy Child and Kant Pan. *Boom:* Kate Morath. *Sound Mixer:* Martin Trevis. *Set Designer:* Andy Nicholson. *Set Decoration:* Judy Farr. *Property Master:* Paul Purdy. *Special Effects:* John Markwell. *Visual Effects Designers:* Mimi Abers and Paddy Eason. *Visual Effects:* Dennis Michelson. *Visual Effects Producer:* Alison O'Brien. *Scanning and Recording Producer:* Kevin Phelan. *Visual Effects Assistant:* Tim Wellspring. *Stunt Coordinator:* Roy Alon. *Unit Manager:* Josh Dynevor. *Location Manager:* David Pinnington. *Second Unit Director of Photography:* Andrew Speller. *Production companies:* BBC; Revolution Films (GB); PolyGram Filmed Entertainment (US). *Distributor:* Gramercy. Filmed on locations in Durham, Northumberland, Yorkshire, Surrey, England; Edinburgh, Scotland; New Zealand; and at Twickenham Film Studios, London. *Sound Mix:* Dolby Digital. *Running time:* 123 minutes. *Premiere:* September 10, 1996, Toronto Film Festival; GB release: October 4, 1996; US release: October 18, 1996.

Cast: Christopher Eccleston (*Jude Fawley*), Kate Winslet (*Sue Bridehead*), Liam Cunningham (*Phillotson*), Rachel Griffiths (*Arabella*), June Whitfield (*Aunt Drusilla*), Ross Colvin Turnbull (*Little Jude; "Juey"*), James Daley (*Jude as a Boy*), Berwick Kaler (*Farmer Troutham*), James Nesbitt (*Uncle Joe*), Mark Lambert (*Tinker Taylor*), Sean McKenzie, Richard Albrecht (*Stonemasons*), Caitlin Bossley (*Anny*), Emma Turner (*Sarah*), Lorraine Hilton (*Shopkeeper*), Amanda Ryan (*Gypsy Saleswoman*), Vernon Dobtcheff (*Curator*), David Tennant (*Drunk Undergraduate*), Darren Tighe (*Punter*), Paul Copley (*Mr. Willis*), Ken Jones (*Mr. Biles*), Roger Ashton-Griffiths (*Auctioneer*), Raymond Ross (*Old Man*), Freda Dowie (*Elderly Landlady*), Dexter Fletcher (*Priest*), Moray Hunter (*Politician*), Adrian Bower (*Blacksmith*), Kerry Shale (*Showman*), Billie Dee Roberts (*Little Sister*), Chantel Neary (*Baby*), James Scanlon (*Newborn Baby*).

The Woodlanders (Great Britain). *Director:* Phil Agland. *Producers:* Phil Agland and Barney Reisz. *Screenplay:* David Rudkin; based on the novel by Thomas Hardy. *Editor:* David Dickie. *Director of Photography:* Ashley Rowe. *Art Direction:* John Frankish. *Production Design:* Andy Harris. *Music:* George Fenton. *Casting:* Susie Figgis, Patsy Pollock, Gail Stevens, and Andy Pryor. *Costumes:* Susannah Buxton. *Makeup and Hair Design:* Aileen Seaton. *Assistant Director:* Konrad Jay. *Second Assistant Director:* Richard Styles. *Third Assistant Director:* Barbara Mulcahy. *Supervising Sound Editor:* Rodney Glenn. *Sound Mixer:* Mark Holding. *Set Designer:* Andy Nicholson. *Set Decoration:* Tracey Gallagher. *Special Effects Supervisor:* Stuart Buidon. *Associate Editor:* Tim Arrowsmith. *Dialect Coach:* Catherine Charlton. *Production Manager:* Mark Huffam. *Unit Manager:* David Boardman. *Location Manager:* Amanda Stevens. *Production companies:* Arts Council of England; Channel Four Films (Films Four International); Pathé Productions; River Films. *Distributors:* Pathé (GB); Miramax (US). Filmed entirely on location in Hampshire, Dorset, and Wiltshire, U.K. Filmed in Technicolor. *Sound Mix:* Dolby. *Running time:* 93 minutes. *Premiere:* February 6, 1998.

Cast: Rufus Sewell (*Giles Winterbourne*), Emily Woof (*Grace Melbury*), Cal MacAninch (*Edred Fitzpiers*), Tony Haygarth (*Mr. Melbury*), Jodhi May (*Marty South*), Polly Walker (*Felice Charmond*), Walter Sparrow (*Old Creedle*), Sheila Burrell (*Grandma Oliver*), Michael Culkin (*Percomb*), Amanda Ryan (*Sukey*), Lara J. West (*Vinny*), Robert Blythe (*Tangs*), William Harry (*Tim*), John Croft (*Upjohn*), William Chubb (*Auctioneer*), Andrew Tansey (*Coachman*), Geoffrey Beevers (*Agent*), Caroline John (*Housekeeper*), Dawn McDavid (*Woodland wife*), Vincent Franklin (*Stable lad*), Sam Rowe (*Street vendor*), Emily Joyce (*Libby*), Kate Blackham, Jennifer Luckraft, Tara Woodward (*Village girls*), Martin Walsh, Justin Gratten (*Village boys*).

The Scarlet Tunic (Great Britain). *Director:* Stuart St. Paul. *Producers:* Daniel Figuero and Zygi Kamasa. *Screenplay:* Colin Clements, Mark Jenkins, and Stuart St. Paul; based on the short story "The Melancholy Hussar of the German Legion" by Thomas Hardy. *Editor:* Don Fairservice. *Director of Photography:* Malcolm McLean. *Production Design:* Richard Elton. *Music:* John Scott. *Executive Producer:* William P. Cartlidge. *Co-Executive Producer:* Tom McCabe. *Co-Producers:* Philip Keenan and Simon Price. *Costumes:* Gary Lane. *Makeup and Hairstylist:* Lesley Lamont-Fisher. *First Assistant Directors:* James Corbett and Beth Elliot. *Second Assistant Directors:* Carwyn Jones and Simon Price. *Third Assistant Director:* Lawrence Thornton. *Sound Re-Recording Mixer:* Ian Tapp. *Special Effects Coordinator:* Graham Aikman. *Location Manager:* Angela Howard-Bent. *Production Supervisor:* Ed Harper. *Historian:* Stephen Guy. *Production companies:* Scarlet Films PLC; Bigger Picture Company, Ltd.; Scorpio Productions, Ltd. *Distributor:* Independent Feature Films. Filmed on location in Dorset, England. Color by Kodak and Fuji. *Running time:* 88 minutes. *Premiere:* June 12, 1998.

Cast: Jean-Marc Barr (*Matthaus Singer*), Emma Fielding (*Frances Grove*), Simon Callow (*Captain John Fairfax*), Jack Shepherd (*Dr. Edward Grove*), John Sessions (*Humphrey Gould*), Lynda Bellingham (*Emily Marlowe*), Thomas Lockyer (*Christoph Singer*), Andrew Tiernan (*Muller*), Gareth Hale (*William Parsons*), Lisa Faulkner (*Amy Parsons*), Roger May (*Fridon*), Laura Aikman (*Dotty Marlowe*), Erich Redman (*Strasser*), Jean Heard (*Lizzie*), Tom McCabe (*Officer Hubbard*), Philip Keenan (*Bone*), Nick Prideaux (*Fisherman*), Mark Sugden (*Hussar Officer*), Charlotte Lemoignan (*Christophine*), Helen Henessey, Evie Fenton, Eva Harvey (*Maids*), George Withers, John Samways (*Gardeners*), Katrina Verdon-Roe, Amy Elton (*Bar Girls*), Paul Villey (*Messenger*), Stephen Blogg (*Army Cook*).

The Claim (Great Britain/France/Canada). *Director:* Michael Winterbottom. *Producer:* Andrew Eaton. *Screenplay:* Frank Cottrell Boyce; inspired by the novel *The Mayor of Casterbridge* by Thomas Hardy. *Editor:* Trevor Waite. *Director of Photography:* Alwin H. Kuchler. *Art Direction:* Ken Rempel. *Production Design:* Ken Rempel and Mark Tildesley. *Set Decoration:* Paul Healy. *Music:* Michael Nyman. *Co-Producer:* Douglas Berquist. *Executive Producers:* Andrea Calderwood, Alexis Lloyd, Mark Shivas, and David M. Thompson. *Line Producer:* Anita Overland.

Casting: Kerry Barden, Wendy Brazington, Billy Hopkins, and Suzanne Smith. *Costumes:* Joanne Hansen. *Makeup:* Bryon Callaghan. *Hairstylist:* Don Olson. *Second Unit Directors:* Douglas Berquist and Matt Palmer. *First Assistant Director:* Nick Laws. *Second Assistant Director:* Kayla Popp. *Second Second Assistant Directors:* Mark Ambury and Pierre Tremblay. *Third Assistant Directors:* Matthew Kershaw and Brad Logel. *Unit Production Manager:* Tom Benz. *Production Supervisor:* Gina Carter. *Unit Production Manager, Colorado:* Tony Schweikle. *Sound Editor:* Ian Wilson. *ADR Mixer:* Peter Greaves. *Sound Re-Recording Mixer:* Adrian Rhodes. *Production Sound Mixer/Sound Recordist:* George Tarrant. *Special Effects Coordinator:* Gordon Davis. *Special Effects:* James Paradis and Maurice Routely. *Assistant Special Effects:* Chad Dolan and Jason Dolan. *Digital Sound Effects Editor:* Peter Christelis. *Digital Effects Producer:* Steve Garrad. *Digital Compositor, Cinesite:* Chris Gibbons. *Stunt Coordinator:* Kirk Jarrett. *Production companies:* Alliance Atlantis Communications (Canada); Arts Council of England; BBC; DB Entertainment (GB); Grosvenor Park Productions (GB); Le Studio Canal+ (France); Pathé Productions (GB); Revolution Films (GB). *Distributor:* United Artists. Filmed on location in Calgary, Alberta, Canada; and in Durango, Colorado. Filmed in DeLuxe Color. *Sound Mix:* Dolby Digital. *Running time:* 120 minutes. *Premiere:* December 29, 2000, in Los Angeles and New York; February 2, 2001, in GB.

Cast: Peter Mullan (*Daniel Dillon*), Milla Jovovich (*Lucia*), Wes Bentley (*Dalglish*), Nastassja Kinski (*Elena Burn*), Sarah Polley (*Hope Burn*), Shirley Henderson (*Annie*), Julian Richings (*Bellanger*), Sean McGinley (*Mr. Sweetley*), Randy Birch (*Priest*), Tom McCamus (*Burn*), Frank Zotter (*Photographer*), Artur Ciastkowski (*Delany*), Barry Ward (*Young Dillon*), Karolina Muller (*Young Elena*), David Lereaney (*Saloon Actor*), Valerie Planche (*Chippie No. 1*), Grant Linneberg (*Miner No. 2*), Jimmy Herman (*Miner No. 3*), Marie Brassard (*French Sue*), Phillipa Peak (*Sarah*), Kate Hennig (*Vauneen*), Fernando Davalos (*Barman*), Marc Hollogne (*Dr. Benoit*), Ron Anderson (*Stagecoach Driver*), Marty Antonini (*German*), Lydia Lau (*Li*), Royal Sproule (*Grimes*), Tim Koetting (*Hotel Clerk*), Billy Morton (*Miner No. 1*), Duncan Fraser (*Crocker*), Landon Hicks (*Young Miner*), Matthew Johnson (*Miner*), Janelle Loughlin (*Beggar Girl*), Linda Eve Miller (*Tobacco Chippie No. 2*), Karen Minish (*Opera Singer*), Trevor Allan Davies, John Goulart (*Members of Saloon Band*), Gil Rivera Blas (*Mexican*), Christopher Hunt (*Assay Clerk*), Jess Maldaner (*Miner No. 6*), Myrna Vallance (*Saloon Girl*).

Appendix C

Television Adaptations of Hardy's Works

The following is a list of the made-for-TV movies and miniseries based on Hardy's novels and stories. Be advised, however, that many of the details on the early adaptations are incomplete. In all likelihood, both *The Distracted Preacher* and *The Woodlanders* were "wiped" by the BBC as part of its policy of junking old programs. Since I was unable to view the actual programs I relied on such sources as the BBC's catalogue of television productions from 1936 to 1975—which provides information on the producers, directors, writers, and air dates, but says nothing of the casts—and on television listings and reviews in The *Times* of London. *Wessex Tales* apparently still exists: it is listed in *The TV Holdings of the National Film and Television Archive, 1936–1979*, eds. Simon Baker and Olwen Terris (London: BFI, 1994), but it has not been re-released to the general public and the information I have received on a few of the individual productions is somewhat sketchy. In cases where I have been able to ascertain that an actor was in a particular production but have been unable to find the name of the character he or she played, I listed only the actor's name. While it is logical to assume that Claire Bloom portrayed Ella Marchmill in "An Imaginative Woman" and that Ben Cross was Mätthaus Tina in "The Melancholy Hussar," there is the possibility that the names of Hardy's characters were changed or that the actor in question actually played a different role. In short, I allowed caution to guide me in the compiling of this list.

The Distracted Preacher (Great Britain). *Production company:* British Broadcasting Corporation. *Producer/Director:* Brandon Acton-Bond. *Teleplay:* John Hale; based on the story by Thomas Hardy. *Length:* 49 minutes. Presumed black and white. *First telecast:* December 26, 1969, on BBC-2.
Cast: Stephanie Beacham, Christopher Gable.

The Woodlanders (Great Britain). *Production company:* British Broadcasting Corporation. *Director:* John Davies. *Teleplay:* Harry Green; based on the novel by Thomas Hardy. *Producer:* Martin Lisemore. *Length:* Four episodes of 45 minutes each. Color. *First telecasts:* Part One, "Giles," February 15, 1970; Part Two, "Grace," February 22, 1970; Part Three, "Felice," March 1, 1970; Part Four, "Marty," March 8, 1970; on BBC-2.
Cast: Unknown.

Jude the Obscure (Great Britain). *Production company:* British Broadcasting Corporation. *Director:* Hugh David. *Teleplay:* Harry Green; based on the novel by Thomas Hardy. *Producer:* Martin Lisemore. *Script Editor:* Lennox Phillips. *Lighting:* John Summers. *Sound:* John Staple. *Costumes:* Odette Barrow. *Makeup:* Elizabeth Lowell. *Design:* Richard Wilmot. *Dialect Coach:* Owen Barry. *Graphics:* Colin Cheesman. *Length:* Six episodes of 45 minutes each. Color. *First telecasts:* February 6 to March 13, 1971, on BBC-2. Telecast in America on *Masterpiece Theatre* (PBS) from October 3 to November 7, 1971.
    Cast: Robert Powell (*Jude Fawley*), Fiona Walker (*Sue Bridehead*), John Franklyn-Robbins (*Richard Phillotson*), Alex Marshall (*Arabella Donn*), Daphne Heard (*Aunt Drusilla*), Sylvia Coleridge (*Miss Fontover*), Mark Praid (*Young Jude*), Charleton Hobbs (*Dr. Tetuphar*), Freda Bamford (*Landlady at Christminster*), Michael Golden (*Tinker Taylor*), Michael Rothwell (*Mr. Dawlish*), Gwen Nelson (*Mrs. Edlin*), Gary Rich (*Juey*), George Woodbridge (*Challow*), Meadows White (*Stonemason*), Edwin Brown (*Blacksmith*), Pamela Denton (*Anny*), Michael Beale (*Chivers*), Christopher Banks (*College Servant*), Eleanor Smale (*Mrs. Hawes*), Hazel Coppen (*Old Crone*), Gladys Spenser (*Mrs. Baize*), Mary Wimbush (*Miss Young*), Jane Tucker (*Sarah Blandford*), Anita Sharp Bolster (*Mrs. Trott*), Mark Dignam (*Vicar of Shaston*), Beth Morris (*Phillotson's Maid*), Ian Ricketts (*Tavern Customer*), John Moore (*Willis*), Christopher Hodge(*Auctioneer*), Owen Berry (*Registrar*), Sheila Fay (*Landlady*), John Scott Marlin (*Doctor*).

Wessex Tales (Great Britain). *Production company:* British Broadcasting Corporation. *Producer:* Irene Shubik. Based on the stories by Thomas Hardy. *Music:* Joseph Horovitz.
    "The Withered Arm." *Director:* Desmond Davis. *Teleplay:* Rhys Adrian. *Camera:* Brian Tufano. *Length:* 49 minutes. Color. *First telecast:* November 7, 1973, on BBC-2.
    Cast: Billie Whitelaw (*Rhoda*), Yvonne Antrobus (*Gertrude*), Edward Hardwicke, William Relton, John Welsh, Esmond Knight.
    "Fellow Townsmen." *Director:* Barry Davis. *Teleplay:* Douglas Livingstone. *Length:* 49 minutes. Color. *First telecast:* November 14, 1973, on BBC-2.
    Cast: Kenneth Haigh, Jane Asher, Terence Frisby, Susan Fleetwood, John McKelvey, Ann Curthoys, Robert Hartley, William Simons, Colin Edwyn, Anthony Edwards.

"A Tragedy of Two Ambitions." *Director:* Michael Tuchner. *Teleplay:* Dennis Potter. *Camera:* Peter Hall. *Editor:* Ken Pearce. *Design:* Richard Henry. *Costumes:* Barbara Lane. *Makeup:* Shirley Channing-Williams. *Length:* 49 minutes. Color. *First telecast:* November 21, 1973, on BBC-2.

Cast: John Hurt (*Joshua Harlborough*), David Troughton (*Cornelius Harlborough*), Paul Rogers (*Joshua Harlborough, Sr.*), Lynne Frederick (*Rosa Harlborough*), Heather Canning (*Selimar*), Edward Petherbridge (*Squire Fellmer*), Betty Cooper (*Mrs. Fellmer*), Dan Meaden (*Countryman*), Andrew McCulloch (*Farm Laborer*), John Rainer (*Clergyman*), Peter Bennett (*Principal*).

"An Imaginative Woman." *Director:* Gavin Millar. *Teleplay:* William Trevor. *Length:* 49 minutes. Color. *First telecast:* November 28, 1973, on BBC-2.

Cast: Claire Bloom, Norman Rodway, Maureen Pryor, Paul Dawkins, Barbara Kellerman, Anne-Louise Wakefield.

"The Melancholy Hussar." *Director:* Mike Newell. *Teleplay:* Ken Taylor. *Length:* 49 minutes. Color. *First telecast:* December 5, 1973, on BBC-2.

Cast: Mary Larkin, Ben Cross, Emrys James, Richard Kay.

"Barbara of the House of Grebe." *Director:* David Hugh Jones. *Teleplay:* David Mercer. *Length:* 49 minutes. Color. *First telecast:* December 12, 1973, on BBC-2.

Cast: Ben Kingsley (*Lord Uplandtowers*), Joanna McCallum (*Barbara*), Nick Bramble (*Willowes*), Leslie Sands (*Sir John Grebe*), Richard Cornish (*Drenkard*), Jean Gilpin (*Mrs. Drenkard*), John Boswall (*Tutor*), Robert Rietty (*Sculptor*), Janet Hanfrey (*Mary*), Charles Rae (*Bailiff*), Paul Imbusch (*Vicar*), Peter Geddis (*Beggar*), Don Henderson, Matthew Guinness (*Tramps*).

The Mayor of Casterbridge (Great Britain). *Production company:* British Broadcasting Corporation. *Director:* David Giles. *Teleplay:* Dennis Potter; based on the novel by Thomas Hardy. *Producer:* Martin Lisemore. *Editor:* Neil Pittaway. *Music:* Carl Davis. *Designer:* Peter Kindred. *Costumes:* Christine Rawlins. *Makeup:* Elizabeth Rowell. *Sound:* Robin Luxford. *Lighting:* Hubert Cartwright. *Script Editor:* Betty Willingale. *Length:* Seven episodes, varying from 50–55 minutes each. Color. *First telecasts:* January 22 to March 5, 1978, on BBC-2. Telecast in America on *Masterpiece Theatre* (PBS) from September 3 to October 15, 1978.

Cast: Alan Bates (*Michael Henchard*), Janet Maw (*Elizabeth-Jane*), Jack Galloway (*Donald Farfrae*), Anne Stallybrass (*Susan Henchard*), Anna Massey (*Lucetta Templeman*), Avis Bunnage (*Mrs. Goodenough*), Richard Owens (*Newson*), Peter Bourke (*Abel Whittle*), Joe Ritchie (*Buzzford*), Douglas Milvain (*Concy*), Clifford Parrish (*Longways*), Ronald Lacey (*Jopp*), Freddie Jones (*Fall*), Alan Rowe (*Mr. Joyce*), Kenneth Waller (*Clerk of Court*), William Whymper (*Commissioner*), Lloyd McGuire (*Prince Albert*), Jeffrey Holland (*Carter*), Leonard Trolley (*Auctioneer*), Deddie Davies (*Nancy*), Patricia Fincham (*Henchard's Maid*), Gilly Brown (*Lucetta's Maid*), John Flint (*Landlord*), Jack Le White (*Fiddler*), Desmond Adams (*Charl*), Charles West (*Doctor*), David Willitts (*Councillor*), Alan Collins (*Laborer*), Alec Bregonzi (*Companion*), Trudie Styler (*Cook*).

❖ ❖ ❖

Exploits at West Poley (aka *Our Exploits at West Poley*) [Great Britain; color]. *Production company:* Children's Film and Television Foundation, Ltd. *Director:* Diarmud Lawrence. *Teleplay:* James Andrew Hall; based on the novella by Thomas Hardy. *Producer:* Pamela Lonsdale. *Executive Producer:* Ian Shand. *Cinematography:* Ray Orton. *Editor:* Chris Ridsdale. *Music:* Nigel Hess. *Production Design:* Keith Wilson. *Costumes:* Reg Samuel. *Makeup:* Elizabeth Moss. *Production Manager:* Jeanne Ferber. *Casting:* Ann Fielden. *Sound Mixer:* Laurie Clarkson. *Boom:* Sam Morris. *Length:* Approx. 55 minutes. Color. *First telecast:* August 31, 1990, on ITV. (Note: Filmed October 7–November 1, 1985.)

Cast: Anthony Bale (*The Man Who Has Failed*), Brenda Fricker (*Aunt Draycott*), Charlie Condou (*Leonard*), Jonathan Jackson (*Stephen*), Jonathan Adams (*Miller Griffin*), Noel O'Connell (*Job Tray*), Frank Mills (*Ned Jones*), Thomas Heathcote (*Farmer Will Gant*), James Coyle (*Millhand*), Jelena Budimir (*Washerwoman*), Diana King (*Old Woman*), Kelita Groom (*Susan*), Brian Coburn (*Branded Man*), Sean Bean (*Scarface*), George Malpas (*Shepherd*), Barry Dromfield (*Fiddler*), Jacob Thomas (*Young Boy*).

The Return of the Native [full onscreen title: **Thomas Hardy's The Return of the Native**] (United States). *Production company:* Hallmark Hall of Fame. *Director:* Jack Gold. *Teleplay:* Robert W. Lenski; based on the novel by Thomas Hardy. *Producers:* Craig Anderson, Nick Gillott, Richard Welsh. *Cinematography:* Alan Hume. *Editor:* Jim Oliver. *Music:* Carl Davis. *Production Design:* Peter Mullins. *Costumes:* Derek Hyde. *Assistant Director:* Kieron Phipps. *Sound Effects:* Eric A. Norris. *Sound Re-recording:* John Asman. *Sound Mixer:* Tony Dawe. *Boom:* Chris Gurney. *Camera Operator:* John Maskall. *Dialect Coach:* Andrew Jack. *Length:* 101 minutes. Color. *First telecast:* December 4, 1994 (CBS).

Cast: Catherine Zeta Jones (*Eustacia Vye*), Clive Owen (*Damon Wildeve*), Ray Stevenson (*Clym Yeobright*), Joan Plowright (*Mrs. Yeobright*), Steven Mackintosh (*Diggory Venn*), Claire Skinner (*Thomasin*), Paul Rogers (*Captain Vye*), Celia Imrie (*Susan Nunsuch*), Richard Avery (*Humphrey*), Peter Wight (*Timothy*), Jeremy Peters (*Sam*), Gregg Saunders (*Charley*), John Boswall (*Grandfer Cantle*), William Waghorn (*Christian Cantle*), Matthew Owens (*Johnny*), Britta Smith (*Olly Dowden*), John Breslin (*Vicar*), Daniel Newman (*Mummer*).

Tess of the D'Urbervilles (Great Britain/United States). *Production companies:* London Weekend Television (GB), Arts and Entertainment Network (US). *Director:* Ian Sharp. *Teleplay:* Ted Whitehead; based on the novel by Thomas Hardy. *Producer:* Sarah Wilson. *Executive Producers:* Delia Fine, Sally Head. *Cinematography:* Richard Greatrex. *Editor:* Peter Davies. *Music:* Alan Lisk. *Production Design:* Gerry Scott. *Art Direction:* Mark Kebby. *Costumes:* Les Lansdown. *Makeup:* Kristin Chalmers. *Assistant Director:* Cliff Lanning. *Sound Editors:* Peter Baldock, Gillian Dodders. *Production Sound Mixer:* Tony Dawe. *Boom:* Chris Gurney. *Script Supervisor:* Sarah Hayward. *Choreographer:* Christine Carter. *Length:* Two parts, approx. 90 minutes each. Color. *First telecasts:* March 8 and 9, 1998, on ITV (GB); September 13 and 14, 1998, on A & E (US).

Cast: Justine Waddell (*Tess Durbeyfield*), Jason Flemyng (*Alec D'Urberville*), Oliver Milburn (*Angel Clare*), John McEnery (*Jack Durbeyfield*), Lesley Dunlop (*Joan Durbeyfield*), Rosalind Knight (*Mrs. D'Urberville*), Anthony O'Donnell (*Crick*), Christine Moore (*Mrs. Crick*), Bryan Pringle (*Kail*), Debbie Chazen (*Marian*), Candida Rundle (*Izz*), Amanda Brewster (*Retty*), Linda Armstrong (*Car Darch*), Hannah Westerman (*Nancy*), Charlotte Bellamy (*Cissie*), Amanda Loy-Ellis (*Sue*), Luke Graham (*Abraham*), Cheryl Heuston (*Liza-Lu*), Trevor Martin (*Parson Tringham*), Penny Morrell (*Rolliver Landlady*), Gerald James (*Narrator*).

Far from the Madding Crowd (Great Britain/United States). *Production companies:* Granada Television (GB), WGBH Boston (US). *Director:* Nicholas Renton. *Teleplay:* Philomena McDonagh; based on the novel by Thomas Hardy. *Producer:* Hilary Bevan Jones. *Executive Producers:* Rebecca Eaton, Gub Neal, Antony Root. *Assistant Producer:* Catriona McKenzie. *Cinematography:* John Daly. *Editor:* Anthony Ham. *Music:* John E. Keane. *Production Design:* Adrian Smith. *Art Direction:* Rosie Hardwick, Paul Kirby. *Costumes:* Nic Ede. *Hair and Makeup Design:* Dorka Nieradzik. *Makeup:* Beverly Binda, Clare Golds. *Assistant Director:* Vincent Fahy. *Sound Effects Editor:* John Rutherford. *Sound Recordists:* Nick Steer, David Hall. *Boom:* Ben Brookes. *Special Effects:* Perry Brahan, Chris Lawson. *Stunt Coordinator:* Peter Brayhan. *Stunts:* Crispin Layfield, Tom Lucy. *Script Editor:* Susie Conklin. *Choreographer:* Jane Gibson. *Dialect Coach:* Julia Wilson-Dixon. *Length:* Four episodes, 54 minutes each. Color. *First telecasts:* Parts One and Two, May 10, 1998; Parts Three and Four, May 17, 1998; on *Masterpiece Theatre* (PBS); July 6 to July 27, 1998; on ITV (GB).

Cast: Paloma Baeza (*Bathsheba Everdene*), Nigel Terry (*Mr. Boldwood*), Nathaniel Parker (*Gabriel Oak*), Jonathan Firth (*Sergeant Troy*), Natasha Little (*Fanny Robin*), Tracy Keating (*Liddy*), Robin Soans (*Henery Fray*), Victoria Alcock (*Temperance Miller*), James Allen (*Will Coggan*), James Ballentine (*Joe Coggan*), David Barrass (*Pennyways*), Tim Bartholomew (*Sam Sammy*), Linda Bassett (*Maryann Money*), Gwynn Beech (*Simeon*), Shannon Bone-Sands (*Lizzie Coggan*), John Boswell (*Timothy*), Reginald Callcott (*Jacob Smallbury*), Neil Caple (*Laban Tall*), Elizabeth Estensen (*Mrs. Coggan*), Philip Fowler (*William*), Sean Gilder (*Joseph Poorgrass*), Robyn Gow (*May Coggan*), Leader Hawkins (*Old Shepherd*), Geoffrey Jenkinson (*Sam Samway*), Phillip Joseph (*Jan Coggan*), Kevin Kibbey (*Billy Smallbury*), Gabrielle Lloyd (*Mrs. Twill*), Prussia Moore (*Annie Coggan*), Rhys Morgan (*Teddy Coggan*), Brian Rawlinson (*Parson Thirdly*), Luke Redbond (*Cainy Ball*), Andy Robb (*Mark Clark*), Charles Simon (*Old Malter*), Paul Sirr (*Barrister*), Linda Spurrier (*Mrs. Hurst*), Sarah Tansey (*Soberness Miller*), Neil Warhurst (*Sergeant Dobbs*).

The Mayor of Casterbridge (Great Britain/United States). *Production companies:* Pearson Television International (GB), Arts and Entertainment Network (US). *Director:* David Thacker. *Teleplay:* Ted Whitehead; based on the novel by Thomas Hardy. *Producer:* Georgina Lowe. *Executive Producer:* Sally Head. *Music:*

Adrian Johnston. *Cinematography:* Ivan Strasburg. *Production Design:* Bruce Macadie. *Costumes:* Lyn Avery. *Assistant Director:* Charlie Leech. *Sound Mixer:* Tim Fraser. *Casting:* Jill Trevellick. *Length:* Two parts, approximately two hours each. Color. *First telecast:* Summer 2001 on ITV (GB).

Cast: Ciarán Hinds (*Michael Henchard*), James Purefoy (*Donald Farfrae*), Jodhi May (*Elizabeth-Jane*), Juliet Aubrey (*Susan*), Polly Walker (*Lucetta Templeman*).

Notes

Introduction: Seeing Hardy, Knowing Hardy

1. Barthes, *The Responsibility of Forms*, pp. 5–8.
2. This does not include the short children's film *The Secret Cave*, based on Hardy's novella "Our Exploits at West Poley," released in Britain in 1953. The low profile of the film—the current status of which is uncertain—has led me to consider it a "minor" adaptation. For more information on this film, see Appendix A.

Chapter 1: "Strange Business": Thomas Hardy, the Cinema, and the Critics

1. Dennis L. Bird, "The First Hardy Film," *Thomas Hardy Journal*, 11.3 (1995), p. 43.
2. Hardy to Florence Henniker, July 2, 1921, in *Collected Letters*, vol. 6, p. 93.
3. Hardy to Sir Frederick Macmillan, February 22, 1911, in *CL*, vol. 4, p. 140.
4. For further information on the 1913 *Tess* and the 1915 *Crowd*, see Appendix A.
5. In the *Life*, Hardy indicates he is most interested in the *lack* of effect the actors had on the Dorchester townspeople. He remarks that in spite of the actors' yellow face make-up and period costumes, the locals "seemed not to notice the strange spectacle" (F. E. Hardy, p. 414).
6. Hardy to Macmillan, February 22, 1911, in *CL*, vol. 4, p. 140.
7. Hardy to Macmillan, September 6, 1913, in *CL*, vol. 4, p. 302.
8. Hardy to Macmillan, February 19, 1921, in *CL*, vol. 6, p. 72.
9. Hardy to Sir George Douglas, October 23, 1913, in *CL*, vol. 4, p. 312.
10. Christian Metz, *Psychoanalysis and Cinema*, translated by Celia Britton, et al. (London and Basingstoke: Macmillan, 1982), pp. 48–9.
11. Roland Barthes writes of a phenomenon he associates (in part) with viewing a disguised actor in a film, which he calls film's "obtuse" meaning (*Responsibility*, p. 48 ff). Derek Attridge has suggested that experiencing "obtusus" is to read deep personal significance into what is being viewed ("Roland Barthes's Obtuse, Sharp Meaning and the Responsibilities of Commentary," in *Writing the Image After Roland Barthes*, edited by Jean-Michel Rabaté [Philadelphia: U of Pennsylvania P, 1997], p. 80 ff). It is possible that Hardy saw actors disguised as his characters as ultimately reverberating with personal meaning for him.
12. Frank M. Laurence, "Hollywood Publicity and Hemingway's Popular Reputation," in *A Moving Picture Feast: The Filmgoer's Hemingway*, edited by Charles M. Oliver (New York; Westport, CT; London: Praeger, 1989), pp. 24–5.

13. I viewed the trailer on the Turner Classic Movies cable network; it is also available on the DVD and on some VHS versions of *Doctor Zhivago.*

14. On the BWE home video; see also Chapter 6.

15. Fred Botting, *Making Monstrous: Frankenstein, Criticism, Theory* (Manchester and New York: Manchester UP, 1991), p. 82.

16. See also Judith Mayne's analysis of how Vincente Minnelli uses Gustave Flaubert (James Mason) as both a character in and the narrator of the film *Madame Bovary* (1949). Flaubert is on trial for obscenity and he both tells the novel's story to the jury (and to the film audience) and offers commentary upon—and a defense of—Emma's actions. Mayne says that "the author is *made accountable* for his work. In that public sphere, the novel is told in such a way that the novelist merges with the characters he has created" (*Private Novels, Public Films* [Athens, GA, and London: U of Georgia P, 1988], pp. 110–11). Hardy has never been portrayed in a similar way in any of the adaptations of his novels—though he is used (in a bizarre way) as the "narrator" of A & E's *Tess of the D'Urbervilles* (see Chapter 7)—but Mayne's overall argument that authors are made "accountable" for their novels within the film versions certainly applies to Hardy.

17. Throughout this study I refer to Hardy's novel by the title he himself used—*Tess of the d'Urbervilles.* Many studies use a capital D in the title, and I have retained the capital letter in referring to those individual studies. Likewise, the A & E *Tess* uses the capital D, and I have respected that (see Chapter 7).

18. For an examination of the extent to which Hardy has been taught—and *how* he has been taught—in Great Britain, see Widdowson, "'Thomas Hardy' in Education," (*Hardy in History,* pp. 77–92). See also Lester D. Friedman, although he uses Hardy mainly to illustrate a general thesis: "Most Americans initially encounter [British] literary works within an academic environment of enthusiastic teachers insistent on communicating the beauty of Wordsworth's verse or the bleakness of Hardy's vision" ("The Empire Strikes Out: An American Perspective on the British Film Industry," in *British Cinema and Thatcherism: Fires Were Started,* edited by Lester D. Friedman [London: University College London P, 1993], p. 5).

19. Eisenstein, *Film Form,* pp. 195–255.

20. Mike Poole, "Dickens and Film: 101 Uses of a Dead Author," in *The Changing World of Charles Dickens,* edited by Robert Giddings (London: Vision; Totowa, NJ: Barnes and Noble, 1983), p. 160.

21. Review of *Great Expectations,* directed by David Lean, *Time,* May 26, 1947, p. 100.

22. Ibid., p. 99.

23. James Agee, "Films," *The Nation,* July 19, 1947, p. 80.

24. Agee, p. 80.

25. Michael A. Anderegg, *David Lean* (Boston: Twayne, 1984), p. 42.

26. Todd McCarthy, review of *Great Expectations,* directed by Alfonso Cuarón, *Variety,* Jan. 19–25, 1998, p. 92.

27. John Wraithall, review of *Great Expectations,* directed by Alfonso Cuarón, *Sight and Sound,* May 1998, p. 45.

28. David Ansen, "Forster Revisited," *Newsweek,* Sept. 21, 1987, p. 66

29. Richard Corliss, "Doing It Right the Hard Way," *Time,* March 16, 1992, p. 72.

30. David Ansen, "A Closet with a View: Forster's Secret Novel," review of *Maurice,* directed by James Ivory, *Newsweek,* Sept. 21, 1987, p. 76.

31. Peter J. Hutchings, "A Disconnected View: Forster, Modernity, and Film," in *E. M. Forster,* ed. Jeremy Tambling (London and Basingstoke: Macmillan, 1995), p. 213 ff; Cairns Craig, "Rooms Without a View," *Sight and Sound,* June 1991, p. 10 ff.

32. Hutchings, p. 223.

33. Hutchings, p. 224.

34. June Perry Levine, "Two Rooms with a View: An Inquiry into Film Adaptation," *Mosaic* 22.3 (1989), p. 74.

35. All quotations related to the film of *An Ideal Husband* come from the Miramax Films Production Notes, available at: <http://movies.yahoo.com/ shop?d=hv&id=1800018653&cf= prod> Accessed Dec. 13, 1999.

36. Roland Barthes, "The Death of the Author," in Barthes, *Image-Music-Text,* p. 143.

37. These are *Far from the Madding Crowd, Tess of the d'Urbervilles, Jude the Obscure, The Woodlanders,* and *The Mayor of Casterbridge* (as *The Claim*).

38. For more information on the "lost" film versions of Hardy's novels, see Appendix A.

39. Thorold Dickinson, *"The Mayor of Casterbridge:* Some Notes," *Sight and Sound,* Jan. 1951, p. 363.

40. Selznick's desire to film *Tess* has been mentioned in many sources—see, for instance, Boyum, p. 138*n.,* and Leaming, p. 193. In his autobiography, Polanski reports that, to start on the film right away, his producer, Claude Berri, had to buy the film rights from the Selznick estate, even though the novel would be out of copyright at the end of 1978—a few months after Polanski's crew was due to start shooting (Polanski, p. 428). Also, Andrew Sarris mentions that *Far from the Madding Crowd* "was once rumored as a vehicle for the late Vivien Leigh" ("Films," *Village Voice,* Nov. 2, 1967, p. 33), but I have been unable to locate any other reference to this proposed film.

41. Hollis Alpert, "A Considerable Measure of Distinction," review of *Far from the Madding Crowd, Saturday Review,* Oct. 21, 1967, p. 46.

42. John Russell Taylor, "Hardy Film Looks Marvellous," review of *Far from the Madding Crowd, The Times* (London), Oct. 17, 1967, p. 9.

43. Sarris, p. 33.

44. Melanie Wallace in *Cineaste,* Winter 1980-81; reprinted in Ozer (1981), p. 954.

45. Tom Milne in *Monthly Film Bulletin,* May 1981; reprinted in Ozer (1981), p. 956.

46. Lawrence Van Gelder, "What's Obscure is Society in a New Tale of Jude," *New York Times,* Oct. 18, 1996, p. C14.

47. Georgia Brown in *Village Voice,* Oct. 22, 1996; reprinted in Ozer (1997), p. 765.

48. "Vivid Victoriana," review of *Far from the Madding Crowd, Time,* Oct. 27, 1967, p. 102.

49. James's dislike of Hardy and his novels is notorious. Of special interest here is James's review of *Far from the Madding Crowd* in The *Nation* (Dec. 24, 1874), in which he castigates Hardy for ballooning his "simple" tale to three volumes and suggests that Hardy in his fiction should observe Aristotle's three unities (quoted in Cox, p. 29).

50. Robert Hatch, "Films," The *Nation,* Jan. 3-10, 1981, p. 29.

51. Stanley Kauffmann, "Mixed Blessings," review of *Tess, New Republic,* Jan. 3-10, 1981, pp. 20-1.

52. Michael Wilmington, "Tragic 'Jude' Remains True to Hardy's Novel," *Chicago Tribune,* Nov. 1, 1996, p. 7J.

53. Millgate, *Thomas Hardy: A Biography,* p. 347.

54. Roger Webster argues that "the dominant critical and popular traditions which have evolved around Hardy's fiction have sought to institutionalize the novels in ways which emphasise a pastoral aspect, producing a very familiar, comfortable version of Hardy which can all too easily predetermine our responses to them" ("Reproducing Hardy," p. 144). He further says that "there are no innocent or uncontaminated readings of Hardy. This familiarity means that the name 'Hardy' has become a cultural trigger for a set of associations: rustic characters and cottages, shepherds playing flutes, and so on" (pp. 144–5). Webster complains that this portrait of the kinds of novels Hardy wrote divorces them from their historical context and renders them "vague, abstract, and sentimental" (p. 145).

55. Widdowson, *Hardy in History,* p. 16.

56. Widdowson, *Hardy in History,* p. 17.

57. Widdowson, *Hardy in History,* pp. 47–55.

58. See, for instance, Simon Gatrell, *Hardy the Creator: A Textual Biography* (New York: Oxford UP, 1988).

59. Widdowson, *Hardy in History,* pp. 53–4.

60. Widdowson, *Hardy in History,* pp. 49–51.

61. I make no claims of originality in this area: more than 20 years ago, James Kincaid wrote that criticism "now acknowledge[s] more fully the tentativeness and inconsistency of a typical Hardy narrator and the ambiguity of the action" ("Hardy's Absences," in Kramer, ed. *Critical Approaches,* p. 202); and Hillis Miller made the elliptical, uncertain quality of *Tess's* narrative the subject of a classic deconstructionist reading of Hardy (*Fiction and Repetition,* pp. 116-46). Even as far back as 1940, Morton Dauwen Zabel argued that Hardy's novels offer a series of contrasts between the aesthetic and the defective—contrasts that present a "truer" picture of life in Hardy's works and which Hardy believed would have the power of enervating fiction and poetry as art forms ("Hardy in Defense of His Art: The Aesthetic of Incongruity," *Southern Review,* 6.1 [1940], p. 125 ff.).

62. Chapters 3, 4, and 5 consider the extent to which the novels *Far from the Madding Crowd, Tess of the d'Urbervilles,* and *Jude the Obscure* have been interpreted by critics as works that fit into, comment upon, or subvert various literary genres. Surprisingly, the only book-length study dedicated *exclusively* to examining Hardy's deployment of genre is Suzanne Ruth Johnson's 1989 dissertation, which has a major premise that Hardy pursued the same themes in different literary genres (fiction, poetry, drama), and that by categorizing Hardy's works according to those genres we are left with an incomplete assessment of his accomplishments as an artist (*Thomas Hardy and the Dynamics of Genre* [Dissertation, University of Virginia 1989], pp. 3–4).

63. M. M. Bakhtin, *The Dialogic Imagination,* edited by Michael Holquist; translated by Caryl Emerson and Michael Holquist (Austin: U of Texas P, 1981), p. 5.

64. My argument here owes a great deal to James R. Kincaid, "Coherent Readers, Incoherent Texts," *Critical Inquiry,* 3.4 (1977), 781–802.

Chapter 2: What You See Is More Than What You Get: The Problem of Adapting Hardy to Film

1. Beach, pp. 143-57.

2. David Cecil, *Hardy the Novelist: An Essay in Criticism* (Indianapolis and New York: Bobbs-Merrill, 1946), p. 81 ff.

3. Miller, *Distance and Desire,* p. 50.

4. David Lodge, "Thomas Hardy as a Cinematic Novelist," p. 80.

5. Lodge, "Cinematic Novelist," p. 80. Lodge doesn't really analyze *why* Hardy utilizes these narrative effects; instead, he entertains Hillis Miller's notion that Hardy wished to "distance" himself from the narrated action and the emotions involved (*Distance and Desire,* p. 43). Lodge concludes that "Hardy's reliance on specified and unspecified observers [is] evidence of the importance he attached to visual perspective. ...These observing eyes act like camera lenses—and if there is often something voyeuristic about their observations, this only reminds us that film is a deeply voyeuristic medium" ("Cinematic Novelist," p. 82).

6. Lodge, "Cinematic Novelist," p. 78.

7. John Wain, Introduction to *The Dynasts* [1904, 1906, 1908], by Thomas Hardy (London: Macmillan; New York: St. Martin's, 1965), pp. ix–x.

8. Wain, pp. xiii, xvii.

9. Joan Grundy, *Hardy and the Sister Arts* (London and Basingstoke: Macmillan, 1979), pp. 107, 109.

10. Eisenstein, p. 205 ff.

11. "Cinematic Novelist," p. 81.

12. Neil Sinyard, *Filming Literature: The Art of Screen Adaptation* (London and Sydney: Croom Helm, 1986), p. 48.

13. Boyum, pp. 138–9.

14. Boyum, p. 15.

15. The following list of adaptation studies is far from exhaustive: a complete list would be too extensive for this study. For the most complete examinations of the history of adaptation studies, see Griffith, pp. 18–35; Boyum, pp. 3–15; and especially Robert Giddings, Keith Selby, and Chris Wensley, *Screening the Novel: The Theory and Practice of Literary Dramatization* (London and Basingstoke: Macmillan, 1990), pp. 1–27.

16. Prior to Bluestone, the only extensive analysis of film adaptation was Lester Asheim's four-part study, published in *Hollywood Quarterly,* 5.3 and 5.4 (1951), and in *HQ*'s successor, *Quarterly of Film, Radio, and Television,* 6.1 (1951) and 6.3 (1952).

17. Bluestone, pp. 20–24.

18. Bluestone, p. 27.

19. Bluestone, p. 48.

20. Bluestone's ideas on editing and on film tenses are based on those of Bela Balázs, *Theory of the Film: Character and Growth of a New Art,* translated by Edith Bone (New York: Dover, 1970), pp. 118–38.

21. Bluestone, pp. 5–11.

22. Bluestone, p. 62.

23. One of the most interesting post-Bluestone studies was by Siegfried Kracauer, who argued that the novel is a "mental continuum," while film is a "material continuum," so that "any attempt to convert the mental continuum of the novel into camera-life appears to be hopelessly doomed" (*Theory of Film: The Redemption of Physical Reality* [1960; Princeton, NJ: Princeton UP, 1997], pp. 237–8).

24. Mitry, pp. 7–8; Mitry's emphases.

25. Mitry, p. 6.

26. Murray, p. 113.

27. Murray, pp. 113–14.

28. Quoted in Roberta F. Green, *"The Scarlet Letter,"* in *Magill's Cinema Annual 1996,* ed. Beth A. Fhaner and Christopher P. Scanlon (Detroit: Gale, 1996), pp. 453, 454.

29. Eidsvik, pp. 31-4.

30. Specifically, Cohen draws from Metz's *Essais sur la signification au cinéma* (Paris: Klincksieck, 1968; Eng. trans. *Film Language*), pp. 67–8 and 117–19. Metz's argument is that the word's double articulation and the film image's simultaneous single articulation make the two forms different, a point Cohen disputes below.

31. Cohen, *Film and Fiction,* p. 88.

32. Cohen, p. 89.

33. Cohen, p. 3.

34. Elsewhere, Cohen calls for filmmakers to *subvert* the novels they are adapting, for "Adaptation is a truly artistic feat only when the new version carries with it a hidden criticism of its model. …The adaptation must subvert its original, perform a double and paradoxical job of unmasking and unveiling its source, or else the pleasure it provides will be nothing more than that of seeing words changed into images" ("Eisenstein's Subversive Adaptation," in *The Classic American Novel and the Movies,* edited by Gerald Peary and Robert Shatzkin [New York: Ungar, 1977], pp. 245, 55). Such a subversive enterprise would also expose the dominant mindsets from which the novels sprang.

35. Orr, p. 72.

36. Barthes, "Death of the Author," in *Image-Music-Text,* p. 146.

37. Orr, pp. 72–3.

38. Larsson, p. 72.

39. Larsson, pp. 72–3.

40. Griffith, p. 38.

41. Griffith, p. 36.

42. Griffith, p. 44.

43. Griffith, pp. 73–4.

44. Barthes, "Introduction to the Structural Analysis of Narratives," in *Image-Music-Text,* p. 86; McFarlane, p. 13.

45. McFarlane, p. 13.

46. McFarlane, pp. 13–14.

47. McFarlane, p. 14.

48. McFarlane, p. 14.

49. McFarlane, p. 14.

50. McFarlane, pp. 26–7.

51. McFarlane believes there are two types of adaptations: those that are "reverently disposed" to being faithful to the original novel's letter and/or spirit; and those that significantly depart from the original. In McFarlane's terms, "Such departures may be seen in the light of offering a *commentary* on or, in more extreme cases, a *deconstruction* … of the original" (p. 22). To McFarlane, a film adaptation should be analyzed according to which kind of adaptation it strives to be.

52. Boumelha, p. 98.

53. For discussion of the often disparate mixture of genres in *The Woodlanders,* see John Bayley, "A Social Comedy? On Re-reading *The Woodlanders,*" *Thomas Hardy Annual,* 5 (1987), pp. 3–21; Lesley Higgins, "Pastoral Meets Melodrama in Thomas Hardy's *The Woodlanders,*" *Thomas Hardy Journal,* 6.2 (1990), pp. 111–25; and especially Boumelha, pp. 98–116.

54. The novel's first plot function is the arrival of Barber Percomb at the home of the Souths, where he presses Marty to sell him her hair (pp. 41–4). This scene is significant in that it

gets the story *started*, but—in my interpretation, at least—a plot function is *cardinal* only if it turns the plot in a new direction. *The Woodlanders* has no real story until Percomb makes his offer to Marty; but I am willing to concede there is a certain cardinality about this function.

55. The most famous study of this feature, of course, is Hillis Miller's *Thomas Hardy: Distance and Desire*. Other significant studies of the modes of overhearing, eavesdropping, and perceiving in Hardy's fiction are Sheila Berger, *Thomas Hardy and Visual Structures: Framing, Disruption, Process* (New York and London: New York UP, 1990); J. B. Bullen, *The Expressive Eye: Fiction and Perception in the Work of Thomas Hardy* (Oxford: Clarendon, 1986); Bruce Johnson, *True Correspondence: A Phenomenology of Thomas Hardy's Novels* (Tallahassee: UP of Florida, 1983); and Penelope Vigar, *The Novels of Thomas Hardy: Illusion and Reality* (London: Athlone, 1974). Individual studies on the modes of overhearing and perception in *Far from the Madding Crowd, Tess of the d'Urbervilles,* and *Jude the Obscure* will be handled in their individual chapters.

56. David Lodge's introduction to the "New Wessex" edition of *The Woodlanders,* which was used for this study, reads the novel in the light of a "pastoral elegy" (pp. 9–30); Robert Y. Drake reads the novel as embracing Elizabethan pastoral values ("*The Woodlanders* as Traditional Pastoral," *Modern Fiction Studies,* 6.3 [1960], p. 253); Charles E. May reads *The Woodlanders* as a "grotesque" pastoral—one that turns the values of the pastoral genre on their heads ("*Far from the Madding Crowd* and *The Woodlanders:* Hardy's Grotesque Pastorals," *ELT,* 17.3 [1974], pp. 152–5). Shirley Stave has read the novel as one in which the Little Hintock residents have fallen from their Pagan, nature-centered past, and where Marty has assumed the role of a nature "goddess" who cannot renew the community (pp. 76–81).

57. Dale Kramer, for instance, identifies in the novel the theme of individual will being restricted by "inevitable frustration" (*Thomas Hardy: The Forms of Tragedy* [Detroit: Wayne State UP, 1975], p. 96), while Bert G. Hornback considers the "Unfulfilled Intention" to be a mere "idea" that is poorly developed in this particular novel (*The Metaphor of Chance: Vision and Technique in the Works of Thomas Hardy* [Athens, OH: Ohio UP, 1971], p. 72).

58. Typically, Hardy's treatment of marriage and divorce in this novel has been of most interest to Marxist and/or feminist critics, both of which largely see marriage as an institution of social domination. See, for instance, Goode, *Offensive Truth,* pp. 101–9.

59. See Millgate, *Career,* where he reads the contrast between tragedy and comedy as illustrating Hardy's own uneasiness about class divisions (pp. 257–60); David Ball, who finds that the comedy is meant is meant to contrast and heighten the sense of tragedy ("Tragic Contradiction in Hardy's *The Woodlanders,*" *Ariel,* 18.1 [1987], p. 19); and Higgins, who argues that Hardy uses conventions and characters from Victorian stage melodrama to allow his readers to distinguish the characters and their behaviors (e.g., noble characters vs. ignoble characters) and to create an elegy for a past way of life that most readers would be able to recognize (pp. 114–16).

Chapter 3: Far from the Madding Crowd: *How Schlesinger Contained the Uncontainable*

1. This observation has also been made by Ian Gregor in *The Great Web: The Form of Hardy's Major Fiction* (London and Boston: Faber, 1974), p. 45, and by Merryn Williams, *Thomas Hardy and Rural England* (London and Basingstoke: Macmillan, 1972), p. 130.

2. F. E. Hardy, *Life,* p. 102.

3. Millgate, *Thomas Hardy: His Career as a Novelist,* p. 96. Hardy's own 1895 Preface to *Far from the Madding Crowd* remarks on the speed with which "Wessex" came to be applied to both southwest England and to its inhabitants after 1874. The currency of the place name was such that George Eliot—named by R. H. Hutton as the probable author of *Crowd* (*Spectator* Jan. 3, 1874)—appropriated it for *Daniel Deronda* (1876).

4. Keith Wilson, *Thomas Hardy on Stage* (New York: St. Martin's, 1995), pp. 25–9.

5. In 1909, the Edison Company released a single-real picture called variously *Far from the Madding Crowd, Far from the Madd'ing Crowd,* and *Far from the Maddening Crowd.* Some sources list this as an adaptation of Hardy's novel, but as a review in the *Moving Picture World* (August 28, 1909, p. 282) reveals, the film was a slapstick farce about a harried city man who

travels to the country and encounters all kinds of bucolic troubles. However, Edison's *Crowd* may have capitalized on the title's association with Hardy.

6. Carl J. Weber, Introduction to *Far from the Madding Crowd* (New York: Oxford UP, 1937), pp. xi–xii.

7. Cox's *Thomas Hardy: The Critical Heritage* offers an excellent digest of early reviews, most of which focus on the book's pastoralism. Henry James's notoriously patronizing review, for instance, still praises Hardy for his "natural relish for harvesting and sheep-washings" (p. 30). In another early study, Henry Charles Duffin waxes rhapsodic, saying *Crowd* and the other Wessex novels create "a Paradise so vast that even the grimy and plastered fingers of man can but soil it here and there" (*Thomas Hardy: A Study of the Wessex Novels, The Poems, and* The Dynasts, revised 3rd ed. [Manchester: Manchester UP, 1937], p. 143).

8. Michael Squires, "*Far from the Madding Crowd* as a Modified Pastoral," *Nineteenth-Century Fiction*, 25.3 (1970), pp. 299 ff. Charles E. May writes in almost direct response to Squires, claiming Hardy's purpose was actually to *distort* the pastoral world by injecting it with grotesque images of death, and that he made Troy a kind of hero, since he is opposed to the deathly world of Nature that Bathsheba lives in ("*Far from the Madding Crowd* and *The Woodlanders*: Hardy's Grotesque Pastorals," *ELT*, 17.3 [1974], p. 151).

9. John Alcorn, *The Nature Novel from Hardy to Lawrence* (New York: Columbia UP, 1977), p. 14.

10. Merryn Williams, *Thomas Hardy and Rural England* (London and Basingstoke: Macmillan, 1972), p. 130.

11. Goode, *Thomas Hardy: The Offensive Truth*, p. 18.

12. Robert Langbaum's analysis of *Crowd* (*Thomas Hardy in Our Time* [New York: St. Martin's, 1995], pp. 78–94) is much on the lines of Squires (and, for that matter, Gregor) in that it argues Hardy shoots through the novel a good deal of violence, tragedy, and eroticism, all of which make the novel's pastoral qualities that much deeper. Judith Bryant Wittenberg and Daryl Ogden each take on the subject of *Crowd*'s use of the gaze, with Wittenberg arguing that Hardy makes Bathsheba and Gabriel at differing times "both helpless and in control, of being both seen and seer, object and subject" ("Angles of Vision and Questions of Gender in *Far from the Madding Crowd*," *The Centennial Review*, 30.1 [1986], p. 40) in order to equalize the roles of men and women; while Ogden argues that Hardy plays with the idea of giving power to Bathsheba through her deployment of the patriarchal "gaze," but ultimately she cannot escape her role as a feminized object and attain a role of power ("Bathsheba's Visual Estate: Female Spectatorship in *Far from the Madding Crowd*," *Journal of Narrative Technique*, 23.1 [1993], p. 12). Samir Elbarbary relies on the writings of Mill and eighteenth- and nineteenth-century feminists to argue that Hardy shows Bathsheba as trying to define herself *against* the way patriarchal male language wishes to define her ("The Male Bias of Language and Gender Hierarchy: Hardy's Bathsheba Everdene and His Vision of Feminine Reality Reconsidered," *Cahiers Victoriens et Edouardiens* 41 [1995], pp. 59–79).

13. Susan Beegel, "Bathsheba's Lovers: Male Sexuality in *Far from the Madding Crowd*," in *Thomas Hardy: Modern Critical Views*, edited by Harold Bloom (New York, New Haven, and Philadelphia: Chelsea House, 1987), pp. 216–9.

14. Stave, *The Decline of the Goddess*, p. 33.

15. Weber, p. xv. Roy Morrell also deals with *Far from the Madding Crowd* as an "introduction" to Hardy's novels, in that Morrell argues the book contains characteristic Hardy themes, including the espousal of pessimism as a practical philosophy—even though Morrell says that pessimism in this novel is presented in a "positive" light (*Thomas Hardy: The Will and the Way* [Kuala Lumpur: U of Malaya P, 1968], pp. 59–72).

16. Elizabeth Drew, *The Novel: A Modern Guide to Fifteen English Masterpieces* (New York: Norton, 1963), p. 143.

17. Phillips, *John Schlesinger*, p. 79.

18. From the original theatrical trailer, included on the MGM/UA home video.

19. My argument here owes something to Rita Costabile, who also says that Hardy's Nature is ungovernable, and that Schlesinger's film reduces Nature to "a glamorous backdrop to a very ordinary love story" ("Hardy in Soft Focus," *The English Novel and the Movies*, edited by Michael Klein and Gillian Parker [New York: Ungar, 1981], p. 164). However, I take issue with many of Costabile's points. In neither the novel nor the film do people try to "rein in" Nature. I believe that, in the novel, people try to validate themselves *through* Nature. I also feel that Costabile's

view that people must be able to "read" Nature in order to survive is disproved by the novel; and, overall, her treatment of Schlesinger's film is unduly dismissive.

20. See, for instance, Squires: "The contrast between rural and urban is frequently noticed in the novel, primarily to show the superiority of the wholly rural Gabriel to the urbanized Sergeant Troy" (p. 39).

21. Richard Carpenter reads this aspect of Norcombe Hill as the "blank face of Nature indifferent to man" ("The Mirror and the Sword: Imagery in *Far from the Madding Crowd*," *Nineteenth-Century Fiction*, 18.4 [1964], p. 339). Essentially, I agree, though ascribing indifference to Nature is a way of humanizing it.

22. "Irony" here can be understood in Wayne C. Booth's terms: a rejection of literal meaning, a proposal of alternative explanations for the meaning of the event in question, a decision on the part of the spectator that irony is intended by the author, and a reconstruction of the event's meaning according to an unspoken "truth" (*A Rhetoric of Irony* [Chicago and London: U of Chicago P, 1974], pp. 10–13).

23. John Goode argues that social circumstances force Gabriel into assuming many "disguises"—bailiff, shepherd, dairyman—before *natural* circumstances allow him an opportunity to play roles that advance his social situation (*Offensive Truth*, p. 29). Other significant studies of role-playing in *Far from the Madding Crowd* are Linda M. Shires ("Narrative, Gender, and Power in *Far from the Madding Crowd*," in Higonnet, ed., *The Sense of Sex*, pp. 49–65), who argues that Gabriel and Bathsheba both subvert the traditional male/female roles, each becoming at times powerful and dependent, in order for Hardy to destabilize power alignments and especially to question the problematic status of women in Victorian society; and William Mistichelli ("Androgyny, Survival, and Fulfillment in Thomas Hardy's *Far from the Madding Crowd*," *Modern Language Studies*, 18.3 [1988], pp. 53–64), who argues that the characters change roles—predominantly gender-related—in order to adapt and evolve.

24. My argument here is somewhat similar to Morrell's, who says that "Nature is one of Gabriel's resources, but he is never controlled by her, nor, in any Wordsworthian sense, does he ever trust her. The essential thing about Gabriel is not that he is in contact with Nature, but that he is in contact with reality. He neither evades it nor resigns himself to it; he makes something out of it" (*Will and the Way*, p. 63). Later, Morrell claims that the Weatherbury peasants' connection to Nature makes them "backward," and that the "outsider" status of Gabriel and Bathsheba "revitalizes" the area (p. 69).

25. Stave, p. 26.

26. See, for instance, Ogden, who argues that Hardy allows Bathsheba to occasionally play the masculine spectator, but that he never gives her complete control over the patriarchal gaze, as Hardy was not yet ready to step outside his age's "patriarchal representations of vision" (pp. 12–13).

27. See Elbarbary, whose essay studies the way "masculine" language is used to appropriate power.

28. James Powers, "Dialogue on Film: John Schlesinger," *American Film*, Dec. 1979, p. 36.

29. The information in the previous sentences was largely gathered from Phillips, *John Schlesinger*, pp. 88–92.

30. James M. Welsh, "Hardy and the Pastoral, Schlesinger and Shepherds: *Far from the Madding Crowd*," *Literature/Film Quarterly*, 9.2 (1981), p. 80.

31. Costabile, p. 156.

32. Gene C. Phillips, *Major Film Directors* (Bethlehem, PA: Lehigh UP), p. 231.

33. Fran E. Chalfont, "From Strength to Strength: John Schlesinger's Film of *Far from the Madding Crowd*," *Thomas Hardy Annual*, 5 (1987), pp. 63 ff.

34. The material in this paragraph was derived from Robert Murphy, *Sixties British Cinema*, pp. 10–33; Phillips, *John Schlesinger*, pp. 41–4; and Alexander Walker, *Hollywood UK*, pp. 23–91.

35. Murphy, p. 25.

36. In addition to their thematic unity, Schlesinger's first six films—with the exception of *Midnight Cowboy*—are all essentially British films, made in England and dealing with English subject matter. After *Sunday, Bloody Sunday*, Schlesinger did most of his work in the United States. Whether because of this or in spite of this, Schlesinger's subsequent films have been a mixed bag.

37. Gene C. Phillips, "The Personal Vision of John Schlesinger," *America*, Oct. 16, 1971, p. 290.

38. Quoted in F. R. Southerington, *Hardy's Vision of Man* (London: Chatto and Windus, 1971), p. 234.

39. Walker, p. 361.

40. According to Murphy (pp. 257–8), by the time *Far from the Madding Crowd* came to be filmed, all things British—Beatlemania, James Bond films, the "myth of Swinging London"—were extremely popular in America, so American film companies were eager to finance British movies. As Walker (p. 361) and Phillips (*John Schlesinger*, p. 80) report, Schlesinger and producer Joseph Janni pitched a "small" film to MGM, but they were told that the film they delivered must be an epic blockbuster. Supposedly, MGM was also interested in having Schlesinger direct a version of *Tess of the d'Urbervilles* as opposed to *Crowd* (Walker, p. 361).

41. Ernest Betts, "Filming Hardy's 'Far from the Madding Crowd,'" the *Times* (London), Aug. 19, 1967, p. 7.

42. McFarland, p. 9.

43. Chalfont, pp. 67–8.

44. The elimination of Hardy's theme of "camaraderie" is significant. In the novel, Gabriel meets Fanny on the road and gives her money—an act that brings these characters together; likewise, Gabriel and Boldwood are brought together over their mutual concern for the whereabouts of Fanny. The elimination of this material in the film renders it unclear how Boldwood knows about the way Troy has treated Fanny, or why Gabriel takes charge of Boldwood's farm. Had this material been included in the film, it might have disarmed Phillips' charge that the characters are lacking in motivation. Fortunately, the material appears in the 1998 television version of *Crowd* (see Chapter 7).

45. Walker, p. 362.

46. Shires claims that Troy dresses like Bathsheba in this scene in order to create an image of "sexual likeness" and to "[seduce] Bathsheba into intimacy with him" (p. 55).

47. Webster, pp. 148–9.

48. Costabile, p. 159.

49. In the novel, Boldwood does not die—Gabriel is instrumental in having Boldwood's sentence commuted to life imprisonment on the grounds of insanity. Chalfont approves of this change, saying that the film "says nothing about Boldwood after showing him waiting stoically in a cell while a gallows is being constructed outside his window, allowing him to leave the film with the dignity he maintained throughout and with a tragic self-awareness and honesty similar to Othello's wish that people speak of him 'as I am, nothing extenuate'" (p. 71).

50. Phillips writes that the film originally ended with "Bathsheba fondly musing over the music box which her dead first husband had given her on their wedding day" (*John Schlesinger*, p. 88), but he notes that this ending was deleted from American prints in 1967 and never restored. I presume that Phillips is referring to the ending that I describe in this paragraph, and that it was restored to the video version (which runs 169 minutes), but I am not entirely sure. Certainly, Bathsheba does not "muse" over the music box in current prints.

51. James Price, review of *Far from the Madding Crowd* in *Sight and Sound*, 37.1 (1967/68), p. 39. See also "Vivid Victoriana," *Time*, Oct. 27, 1967, p. 102: "As Hardy did, Schlesinger relies on the countryside to give the story its character"; and John Coleman ("The Wessex Set," review of *Far from the Madding Crowd*, in *New Statesman* [Oct. 20, 1967], p. 517), who feels the film creates "fine visual metaphors for those underlying Hardy themes of man's isolation and the brute workings of destiny."

Chapter 4: Tess *by Hardy,* Tess *by Polanski: Convergence and Fulfillment*

1. Arnold Kettle, "Introduction to *Tess of the D'Urbervilles*," in *Twentieth Century Interpretations of Tess of the D'Urbervilles*, edited by Albert J. LaValley (Englewood Cliffs, NJ: Prentice Hall, 1969), p. 15.

2. Kettle, "Introduction," pp. 14–5.

3. Kettle, "Hardy: *Tess of the D'Urbervilles* (1891)," in *An Introduction to the English Novel*, vol. 2 (New York: Harper, 1951; reprint 1960), pp. 14–29.

4. James to Robert Louis Stevenson, March 19, 1892: "The good little Thomas Hardy has scored a great success with *Tess of the d'Urbervilles*, which is chock full of faults and falsity and yet has a singular beauty and charm" (reprinted in Lerner and Holmstrom, p. 85).

5. See, for instance, Springer, *Hardy's Use of Allusion*: "Hardy's public problems with *Tess* have become a familiar metaphor for the Grundian pressures which Victorian novelists faced and feared" (p. 122).

6. Goode, *Offensive Truth*, p. 10.

7. Reprinted in Cox, p. 190.

8. *Life*, p. 246. Hardy's response is to Mowbray Morris, "Culture and Anarchy," in *Quarterly Review* (April 1892), pp. 319–26; reprinted in Cox, pp. 214–221. Unknown to Hardy, Morris was the editor who first rejected *Tess* for serial publication in *Macmillan's Magazine*.

9. See, for instance, the biographical sketch of Hardy that has been published in every Signet Classic edition of his novels—unchanged—for decades: "In 1896, disturbed by the public outcry over the unconventional subjects of two of his greatest novels, *Tess of the D'Urbervilles* and *Jude the Obscure*, he announced that he would never write fiction again, and after that he wrote only poetry."

10. Among the most appreciative reviews are the *Speaker* (December 26, 1891), William Watson in the *Academy* (February 6, 1892), and D. F. Hannigan in *Westminster Review* (December 1892).

11. Reprinted in Lerner and Holstrom, pp. 81–2.

12. Reprinted in Cox, p. 193.

13. D. H. Lawrence, *Study of Thomas Hardy*, in *Phoenix: The Posthumous Papers, 1936*, edited by Edward D. McDonald (New York: Penguin, 1978), p. 483.

14. Simon Gatrell, *Thomas Hardy and the Proper Study of Mankind* (London and Basingstoke: Macmillan, 1983), p. 100.

15. In Kathleen Blake's assessment, Hardy essentially falls victim to his own project of critiquing the way Tess is apprehended as an archetype: "Throughout the novel Hardy alternates between idealizing and particularizing Tess. By alternating in this way while also calling attention to it, he may be said to exhibit while also examining the epistemological sources of her tragedy" ("Pure Tess: Hardy on Knowing a Woman," in Bloom, ed., p. 97). Morgan, however, believes Hardy is mostly successful in challenging the ways Tess is supposed to be viewed, and she finds particular meaning in the "Garden" scene from chapter 19: "Tess is drawn close to the 'Garden' yet remains withdrawn from it throughout. This emphasis suitably fulfils the promise of the subtitle, 'A Pure Woman Faithfully Presented'. There is no fall, for Tess, that renders her impure, just as there is nothing to render her impure by association. In Hardy's eyes (if not in Angel's), she remains beyond the boundary of sin-laden archetypes and man-made 'Gardens' of diabolism and sexual shame" (*Women and Sexuality*, pp. 86–7).

16. Mary Jacobus, "Tess: The Making of a Pure Woman," in Bloom, ed., p. 46.

17. Boumelha, p. 129.

18. See Joseph Warren Beach, p. 209; and especially Douglas Brown, who calls Tess "the agricultural community in its moment of ruin" (*Thomas Hardy* [London: Longmans, Green, 1954], p. 91).

19. Bernard J. Paris, "'A Confusion of Many Standards': Conflicting Value Systems in *Tess of the d'Urbervilles*," *Nineteenth-Century Fiction*, 24.1 (1969), p. 64.

20. Paris, p. 64.

21. Lodge, who (in 1966, at least) also argues that Hardy "undertakes to defend Tess as a pure woman by emphasizing her kinship with Nature" (*The Language of Fiction* [London: Routledge and Keegan Paul; New York: Columbia UP, 1966], p. 176), sees conflict in Hardy's attitude toward Romanticism. By associating Tess with Nature, Lodge argues, Hardy is drawn "towards the Romantic view of Nature as a reservoir of benevolent impulses, a view which one side of his mind [i.e., that of the Darwinian rationalist] rejected as falsely sentimental" (*Language*, p. 176). J. R. Ebbatson argues that Hardy's language in regard to Nature is itself Romantic, suggesting that Hardy effectively embraced Darwin's "Romantic" view of Nature as a "teeming family" ("The Darwinian View of Tess: A Reply," *Southern Review*, 8.3 [1975], p. 250–1).

22. J. T. Laird, *The Shaping of Tess of the D'Urbervilles* (Oxford: Oxford UP, 1975), p. 44.

23. See Cox, p. 183.

24. Peter Morton, "*Tess of the D'Urbervilles:* A Neo-Darwinian Reading," *Southern Review*, 7.1 (1974), pp. 47–8.

25. Ebbatson, pp. 249–51. See also Eliot Gose, who sees Tess's attempt to reach "psychic evolution" pulled down by the brutality of natural selection ("Psychic Evolution: Darwinism and Initiation in *Tess of the d'Urbervilles*," in Hardy, *Tess*, edited by Scott Elledge, pp. 427–8); and Bruce Johnson, who reads Tess as an organism that has evolved to a point of near-perfection—but she is prevented from evolving further by Angel and the forces of modern society ("The 'Perfection of Species' and Hardy's *Tess*," in *Nature and the Victorian Imagination*, edited by U. C. Knoepflmacher and G. B. Tennyson [Berkeley, Los Angeles, and London: U of California P, 1977], p. 275).

26. See, for instance, the anonymous reviewer in *Pall Mall Gazette* (December 31, 1891), who says Tess is done to death "not by slanderous tongues, but by the tyranny of man, of nature, which makes woman emotionally subject to man, and of social circumstance" (reprinted in Cox, p. 182).

27. Beach, p. 208.

28. Margaret R. Higonnet argues that Hardy struggled with various means to convey the woman's "voice," and she concludes that Hardy's real accomplishment is his allowance of gaps and elisions within the narrative. To Higonnet, "Hardy's silences reproduce but displace Tess's difficulty in coming to speech. We have been asked whether her story will 'bear' telling, a burden, it seems, that Tess alone must take on. A curious inversion takes place: the narrative becomes the margin for her silently spoken secret, raising the question of the propriety of narrative-making itself. The problem of giving voice to a woman's story ironically becomes a figure for the problem of giving voice to experience and to the Other at all" ("A Woman's Story: Tess and the Problem of Voice," in Higonnet, ed., p. 27).

29. Morgan, pp. 92 ff.

30. Arnold Kettle reads Tess as a symbol of the destruction of the English peasantry at the hands of capitalists who intrude into a traditional agricultural society ("Hardy: *Tess*," pp. 49 ff). Merryn Williams dismisses this reading—arguing that there were no "peasants" in 1891—but argues that the novel is a study in "false consciousness," since the characters are so deluded by Tess's noble ancestry and Angel's ideals that they cannot see the "dead weight" of bourgeois Victorian culture (*Thomas Hardy and Rural England* [London and Basingstoke: Macmillan, 1972], p. 172).

31. Terry Eagleton, "Thomas Hardy: Nature as Language," *Critical Quarterly*, 13.2 (1971), p. 161.

32. Goode, *Offensive Truth*, p. 120.

33. Jennifer Wicke, "The Same and the Different: Standards and Standardization in Thomas Hardy's *Tess of the d'Urbervilles*," in Riquelme, ed., p. 575 and 574 ff. I have put Wicke's study together with Marxist analyses because her consideration of the commodification of Tess and of Hardy's novel falls more or less along Marxist lines. In point of fact, Wicke's essay is published expressly as "a cultural perspective" on *Tess*, and Wicke herself—though she endorses Lukács's theory of reification—warns against the Marxist fault of "sentimentally disposing of Tess and her tribe as the predestined victims of capitalism" (p. 585).

34. Among readings along this line are Kaja Silverman, who sees Tess as the subject of the "constructing gaze," which establishes that she is a "canvas" upon which patterns (of desire) are imposed ("History, Figuration, and Female Subjectivity in *Tess of the d'Urbervilles*," *Novel*, 18.1 [1984], pp. 7–8); Helena Michie, who considers the rape of Tess an "inscription" that provides her with a bodily history that men and culture must interpret (*The Flesh Made Word: Female Figures and Women's Bodies* [New York and Oxford: Oxford UP, 1987], pp. 112–13); and Ellen Rooney, who sees Hardy as selecting "the opposition between rape and seduction as the mechanism for articulating Tess's purity," thus "textualizing" Tess's body and making it impossible for him to represent her as both pure *and* raped ("Tess and the Subject of Sexual Violence: Reading, Rape, Seduction," in Riquelme, p. 465).

35. Bayley says Hardy's "erotic image of Tess is fixed and overmastering; and it also represents, which is perhaps unfair on Angel as a character, the culmination of Hardy's own locality-centered daydreams on a womanly image" (*An Essay on Hardy* [Cambridge: Cambridge UP, 1978], p. 167).

36. Janet Freeman, "Ways of Looking at Tess," *Studies in Philology*, 79.3 (1982), p. 315.

37. Freeman, p. 323.

38. Judith Mitchell, *The Stone and the Scorpion: The Female Subject of Desire in the Novels of Charlotte Brontë, George Eliot, and Thomas Hardy* (Westport, CT; London: Greenwood, 1984), p. 189.

39. Mitchell, p. 193.

40. Mitchell, p. 188.

41. James R. Kincaid, "'You did not come': Absence, Death and Eroticism in *Tess*," in *Sex and Death in Victorian Literature*, edited by Regina Barreca (London and Basingstoke: Macmillan, 1990), pp. 13–14.

42. Kincaid, "'You did not come,'" p. 29.

43. Lionel Johnson, *The Art of Thomas Hardy* (London: Bodley Head, 1923 [reprint]), p. 230.

44. Dorothy Van Ghent, *The English Novel: Form and Function* (New York: Harper, 1953; repr. 1961), p. 196.

45. Kettle, "Hardy: *Tess*," p. 61.

46. See Ian Gregor, *The Great Web: The Form of Hardy's Major Fiction* (London and Boston: Faber, 1974), pp. 196–204. Peter J. Casagrande in *Tess of the D'Urbervilles: Unorthodox Beauty* (New York: Twain, 1992) creates a bizarre term—"beaugly"—to describe Hardy's new aesthetic. To Casagrande, beaugliness can be found in such contrasts as the fact that Tess is "a woman pure with unavoidable impurity" (p. 103).

47. See Miller, *Fiction and Repetition*: "There is no 'original version,' only an endless sequence of [causes for Tess's fate], rows and rows written down as it were 'in some old book,' always recorded from some previously existing exemplar" (p. 141). This repetition causes the reader to make connections and to find a pattern, thus contributing to the narrative process (p. 144). Garson reads the overdeterminance in the novel as showing a tension in genres, between the "foundling novel" and the "fallen woman novel," and as showing Hardy's conflicted feelings about his own class background (*Hardy's Fables of Integrity*, pp. 130–6). Kaja Silverman's perspective is that "the very density of [*Tess*'s] representational activity attests to difficulties of containment—to a certain slippage of Tess out of the paradigms that structure her" ("History," p. 21). To Linda M. Shires, Hardy overdetermines Tess's fate so as to "aggressively [assault] an audience whose subtlety of understanding he repeatedly tests. Alec-like, he lures us into a fictional world to raise and violate our Angel-like desire for some monolithic essence of female purity. And he challenges our narrator-like sentimental and patriarchal wishfulness by showing that a violated woman can not 'get over' her ordeals, as if she were just putting on new clothes" ("The Radical Aesthetic of *Tess of the d'Urbervilles*," in *The Cambridge Companion to Thomas Hardy*, ed. Dale Kramer [Cambridge: Cambridge UP, 1999], p. 151).

48. I have found only one article that deals entirely with the sign painter sequence (see note 49). Usually, this character and his messages are glossed by critics simply to support a larger point: i.e., that the painter's is another masculine voice used to oppress women (see, for instance, Higonnet, "Woman's Story," p. 18); or that he fits into a definite "pattern" in the novel, such as in Hillis Miller's contention that "Each episode of the novel is, like one of the words in the [painter's] sign, separated from the others, but when all are there in a row the meaning emerges. This meaning is not outside the words but within them" (*Fiction and Repetition*, p. 141). The painter sequence has been most commonly read in humanistic terms, such as in Bert G. Hornback's statement that the painter's message "describes the whole philosophical and argumentative thesis of the novel— that the past is never dead—and at the same time creates a significant dramatic movement out of this oracular confrontation between Tess and the voice of her fate" (*The Metaphor of Chance: Vision and Technique in the Works of Thomas Hardy* [Athens, OH: Ohio UP, 1971], p. 112).

49. To my knowledge, the only previous critic to make this observation is Ronald J. Nelson, in the sole article I've found that deals specifically with the painter. Nelson's argument is that the painter's misquotation makes him "a false prophet—the very kind of person being warned against in 2 Peter" ("Stirring Up Trouble: The Sign Painter in Hardy's *Tess of the d'Urbervilles*," *Thomas Hardy Journal*, 15.2 [1999], p. 66), but Nelson takes 2 Peter at face value, ignoring its problematic history.

50. Nelson believes that the painter *himself* is a false prophet, as the character gives the passage "his own private interpretation," which goes directly against the lessons of 2 Peter. Point taken, but again the epistle itself is problematic: *whose* authority, exactly, does the painter misrepresent?

51. David F. Payne, for instance, argues that the text's concern with heresy and its acceptance

of the canonicity of Paul's letters suggests it dates from the second century ("The Second Letter of Peter," in *A Bible Commentary for Today,* general editor G. C. D. Howley [London and Glasgow: Pickering and Ingles, 1979], p. 1465). Richard Nemesvari demonstrates that Hardy was aware of the New Testament "Apocrypha"—if only through his familiarity with the writings of Arnold—and he suggests that *Jude the Obscure* is essentially an ironic rewriting of the apocryphal epistle of St. Jude ("Appropriating the Word," p. 52 ff; see also Chapter 5). If Hardy was aware that 2 Peter and Jude have long been considered to be by the same author, it is possible he intended *Tess* and *Jude* to be companion pieces, with each novel reflecting upon a different—though related—apocryphal epistle.

52. John Calvin, "Commentaries on the Second Epistle of Peter," in *Calvin's Commentaries,* vol. 22, translated by John Owen (Grand Rapids, MI: Baker, 1984), p. 363; Robert Jamieson, A. R. Fausset, and David Brown, *A Commentary, Critical and Explanatory, on the Old and New Testaments,* vol. 2 (Hartford, CT: Scranton, 1871), p. 515.

53. My argument here owes a good deal to Charlotte Thompson, "Language and the Shape of Reality in *Tess of the D'Urbervilles,*" *ELH,* 50.4 (1983), pp. 740–44. Thompson, however, does not deal with the sign painter sequence.

54. This is the view espoused by Nelson, p. 67.

55. Charlotte Thompson, p. 740.

56. Recently, Linda Shires has argued that The Chase scene is "blurred" by Hardy so that he can force the readers to face the fact that their own judgments of the situation—whether they blame Alec or Tess for what happens—are socially constructed ("Radical Aesthetic," pp. 153–4), a view that is in keeping with my own.

57. A similar point is made by Garrett Stewart: "Just as the far horizons of *Tess's* plot lie with the reader in the impure security of reception, so does its other vanishing point reach back behind the story to those textual prototypes from which it—along with much of the reader's intellectual invigoration, and none of the heroine's—derives" ("'Driven Well Home to the Reader's Heart': *Tess's* Implicated Audience," in Riquelme, ed., p. 539).

58. A slightly different argument is made by Shires, who finds Alec to be such an *obvious* stereotype that Hardy manages "to subvert that stereotype's very obviousness" ("Radical Aesthetic," p. 152).

59. See, for instance, Hardy's comparison of the scorching summer to Angel's inward passion for Tess (p. 116), and Tess's growing "acquiescence" in Nature's call that she "revolt against her scrupulousness" (p. 139).

60. This point was perhaps best made by Lodge, who says Angel "is constantly trying to dignify the homely pastoral in which he is involved—the country wooing of a milkmaid—by Art, by talking to [Tess] about 'pastoral life in ancient Greece' and calling her by classical names..., thus demonstrating that he is not really prepared to accept a mate from unconstrained Nature" (*Language of Fiction,* p. 184). It is interesting that, though he is critical of Angel's pastoralizing of Tess, Lodge himself reads her in essentially pastoral terms.

61. Blake also argues that Angel sees Tess as a generic type, though her focus is primarily on Angel's conception of Tess as a *woman.* Blake complicates the issue of purity in the novel in an interesting way, arguing that Angel's "horror of Tess's un-intactness bespeaks his allegiance to the purity of the generic as such, as well as to the feminine principle of erotic purity that furnishes the dramatic text" ("Pure Tess," p. 94–5).

62. Charlotte Thompson makes a similar case, arguing that Hardy uses both allusions and certain "trigger words" (my phrase) such as *ascent, descent,* and *Fall* to play upon the readers' private tendency to link human experience with the natural world. In the readers' minds, Thompson argues, certain "upward"-directed words and images connect the story to transcendence, while "downward"-directed words point to Tess's "fall" (pp. 745–6).

63. H. M. Daleski, *Thomas Hardy and Paradoxes of Love* (Columbia, MO; London: U of Missouri P, 1997), pp. 153–4.

64. Goode sees Tess's attempts to narrate in a positive light, since they turn her into a *maker* of authoritative texts (*Offensive Truth,* p. 130). On the other hand, Ellen Rooney argues that Tess's attempts to write "like a man" erase her story as a *woman* ("Tess and the Subject of Sexual Violence: Reading, Rape, Seduction," in Riquelme, ed., pp. 472–3).

65. Peter Widdowson, "'Moments of Vision': Postmodernising *Tess of the d'Urbervilles;* or, *Tess of the d'Urbervilles* Faithfully Presented by Peter Widdowson," in *New Perspectives on Thomas*

Hardy, ed. Charles P. C. Pettit (London and Basingstoke: Macmillan, 1994), pp. 97–8; Widdowson's emphases.

66. The year of release for *Tess* is variously listed as 1979, 1980, and even 1981. The film was completed in 1979 and released in Europe that year. Columbia Pictures agreed to distribute the film in America, and put the film in limited release in the U. S. at the end of 1980 to qualify for the Academy Awards. *Tess* was given its general American release later in 1981. I have chosen to use 1979 as the year of *Tess*'s release, since this is the year the film premiered.

67. See, for instance, Carrie Rickey's review in *Village Voice,* in which she confesses to fearing that the film would be "three hours of blood-stained, lugubrious Late Victoriana," but then expresses her admiration for Polanski's restraint and speculates that the film is an "apology" for the director's earlier "excesses" (reprinted in Ozer [1981], p. 961).

68. David Ansen in *Newsweek,* Dec. 22, 1980; reprinted in Ozer (1981), p. 960.

69. Aljean Harmetz, "Polanski Sends Us 'Tess' as His Envoy," *New York Times,* Dec. 11, 1980, p. C19. Polanski's statement is remarkably similar to John Schlesinger's reported comment that he wished to break away from realistic pictures and to make "something more romantic about another age," which led him, of course, to *Far from the Madding Crowd* (see Chapter 3). It is interesting that two directors should find Hardy's works to be an "escape" from realism, violence, and "dark" subject matter in general.

70. Jane Marcus, "A Tess for Child Molesters," in *New Casebooks: Tess of the d'Urbervilles,* edited by Peter Widdowson (London and Basingstoke: Macmillan, 1993), pp. 90–3. To be fair, more than ten years after Marcus's review first appeared, she characterized it as a "pretty rough piece" on *Tess,* so she may have since moved away from some of the views she expressed. See Marcus, 93*n.*

71. Frequently, critics and viewers have seen in Polanski's films parallels to specific events in his life. Barbara Leaming's study is filled with instances where she reads Polanski's films as straight autobiography; e.g., she argues that *Cul-de-Sac* is "Polanski's fictionalized portrait of his marriage to Basia [Kwiatkowska], his humiliation by her, and his continued longing" (p. 67). In February 2000, the Arts and Entertainment Network ran a profile of Polanski as part of its "Biography" series, and the program contains a number of instances where Polanski's life is read into his films. Thom Mount, the producer of *Death and the Maiden* (1994), identifies the claustrophobic images that appear in Polanski's films as originating with his memories of the shrinking of the Krakow ghetto; and Richard Sylbert, the production designer on *Chinatown,* says of the character of Evelyn Mulwray (Faye Dunaway) in that film: "The girl dies. Of course the girl dies. That's what happened to Sharon [Tate]" ("Roman Polanski: Reflections," first aired Feb. 7, 2000). Polanski often dismisses autobiographical readings of his films, but at the time of this writing, he is preparing a Holocaust drama, *The Pianist,* which he admits relates to his own childhood experiences.

72. Polanski's preferred title—and the title under which the film originally appeared in Britain—was *Dance of the Vampires.* Its American distributor recut the film and changed its title to *The Fearless Vampire Killers or: Pardon Me, But Your Teeth Are in My Neck*—which earned Polanski's displeasure (Wexman, p. 57). The uncut version of the film is now generally available in the U.S., but its altered title remains, and I use it here because of its familiarity.

73. David Thompson, "'I Make Films for Adults,'" interview with Roman Polanski, *Sight and Sound,* April 1995, p. 9.

74. Leaming, p. 61.

75. Wexman, p. 5.

76. Polanski, p. 265.

77. Polanski's take on *Macbeth* also suggests that much of what happens could be in the mind of Macbeth (John Finch). Banquo's ghost and the dagger that appears before Macbeth's hand could either be supernatural or just hallucinations; but the "show of kings" is clearly brought on by a hallucinogenic drink given to Macbeth by the witches.

78. Polanski, pp. 272–3.

79. Leaming, p. 12.

80. Molly Haskell, *From Reverence to Rape: The Treatment of Women in the Movies,* 2nd ed. (Chicago and London: U of Chicago P, 1987), pp. 346, 347.

81. There are other, perhaps less significant, omissions, but they have still generated complaint. William V. Costanzo and Margaret Harris, perhaps influenced by Hillis Miller's essay in

Fiction and Repetition, both criticize Polanski for leaving out the novel's patterns of red (Costanzo, "Polanski in Wessex: Filming *Tess of the d'Urbervilles*," *Literature/Film Quarterly*, 9.2 [1981], p. 74; Harris, "Thomas Hardy's *Tess of the d'Urbervilles*: Faithfully Presented by Roman Polanski?" *Sydney Studies in English*, 7 [1981–2], pp. 121–2). Nell Kozak Waldman faults the film for omitting the fact that Angel leaves Tess with £50, which is wasted by her family ("'All That She Is': Hardy's Tess and Polanski's," *Queen's Quarterly*, 88.3 [1981], p. 431). Finally, Charles L. Fierz's whole essay is built on the charge that Polanski entirely "misses" the fact that Tess's tragedy stems from her being the product of an alcoholic father and of a dysfunctional family ("Polanski Misses: A Critical Essay Concerning Polanski's Reading of Hardy's *Tess*," *Literature/Film Quarterly*, 27.2 [1999], p. 103 ff; see also note 90 below).

82. Waldman, p. 433.

83. Gladys V. Veidemanis, "*Tess of the D'Urbervilles*: What the Film Left Out," *English Journal*, 77.7 (1988), p. 56.

84. Dianne Fallon Sadoff, "Looking at Tess: The Female Figure in Two Narrative Media," in Higonnet, ed., p. 167.

85. Brach has collaborated with Polanski on the screenplays for most of his films, beginning with *Repulsion*. John Brownjohn was hired to translate Polanski's and Brach's French script for *Tess* into English and to make the dialogue more true to the Dorset idiom; and both Burrill and Polanski have taken pleasure in pointing out the remarkable coincidence that Brownjohn's hometown is Marnhull, the model for Marlott (Timothy Burrill, "Wessex Tales," *Sight and Sound* [July 1996], p. 59; Polanski, p. 429). Brownjohn has collaborated on the scripts for most of Polanski's films since *Tess*.

86. Polanski, p. 435.

87. Burrill, "Wessex Tales," p. 59.

88. Both Harris and Widdowson point out that Marx was unavailable in English during the 1880s. Harris considers the inclusion of Marx's book to be a rather simple-minded literalization of Hardy's description of Angel as "sticking communistically" to the concept of working with others ("Faithfully Presented," p. 122); and Widdowson presumes the book is used in the film to illustrate Angel's "half-baked socialism" (*Hardy in History*, p. 121).

89. Wexman, p. 115.

90. After considering these scenes, it is difficult to understand how Charles Fierz in "Polanski Misses" can argue that Polanski fails to understand Jack's alcoholism and how it effects Tess and her family.

91. Pauline Kael, *Taking It All In* (New York: Holt, Rinehart and Winston, 1984), p. 135.

92. This is yet another sore point for Margaret Harris, who calls the buildings "uncompromisingly French" (p. 119).

93. See Martin Donougho, "West of Eden: Terrence Malick's *Days of Heaven*," *Post Script*, 5.1 (1985), p. 17 ff. for a fuller analysis of Malick's techniques.

94. See Wexman, p. 121.

95. Widdowson, *Hardy in History*, pp. 124–5.

96. Wexman, p. 123.

Chapter 5: Hardy's Jude the Obscure *and Winterbottom's* Jude: *Coherence and Codification*

1. The most complete analysis of allusion in *Jude* is, of course, to be found in Marlene Springer's *Hardy's Use of Allusion*. Among other things, Springer locates over 100 allusions that are associated with Jude alone (p. 166). Other treatments of the allusive qualities of *Jude*'s language include Frederick P. W. McDowell, "Hardy's 'Seemings or Personal Impressions': The Symbolic Use of Image and Contrast in 'Jude the Obscure,'" *Modern Fiction Studies*, 6.3 (1960), pp. 233–50; Eleanor McNees, "Reverse Typology in *Jude the Obscure*," *Christianity and Literature*, 39.1 (1989), pp. 35–49; and Richard Nemesvari's "Appropriating the Word." All of these studies examine the biblical nature of the allusions. Ramon Saldívar, in "*Jude the Obscure*: Reading and the Spirit of the Law," *ELH*, 50.3 (1983), pp. 607–25, deconstructs the referential ability of language.

2. Joe Fisher, *The Hidden Hardy*, pp. 7–8.

3. I am in this sense referring to Fisher's *system*, and not his actual *analysis* of *Jude*. Like me, Fisher examines *Jude* as something of a satire, but I find his mixture of Marxism and nature-worship a bizarre combination. Fisher's argument also begs the question: since satire *is* subversive, what, then, is "hidden" about *Jude the Obscure*?

4. Reprinted in Cox, p. 260.

5. Reprinted in Cox, p. 260.

6. Lascelles Abercrombie, *Thomas Hardy: A Critical Study* (1912; New York: Russell and Russell, 1964), p. 161.

7. This division of thought can be seen in two of the most influential feminist readings of *Jude*. Kathleen Blake ("Sue Bridehead, 'The Woman of the Feminist Movement,'" *Studies in English Literature, 1500-1900* 18.4 [1978]), after disentangling Lawrence from "his offensive definitions of what it means to be a woman or a man, and from his idea that Sue was born with an unhealthy overbalance of the masculine"(p. 721), finds that he is essentially correct in saying that Sue channels her sexuality into more intellectual areas, which leaves her feeling guilty over keeping Jude unsatisfied (p. 722). However, Mary Jacobus in "Sue the Obscure," *Essays in Criticism*, 25.3 (1975), feels that "Lawrence recreates [*sic*] the novel with such imaginative intensity that it is easy to substitute his version for Hardy's" (p. 306), and faults him for creating an image of Sue that allows her to be cast as a villain in other critics' readings (p. 307).

8. D. H. Lawrence, *Study of Thomas Hardy*, in *Phoenix: The Posthumous Papers, 1936*, edited by Edward D. McDonald (New York: Penguin, 1978), pp. 495, 496.

9. These interpretations are echoed in 1922 by Joseph Warren Beach, who claims that *Jude* is built on a "militantly" naturalistic scheme in which Arabella's animal qualities and Sue's "morbidity" both play a role in undermining Jude (pp. 218–22); in 1928 by Patrick Braybrooke, who casts Jude as a Peter Pan character (!) and renders the story as "a conflict between Jude and his ideals and Jude and two women. That the women win is only to be expected, as it seems to be an inevitable law that they should" (*Thomas Hardy and His Philosophy* [1928; New York: Russell and Russell, 1969], p. 91); and in 1946 by David Cecil, who criticizes Jude for forgetting his intellectual ambitions and becoming absorbed in his passion for Sue (*Hardy the Novelist: An Essay in Criticism* [Indianapolis and New York: Bobbs-Merrill, 1946], p. 42). In 1971, Bert Hornback argued that Jude's marriage to Arabella is the *single* action that keeps him from obtaining his goals—he remains "tied" to Arabella and to Marygreen, and he robs himself of a future—forcing himself and Sue to live a "static nonexistence" (*The Metaphor of Chance: Vision and Technique in the Works of Thomas Hardy* [Athens, OH: Ohio UP, 1971], pp. 130, 135).

10. A. Alvarez, "Afterword" in *Jude the Obscure* by Thomas Hardy (New York: Signet, 1980), p. 408.

11. Jacobus, "Sue the Obscure," p. 313.

12. Blake, "Sue Bridehead," pp. 709–11 ff.

13. Elizabeth Langland, "Becoming a Man in *Jude the Obscure*," in Higonnet, ed., p. 32 ff.

14. James M. Harding, "The Signification of Arabella's Missile: Feminine Sexuality, Masculine Anxiety and Revision in *Jude the Obscure*," *The Journal of Narrative Technique*, 26.1 (1996), p. 97. Other significant feminist readings include John Goode, who defines Sue by her "incomprehensibility" and claims that the attempts by the men in her life to assign meaning to her is also an attempt to render her subversive ideology as "false consciousness" ("Sue Bridehead and the New Woman," *Women Writing and Writing About Women*, edited by Mary Jacobus [London: Croom Helm, 1979], pp. 107–8); Penny Boumelha, who argues that Sue's tragedy is her growing understanding that she is not free (p. 144 ff.); Laura Green, who claims that the novel "attempts to rescue the androgynous intellect, figured in Sue Bridehead, from the [1890s] discourse of gynecological anti-feminism" ("'Strange [in]difference of sex': Thomas Hardy, the Victorian Man of Letters, and the Temptations of Androgyny," *Victorian Studies*, 38.4 [1995], p. 540); Rosemarie Morgan, who sees Sue as voicing Hardy's militantly anti-marriage argument and not being silenced for doing so (p. 110 ff.); and Talia Schaffer, who argues that Hardy presents the novel through the eyes of a staring *man*, thus robbing Sue of an awareness of her own body and creating a parody of feminist self-consciousness ("Malet the Obscure: Thomas Hardy, 'Lucas Malet' and the Literary Politics of Early Modernism," *Women's Writing*, 3.3 [1996], p. 269).

15. Reprinted in Cox, p. 283.

16. Terry Eagleton, "The Limits of Art," in *Thomas Hardy's Jude the Obscure*, edited by Harold Bloom (New York, New Haven, Philadelphia: Chelsea House, 1987), pp. 65, 70.

17. Reprinted in Cox, p. 250.

18. Howells, *Harper's Weekly*, Dec. 7, 1895; reprinted in Cox, p. 253.

19. Some durable humanist readings of *Jude* are Hornback, who identifies Jude's fatal mistake as marrying Arabella (p. 127 ff), and Ian Gregor's *The Great Web* (London and Boston: Faber, 1974), in which the tragedies of Jude and Sue are said to be significant because the couple is part of an overarching human design—to diminish one person is to diminish all.

20. Lodge, "*Jude the Obscure*: Pessimism and Fictional Form," in Kramer, ed., p. 193.

21. "FIR Chats With Director Michael Winterbottom," *Films in Review*, Jan./Feb. 1997, p. 74.

22. Richard Carpenter, *Thomas Hardy* (New York: St. Martin's, 1964), p. 139. Similarly, Lodge claims that "so much attention is given to the use of the railway, especially by Jude, to the problems, ironies, and frustrations of such travel—waiting for connections, missing trains, planning cross-country journeys—that it does not seem fanciful to interpret the railway (a 'closed system' which allows its users a strictly limited mobility) as a symbol for life itself in this novel" ("Pessimism," p. 201*n*); while John Goode argues that "'At', the word which links the title of each part, implies a double negation of the subject since although it defines a location it does not suggest, in fact in most cases positively denies accommodation—thus at various stages the characters are placed but have no place" (*Offensive Truth*, p.141).

23. For representative arguments see Richard Benvenuto, "Modes of Perception: The Will to Live in *Jude the Obscure*," *Studies in the Novel*, 2.1 (1970), pp. 32–3; Frank R. Giordiano, Jr., "*I'd Have My Life Unbe*": *Thomas Hardy's Self-Destructive Characters* (Tuscaloosa: U of Alabama P, 1984), p. 125; and Dale Kramer, *Thomas Hardy: The Forms of Tragedy* (Detroit: Wayne State UP, 1975), pp. 152–5.

24. Ronald P. Draper has also analyzed the novel in terms of its comedy; however, he feels that the humor is always deflated by disillusionment ("Hardy's Comic Tragedy: *Jude the Obscure*," in Kramer, ed., p. 246). Joe Fisher sees *Jude* both as a satire on Christianity and capitalism, with Jude and Sue "trying to enact bourgeois myths of autonomy without bourgeois money and power" (*The Hidden Hardy*, p. 182).

25. Barbara DeMille, "Cruel Illusions: Nietzsche, Conrad, Hardy, and the 'Shadowy Ideal,'" *Studies in English Literature, 1500-1900*, 30.4 (1990), p. 707.

26. Ramón Saldívar argues that Jude's idealization of the city is representative of his overall tendency to misread the world around him: Jude "sees in Christminster and its university the image of an attainable ideal world. His desire for this ideal vision involves a rejection of reality. For his own sporadically controlled, partially understood world, he substitutes the image of a unified, stable, and understandable one" (p. 609).

27. McNees argues that one of *Jude's* central themes is "Jude's lifelong search for a master text. This master text is housed in the inaccessible Christminster where Jude believes the 'tree of knowledge' grows" (p. 39).

28. Frederick P. W. McDowell and Alexander Fischler both argue that Jude's—and Hardy's—biblical allusions add depth and universality to Jude's tragedy (McDowell, p. 245; Fischler, "A Kinship with Job: Obscurity and Remembrance in Hardy's *Jude the Obscure*," *Journal of English and Germanic Philology*, 84.4 [1985], p. 516). However, McNees and Nemesvari both see these allusions as a form of social criticism. To McNees, the biblical quotes are devoid of meaning, yet Jude clings to their *form*, illustrating the hollowness of Victorian beliefs (p. 36–7), while Nemesvari argues that Jude tries to "rewrite" the Bible as a kind of subversive apocrypha that undercuts the Victorian reliance on "stable" religious texts to create a cohesive cultural identity ("Appropriating the Word," p. 48 ff).

29. Matthew Arnold, "Hebraism and Hellenism," in *Culture and Anarchy, with Friendship's Garden and Some Literary Essays*, edited by R. H. Super (Ann Arbor: U of Michigan P, 1965), pp. 163-75. For analyses of the Hellenic/Hebraic dichotomy in *Jude* see, for instance, Lennart Björk, who argues that Sue is "trying" to be a pagan, just as Jude is "trying" to be a Christian ("Thomas Hardy's 'Hellenism,'" in *Papers on Language and Literature: Presented to Alvard Ellegård and Erik Frykman*, edited by Sven Bäckman and Göran Kjellmar [Göteborg, Sweden: Acta, 1985], p. 49); and Barbara Fass, who sees the Hellenic/Hebraic split as being entirely within Sue ("Hardy and St. Paul: Patterns of Conflict in *Jude the Obscure*," *Colby Library Quarterly*, 10.5 [1974], p. 274 ff.).

30. Oscar Wilde, "The Critic as Artist," in *The Complete Works of Oscar Wilde* (New York: Barnes and Noble, 1994), p. 1021.

31. Wilde, p. 1058. For a further discussion of Wilde's "evolutionary" theory of art, see Julia Prewitt Brown, *Cosmopolitan Criticism: Oscar Wilde's Philosophy of Art* (Charlottesville, VA, and London: UP of Virginia, 1997), pp. 54–55.

32. That Hardy read and appreciated Wilde is certain. In a fine appreciation—apparently meant as an introduction to a 1908 collection of Wilde's works—Hardy praised Wilde's use of levity to attack materialism in literature, and his holding criticism to more rigid standards (*Literary Notebooks*, vol. 2, pp. 255–7).

33. Marjorie Garson, p. 158.

34. In a letter to Edmund Gosse, Hardy wrote that "one of [Sue's] reasons for fearing the marriage ceremony is that she fears it wd be breaking faith with Jude to withhold herself at pleasure, or altogether, after it; though while uncontracted she feels at liberty to yield herself as seldom as she chooses" (November 20, 1895, in *Collected Letters*, vol. 2, p. 99). The marriage *contract*, then, has the power of reining in Sue's behavior and forcing her into a mode of being she does not like.

35. This observation was made by Fass, p. 281. See also Marlene Springer, who argues Sue is repressed by the Hebraism in her (*Hardy's Use of Allusion*, p. 161).

36. For a complete and fascinating analysis of divorce among the classes in Victorian England and how it relates to the themes in *Jude*, see William A. Davis, "Happy Days in *Jude the Obscure:* Hardy and the Crawford-Dilke Divorce Case," *Thomas Hardy Journal*, 13.1 (1997), pp. 64–74.

37. Hardy to Gosse, November 20, 1895, in *CL*, vol. 2, p. 99.

38. Dale Kramer apparently believes so: in his reading, Jude does not appreciate or take advantage of the land; and Jude makes no effort to become involved in the life of the Marygreen community (*Forms*, pp. 158–9).

39. John Sutherland, "A Note on the Teasing Narrator in *Jude the Obscure*," *English Literature in Transition (1880-1920)*, 17.3 (1974), p. 160.

40. Harding argues that Hardy's subsequent revisions of this sequence to remove most direct references to the severed penis are all concessions to conventional morality. The revisions undercut Hardy's intention of satirizing Jude's academic goals, and they result in Hardy expressing a stereotypical fear of the feminine ("Signification," p. 86 ff).

41. Peter Widdowson, *On Thomas Hardy: Late Essays and Earlier* (London and Basingstoke: Macmillan, 1998), p. 168. Widdowson's essay on *Jude* appears as a "postscript" to this book (pp. 188–95), and he later reprinted it as "Obscuring *Jude the Obscure*" (*Critical Survey*, 9.1 [1997], pp. 96–103). All references to the Widdowson essay will be from *OTH*.

42. Pamela Church Gibson reports that in Britain the film "was not successful" ("Fewer Weddings and More Funerals: Changes in the Heritage Film," in *British Cinema of the 90s*, edited by Robert Murphy [London: BFI, 2000], p. 120). In America, *Jude* played mostly in arthouses and earned just $408,000 in its entire U.S. run (James M. Welsh, "*Jude*," in *Magill's Cinema Annual 1997*, edited by Beth A. Fhaner [Detroit, New York, Toronto, London: Gale, 1997], p. 298).

43. According to Gibson, Winslet was cast as Sue before she played in *Sense and Sensibility* (p. 119), but *Jude* was released after the Ang Lee film.

44. See, for instance, Mike Clark, who claims that "Winslet's performance is effective enough to make an unsatisfactory movie tough to dismiss" ("Winslet Lends Heart to Detached 'Jude,'" *USA Today*, Oct. 18, 1996, p. 5D). Richard Corliss calls *Jude* "a handsome showcase for [Winslet's] gifts" ("Grim Rapture: A Flinty Adaptation of Hardy's Last Novel," *Time*, Oct. 28, 1996, p. 113).

45. Amini has said that his intention in *Jude* was to "destroy the heritage film from within" (quoted in Gibson, p. 119).

46. Andrew Higson, "Re-presenting the National Past: Nostalgia and Pastiche in the Heritage Film," in Lester Friedman, ed., *British Cinema and Thatcherism: Fires Were Started* (London: University College London P, 1993), p. 109 ff.

47. Cairns Craig, "Rooms Without a View," *Sight and Sound*, June 1991, p. 13.

48. Widdowson, *On Thomas Hardy*, p. 188.

49. Rosemary Ashton, "At a Loss for Words," review of *Jude*, *Times Literary Supplement*, Oct. 11, 1996, p. 22.

50. Many critics say that Sue's character is similar to Catherine, the brainy, chain-smoking rebel from Truffaut's *Jules et Jim* (1961). See Corliss, "Grim Rapture"; Gibson, p. 120; and Michael Wilmington, "Tragic 'Jude' Remains True to Hardy's Novel," *Chicago Tribune*, Nov. 1, 1996, p. 7J.

51. Blake, "Sue Bridehead," pp. 709–11.

52. On video, Eccleston is practically cropped out of the scene, so Winslet occupies the *entire* shot. This is an interesting commentary on what editors choose to favor when a wide-screen movie is forced into the "pan-and-scan" format for video. As of this writing, *Jude* is not available in the "letterbox" format and there is no DVD version, but it does exist on Japanese laserdisc.

53. Laura Mulvey, "Visual Pleasure and the Narrative Cinema," in *Feminism and Film Theory*, edited by Constance Penley (New York: Routledge, 1988), p. 58.

54. Marcia Landy, "The Sexuality of History in Contemporary British Cinema," *Film Criticism*, 20.1-2 (1995–96), p. 82.

55. Landy, p. 81.

56. Landy, pp. 83–6.

57. Wilmington, p. 7K.

58. Welsh, *"Jude,"* p. 300. Some reviews that were not favorable to the film are interesting here, as they fault *Jude* precisely because it *doesn't* stay faithful to popular social constructions of the novel. See, for instance, Lloyd Rose: "Thomas Hardy's novel—a sexually frank, anti-marriage diatribe—raised such vitriolic criticism in the 19th century that he turned the rest of his career to the safer art of poetry. Watching the wan Christopher Eccleston as Jude and Kate Winslet as his cousin and lover Sue Bridehead, an audience might well wonder what all the fuss was about" ("'Jude': Loss of Innocents," *Washington Post*, Nov. 1, 1996, p. D7). Lawrence Van Gelder says that, in the film, "the inevitability of tragedy seems to have been mislaid," and that "the role of society has been shrunk. From this imbalance emerges not a great tragedy but a tale of doomed romance" ("What's Obscure is Society in a New Tale of Jude," *New York Times*, Oct. 18, 1996, p. C14).

Chapter 6: The Lesser Known Hardy Adaptations: The Woodlanders, The Scarlet Tunic, *and* The Claim

1. Ali Kayn, review of *The Woodlanders*. Festivale Online magazine. Feb. 1998. Available at: <http://www.festivale.webcentral.com.au/filmvu/9804frvb.htm>

2. See Chapter 2 for a full discussion of *The Woodlanders* and its often problematic critical history.

3. Patrick Tolfree's review of *The Woodlanders* (*Thomas Hardy Journal*, 14.2 [1998]: 86–8) also notes the loss of the sense of community and the transformation of Felice into a "caricature of the *femme fatale* of the Victorian romance," but Tolfree feels that most of the cuts and changes are only noticeable in hindsight (p. 87).

4. For an interesting reading, see Jonathan Bate, "Culture and Environment: From Austen to Hardy," *New Literary History*, 30.3 (1999): pp. 541–60. Bate identifies Austen and Hardy as "the two most popular English writers of the nineteenth century" who are still being read today, and he says that the authors are united in that "they stand for the imagined better life of both the higher and lower classes in a world where there is no place for the motor car" (p. 541).

5. Unfortunately, I have been unable to locate a print of this film, and there is surprisingly little information on it. However, as this study is primarily concerned with British and American interpretations of Hardy, I am not sure how much an analysis of the Kashyap film would add.

6. Interview with Frank Cotrell Boyce. Available at <http://www.theclaimmovie.com>. Accessed Sept. 1, 2000.

7. Ibid.

8. See Fred Reid, "Wayfarers and Seafarers: Ideas of History in *The Mayor of Casterbridge*," *Thomas Hardy Journal*, 13.3 (1997):47–57. See especially p. 51: "Like 'old Rome' ... Casterbridge has subjugated the surrounding communities, linking them to itself by roads running straight out of the town, like those by which Rome dominated Latium."

9. Michael Valdez Moses, for instance, contends that Henchard abandons sound business practices in favor of following superstition, and that he foolishly wages an economic war against Farfrae that results only in his own bankruptcy ("Agon in the Marketplace: *The Mayor of Casterbridge* as Bourgeois Tragedy," in *New Casebooks: The Mayor of Casterbridge*, ed. Julian Wolfreys [London and Basingstoke: Macmillan, 2000], pp. 187, 191).

10. Michael Coyne argues that the Western constructs a particularly white and male version of America, and that Westerns marginalize Indians because Westerns are not *about* Indians (*The Crowded Prairie: American National Identity in the Hollywood Western* [London and New York: Tauris, 1997], p. 4 ff).

Chapter 7: "Moments of Television"; or, Thomas Hardy Is Brought to You By...

1. Robert Giddings and Keith Selby, *The Classic Serial on Television and Radio* (Houndsmills, Eng: Palgrave, 2001), p. 32.

2. Widdowson, *Hardy in History*, pp. 95–6.

3. Andrew Crisell, *An Introductory History of British Broadcasting* (London and New York: Routledge, 1997), pp. 28–9.

4. Paul Kerr, "Classic Serials—To Be Continued," *Screen*, 23.1 (1982), p. 15.

5. Kerr, p. 9 ff.

6. For the sake of convenience, I refer to the program merely as *Masterpiece Theatre*. In point of fact, in the early 1990s the program's sponsor changed the title to *Mobil Masterpiece Theatre*. Following Mobil's merger with another oil giant in 1999, the program became *Exxon/Mobil Masterpiece Theatre*.

7. See Laurence A. Jarvik, *Masterpiece Theatre and the Politics of Quality* (Lanham, MD, and London: Scarecrow, 1999), pp. 9 and 29–33, for the influence of the success of *The Forsyte Saga* in inspiring *Masterpiece Theatre*; pp. 36–44 and pp. 165–202 for Mobil's sponsorship of the program; and pp. 204–17 for Nixon's hostility toward PBS and his desire to promote "Classic" learning through public television.

8. Jarvik, p. 117 ff.

9. For a complete list of television productions based on Hardy's works and for further commentary on their availability, see Appendix C.

10. F. E. Hardy, *Life*, p. 273.

11. *Native*, however, is not the first adaptation of a Hardy *work* in that time. In late 1985, the Children's Film and Television Foundation, Ltd., produced *Exploits at West Poley*, based on Hardy's novella, starring Brenda Fricker and—in a small role—Sean Bean. The short production—less than an hour long—apparently stayed on the shelf for nearly five years until it was aired by ITV in 1990. The production is not listed as being available on either video or DVD, and I am not certain if it has aired in America. For information on the cast and crew, see Appendix C.

12. John Kiesewetter, "Hallmark's Hall of Fame Tradition," available at <http://enquirer.com/columns/kiese/1999/02/07/jki_hallmarks_hall_of.html>. Accessed Aug. 17, 2000.

13. Patricia O'Hara reads such continuing rituals in light of the anthropological theory of "survivals." Accordingly, Victorian anthropologists saw "savages" or—closer to home—"rustics" as carrying on traditions that date from the "childhood" of mankind. O'Hara argues that Hardy's treatment of this theme in *Native* is split between viewing survivals as satisfying an innate need, and showing the heath folk as impediments to progress ("Narrating the Native: Victorian Anthropology and Hardy's *The Return of the Native*," *Nineteenth-Century Contexts*, 20.2 [1997], pp. 155–6). My own view, explained below, is that the heath folk themselves *are* progressing.

14. Simon Trezise points out that the novel is set during "the period of Chartist unrest from 1840 to 1850," when widespread education was either hailed as a means of social control or feared as fomenting revolution ("Ways of Learning in *The Return of the Native*," *Thomas Hardy Journal*, 7.2 [1991], p. 57).

15. O'Hara reads the novel more cynically than I do (though she attributes the cynicism to Hardy): "Clym will never be able to elevate the 'clowns' because they aspire to luxury, and not the sweetness and light of 'culture'" (p. 157).

16. Eustacia's voice-over monologue is a nearly direct transportation from the novel of Eustacia's "prayer": "O deliver my heart from this fearful gloom and loneliness: send me a great love from somewhere, else I shall die" (p. 122). The passage occurs toward the middle of the "Queen of Night" chapter, in which Hardy reveals Eustacia's background (barely mentioned in the TV movie) and systematically deconstructs her romanticism. After Hardy records Eustacia's prayer, he writes, "Her gods were William the Conqueror, Strafford, and Napoleon Buonaparte, as they had appeared in the Lady's History used at the establishment in which she was educated" (p. 122). Certainly no "great love" can live up to the heroes of Eustacia's imagination; and Hardy clearly condemns education for fostering her wildest dreams—an indication that he saw the negatives in universal education.

17. Here again we see how Hardy's narrative voice is sorely needed. The movie shows a crowd gathered around Clym, clearly transfixed by his words, while in the novel, the people "listened to the words of the man in their midst ... while they abstractedly pulled heather, stripped ferns, or tossed pebbles down the slope" (p. 473). Hardy closes the novel by reporting that Clym preaches all over Wessex, where "Some believed him, and some believed not; some said that his words were commonplace, others complained of his want of theological doctrine; while others again remarked that it was well enough for a man to take to preaching who could not see to do anything else. But everywhere he was kindly received, for the story of his life had become generally known" (p. 474). Clym has become chastened by events, but he has not gained knowledge; he continues trying to spread a message that the heath folk neither want nor need. The final image of Clym in the movie, however, is of a man who has gained enlightenment.

18. Although *Far from the Madding Crowd* is analyzed first, the serial of *Tess* was actually filmed first and in Britain it aired months earlier than *Crowd*. I have chosen to follow the dates when the serials were first aired in America. Incidently, *Crowd* was shown in the U.S. before it appeared in Britain.

19. This is certainly the position of Giddings and Selby, who argue that MacDonagh has shifted the focus of Hardy's story to "money and sex," and that it is Gabriel's coming into money that makes him "sexy" to both Bathsheba and the audience (*Classic Serial,* p. 171). Giddings and Selby's opinion of the serial is the opposite of mine.

20. Interestingly, in 1999 Natasha Little starred as Becky Sharp in A & E's serial of *Vanity Fair.* Between Fanny and Becky, Little has portrayed the "extremes" in the Victorian conception of womanhood.

21. Compare this to the way Schlesinger handles the scene: he has Troy running up and down the ramparts of the old fort, and—through Bathsheba's eyes—he is transformed into the head of a charging cavalry. Again, romantic spectacle rules the 1967 film, while the serial creates a sense of intimacy and immediacy.

22. A & E also contracts with American and Canadian production companies to create original movies and miniseries—most of which seem to be mysteries; e.g., adaptations of Robert B. Parker's "Spenser" novels and even a new take on Nero Wolfe.

23. AandE.com On TV: Tess of the D'Urbervilles, available at <http:// www.AandE.com /tv/shows/tess/html> Accessed Aug. 17, 2000.

24. AandE.com.

25. AandE.com.

26. Jane Marcus, "A Tess for Child Molestors," in *New Casebooks: Tess of the d'Urbervilles,* edited by Peter Widdowson (London and Basingstoke: Macmillan, 1993), p. 90 ff.

27. AandE.com.

28. For a radically different reading of the A & E *Tess,* see Giddings and Selby, *Classic Serial,* pp. 163–6. The authors find both the serial's imagery and use of the narrator complementary to Hardy's novel.

Postscript: Hardy on the Horizon

1. Available at: <http://www.acornonline.com/CFForum2000/viewmessages.cfm?Forum= 5&Topic=96>. Accessed January 24, 2002.

Appendix A: The "Lost" Hardy Adaptations, 1913–1953

1. Hardy to F. A. Duneka, April 8, 1913, in *Collected Letters*, vol. 4, p. 265.
2. "Mrs. Fiske on 'Movies' Film," *New York Times*, July 1, 1913, p. 9.
3. "Mrs. Fiske in 'Tess of the D'Urbervilles,'" *Moving Picture News*, Aug. 2, 1913, p. 12.
4. Adolph Zukor with Dale Kramer, *The Public is Never Wrong* (New York: Putnam, 1953), p. 90.
5. George Blaisdell, "Mrs. Fiske Triumphs as 'Tess,'" *Moving Picture World*, Sept. 13, 1913, p. 1155.
6. "Another Famous Players Achievement," review of *Tess of the D'Urbervilles*, *Motography*, Sept. 20, 1913, p. 212.
7. Hardy to Sir George Douglas, October 23, 1913, in *CL*, vol. 4, p. 312.
8. Hardy to Edward Clodd, December 10, 1913, in *CL*, vol. 4, p. 328.
9. Florence Hardy on behalf of Thomas Hardy to John Langdon-Davies, October 25, 1922, in *CL*, vol. 6, p. 163.
10. Details of the contract are in Hardy's letter to Frederick Macmillan, November 26, 1913, in *CL*, vol. 4, p. 324 and *n*.
11. Hardy to Florence Henniker, December 21, 1913, in *CL*, vol. 4, p. 330.
12. Richard Little Purdy, *Thomas Hardy: A Bibliographic Study* (London: Oxford UP, 1954), p. 318.
13. "A Wessex Film," *Times* (London), Nov. 17, 1915, p. 5.
14. Hardy to Macmillan, November 17, 1915, in *CL*, vol. 5, p. 133.
15. *Variety Film Reviews*, vol. 1: 1907–1920 (New York and London: Garland, 1983).
16. Hardy to Macmillan, October 9, 1920, in *CL*, vol. 6, p. 42.
17. Rachael Low, *The History of the British Film, 1918-1929* (London: Allen and Unwin, 1971), p. 221.
18. Hardy to Macmillan, February 19, 1921, in *CL*, vol. 6, p. 72.
19. Hardy to Sidney Morgan, March 22, 1921, in *CL*, vol. 6, p. 78.
20. Dennis L. Bird, "The First Hardy Film," *Thomas Hardy Journal*, 11.3 (1995), p. 44.
21. Hardy to Henniker, July 2, 1921, in *CL*, vol. 6, p. 93.
22. "The Mayor of Casterbridge," review in the *Times* (London), December 5, 1921, p. 8.
23. Bird, p. 44.
24. Hardy to Macmillan, September 13, 1922, in *CL*, vol. 6, p. 152. Details of the 1919 contract with Metro can also be found in this letter.
25. See note 9.
26. *Variety Film Reviews*, vol. 2: 1921-1925 (New York and London: Garland, 1983).
27. Gary Carey, *Lost Films* (New York: MOMA, 1970), p. 76.
28. Hugh Castle, "Lachman and Others," *Close Up*, 5.4 (1929), p. 288.
29. "A New British Talking Picture," The *Times* (London), September 7, 1929, p. 10.
30. Ibid.
31. Castle, pp. 288, 289.
32. Castle, p. 289.
33. *Variety Film Reviews*, vol. 4: 1930–1938 (New York and London: Garland, 1983).
34. Hal Enderson, *All Movie Guide*, quoted on the Blockbuster.com site for *The Greenwood Tree*. Available at <www.blockbuster.com/bb/details/0,7286,VID-V++++93909,00.html?> Accessed February 11, 2002.
35. Jay Robert Nash and Stanley Ralph Ross, eds., *The Motion Picture Guide*, vol. 7 (Chicago: Cinebooks, 1987), p. 2799.

Works Cited

I. Primary Sources

A: Principal Works by Thomas Hardy

Far from the Madding Crowd (1874). London: Penguin, 1978; reprint 1985.
Jude the Obscure (1895). London: Penguin, 1978; reprint 1986.
The Mayor of Casterbridge (1886). London: Penguin, 1978; reprint 1985.
"The Melancholy Hussar of the German Legion," in *Wessex Tales* (1912). Oxford: Oxford UP, 1991.
The Pursuit of the Well-Beloved and the Well-Beloved (1892, 1897), edited by Patricia Ingham. London: Penguin, 1997.
The Return of the Native (1878). London: Penguin, 1978; reprint 1985.
Tess of the d'Urbervilles (1891), edited by Scott Elledge. 3rd ed. New York and London: Norton, 1991.
The Woodlanders (1887), Introduction by David Lodge. London and Basingstoke: Macmillan, 1974.

B: Other Writings by Hardy

The Collected Letters of Thomas Hardy, Vols. 2–6, 1893–1925; edited by Richard Little Purdy and Michael Millgate. Oxford: Clarendon, 1980–1987.
"General Preface to the Wessex Edition of 1912," in *The Woodlanders*, pp. 392–7.
The Literary Notebooks of Thomas Hardy, Vol. 2, edited by Lennart A. Björk. London and Basingstoke: Macmillan, 1985.

C: Films and Television Programs

The Claim (2000). Metro-Goldwyn-Mayer videocassette.
Far from the Madding Crowd (1967). MGM/UA videocassette.

Far from the Madding Crowd (1998). WGBH Boston videocassette.
Jude (1996). PolyGram videocassette.
Jude the Obscure (1971). CBS/Fox videocassette.
The Return of the Native (1994). Republic videocassette.
The Scarlet Tunic (1998). BWE videocassette.
Tess (1979) RCA/Columbia videocassette.
Tess of the D'Urbervilles (1998). A & E videocassette.
The Woodlanders (1998). Pathé videocassette.

II: SECONDARY SOURCES

A: *Biographical*

Hardy, Florence Emily (pseudonym of Thomas Hardy). *The Life of Thomas Hardy, 1840-1928*. Hamden, CT: Archeron, 1970.
Millgate, Michael. *Thomas Hardy: A Biography*. New York: Random House, 1982.
_____. *Thomas Hardy: His Career as a Novelist*. New York: Random House, 1971.

B: *Studies on Hardy's Fiction*

Beach, Joseph Warren. *The Technique of Thomas Hardy* (1922). New York: Russell and Russell, 1962.
Bloom, Harold, ed. *Modern Critical Interpretations of Thomas Hardy's* Tess of the D'Urbervilles. New York, New Haven, Philadelphia: Chelsea House, 1987.
Boumelha, Penny. *Thomas Hardy and Women: Sexual Ideology and Narrative Form*. Sussex: Harvester, 1982.
Fisher, Joe. *The Hidden Hardy*. London and Basingstoke: Macmillan, 1992.
Garson, Marjorie. *Hardy's Fables of Integrity: Women, Body, Text*. Oxford: Clarendon, 1991.
Goode, John. *Thomas Hardy: The Offensive Truth*. Oxford: Blackwell, 1988.
Higonnet, Margaret R., ed. *The Sense of Sex: Feminist Perspectives on Hardy*. Urbana and Chicago: U of Illinois P, 1993.
Kramer, Dale, ed. *Critical Approaches to the Fiction of Thomas Hardy*. London and Basingstoke: Macmillan, 1979.
Lodge, David. "Thomas Hardy as a Cinematic Novelist." *Thomas Hardy After Fifty Years,* edited by Lance St. John Butler. London and Basingstoke: Macmillan, 1977. 78–89.
Miller, J. Hillis. *Fiction and Repetition: Seven English Novels*. Cambridge: Harvard UP, 1982.
_____. *Thomas Hardy: Distance and Desire*. Cambridge: Harvard UP, 1970.
Morgan, Rosemarie. *Women and Sexuality in the Novels of Thomas Hardy*. London and New York: Routledge, 1988.
Nemesvari, Richard. "Appropriating the Word: *Jude the Obscure* as Subversive Apocrypha." *Victorian Review*, 19.2 (1993): 48–66.
Riquelme, John Paul, ed. Tess of the d'Urbervilles: *Complete Authoritative Text with Biographical and Historical Contexts, Critical History, and Essays from Five Contemporary Critical Perspectives*. Boston and New York: Bedford, 1998.

Springer, Marlene. *Hardy's Use of Allusion*. Lawrence: UP of Kansas, 1983.

Stave, Shirley A. *The Decline of the Goddess: Nature, Culture, and Women in Thomas Hardy's Fiction*. Westport, CT, and London: Greenwood, 1995.

Webster, Roger. "Reproducing Hardy: Familiar and Unfamiliar Versions of *Far From the Madding Crowd* and *Tess of the d'Urbervilles*." *Critical Survey*, 5.2 (1993): 143–51.

Widdowson, Peter. *Hardy in History: A Study in Literary Sociology*. London and New York: Routledge, 1989.

C: Contemporary Reviews of Hardy's Novels

Cox, R. G., ed. *Thomas Hardy: The Critical Heritage*. New York: Barnes and Noble, 1970.

Lerner, Lawrence, and John Holstrom, eds. *Thomas Hardy and His Readers*. New York: Barnes and Noble, 1968.

D: Studies on Film, Film Theory and History, and Film Adaptation

Barthes, Roland. *Image-Music-Text*, edited and translated by Stephen Heath. New York: Hill and Wang, 1977.

_____. *The Responsibility of Forms: Critical Essays on Music, Art, and Representation*. Translated by Richard Howard. New York: Hill and Wang, 1985.

Bluestone, George. *Novels into Film* (1957). Berkeley and Los Angeles: U of California P, 1966.

Boyum, Joy Gould. *Double Exposure: Fiction into Film*. New York: Universe, 1985.

Cohen, Keith. *Film and Fiction: The Dynamics of Exchange*. New Haven and London: Yale UP, 1979.

Eidsvik, Charles. "Toward a Politique des Adaptations," in *Film And/As Literature*, edited by John Harrington. Englewood Cliffs, NJ: Prentice-Hall, 1977. 27–37.

Eisenstein, Sergei. *Film Form*. Edited and translated by Jay Leyda. New York: Harcourt, Brace, and World, 1949.

Larsson, Donald F. "Novel into Film: Some Preliminary Reconsiderations," in *Transformations in Literature and Film*, edited by Leon Golden. Tallahassee: UP of Florida, 1987. 69–83.

McFarlane, Brian. *Novel to Film: An Introduction to the Theory of Adaptation*. Oxford: Clarendon, 1996.

Metz, Christian. *Film Language: A Semiotics of the Cinema*. Translated by Michael Taylor. New York: Oxford, 1974.

_____. *Psychoanalysis and Cinema*. Translated by Celia Britton et al. London and Basingstoke: Macmillan, 1982.

Mitry, Jean. "Remarks on the Problem of Cinematic Adaptation." Translated by Richard Dyer. *Bulletin of the Midwest Modern Language Association*, 4.1 (1971): 1–9.

Orr, Christopher. "The Discourse on Adaptation." *Wide Angle*, 6.2 (1984): 72–6.

E: Studies on Filmmakers and Film Eras

Leaming, Barbara. *Polanski: The Filmmaker as Voyeur.* New York: Simon and Schuster, 1981.

Murphy, Robert. *Sixties British Cinema.* London: BFI, 1992.

Phillips, Gene C. *John Schlesinger.* Boston: Twayne, 1981.

Polanski, Roman. *Roman by Polanski.* New York: Morrow, 1984.

Walker, Alexander. *Hollywood UK: The British Film Industry in the Sixties.* New York: Stein and Day, 1974.

Wexman, Virginia Wright. *Roman Polanski.* Boston: Twayne, 1985.

F: Film Review Anthologies

Ozer, Jerome S., ed. *Film Review Annual 1981.* Englewood, NJ: Film Review, 1981.

———, ed. *Film Review Annual 1997.* Englewood, NJ: Film Review, 1997.

Index